# THE JOURNALS OF
# FATHER ALEXANDER SCHMEMANN
# 1973-1983

# The Journals of Father Alexander Schmemann 1973-1983

*Translated by*
Juliana Schmemann

ST VLADIMIR'S SEMINARY PRESS
CRESTWOOD, NEW YORK
2000

This publication is made possible by the generosity of the Lex Hixon family.

LIBRARY OF CONGRESS CATALOGING-IN-PUBLICATION DATA

Schmemann, Alexander, 1921-1983
    [Journals. English. Selections.]
    The journals of Father Alexander Schmemann, 1973-1983 / translated by Juliana
Schmemann.
        p.    cm
    Includes bibliographical references.
    ISBN 0-88141-200-7
    1. Schmemann, Alexander, 1921-1982—Diaries. 2. Orthodox Eastern Church—
Clergy—Biography. I. Title.

Bx395.S34 A313 2000
281.9'092—dc21
[B]                                                                        00-022106

THE JOURNALS OF
FATHER ALEXANDER SCHMEMANN
1973-1983

ISBN 0-88141-200-7

PRINTED IN THE UNITED STATES OF AMERICA

# CONTENTS

# FOREWORD

∾

The existence of these journals was discovered only after Father Alexander Schmemann's death on December 13, 1983, when the eight notebooks were found in his desk at St Vladimir's Seminary. More than a diary, they recorded his thoughts, his spiritual struggles, his occasional frustration with the weight of daily duties, and above all his profound joy in the glory of God's Creation.

Father Alexander never explained in the journals what he intended to do with them. Some passages suggest an inner debate, but others are written as for publication. The overall impression is that Father Alexander always intended some further use for these writings, whether as a spiritual journal, or an autobiography. In any case, the reader of the passages in this volume must always bear in mind that these are highly personal and private writings, in which a priest and teacher of unwavering faith, great energy and firm discipline confesses, to himself and to God, the private pains and doubts that are an indelible factor of the human condition. Many readers may find some of the passages troubling—those critical of various forms of spirituality, or the institutions of the Church, or the science of theology, or even of himself and his colleagues.

But what is instructive in the journals, and what ultimately persuaded those closest to Father Alexander that they should be published, is that however strong the doubts and pains, he always returns—even from the anguish of impending death—to joy: the joy of the beauty of an autumn day, the joy of friendships, the joy of the Liturgy, joy in the certainty of the Kingdom and the love of God.

Father Alexander began keeping this journal in 1973, and continued making entries until the onset of his final illness, pausing only during his annual summer vacation on Lac Labelle in Quebec. He wrote largely in Russian, but sometimes in English and in French. The entries included in this volume were painstakingly selected, edited and translated by Father Alexander's wife, Juliana Schmemann, who appears on virtually every page of the journals as his beloved "L." (from Liana, the diminutive form of her name). Ann Zinzel, Father Alexander's long-time secretary, typed the translation, and other former students and colleagues helped edit the final text. For all who worked on the *Journals*, it was an act of love.

Many of the people and events referred to in the text will not be familiar to the reader, though often they will become clear through the context. Though the journals were written over the final ten years of Father Alexander's life, the entries range over his entire life. He writes of his childhood and youth in Paris: of the love of poetry inculcated in him by the director of the Russian school he attended, General Rimsky-Korsakov; of an illness that awakened him to mortality and eternity; of a growing attraction to the Church; of friends and teachers at the St Sergius Theological Institute in Paris, including his mentor, Father Cyprian (Kern) and his lifelong friend, Nikita Struve. He writes of the early years in the United States, where Father Schmemann arrived with his family in 1951, when St Vladimir's Seminary was ensconced in a few modest apartments on West 121st Street in New York. He writes of the tragic clashes with Father Georges Florovsky, of old colleagues like Serge Verhovskoy and Nicholas Arseniev, of his friend and successor as dean, the late Father John Meyendorff, and, with warmth and tenderness, of the students who became his colleagues at the Seminary— Father Thomas Hopko, David Drillock, Father Paul Lazor, John Erickson, Constance Tarasar. He writes of the vicissitudes of his Church, of its achievement of autocephaly as the Orthodox Church in America, and of its leaders—the late Metropolitan Ireney, Metropolitan Theodosius, Father Daniel Hubiak, Father Leonid Kishkovsky, and many others with whom his life was inextricably intertwined in those tumultuous years.

The journals also follow Father Alexander into his many trips around the United States, to Church Councils, to the weekly taping of the broadcasts he made for thirty years to Russia via Radio Liberty, to his dramatic encounter with a newly exiled Alexander Solzhenitsyn. They show him wrestling painfully with the writing of his book, *The Eucharist: Sacrament of the Kingdom*, which was to prove his last. And they give us loving glimpses into his family—of the agony of his wife's battle with cancer and his joy in her appointment as headmistress of a private school in New York; of visits to his daughters, Anne Hopko and Mary Tkachuk, both married to priests; of the departure of his son Serge, a reporter, to South Africa; of his niece Elizabeth Vinogradov and her husband Father Alexis; of the births and birthdays of their children.

The Afterword by Father John Meyendorff and the notes added to the text provide more information on the people and events covered in the journals. Where Father Alexander himself avoided naming specific people, or where the editors thought it best to keep them anonymous, they are identified as N. or NN. Brackets "[ ]" have been added by the editors; parentheses "( )" are Father Alexander's.

Father Alexander was diagnosed with terminal cancer on September 21, 1982. After several months of silence in the journal, he made one final entry on June 1, 1983, describing how even those months became, in the end, almost a celebration. Six months later, Father Alexander died at home in Crestwood, New York, with his family and colleagues around him. His last words, after receiving Holy Communion a day earlier, before lapsing into a coma, were, "Amen! Amen! Amen!"

Serge Schmemann

# CHAPTER I

# 1973

∾

*Monday, January 29, 1973*

Yesterday, on the train coming back from Wilmington, Delaware, I thought: "Here I am, fifty-two years old, a priest and a theologian for more than a quarter of a century—what does it all mean? How can I put together, how can I explain to myself what it all implies, clearly and distinctly; and is such a clarification needed?"

Twenty-five years ago, when my life such as it is now was just beginning, it seemed to me that, either today or maybe tomorrow, I would sit down, think a little, and sort it all out. I thought I just had to find some leisure. But after twenty-five years, when without any doubt the greater part of my life is over, there is less clarity than ever.

What is there to "explain"? The surprising combination in me of a deep and ever-growing revulsion at endless discussions and debates about religion, at superficial affirmations, pious emotionalism and certainly against pseudo-churchly interests, petty and trifling, and at the same time an ever-growing sense of reality. Just yesterday, I felt this reality while walking to church for the Liturgy, in the early morning, through the emptiness of winter trees; and then this precious hour in the empty church, before the Liturgy. Always the same feeling of time filled with eternity, with full and sacred joy. I have the feeling that church is needed so that this experience of reality would exist. Where the church ceases to be a symbol, a sacrament, it becomes a horrible caricature of itself.

*Friday, February 16, 1973*

"Religion" is the best and the worst in man. Not only the best, but also the worst: the falseness of religiosity, the pettiness of some "believers," their joyless, talentless seriousness. Is it really possible if one believes in God? In the Eternal and the Essential? "All is elsewhere." (Julien Green: "Tout est ailleurs.")

I

T. S. Eliot:

I am not myself very much concerned with questions of influence, or with the publicists who have impressed their names upon the public by catching the morning tide and rowing very fast in the direction in which the current was flowing, but rather that there should always be a few writers preoccupied in penetrating to the core of the matter, in trying to arrive at the truth and to set it forth, without too much hope, without ambition to alter the immediate course of affairs and without being downcast or defeated when nothing appears to ensue.

I spent the whole morning at home. After a week in California, after the feast in Wilkes-Barre (consecration of Bishop Herman*), after a trip to Philadelphia (funeral of Ivan Czap). What pure joy! Working in the dining room is Tom Hopko,** with whom I always feel the presence of light and goodness. Snow outside my window.

### Saturday, February 17, 1973

On Friday, I spent a long evening with my son Serge and the poet Joseph Brodsky [Brodsky died in January 1996]. At home, Brodsky is straightforward, simple and nice. Serge says that in the afternoon at the PEN Club, after the reading of his poetry, a Jewish man approached Brodsky and asked him why he used Christian symbolism. Brodsky answered: "Because I am not a barbarian..." Terribly nervous, he gives the impression of being lost, does not know how to behave.

I walked home from the train in the middle of the night, in the snow and terrible cold.

This morning—total bliss—I spent reading *Chevengur*, by Andrei Platonov. What an amazing book!

### Sunday, February 18, 1973

Liturgy in East Meadow. I have a joyful feeling that "American Orthodoxy," after endless struggles, is a reality, a thousand times more a reality than the cheap pseudo-spirituality of many "spiritual centers." But, alas, people enjoy cheapness, as long as it is covered with beards, crosses, and comfortable words.

* Herman (Swaiko), Bishop—Presently the Archbishop of the Diocese of Eastern PA and Rector of St Tikhon's Seminary.
**Hopko, Father Thomas—Married Father Schmemann's daughter Anne (Anya in the journals). Appointed Instructor and later Professor of Dogmatic Theology at St Vladimir's Seminary, 1968–present. Became Dean in 1992.

## *Tuesday, February 20, 1973*

I learned today about the sudden death in Los Angeles (during a banquet at a parish, while he was giving a speech) of Illarion Vorontsov*. Two weeks ago, I had lunch with him in L.A. Fifty-three years old. He is part of the happy, even piercing memories of my childhood: We were together at camp on the French Riviera, we were friends under the cloudless sky of those early years of my life, a blinding sunshine, the warm inviting sea. Then, many years later, we met again in California. He had an amazing beauty, the beauty of his whole being, his quietness, love of poetry, our shared love for the Church, his constant dissatisfaction with earthly things, without any claim in pseudo-spirituality. We met several times over the years. Two weeks ago, he told me about his trip to Mount Athos, which he had just visited. And again, without big words, even with humor, he saw everything, understood, and felt everything about this complex place. His wife told me: "He sits in the bathtub and loudly reads poetry!" I have a feeling of sad loss. Although we hardly ever saw each other, every encounter was filled with joy.

## *Thursday, February 22, 1973*

Confession. One guides another human being. One must start from the bottom, then build, gather one's self, detach, and liberate. But what about me?

I have incredible difficulty having "personal" conversations, and almost feel irritation with any "intimacy." I have intense difficulty hearing confessions. What is there in Christianity that one must constantly talk about? And what for?

## *Friday, February 23, 1973*

Last evening, feeling very tired, I read several chapters of Alan Watts, *In My Own Way* (an autobiography given me for Christmas by my son-in-law, Father John Tkachuk). I never had any interest in learning about Eastern religions, Zen, etc. In Watts's book I find interesting only the fact that he was a priest and left for an Orientalism that, to me, seems rather shallow. Therefore I read only those chapters that dealt with his priesthood for five years in the Anglican Church. Watts himself appears to me as a rather superficial thinker with his references to a "mystical experience" (!) But some of his criticism of Christianity deserves attention. About prayer: He interpreted St Paul's "pray without ceasing" as "chattering to Jesus all the time, mostly about how horribly one has sinned" (p. 180). About the belief in the

* Voronstov, Illarion—A personal friend of Father Schmemann from his childhood.

3

forgiveness of sins, he "seems to aggravate rather than mitigate the sense of guilt, and the more these people repented and confessed, the more they were embarrassed to go creeping to Jesus again and again for His pardon. They feel simply terrible about drawing so heavily on the merits of the Cross—infinite as they might be and idealized being good children in their paternalistic universe"(p. 181).

One of his friends gave a good answer about his syncretism: "There are many religions, but only one Gospel." Watts is a good example of how Christianity, diluted in "religion" and "mysticism," is losing its uniqueness, its meaning and strength as a judge over religions.

### Tuesday, February 27, 1973

Yesterday afternoon, in the Trinity Church on Wall Street, I lectured on prayer. And immediately, a question: "Is not it more important to feed the hungry...?" Why the either/or of our times?

Quite a pleasure to find myself in that extraordinary area of Manhattan with its hustle, noise, crowds.

This morning, a package from Finland; a translation of my *Great Lent.*

### Wednesday, February 28, 1973

Yesterday I had a talk with Father Tom about N. We agreed that the source of his most glaring defects in theology lies in his arrogance. Essentially, all sins come from two sources: flesh and pride. But pride is more frightening (after all, it ruined the angelic powers). Christians have focused their attention, their religious "passion," on flesh, but how easy it is to succumb to pride. Spiritual pride (truth, spirituality, maximalism) is the most frightful of all. The difficulty of the fight against pride lies in the fact that pride, unlike the flesh, appears in so many different forms and most easily appropriates that of the angel of light. In humility, people gain the knowledge of their unworthiness and defects, yet humility is the most divine of all possible qualities. We become humble, not because we see ourselves (one way or another, that always leads to pride because false humility is just another aspect of pride, perhaps the most difficult to conquer), but only if we see God and His humility.

### Saturday, March 3, 1973

All these days an endless amount of work and concerns. I feel tired and dried up from all this bustle. One ray of light: A two-hour drive to South Canaan yesterday, on a wonderful, sunny spring day. I arrived there early and walked for a whole hour along country roads in the midst of a transparent forest.

Melting snow, water, sunshine, quiet. The same on the way back. Otherwise my time is fragmented. I feel stressed and drowning in pettiness and weariness.

## Tuesday, March 6, 1973

On Saturday I heard a confession that made me painfully reflect: What is right, what is not? Any principle is shattered by the unique experience of every life. I am but a witness.

On Sunday—Liturgy in Paramus, New Jersey.

Yesterday I spent the whole morning and until four o'clock at home, writing an article for a liturgical seminar. Once more, I feel convinced of the falseness of academic theology. But mine is a cry in the wilderness…

*Any* purely logical thinking is frightening; it is without life, without fruit. A rational and logical person is hardly able to repent.

I just had a phone conversation with N. How easily people become discouraged, depressed, and come to see everything as hopeless. Patience is strength divine. For fighting with the devil, one needs patience more than anything else. But there is so little patience in a human being, especially a young one. The main danger in youth is impatience. Why does God have patience? Because God knows and loves.

Tragedy in Khartoum (diplomats killed by terrorists). I am repelled by all "ideologies." So-called human "convictions" are hopelessly narrow. What is even more hopeless is the fact that "faith" is often identified with "convictions." This is the harmful trend of theology, to reduce faith to ideas and convictions based on scientific reasoning.

## Friday, March 9, 1973

Tragic news about Father N.'s breakdown. So the symptoms I had noticed three weeks ago were real. I am afraid that the reason is clear: "He buried himself in his activity." And that is just what one should not do. One becomes unable to put things in perspective, to detach oneself, to push away all the fuss and the petty details that encumber our life and can devour our hearts. Actually, the cause is the same arrogance that seeks to convince me that all depends on *me*, all relates to *me*. Then the "I" is filling all reality, and the downfall begins. The essential error of the modern man is to identify life with activism, with thought, etc., hence an almost complete inability simply to "live," i.e., to feel, to appreciate, to live life as a continuous gift. To walk to the train station in a light that feels like spring, in the rain, to be able to see, to sense, to be conscious of a morning ray of sun on the wall—all of these *are* the reality of life. They are not the conditions

5

*for* activism or for thought, they are not just an indifferent background, they are the reason one acts and thinks. Only in that reality of life does God reveal Himself, and not in acts and thoughts. That is why Julien Green is right when he says: "all is elsewhere"—"the only truth lies in the swaying of bare branches in the sky." The same is true of communication. One does not communicate through talks and debates. The deeper and more joyful the communication, the less it depends on words. On the contrary, one is almost afraid of words because they might destroy the communion, cut off the joy.

I felt that most acutely on that New Year's eve, when I sat in Paris, in Adamovich's* mansard. I had always heard that he preferred to talk about unimportant little events. True. But not because there was nothing to talk about, but because communication was so clearly what was happening so vividly between us. Hence my dislike for "profound" and especially spiritual conversations. Did Christ converse with his twelve followers while walking along the roads of Galilee? Did he resolve their problems and difficulties? Christianity is the continuation of that communication, its reality, its joy and effectiveness. "It is good to be here."

Outside, a beautiful spring like day! It is almost hot. I spent the whole day home at my desk. Happiness.

### Saturday, March 10, 1973

#### About depression

Yesterday I had a long pastoral talk with a woman in deep depression. Her husband left her. Her son joined some hippies, dropped out of school, lives nobody knows where. Her twelve-year-old daughter is also beginning to feel depressed. All is pointless. The woman has lost any interest in her profession. Total darkness, a state of blasphemy. While we were talking I felt quite clearly the demonic character of a depression. I felt her acceptance, willing acceptance of blasphemy. I felt also the weakness and inadequacy of psychiatry and psychoanalysis. There is no way that they can drag people out of this darkness "if the light that is in you is darkness…" I told her: you can do only one thing, renounce blasphemy, eject yourself out of this lie, this surrender. You cannot do more, but this is the beginning.

### Wednesday, March 14, 1973

Beautiful spring day. And as soon as I am alone—like yesterday, in Harlem, late for my train—happiness, completeness, joy.

* Adamovich, Mark—Literary critic from Paris.

## *Thursday, March 22, 1973*

Yesterday and today, little Sasha Schmemann is with us. "A child, a bird, a flower...the words I love."

Where there is no sadness for God, no peace, no memory of mysterious light, no mysterious "taste" for joy, there is no God. There might be piety, but no God. Where is this awful nervousness coming from that dominates people?

## *Monday, March 26, 1973*

### *The Temptation of Idols*

Today, I thought about it all: about the low level of church life, about fanaticism, lack of tolerance, the enslavement of so many people. A "New Middle Ages" is engulfing us in the sense of a new barbarian era. Many churchmen are choosing and, what is worse, love Ferapont.* He is easy to love because with him all is clear. Especially "clear" is the fact that all that is higher, more complex, more difficult to comprehend—all this is a temptation and has to be destroyed. We should have understood long ago that there is, in this world, religion without God, religion as a center of all idols that possess fallen man, religion that is the justification for these idols. Hence the eternal question: What to do?

If one remains in the system, one accepts it, albeit unwillingly, along with its methods. If one leaves—in the role of a prophet or an accuser—one slides into arrogance and pride. I feel constantly tortured and torn.

## *Friday, March 30, 1973*

### *Transmission of experience*

Only when we write it down do we understand how much of our time is spent empty, how much fuss there is, not worthy of our attention, unimportant yet devouring our time and our hearts. All these days, in a state of total exhaustion as well as revulsion at the duties I need to be performing. I find myself passively watching television. But at the same time, when lecturing in the morning, I feel inspired again and again. I always have the feeling that something essential is being revealed to me while I lecture. It is as if someone else is lecturing for me!

---

* Ferapont is the spiritual adversary of the Elder Zosima in Dostoevsky's novel *The Brothers Karamozov*. He is an illiterate, rigid, demon-obsessed ascetic who condemns Zosima's spiritual teaching of humble love and joy.

7

On Tuesday I had a class on the "Polyeleos," on Wednesday, about the cosmic character of the Virgin Mary and yesterday—Thursday—about confession and repentance. Whether one is writing notes or books or articles, nothing is ever revealed as when one speaks. It is clear that in Christianity, "the Good News" is of primary importance. Christ did not write. And all that is written—the Bible, etc.—is the record of "experience"; not of individual experience, but supra-individual, precisely cosmic, ecclesial and eschatological. It is a common mistake to think that education is on the level of ideas. No! It is always a transmission of experience. How much sadness, emptiness and banality there is in the game of academia and footnotes. People are not convinced by reasoning; either they catch fire or they do not.

Yesterday, on television, terrible stories by former prisoners about torture in Vietnam. All these people seemed deeply marked and somehow illumined from inside. Christianity is destroyed not by bourgeoisie, capitalism or the army, but by rotten intellectualism, based on a firm trust in one's own importance. Where there is talk about "rights" there is no faith.

## Monday, April 2, 1973

*"We praise Thee..."*

On Friday, children's confessions, then a lecture at the Bergenfield parish. Yesterday, Watervliet, tomorrow, Buffalo. On Wednesday, Toronto, on Friday, Philadelphia... Then minutes of paradise: Yesterday, during the Liturgy in Wappingers Falls, then when we drove with Father Tom under pouring rain to Watervliet along the same Route 9 that we took many times with the children on our way to Labelle, where we spent our summers.*

Spring is quiet, an almost humble beginning. A rainy Sunday. The silence, the emptiness of these small villages. The joy of the living life that lives beyond all superficial activism, joy that is the true substance of life... And late at night, rain, lights and life behind brightly lit windows. If we are not given to feel all this, what do the words mean, "We praise Thee, we bless Thee, we give thanks unto Thee..."? This is the essence of religion, and its absence is the beginning of an awesome treachery. Who invented the idea that religion is the resolution of problems? Religion is always a transfer to another dimension, another level, and is therefore the annihilation of problems, not their solution. Problems also come from the Devil, who filled religion with his fuss and vulgarity—thus religion became a problem in the

---

* Father Alexander spent his summers on a lake in the Canadian Laurentian Mountains, Lac Labelle, where he served in a little chapel built on the land of Serge Troubetzkoy.

modern world. All these words have nothing to do with the essence of life, with bare rows of apple trees under a rainy, spring-like sky, with the reality of the heart and the soul.

## *Tuesday, April 3, 1973*

### *The Orthodox Service*

This morning I lectured about the Sunday *Prokeimenon* of Matins, on the preparation and the reading of the Gospel. How much I joyfully discover for myself when trying to transmit to others something so utterly untransmittable. People have forgotten how to understand, feel and realize what church services are about, into what reality they introduce us, how they create a different dimension. Before explaining a service, one should realize this different dimension. To reveal this dimension is the reason the Church exists. Without this different dimension, the whole teaching, structure and order of the Church mean nothing.

## *Thursday, April 5, 1973*

### *Church services—revelation of the Kingdom*

Yesterday, in Toronto, after the Passion service, lecture about the spirit of the Orthodox service, about what is most obvious to me about Orthodox worship as truly the revelation of the Kingdom of God; revelation that enables us to love the Kingdom, pray for its coming, feel it as "the only thing needful." Beauty as a revelation of truth and goodness; Church as the place of that revelation. Quiet, breathless attention—it seems contagious.

During the Passion, standing at the altar, I thought: What an immense part of life, from my early childhood, I have spent in that air, that melody, that state—it seems like the same, unbroken moment: the altar, the priest in Lenten vestments, the censing, the same joyful, humble, sad melody of the Lenten, "Lord, have mercy." A little later in the service, the choir sang: "O Thou Who didst clothe Thyself with light as with a garment..." They sang clumsily, slowly, earnestly directed by a very young girl. And again, the wonderful, "Woe is me, my Light." At the hour of death, what will remain of life is a unique vision of an unchanging altar, an eternal gesture, a continuous melody. There is really nothing better; truly a revelation.

The day before, in Buffalo, I heard a surprising story told by Father Thaddeus Wojcik,* about a woman in his parish, a sober, straightforward widow with two children. Without any hysteria, without ecstasy or

* Wojcik, Father Thaddeus—priest of the OCA and alumnus of St Vladimir's Seminary.

sentimentality, she said that during the service she saw the altar and the priest lit by a blinding light. It lasted a few moments. Ineffable joy from that story, especially as told by Father Ted himself, so humble, so clear, so transparent.

From Buffalo to Toronto I took the bus, alone, for three hours. The entire drive was along the lake, as large as the sea. It was raining; we were passing villages, little houses. Here and there yellow paschal forsythias were beginning to bloom. I love to commune with humble human lives, in their simplicity, quiet and humility. Only in these lives can there be the revelation of God.

## Friday, April 6, 1973

### Happiness—no need for words

Yesterday was little Vera's birthday. Three years have gone by since that night at that Derby hospital when we prayed for her mother's life. How petty and pitiful all "serious" discussions seem, all the fuss over problems, when compared with that night.

What is happiness? It is to live as we do now, with L., just the two of us, savoring every hour—morning coffee; two, three hours of quiet in the evening. No "special" conversation. All is clear, and therefore so good! If we were to start trying to define the essence of that obvious happiness, we would each do it differently; we might even have an argument! My words would not seem right to her, and vice-versa. Misunderstanding! And happiness would become clouded. As one approaches the essence of a thing, fewer and fewer words are needed. In eternity, in the Kingdom, only "Holy, Holy, Holy" will be needed, only words of praise and thanks, only prayer and the brightness of fullness and joy. This is why the only profound and needed words are not the ones which are about reality (discussions), but which are real in themselves, and as such are the very symbol, presence and mystery of reality.

The word of God, prayer, art—there was a time when theology was that "word of God," not just words *about* God, but divine words, a revelation.

What is prayer? It is the remembrance of God, the feeling of His presence; it is joy from that presence. Always, everywhere, in all things.

## Friday, April 13, 1973

### Memory. Remembrance

"To accept not to be loved, it is at this price that one leaves one's mark on things" (from an article by Michel Debré).

Friday of the fifth week of Lent. From early childhood, I always felt this day to be the beginning of the ultimate approach to Pascha. This morning, I remembered so clearly one of the years that I spent at Lycée Carnot (probably in 1938—I was fifteen). I was walking from home to school and eagerly anticipating how, in four hours, I would go to the cathedral on the rue Daru, to the Akathist to the Virgin Mary. I remember everything: the light; the trees, just beginning to open young, green leaves; children's cries and laughter in the little square. I did not know then that standing on that same street I would see my father for the last time in the summer of 1957—I was leaving for New York and he looked down, waving down to me from his window on the fourth floor.

With a slight effort, I can recall many things: I can restore a sequence of events, the when and the how. But for some reason, some things (days, minutes) I do not recall, but remember, as if they had a life of their own in me. They are not remarkable or important events, not even events at all, but particular moments and impressions. They have become the very fabric of my consciousness, a constant part of *me*. I am quite convinced that these memories are revelations (epiphanies) from deep within, contacts with the "other," the deeper and higher level of consciousness. Later, much later, one realizes that in these moments was given a kind of absolute joy. Joy about nothing concrete, but joy nonetheless; the joy of God's presence and openness to the heart. And the experience of this close contact, of this joy (which will never be taken away since it has become the deepest part of the heart) will determine the thoughts and vision of one's whole life.

*Holy Saturday. A memory*

For example, that Holy Saturday in Paris, I was standing on my balcony before going to church. I saw a car passing by, and there was a quick, blinding reflection of sunlight from one of the windows. All I have ever felt and learned about Holy Saturday, and through that day about the essence of Christianity; all that I have tried to say or write, has always been an inner need to transmit to myself and to others what burst forth, what was illumined and revealed to me in that moment. One speaks about this when one speaks of eternity. Eternity is not the negation of time, but time's absolute wholeness, gathering and restoration. Eternal life is not what begins after temporal life; it is the eternal presence of the totality of life.

Christianity is a blessed memory; it is really the conquering all of fragmented time; it is the experience of eternity, here and now. All the religions and spiritualities which tend to annihilate time are false religions and pseudo-spiritualities.

A radiant, sunny spring day. It seems that the day itself is singing: "In you alone do we rejoice!"

## Monday, April 16, 1973

I remember the Akathist on Friday evening and the Liturgy on Saturday. While we were having communion in the altar, the choir was singing: "Hail, Mary, whose joy is radiant." The choir sang beautifully and the whole service was like rain on my heart after a drought.

We spent Saturday afternoon in Wappingers Falls with Father Tom, Anya and the children. Mainly because we could not sit at home on such a day with so much light, such blueness, such joy. And yesterday, on Sunday again: choking with blissful joy.

The mixed choir was singing—two, three students, some girls. A feeling of complete certainty: man is *capax Dei*—capable of being with God. In the middle of this, a talk with N. about his depression. It is such an obvious, demonic revolt against light.

## Thursday, April 19, 1973

All these days I have an endless accumulation of business, concerns, hurry, distress from gossip, from the painful level at times of our little seminary world. I feel as if some gray dust was lying on my heart. I cannot feel any joy, nor see any light. All I want is to be able to "squeeze through," to live through this wave.

Some rays of light: a lecture on Wednesday about the Virgin Mary, when I feel that I am talking to myself.

Today a sudden feeling of relief: All is well again. Tomorrow is the last day of Lent, and we will be singing: "Having completed the forty days..."

It is the beginning of the most blessed days of the year. I pray that they will be peaceful and pure.

During the whole day, a violent thunderstorm was coming. Now it is here—a spring shower.

## Palm Sunday, April 22, 1973

Joy! How it flows out of these unique days, Lazarus Saturday and Palm Sunday. Today's epistle reading: "Rejoice, and again I say rejoice..." The feast of the Kingdom.

## *Bright Tuesday, May 1, 1973*

Pascha. Holy Week. Essentially, bright days such as are needed. And truly that is all that is needed. I am convinced that if people would really hear Holy Week, Pascha, the Resurrection, Pentecost, the Dormition, there would be no need for theology. All of theology is there. All that is needed for one's spirit, heart, mind and soul. How could people spend centuries discussing justification and re-demption? It is all in these services. Not only is it revealed, it simply flows in one's heart and mind. The more I live, the more I am convinced that most people love something else and expect something else from religion and in religion. For me this is idolatry, and it often makes contact with people so difficult.

## *Monday, May 7, 1973—After Pascha*

On Saturday, after the last Paschal Liturgy, we left for Montauk Point, Long Island, for some rest. We spent the night in the same motel in East Hampton. What a delight, what a thoroughly enjoyable weekend. We spent the morning on the rocks near the lighthouse. The ocean, sunshine, silence, a delicious lunch in a German restaurant on the pier of Sag Harbor.

One counts the days until Pascha, then until the end of the school year, then the blessed departure for Labelle. If only one would count the days with the same eagerness, hope, joy and anticipation until the "day without evening." But instead, fear, despondency.

## *Monday, May 14, 1973*

"Principles are what people have instead of God... "Principle is an even duller word than 'Religion.'" (From the review of Frederic Buecher, *Theological ABC*, in the *New York Times*).

"Religion"—how much is covered by that word. I thought about it while reflecting on N.—a rather ordinary middle-aged woman whom I see every two or three weeks, as her "spiritual father." She wants to lead a good spiritual life, but O Lord, what a total concentration on herself, on how everyone—son, husband, neighbors, everything—stand in the way of her efforts, what complete blindness to everything around her.

What attracts this kind of person to religion? Or rather, what kind of compensation do they seek?

## *Facing sins*

"One has to understand...!" One reaches a point when it becomes clear that there is nothing to understand, that all complexities are imagined, that it is all a sort of fog we raise to cover up our sins and to avoid having to face them. The problems of contemporary consciousness, of young people, are often rubbish. There are two sources of sin: flesh and pride. And people are often trying to cover them up with complexities so that they look nice and deep ("He has great problems...") And one can always find helpful spiritual guides ready to solve problems, mainly by discussing them endlessly. The truth is much simpler: flesh and pride. They are the true keys to problems and difficulties, the root of endless discussion, of whispers during the dullest confessions, of all the introspection and morbid self-indulgence. Christianity is not "effective," it does not sound right. The inadequacy and falsity of pastoral counseling, of religious "therapy," is quite often as false as the refusal to face sin. Real faith always consists of growing in the virtue of simplicity—joyful, wholesome and liberating. "Difficulties," "complexities" and "problems" are trivial alibis of a self-centered human being enamored with his self-image of a tormented, complex man.

### Friday, May 25, 1973

I was rereading my very favorite diary of Julien Green (*What Remains of the Day*). He writes: "Without communion, life changes and faith leaves. It happens without exception" (p. 14). How true! For the last two days I have rejoiced in thinking that tomorrow I will celebrate the Liturgy. What else can be "interesting" in the Church?

### Monday, September 17, 1973

This notebook remained in my office desk this whole summer. Labelle—I love it more and more acutely, almost painfully. My brother Andrei spent three weeks with us. We visited Québec, spent a morning with L. on Lac Grand Caché. Children, grandchildren—then a trip to Switzerland and Paris.

Now, back to normality: The seminary, the usual fuss of the beginning of the school year.

Beautiful, early fall day.

### Thursday, September 27, 1973

Each September I make a few resolutions: I will organize my life differently, without fuss, without wear on the nerves. I will adopt some rhythm, with layers of quiet, work, concentration. And after only three weeks everything has gone to wrack and ruin: Fuss at the seminary, endless phone calls, meetings. Today I called in sick and did not go anywhere. But my conscience is bothering me...

I sometimes think that every person is called to say or do something, albeit small, but genuine and something that is *his* calling. But life is such that one is plunged headlong into everything. Then one loses oneself and one's own and does not fulfill this calling.

I am quite convinced that I have no calling to be a personal guide. I dislike "intimate" effusions. When I hear confession, I often have the feeling that it is not me, but someone else, and that all the things that I say are impersonal clichés, not *it*, not *it* at all… I see a lot of harm being done, from encouragement of self-centeredness and spiritual pride (on both sides), to the reduction of faith to one's self and one's problems. Christianity is always a preaching, a *revelation* of that other, higher level, of reality itself, and not an "explanation." But then what about the *starets* (an elderly monk, adviser and spiritual guide)? To be a *starets* is a special calling. If we take seriously all that we know about the *startsy*, we see that they indulge neither in intimate guidance nor in solving problems, but in revealing the Lord's reality. That's why a *pseudo-starets* is so dangerous—there are so many of them nowadays and they are usually full of lust for power.

I am quite convinced that genuine preaching is always an answer to doubts and to temptations as well as their healing. It is always preaching about Christ, and only about Christ—knowing Him, meeting Him, obeying Him, loving Him—which can remove doubts and problems. What makes a genuine preacher strong is that he directs his sermon also to himself, to his own despondency, lack of faith, his own lukewarm heart. What can "talks" add to it?

## *Wednesday, October 3, 1973*

### *Fear of Death*

My usual headache from exhaustion. Coming back from the seminary, I suddenly remembered very clearly my crisis of 1935-36. At the age of 14-15, I was in the hospital after a life-threatening operation. The "crisis" consisted in a real encounter with death. Not the fear of death, but the feeling of death's presence. How can one live knowing that all will die? It seems banal, like a cliché, but for several months I literally did not live. I remember how I could not listen to my family's conversations. I went to another room and, looking down from our balcony on the sixth floor, I felt that I was in an awesome, frightening hole. It is hard to describe: not despair, not fear, but a fearful contradiction. My home, people, life—and it is all mortal! I had never experienced such torture, nor have I since. It went away suddenly, and has never come back. Right now I remember not so much the content but the horror of that touch of death. I was quite sick, I nearly died, and I lived *in extremis*. Death touched me and left. I do not know; it makes sense: "Darkness covered me." We must always realize that this darkness is real, that it is here, ready to engulf us, and God saves us from it.

This was the time in my life when I truly prayed. I prayed for salvation and nothing else, as I felt I could no longer bear this darkness.

### Friday, October 12, 1973

There is no point in converting people to Christ if they do not convert their vision of the world and of life, since Christ then becomes merely a symbol for all that we love and want already—without Him. This kind of Christianity is more terrifying than agnosticism or hedonism.

Theologians have connected their fate with erudition, with learning, whereas they would be better off following poetry, poets and art. Genuine poetry is hard to come by, while erudition is endlessly easy...

Dean, Protopresbyter, professor: I sometimes feel (especially on a sunny, solitary morning like today) that it has nothing to do with me personally, that it is a poor mask, and yet, 90 percent of my life is determined by these titles. When I take off the mask, people are shocked—how can he be himself? When I wear the mask, whatever I say or do is justified. How easy it is to dilute one's personality under a mask and even become fond of it...

### Friday, October 19, 1973

"The curse of labor." But many people, if not the majority, are wallowing in furious activity, because they are afraid of remaining face-to-face with life, with themselves, with death. They are bored, and boredom is the kingdom of the Devil. Bored and afraid, they deafen themselves with action, with ideas and ideologies. The key to our culture is an optimistic activity with traces of fear and boredom. Without God, all is possible, but this "all" is endlessly frightening and boring. It seems to me that the first duty of the Church is to refuse any part in the logic and the keys of this world. One cannot enlighten the world without first wholly rejecting it. What is needed in contemporary Christianity is courage and spiritual freedom: Never give in to "understanding," "involvement," "survival of the world" at all cost.

### Saturday, October 20, 1973

I had to visit the widow of the architect A. Neratov, who has taken over painting icons for the cathedral in Washington. The trip along the sunny

Taconic Parkway was accompanied by a blaze of autumn leaves. I was thinking: Why do we know that besides this world—sinful and fallen—there is without a doubt another one, one for which we long? Above all we know it through nature, through her witness, her wounded beauty. The testimony, the beauty of nature is about the Other.

Theology is the study of God as science is the study of nature—without mystery.

### Wednesday, October 24, 1973

I am thoroughly enjoying Malcolm Muggeridge's book, *Chronicles of Wasted Time*, and Simone Weil: "No desert is so dreary, monotonous and boring as evil," and "Nothing is so beautiful and wonderful, nothing is so continually fresh and surprising as the good."

### Thursday, November 1, 1973

Lately, I have a pile of work, meetings, reunions. In spite of that, I have a feeling of inner peace and courage, perhaps because I am so continually inspired by writing and thinking about Confession and Communion.

### Sunday, November 4, 1973

Twenty-seven years have passed since my ordination to the diaconate, in Paris. I hardly remember the service. I remember that we came home to Etang la Ville* and I slept. That evening I celebrated my first Vespers at St Sergius.**

I remember a gray autumn day.

Yesterday and today—many confessions. So much sadness, loneliness, dead ends, life's failures.

### Wednesday, November 7, 1973

On Saturday I heard the confession of a pious man who told me that "general confession" was too easy for him. "I prepare for my personal confession, I do not sleep half a night..." But after that comes a series of superficial words and reasoning, torturous and needless spiritual chatter and condemnation of all those who do not "understand" him... And *that* is piety?

---

* Etang la Ville was the Paris suburb where Father Schmemann and his family lived in France, in a log cabin.

**Founded in 1925 in Paris, St Sergius Theological Institute was the primary link with the Russian religious renaissance. Father Schmemann was a graduate and faculty member until 1951.

*Saturday, November 17, 1973*

I spent this whole week—from Monday to Thursday night—in Pittsburgh, at the All-American Council. I am completely exhausted, but unexpectedly lightened. I felt a close contact with the mystery of the Church—and that is neither rhetorical nor exaggerated. I went to the council quite downcast and with a lack of any enthusiasm, not expecting much. After three days of incredible effort and tension (I was chairman again), suddenly it became quite clear: Our Church is alive in spite of everything, and an assembly of rather "little" people is transfigured into the Church. Wonderful prayer services. Hundreds of communicants and, mainly, a kind of common inspiration. I still feel elated by the Council. The miracle of the Holy Spirit in an American Hilton Hotel!

*Monday, November 26, 1973*

Yesterday after the Liturgy, N., from Oxford, came to visit us. Such a nice, lovely lady. The conversation was mostly about their church in Oxford, about Greeks, priests, church life in general. I know, of course, when I think rationally, that the church is needed as well as all the hard work and the all-too-human activity that accompanies it. But what remains from that conversation is an unpleasant aftertaste. All this rushing about, either to Byzantium, or to the *Philokalia*, or to the island of Patmos, or to icons, makes Orthodoxy look like a supermarket. Each chooses what he wants: the era, the style and identification. It becomes impossible to be oneself. One has to belong to a "style." I have a rather sad feeling that what is essential in Orthodoxy, in my opinion, "the one thing needful," important and precious, is left by the wayside—it does not have style!

"Little children, keep yourselves from idols!" (1 John 5:21). Sometimes I see Orthodoxy in a thicket of idols. To be attached to the past always leads to idolatry, and I see many people living by the past, or rather, by many pasts. An Old Believer lies deeply buried in an Orthodox person.

*Wednesday, November 28, 1973*

I just reread Chekhov's *The Darling, The Bishop*, etc. I always thoroughly enjoy reading him.

I long to be free, free to "live": my wife and family (no time), friends (no time), nature (no time), cultural reading (no leisure). I would like to live in such a way that every particle of time would be fullness (and not fuss); and being full, time would be prayer, a tie, a relationship with God, transparency for God who gave us life, not fuss.

## *Friday, December 7, 1973*

Yesterday we celebrated the feast of St Nicholas—new calendar. By the old calendar it was St Alexander Nevsky, my saint's day. I remembered that day, forty years ago; I woke up in my boarding school dormitory and found on the little stool next to my bed a very precious gift, a Waterman fountain pen. I remember its color, its feeling in my fingers. On the same day, Father Sergius M[oussin-] P[ushkin] was ordained to the priesthood. Why do some days, in all their detail—weather, light, etc.—become engraved in one's memory and remain there?

Outside it is gray, quiet, freezing. I enjoy this quiet after a few stormy days.

Yesterday, the annual Board of Trustees meeting at the seminary.

## *Monday, December 10, 1973*

On Sunday, I preached at the Cathedral of St John the Divine: a "dialogue" with the Rev. James Morton. Listening to my favorite Anglican hymn, "Let All Mortal Flesh Keep Silence," I remembered my first trips to England, in 1937 and 1938, especially the weeks spent in Stamford, when I attended a High Church Mass every day. During my school years in Paris, on my way to the Lycée Carnot, I would stop by the Church of St Charles of Monceau for two or three minutes. And always, in this huge, dark church, at one of the altars, a silent Mass was being said. The Christian West: it is part of my childhood and youth, when I lived a double life. On the one hand it was a worldly and very Russian émigré life; on the other, a secret, religious life. Sometimes I think of the contrast: a noisy, proletarian rue Legendre (a small street in the 19th *arrondissement*, in Paris) and this never-changing Mass (…a spot of light on the dark wall…)—one step, and one is in a totally different world. This contrast somehow determined in my religious experience the intuition that has never left me: the coexistence of two heterogeneous worlds, the presence in this world of something absolutely and totally "other." This "other" illumines everything, in one way or another. Everything is related to it—the Church as the Kingdom of God among and inside us. For me, rue Legendre never became unnecessary, or hostile, or nonexistent—hence my aversion to pure "spiritualism." On the contrary, the street, as it was, acquired a new charm that was understandable and obvious only to me, who knew at that moment the Presence, the feast revealed in the Mass nearby. Everything became alive, intriguing: every storefront window, the face of every person I met, the concrete, tangible feeling of that moment, the relationship between the street, the weather, the houses, the people.

19

This experience remains with me forever: a very strong sense of "life" in its physical, bodily reality, in the uniqueness of every minute and of its correlation with life's reality. At the same time, this interest has always been rooted solely in the correlation of all of this with what the silent Mass was a witness to and reminder of, the presence and the joy. What is that correlation? It seems to me that I am quite unable to explain and determine it, although it is actually the only thing that I talk and write about ("liturgical theology"). It is not an "idea": I feel repulsed by "ideas"; I have an ever-growing conviction that Christianity cannot be expressed by "ideas." This correlation is not an "idea" of the Christian world, Christian marriage, etc. This correlation is a tie, not an idea; an experience. It is the experience of the world and life literally in the light of the Kingdom of God, revealed through everything that makes up the world: colors, sounds, movements, time, space—concrete, not abstract. When this light, which is only in the heart, only inside us, falls on the world and on life, then all is illumined, and the world becomes a joyful sign, symbol, expectancy. That's why I love Paris, why I need it! It is because it was in Paris, in my Parisian childhood that this experience was given to me, became my being. And now that I no longer live there, nor have any work or obligations there, Paris has become for me an immersion into that first experience, its renewal. When I am in Rome, where I took many walks in the fall of 1963* I feel that Rome is fragmented into beauties of many eras and cultures, and everything reminds us of the perishable past. In Athens I feel quite acutely the ever-present paganism, the "sacred flesh," which provokes pure spiritualism as a reaction to it, Manichaeism, or a "sacred orthodox way of life." This spiritualism, in my opinion, sadly leads to a self-righteous denial of the world. Whereas in Paris, in its fabric and tonality, I feel the presence, the existence of the other level. In Rome there is a sense of pleasure and of tragedy. In Paris there is sadness and there is joy, and both are always there. The beauty of Paris reflects its place in another level, neither self-satisfied nor triumphant, neither pompous nor heavy. It is a beauty that belongs to a world where Christ lived.

I have just finished a huge book by Gay Talese, *The Kingdom and the Power,* about the *New York Times,* and *An Age of Mediocrity* by C. L. Sulzberger. Both authors describe the strength of lust for power—a never-ceasing, wild struggle for power, for success. While reading, I felt really frightened by the force, the energy of that struggle, even in the smallest worlds—a force that can move mountains and be quite poisonous. The struggle for power is the quintessence of our world. In order to be saved, one has to run away from it. How humane are the people who do not have any power and do not pretend, nor attempt, to have it.

* Father Schmemann was an Observer at the Second Vatican Council in 1963.

*Wednesday, December 12, 1973*

Yesterday was a day of very special encounters. At 1:00 PM I had lunch with Father George Grabbe (of the Russian Orthodox Church Outside of Russia) at the Hotel Commodore. The meeting had been arranged a long time before and was more pleasant than I anticipated. We agreed right away that obstacles against not only unity, but also even a simple *détente* were quite substantial. We agreed with Talleyrand that "politics is the art of what is possible." But I had the feeling that something was happening, was moving—as long as we did not discuss the devil in the Moscow Patriarchate, or apostasy, or the usual rhetoric of the Russian Church Abroad; as long as we tried to talk about how to achieve some agreement without rejecting autocephaly on one hand and, on the other, without rejecting the ideas of the Church Abroad. We mainly agreed to continue our discussions and meetings.

After the Commodore, I went to the Hotel Latham where I met Misha Meerson,* who recently came from Paris. A thoroughly charming young man obsessed with the idea of a mission. He has projects, ideas; he will publish a magazine and open a research center. A Russian boy who is energetically correcting all the evils of the world and doing it with great assurance and eagerness. He is courageous, pure, idealistic.

I just reread these pages and felt a strange satisfaction, almost happiness, when able to look around me with a sense of perspective. No need to leave or become indifferent; just be detached. I remember when in boarding school one Saturday, when we did not go home for the weekend, I would walk into an empty classroom, or an empty church, or to the woods around the school. To be close to people, but alone, and suddenly to feel with extraordinary force these woods, these empty wet branches against the gray sky, all the things that are stifled by the presence of people coming to life, living their own independent existence, every minute whole, not fragmented. Later on, when I went to the Lycée in Paris, I remember street lights, empty roads on my way to church. It took me only ten minutes, but they remain in my memory with more light and brightness than any other time.

*Thursday, December 13, 1973*

*The beginning of the Bilateral Commission*

Yesterday I spent the evening at the Princeton Club with Archbishop

---

* Fr Michael Meerson—An emigrant from the Soviet Union, he was subsequently ordained a priest in the OCA at St Vladimir's Seminary.

Iakovos,* two of his vicars and three priests. Our Metropolitan was a most gracious host. Everything was friendly, even somehow sweet. I was thinking, This is the triumph of diplomacy in the Church. We met with a complete prepared agenda. After such diplomatic meetings there remains a sad after-taste. This dinner laid the basis for "bilateral conversations."

## Friday, December 14, 1973

### Laughter, Childhood, Life

"Christ never laughed." I thought about this yesterday during the seminary Christmas party when we watched clever and very funny skits about daily life at the seminary. The party was like an exorcism from all misunderstandings, all the unavoidable clouds hanging over our little school world. There are all kinds of laughter, but there is one kind that shows a sort of unassuming modesty. In the East, people are often devoid of any sense of humor; therefore they are often pompous, proud, prone to dramatize. I am always sad when meeting people without humor, often tense, easily offended. If we have to "be like children," it is impossible to do it without laughter. But laughter also fell and can be demonic. In dealing with "idols," however, laughter is salutary, since it allows us to see them in perspective.

### Childhood

Last evening I had a long talk with L. about my childhood, about my brother Andrei and our life before my marriage. How far apart we were in those days! And how close we became. When I remember my life, I remember mainly being drawn in so many directions, so many various worlds. But I was never engulfed totally in any of them; I never identified with any one. I always felt that I could leave them any minute. I was never a loner; on the contrary, I was quite a worldly person. But I always knew that I could not get totally involved. I kept my head free and aloof. Even in the Corps of Cadets school,** I accepted without question the military, Russian, romantic, heroic world that the school conveyed to us. At the same time, I loved to escape to the opposite pole: talks about the St Sergius Institute, about the Church and theology. The charm of every aspect of my mundane life consisted in the feeling that I could at any moment leave and know that "All is elsewhere" (Julien Green).

* Iakovos, Archbishop—Archbishop of the Greek Archdiocese of North and South America, 1958-1996.

**As a youth, Father Schmemann attended the Corps of Cadets school, run by Russian émigrés in Paris.

*Home*

I love my home, and to leave home and be away overnight is always like dying—returning seems so very far away! I am always full of joy when I think about home. All homes, with lit windows behind which people live, give me infinite pleasure. I would love to enter each of them, to feel its uniqueness, the quality of its warmth. Each time I see a man or a woman walking with shopping bags, that is, going home, I think about them: they are going home, to real life, and I feel good, and they become somehow close and dear. I am always intrigued: What do people do when they do not "do" anything, when they just live? That's when their life becomes important, when their fate is determined. Simple bourgeois happiness is often despised by activists of all sorts who quite often do not realize the depth of life itself; who think that life is an accumulation of activities. God gives us His Life, not ideas, doctrines, rules. At home, when all is done, life itself begins. Christ was homeless not because He despised simple happiness—He did have a childhood, family, home—but because He was at home everywhere in the world, which His Father created as the "home" of man. "Peace be with this house." We have our home and God's home, the Church, and the deepest experience of the Church is that of a home. Always the same and, above anything else, life itself—the Liturgy, evening, morning, a feast—and not an activity.

## *Monday, December 17, 1973*

*Everyday life*

Last Tuesday I met again with Father George Grabbe to continue our dialogue about contacts between the Russian Orthodox Church Outside of Russia and the OCA [Orthodox Church in America]. He says, "Our goal is to keep Orthodoxy pure." This is where the essential disagreement is. The purity of Orthodoxy for them consists in an "orthodox way of life"—no thought, no problems. On the contrary, they are organically repelled by them, they deny them. They are convinced that to deny problems is right, for any thought, any problem is a threat to this "orthodox way of life," whereas the crisis of Christianity consists precisely in the collapse of the orthodox way of life, to which Christianity found itself bound and submitted. The question is not whether this way of life was good or bad; it probably was both. The question is whether one can and should hold on to it as a *sine qua non* of Christianity, of true Orthodoxy. They answer that question with a total, unconditional "Yes." Hence comes their instinctive fear of sacraments (frequent Communion, etc.), because sacraments are eschatological; they do not fully fit in an orthodox way of life. For the sake of the preservation of this way of life, they stay away from culture and theology, which might raise problems, questions, searches and struggles, which would constantly threaten the static character of their way of life. The defenders of this way of life accept culture only when it has become stabilized and when it has become fixed, made harmless by being part of their way of life; when they know *what* one should think about that culture, or rather not think. These people, stifled by their own chosen limitations, are quite unable to accept or try to understand any creativity. Christianity and Orthodoxy are good and acceptable because they are ancient, because they are in the past, because they are the substance and the sanction of the "orthodox way of life." Therefore, they simply do not accept any words, any creative works, even genuine and true, that do not have a familiar "sacred form." They feel threatened, endangered, they feel that some essential foundations have been shaken. The fruits of this sort of mind-set are fear, narrow-mindedness, a total inability to discern the spirits.

Christianity in general, and Orthodoxy in particular, are now undergoing a real test to determine what will enable them to remain alive in the world of today. The defenders of the orthodox way of life express one clear and profound answer as they define it. But there is no clear, total answer from any other side except reductions, like return to "Byzantium," or spiritual individualism, or reading the ascetics, or escapism from reality. I hesitate to come forward with my feeling—it sounds arrogant—that I have an answer! In everything that I preach, or teach, or write, I want this answer to appear, hopefully to shine through. But that answer cannot be squeezed into any system, any recipe, any defined way of life. No rules come out of that answer. It is simply a vision of life, and what comes from that vision is the light, the transparency, the referral of everything to the "Other," the eschatological character of life itself and all that is in it. The source of that eschatological light, the lifting up of all life, is the sacrament of the Eucharist. The error of the defenders of a concrete and clearly defined way of life is not in attributing great importance to the external forms of life. In that, they are right against all the pseudo-spiritual people, whether religious or cultured, who are obsessed by the idea of breaking with any forms or destroying them altogether. It does not mean that Christianity leads us into some sort of "other-worldliness." It means that the image of this world in Christ and through Christ becomes passing, dynamic, open, outreaching.

To understand St Paul when he says, "The image of this world is passing away," to make it real, we need in *this* world the experience of the *other* world, its beauty, depth, treasure, the experience of the Kingdom of God and its Sacrament—the Eucharist. The Church has been established in this world to celebrate the Eucharist, to save man by restoring his Eucharistic being. The Eucharist is impossible without the Church, that is, without a community that knows its unique character and vocation—to be love, truth, faith and mission—all of these fulfilled in the Eucharist; even simpler, *to be* the Body of Christ. The Eucharist reveals the Church as a community—love for Christ, love in Christ—as a mission to turn each and all to Christ. The Church has no other purpose, no "religious life" separate from the world. Otherwise the Church would become an idol. The Church is the home each of us leaves to go to work and to which one returns with joy in order to find life, happiness and joy, to which everyone brings back the fruits of his labor and where everything is transformed into a feast, into freedom and fulfillment, the presence, the experience of this "home"—already out of time, unchanging, filled with eternity, revealing eternity. Only this presence can give meaning and value to everything in life, can refer everything to that experience and make it full. "The image of this world is passing away." But only by passing away does the world finally become the "World": a gift of God, a happiness that comes from being in communion with the content, the form, the image of that "World."

### Thursday, December 20, 1973

Snow. Ice. Frost. Yesterday we started the canon of the Pre-Feast of Christmas. "Prepare, O Bethlehem..." At the seminary, everyone talks of the end of the year, of vacation.

# CHAPTER II

# 1974

～

### Thursday, January 10, 1974

Our Anya is 30 today. It seems like only yesterday we had our firstborn in Clamart (France). The Lord gave me such wonderful, good children! I was thinking about it with unending gratitude after a dinner at "Le Bistro" in New York with my son, Serge, and his wife Mania.

Yesterday I sent to N. Struve,* the editor of *Vestnik* (*Messenger*) in Paris, my article about *The Gulag Archipelago*. I managed to write it very fast as a reaction to a literally fairy-talish book. I am still strongly impressed, or rather surprised, joyfully and gratefully, by the phenomenon of Solzhenitsyn. It seems to me that I have not encountered such a broad mind, such a heart, such an approach to life since Pushkin. Even Dostoevsky and Tolstoy do not have it; they have often a hint of ideology, a message.

Yesterday I met for three hours with Father N., a young priest, nice, sincere, convinced, even broadminded. But, Lord, what confusion, not only of thoughts but precisely of experience, of consciousness. People like him seem to like such a small "orthodoxy," with many idols, fetishes, inner constraints. One has the impression that were they to go off their rails, everything would disintegrate. So they cling to those rails, not even questioning where they are going or where they came from. After such a meeting, I get an acute feeling of loneliness, of inability to say what is really needed. I cannot escape a thirst for freedom that would liberate me to act responsibly. When I am in such a mood, I give in to a sense of totally ignoble despondency. How can I cure it? I read the 14th volume of P. Leautaud's diary,** one of my very favorite authors.

What is real culture? Communion. Participation in that which conquered time and death.

* Struve, Nikita—Professor of Russian Studies at the Univesity of Paris. His wife Marie is the daughter of Father Alexander Elchaninov and an iconographer.
**Léautaud, Paul, *Journal littéraire*, 27 volumes.

*Monday, January 14, 1974*

On Saturday we went to Wappingers Falls to celebrate Anya's birthday. Very cold, frosty, winter evening. Lots of snow on every tree and every branch and over all of it an incredible triumphant sunset. I have not seen such beauty in a long time. That beauty speaks, but we forgot how to hear it.

All these days I am in a creative mood. I am writing in my book on baptism a paragraph about the aspect of dying in baptism (the image of death), a paragraph that has been blocking my writing for more than a year. As usual, the solution, the unblocking, does not come out of me, but is somehow suddenly opened up to me. It is always a wonderfully happy feeling.

Yesterday, before the Liturgy, I went to Mt. Vernon Hospital and took communion to David D[rillock]'s* mother—72 years old, she had a serious operation. The appearance of a humble, almost subconscious Christianity, self-evident faith, clarity, joy. No theories, but everything that theologians write about with so much anguish, hard work and argument. One begins to think how serious a sin is being committed toward such people by all the religious professionals obsessed with their righteousness, disputes, etc. True, such humble people are not concerned about it all. Thank God!

*Wednesday, January 16, 1974*

Léautaud is a man who, day after day, "tells" his life, who is always truthful. After a while (15 volumes) he becomes a friend. I neither agree with him nor are we of the same mind. It is quite strange, actually rather mysterious, how one comes to love a person for no other reason than because of what he is. He writes in such a way that I begin to regret I was not part of his life, nor he of mine. But that I was not part of Hegel's or Kant's life leaves me completely indifferent. The gift of life is in inverse proportion to the gift of ideas.

*Saturday, January 19, 1974*

*Denial of Change*

"Historical crisis of Orthodoxy." Historically, Orthodoxy was always not only a church, but also an Orthodox world, a sort of Orthodox universe. *Any* change of circumstances in this world causes a negative reaction, a denial of change, reducing it to evil, temptation, demonic pressure. This reaction is not due to loyalty, faith or dogma—which remain unchanging amidst all changes. Actually, the Orthodox world has ceased to be overly interested in

* Drillock, David—Professor of Liturgical Music and Provost of St Vladimir's Seminary, 1962–present.

dogmas, in the content of the faith. It is rather the denial of change as a category of life. A new situation is bad, because it is new. This *a priori* denial does not allow an understanding of change, to evaluate it in the context of the faith, to "meet" it realistically. Leave and deny, not understand. Since the Orthodox world was and is inevitably and even radically changing, we have to recognize, as the first symptom of the crisis, a deep schizophrenia which has slowly penetrated the Orthodox mentality: life in an unreal, nonexisting world, firmly affirmed as real and existing. Orthodox consciousness did not notice the fall of Byzantium, Peter the Great's reforms, the Revolution; it did not notice the revolution of the mind, of science, of lifestyles, forms of life… In brief, it did not notice *history*. This denial of the significance of the historical process did not serve the cause of Orthodoxy. Instead of understanding change, and therefore dealing with it, Orthodoxy found itself crushed by it. People *escaped*—to the Fathers, to the *Typikon*, to Catholicism, to Hellenism, to spirituality, to a strictly defined way of life, anywhere. Fundamentally, one escaped. To escape or to deny is stronger than to affirm. It is easier to cling to the old calendar, to the letter of the law, to fear and angry defense. This struggle with history, which inevitably follows its course, comes from an inability to come to terms with the basic Christian antinomy: "in this world, but not of this world" and to understand that the Orthodox world is of this world. To proclaim it as the ultimate absolute is a betrayal. We are paying the price of the crisis of Orthodoxy because we created so many idols, hundreds of idols. We never incorporated our own Orthodox world in the "passing image of the world." Now that this Orthodox world is breaking down, we try to regenerate and revive it. We are deeply concerned with the fate of many Patriarchates, with the survival of Mt. Athos; we busy ourselves with Byzantium and the Byzantine texts so important to theologians. We are engulfed in many jurisdictions, all of them brandishing various canons. We try to conquer the West with what is weak and ambiguous in our heritage. This arrogance, self-satisfaction and pompous triumphalism are frightening. Perhaps most frightening is the fact that few people see it, feel it, know it. People are horrified by the fallen world, but not enough by the falling of Orthodoxy. We condemn heresies, violations of canons, the sins of others and all that at a time when the essence of Orthodoxy, its Truth, could, perhaps for the first time in history, be heard as salvation. All that remains is to believe that God cannot be desecrated. In a personal way, what remains is the same agonizing question: What to do?

## Monday, January 21, 1974

When reading about writers, about the academic milieu, I came to the rather pleasant conclusion that I never suffered from any form of careerism: I never sent any books with my inscriptions, nor sought book reviews. I avoided meeting influential people who could help to promote my "career." I never imposed on anyone my books, articles, convictions. I can say with a clear conscience that I am neither proud of this, nor am I attempting to show off my humility. No! I think that my main reason for this is to avoid being tied down, and a secret and constant thirst for freedom.

Another thought came to my mind yesterday on my way to give a lecture in Wilmington, Delaware. I was reading the journals of Mircea Eliade and I realized that I am really not interested at all in any of the Eastern religions that are provoking such interest in Eliade and others around him. My mind and tastes are somehow totally impermeable to them. I am certain that the meeting of East and West is necessary (Eliade's dream), and what he writes about it is quite noteworthy, but I do not find any in Tibet, India, et al. I feel stifled by these eerie and scary worlds, in spite of their liberating and cosmic character.

This was my fourth year of going to Wilmington to lecture at their cultural center. Before my lecture, I had dinner at an old-fashioned hotel. Sometimes it seems to me that during these trips my secret joy comes from the two hours spent in that enormous, old, lordly hall with its huge windows. Respectable, quiet couples find there a festive conclusion to an idle Sunday. Blinking candles, old unhurried waiters and frosty twilight behind well-insulated windows. My lecture was attended by 300 people—but it was not I, it was Solzhenitsyn, who was the topic of the lecture. I spent the night at the Statler-Hilton across from the station. Strange feeling: to be completely lost, quite alone in the world.

Checkup at the doctor: hopelessly healthy!

## Wednesday, January 23, 1974

I feel discouraged. Not personally. I can safely and boldly say that I am very happy—with my family, my children, etc. But in matters concerning the church, its situation, my involvement in it, I am discouraged. I am becoming allergic to the pseudo-churchly and the pseudo-religious content of the church and of church life, which more and more seems to me a distortion of Orthodoxy and Christianity. At the same time, I am totally involved and engulfed in it: endless phone calls, letters, talks, meetings. All of these are neither genuine nor real; they are outside the reality of God, man, world, life. I feel that my heart cries for something "other." But I do not see any way out. To leave? Where to? I cannot leave the church—the church is my life. But as I am now, I cannot serve the church as I understand that service. I firmly believe that Orthodoxy is Truth and Salvation and I shudder when I see what is being offered under the guise of Orthodoxy, what people seem to like in it, what they live for, what the most orthodox, the best people among them see in Orthodoxy. "Save yourself and you will save thousands around you." Each one saves himself in his own way; salvation consists in fulfilling one's vocation. But what if circumstances do not allow this salvation; what if one's whole involvement, one's activity is constantly denying the level where salvation is possible?

### Thursday, January 24, 1974

I am about to finish Mircea Eliade's book, *Fragments of a Journal.* A great deal is quite true, but at the same time, somehow quite erroneous. In our world, any religion without Christ (even Christianity and Orthodoxy) is a negative phenomenon, even frightening. *Any* contact with such a religion is dangerous. One can study it to better understand Christianity, or Christ. But by itself, it cannot be salvation, however one understands this word.

For the early Christians, the Body of Christ is on the altar because He is among them. For the contemporary Christians, Christ is here because His Body is on the altar. It seems to be analogous, but in fact, there is an essential difference between the early Christians and us. For them, everything is in knowing Christ, loving Him. For us, everything is in the desire to be enlightened. The early Christians came to Communion to follow Christ, whereas now Christ is not the unique reason for partaking of Communion.

Three o'clock. Children are walking home from school. And suddenly I remember the acute joy of that coming out of school, the blissful moment of the end of the school day. Freedom, even the sun seems brighter, an almost painful feeling of life, youth, happiness.

### Friday, February 8, 1974

I just spent six days in sunny California. In spite of being exceedingly busy (seven lectures about Solzhenitsyn, meetings, dinners, conversations), what dominated during my stay was a wonderful festal light, a deep blue sky, a deep blue ocean, a white city, blooming cherry trees. How many times have I been in San Francisco and every time I have an impression of paradise. Large crowds attended the lectures. I had lost contact with that old Russian émigré crowd, but suddenly I was impressed by these transparent wonderful faces with the genuine Russian culture and strong roots.

## Monday, February 11, 1974

This morning from 6 to 8 AM, in total darkness, I was in line to get some gas for my car. I spent blissful hours fascinated by the world of simple people, the morning hustle, life in its daily mixture of colors. I took a book, but did not read. Instead, I happily contemplated.

All these days are full of news about Solzhenitsyn. On Tuesday in Washington, where I flew to give a talk about S. at the American University, I learned about his arrest and, the next day, about his expulsion from Russia to Switzerland. At night I saw him on television getting off the plane. I have one wish: that Solzhenitsyn will be able to remain himself, which might be difficult in the West. To be an émigré is so much more difficult than to be in one's own country. If S. were to ask my advice, what to do in exile, I would tell him that the Russia which expelled you is not Russia, but the Russia "abroad" is not Russia either. Remain what you are. Be responsible; do not identify yourself with anyone or anything in the West.

After hearing a confession this morning, I thought, how easy it is to give advice to others, that one should address to oneself.

## Saturday, February 16, 1974

A strong faith attenuates the intensity of problems. In those rare moments when through religion one manages to reach God, there are no problems, because God is not part of the world. In those moments the world itself becomes life in Him, meeting with Him, contact with Him. The world does not become God, but life with God, joyful and full. This is God's salvation of the world. It is fulfilled every time that we believe. The church is not a religious establishment, but the presence in the world of a saved world. But so often the church is entangled in problems that in faith are nonexistent and harmful. "Spirituality," "churchiness"—dangerous and ambiguous concepts. So often many people whom I knew as seekers of spirituality were narrow-minded, intolerant and dull, joyless, quite often accusing others of not being spiritual enough. They were often the center of their conscience, not Christ, not the Gospel, not God. In their presence, one does not bloom; just the opposite, one crouches. Pride, egocentricity, self-satisfaction and narrow-mindedness; but then, what is the use of spirituality? One will say to me that this is not genuine spirituality, that it is pseudo-spirituality. But where is true spirituality to be found? —Maybe in the desert or in lonely monastic cells. Yet the spirituality found in the church somehow frightens me. There is nothing worse than professional religiosity. All this fingering of a rosary in the midst of church gossip, the whole style of sighs and lowered eyes, seem so often terribly fake.

## *Wednesday, February 20, 1974*

Yesterday was for me a truly joyous paschal day. At 4 o'clock, Nikita Struve called from Paris, having just spent two days with Solzhenitsyn. N. S. said that Solzhenitsyn wants to meet me, that he feels that we are "related." He liked my radio scripts about the Gulag. Struve: "He is a superman!"

## *Thursday, February 21, 1974*

To touch base—this is the meaning, the purpose of this journal; not so much a desire to record everything, but a kind of visit with myself, albeit quite brief. You are here? Yes. Well, thank God. Then it becomes easier not to be completely dissolved in the fuss of my life. Deep down, what tortures me is not busyness *per se*, but an inner doubt about most of what I do, about the role that I have to play. It is hard to believe how much I dislike this role, somehow imposed on me by circumstances.

Fear of death comes from bustle, fuss, not from happiness. When one bustles around and suddenly remembers death, death seems totally absurd, horrible. But when one reaches quiet and happiness, one contemplates and accepts death quite differently. For death itself is on a high, "important" level, and seems frightening only when associated with mediocre, low, unnecessary fuss. In happiness, in genuine happiness, one always feels the presence of eternity in the heart, so that happiness is open to death. They are alike, they touch eternity. In fuss, there is no eternity and therefore fuss rejects death. "In blessed repose…"—it means *in death*, as perceived by a happy man.

Being in church should be liberating. But in the Church's contemporary tonality, church life does not liberate, but narrows, enslaves, weakens the man. One starts to be interested in the Old and New Calendars, in what the bishops are doing, one assumes a kind of unctuous sweetness. A great deal of so-called spiritual literature is of dubious quality. Instead of teaching man to look at the world through the Church's vision, instead of transforming man's view of himself and his life, one feels obliged—in order to be "spiritual"—to clothe oneself in an impersonal, soiled "garment of piety." Instead of at least knowing that there is joy, light, meaning, eternity, man becomes irritated, narrow-minded, intolerant and often simply mean. He does not even repent of it because it all comes from "churchliness," whereas the meaning of religion consists only in filling life with light, in referring it to God, transforming it into a relationship with God.

### Monday, February 25, 1974

"Clean Monday"—first day of Great Lent. I spent Saturday and yesterday in Endicott, NY. Joyful impression from the services and the people. After days of inner rebellion, such a clear indication: Stop rebelling, there is nowhere to go. The Church is your body and blood; you are wedded to the Church through your priesthood.

Sunday evening, Forgiveness Vespers at the Seminary.

### Thursday, February 28, 1974

First Liturgy of the Presanctified Gifts yesterday. Before the Liturgy, two hours of confessions. The usual impression: the narrowing of man's conscience through piety and, therefore, what one hears is not a confession of sins but of "difficulties" that should not occupy our attention. I always try to call people to live higher, more openly. This morning I lectured about sin—a reconstruction of the sacrament of repentance, its true dimension, ecclesiastical, eschatological. How far is that dimension from the habitual view of confession which leads to a rather dull, gray digging into one's self. How much unnecessary fuss in the Church, how little air, quiet, light. Today, during my lecture, I commented on the wonderful epistle of Palm Sunday—Philippians 4:4: "Rejoice in the Lord always; again I will say, Rejoice…" What a call! Flooded in sun, radiant days announcing spring.

### Friday, March 1, 1974

(Julien Green—*Journal*):

> To love to the point of dying, someone whose voice one never heard, whose face one never saw, this is the whole of Christianity. A man stands next to a window and looks at the snow falling and suddenly, he is filled with a nameless joy. In the deepest instant, he feels a mysterious peace without any personal care: there is the refuge, the only one; for Paradise is nothing other than to love God, and there is no other Hell than to be without God.

### Thursday, March 7, 1974

I spent two days in Syosset at a meeting of the Synod of Bishops. The bishops celebrated and sang the Liturgy of the Presanctified Gifts. They sang together, so well, with such simplicity. I was inspired by their strong attachment to the Church, their firm loyalty, a sort of humility. We do not always understand, nor do we always think about it, but we "preserve" the Church and we rejoice in how well we preserve her. This is the Old Testament and the preservation of memory. It is so important because it is so deep. I feel gratitude for it because without it, how could people be inspired—set on fire?

## Saturday, March 9, 1974

Beautiful Liturgy with Bishop Gregory* of Alaska. After a quiet working day at home, dinner at my son's (Serge). Late at night Anya, Tom and all their children are with us.

Beauty and truth of little details of life, little joys—spring is early this year. I thought about it all while going to church and remembered the verse: "O beautiful March, full of spring, sadness and promise, you give me hope…"

## Tuesday, March 12, 1974

"The Lord is my shepherd, I shall not want…" The strength of prayer, when I say to God: I cannot but You can; help me; when with all my being, I know that, "Without Me, you can do nothing…"

## Wednesday, March 13, 1974

Yesterday, I met for a long time with N. He told me that two people—a girl he loved, and someone else, broke up with him because he did not believe in God in the "Orthodox way." He was explaining to me his reticence toward the Church; his inability to accept faith as it is lived in the Church, his imperviousness to the teachings of the Church. He is a radiant boy, full of light, goodness and love for peace. What can one say to such people, or rather how can one defend a Christianity in which Christ is somehow obscured from view by an accumulation of inexplicable obstacles and taboos? Those people who have the gift of life, life's religious sense, often do not need a "religion" which fills a void, which takes away fear. This kind of joyless, lifeless religion repels people, mainly because its outlook on life is often mean, censorial and judgmental.

"Rejoice evermore…In everything give thanks…" Is it heard clearly enough in our Christianity, tired and suffering from its own history?

## Sunday, March 17, 1974

All these days I managed to find time, in snatches, to write my *Of Water and the Spirit*. I feel so inspired and full of joy when I can work on what I love, when I touch "the one thing needful."

* Gregory (Afonsky), Bishop—Bishop of the Diocese of Alaska (OCA), 1973–1995.

Yesterday, a retreat in Yonkers. I did not want to go, started the day in a mean mood. But on the way, the rain and the dear familiar ugliness of rows of simple little houses when approaching our church miraculously converted me. I suddenly felt how sinful is my lack of enthusiasm, a real treason. This is *my* job—whether the timing is bad or good. And the retreat and the whole day after it were good and full of light.

In the evening, the service of the Cross. I continue feeling lifted up and lit up inside. There is the whole truth, the only victory. I feel it quite acutely.

## Monday, March 18, 1974

A radiant, windy, spring day. In New York City, on Fifth Avenue, huge flags are swinging and slapping in the wind. A feast in the sky, the air, the people.

Yesterday, I served the Presanctified Liturgy in East Meadow, followed by a lecture about Solzhenitsyn. The church was full. We gave Communion from two chalices. A wonderful feeling of being in communion with the reality of the Church. This morning I lectured at the seminary about repentance, one of the rare lectures when I was completely satisfied. In the afternoon, a few hours of writing about Baptism—also with real joy. Finally, late at night, an hour with the Kobloshs* and the Hubiaks —a wonderful feeling of brotherhood, togetherness, friendship. Why am I writing all of this down? Because it is important to know, to realize, how much God is giving me all the time, and also to know how sinful is despondency, grumbling, joylessness.

Watching the crowd in church, I thought, "Thou has hidden these things from the wise and understanding, and revealed them to babes…" (Matthew 11:25). Complexity, snobbism, the cheap sentimentality of sophisticated parishes—transparent simplicity of a classic American parish.

## Sunday, March 24, 1974

On Friday I received a joyful letter from N. Struve: Solzhenitsyn wants to see you and is inviting you to celebrate the Liturgy and give Communion to his whole family. Until this, he says he will not start his "church life"—now I await his invitation.

## Wednesday, March 27, 1974

Sunday night and Monday we celebrated the Feast of the Annunciation—a breakthrough of radiant eternity with the voice of the Archangel. How

---

* Koblosh, Father Michael—Priest of the OCA, currently rector of St Nicholas Church, Whitestone, NY.

difficult to preserve the feast, to live by its light! Once the celebration is over, everything contrives to stifle the silence, the peace, the light of the feast and pushes one into the usual hustle.

## Thursday, March 28, 1974

To dream, to indulge in reverie—is it sinful or is it good? I know for sure that it is my favorite way of spending time: half-thinking, half-contemplating. I very easily and willingly indulge in it, and how hard it is to let it go!

Early this morning—Vigil of Mary of Egypt, then a Presanctified Liturgy celebrated by Bishop Iakovos with me and Father John M[eyendorff*].

I used to be quite vulnerable to what people said about me. I was distressed by misunderstandings, unfairness, animosity, always undeserved, I thought. I am happy to realize that I am more and more liberated from that sensitivity. I do not see any merit in it—it is a habit that I think that the Lord Himself is teaching me.

One after another, radiant, cool days. Tomorrow we will hear: "Rejoice, for through you joy shall shine forth. Rejoice O dawn of a mysterious day." From childhood it has been one of my most beloved days.

## Saturday, March 30, 1974

Yesterday, a fierce snowstorm. I spent the day at home, warm and cozy. In the evening—the *Akathistos* hymn, a surge of joyful love, of generous praise. I watched on television the arrival of Solzhenitsyn's family in Zurich. He was carrying his boys. A vision of something simple, clear, eternal—of the life that is being corrupted and demonically ruined by the fuss and the evil of this world. But, "in vain are the mortals rushing about...simple life prevails and lives."

## Tuesday, April 2, 1974

On Sunday I lectured to a Russian audience in Boston: "I am so glad that they listened to you, if you only knew what people say about you..." At first I feel surprised: from where comes this hatred? All the stories about me, sometimes a sort of obsession about me. But quite quickly I realize that it does not throw me off track any more, it does not deprive me of peace. I am slowly learning to know the worth of popularity or unpopularity—both worthless.

Yesterday, L. and I stopped by in Wappingers Falls at the Hopkos, then went to Kent. A nostalgic trip: how much we loved these trips to Serge's

* Meyendorff, Father John, †1992—Appointed Professor of Church History (1959) at St Vladimir's Seminary and Dean from 1984–1992. Friend and colleague of Father Schmemann.

boarding school (Kent School, 1957-1963). We took little roads through the Berkshires, enjoying the special coziness of New England. The trees are still bare, but we can unmistakably feel that spring is breaking through.

## Friday, April 5, 1974

A letter from Solzhenitsyn:

30/3/74

Dear Father Alexander:

Please forgive me for not writing sooner. It is quite difficult to live until you feel at home. I do not mean serious work, or answering letters, but even to unpack and sort things out—is beyond my power.

Nikita told me that you were planning a trip to Europe. Why not come for a few days, there is so much to talk about. I am facing a problem that I cannot really understand—the number of Orthodox Churches abroad. But more important, I want to say Confession to you and take Communion. So does my whole family. Is it possible?

Sincerely yours,<br>AS

I am so happy with the simplicity, modesty, directness of this letter.

On Wednesday morning I flew to Montreal, on a clear spring day. I was in no hurry, so I took a bus to the city from the airport. My favorite feeling: solitude and freedom on a sunny day in a strange city. The city and its people live their everyday lives—which for me is a feast. A lecture at McGill University. In the evening a wonderful Liturgy of the Presanctified Gifts with a choir directed by Liz Vinogradov.

I was touched to tears by the whole group of young people. In spite of a dull opposition of the older generation, they reach out for what is genuine, find it and again set it on fire.

In Montreal, our granddaughter, little Vera Tkachuk. Paradise is open to children; it shines from them.

Today—the last Lenten Matins. Lazarus Saturday slowly comes into being and with it the "high place" to which we are ascending.

## Lazarus Saturday, April 6, 1974

"By raising Lazarus from the dead before Thy Passion, Thou didst confirm the Universal Resurrection…" really proclaim, really devour death with victory. This feast is the height of Orthodoxy, intimately authentic, its deepest experience. Children's procession with palms.

### Holy Monday, April 8, 1974

Beautiful celebration of Palm Sunday. Festive services, many people in church. Yesterday I spent the whole day at home with my grandchildren—Anya's and Serge's. In the evening, Bridegroom service. All the gardens in Crestwood are full of blooming forsythias.

Chekhov's *Letter*—"You will always find enough people who punish …try to find merciful ones."

### Bright Tuesday, April 16, 1974

Holy Week and Pascha—filled with their usual tension, growth, fullness. I am always anxious that all should go well, and thanks to God, always the same gift from heaven! Again the same feeling: how easy it is to transform all that beauty, fullness, depth, to transform it into a goal in itself, into an idol! As soon as one tries to apply it all to life, one realizes with fear and awe that in one's life—it is a cross. Holy Week and Pascha open for us a vision of life and of victory that truly pierces the heart like a sword.

Two busy days at home, children and grandchildren.

Yesterday, in the *New York Times,* Sakharov's answer to Solzhenitsyn's "Letter to the leaders in Russia." I feel all around a growing irritation with Solzhenitsyn and rationally I do not know how to react to it. I can understand all of Sakharov's objections—moderate, reasonable, well founded—the perpetual conflict between the prophet and the Levite. The prophet is always defenseless because against him stands an arsenal of ready, tested ideas. A prophecy does not fit into ready-made frames and destroys them. That's why a prophecy must be interpreted.

### Bright Wednesday, April 17, 1974

I do not remember ever seeing such a bright sun, such clear skies as in these last days. Every morning we celebrated a Paschal Liturgy with a procession. If only one could let everybody see the victorious power that flows so generously from these Paschal services.

### Tuesday, April 23, 1974

Sudden death of Serge B[outeneff] last Thursday. I brought him Communion Wednesday night in the hospital, then he died. We buried him on Bright Saturday; it was a beautiful, joyful, triumphant Paschal burial service. How strange that the Church has lost—except during that special week—what should always be the Christian burial. People prefer the morbid tonality, the gloomy delight of

39

a contemporary funeral. Young Peter B[outeneff] to his mother: "I see now the connection between Pascha and death." That connection *is* Christianity, but one has ceased to understand that death has been trampled by victory.

### Monday, April 29, 1974

This morning I went to New York with L. It was too early to go to Radio Liberty for my weekly script taping, so we stopped in at St Patrick's Cathedral. The Mass was ending with about forty communicants. A lot of people praying, quietly kneeling on that weekday morning, in the middle of the hustle and bustle of Fifth Avenue. Being with them, I felt "peace and joy in the Holy Spirit" (Romans 14:17).

Summer seems to be here. Our Crestwood is drowning in blooming trees—magnolias, dogwood, cherry trees, flowers. Yesterday I spent the day at home trying to put my office in order. I couldn't continue working in such chaos. A quiet walk with L.

### Monday, May 6, 1974

Yesterday I was in Binghamton where I preached at Matins, then again at the Liturgy, and had talks with parishioners; finally a meeting with the local clergy. I love those immersions into the basics and roots of our Church. I am never taken aback by the elementary questions which concern people (calendar, rites, head covering for women, etc.). These questions are more genuine than discussions about spirituality.

### Monday, May 13, 1974

A card from Solzhenitsyn—

> Dear Father Alexander:
>
> As soon as you land in Zurich, take a taxi to our home. We will immediately proceed into the mountains where we will spend a few days and you will be able to sleep. There we will talk. I can have real conversations only out of the city. On your last day, we will go back home and there you will serve.
>
> Believe me, it is the best plan which I never offer anyone. No hotels! I am waiting for you.
>
> A.S.

### Tuesday, May 14, 1974

Flying back from Boston, I thought about my life. I like most a contemplative life—No! not in the sense of an intense spiritual life, but in my daily life.

I love to read, to think, to write. I like my friends and peace, and I am endlessly happy alone at home with my family. But all the time I am condemned to activity—in the church, at the seminary; to make decisions, to be "responsible." How can I say it? I am constantly caught up in things that I do not want to be mixed up in. I am often regarded as power hungry, ambitious, an activist. But in my conscience, I know that I do not want power, nor do I seek it. Then why, how come I am involved in everything and everywhere? I end up being responsible and even a scapegoat. I am 52 and I can not decide what to do. Accept it and carry on, or liberate myself? What is right and what is faintheartedness? "Everybody must follow one's own way as long as it goes upward." (André Gide) But what to do, when I do not know what my own way should be?

## Tuesday, May 21, 1974

Yesterday, Monday, the 20th, I drove to St Tikhon's to have a talk with Bishop Herman and Bishop Kyprian.* The drive on that unbearably beautiful day with blooming trees and sunny fields was wonderful. I took a bath of solitude, happiness, quiet. After all these fussy days it was sheer bliss. The talk was about unifying our two seminaries—a talk that will have to continue in order to pave the way.

## Thursday, May 23, 1974

*Ascension*

After Vespers, confessions. I try to tell everyone the same thing: to liberate oneself from "pounds" of pettiness. Pettiness—of the heart, of relationships, of cares—does not leave room in the heart for God, it is truly demonic. The fallen world is a petty world, a world in which a high vision is not perceived, a high note is not heard. In a petty world, even religion becomes petty. The perversion of Christianity does not come from heresies, but from the fall. A fall downward, and pettiness is down there.

I would like to write down for myself, very truthfully if possible, what my faith is. I would like to envision the order of symbols, words, moods, etc. that express the faith in me and for me. The most important question is how does objective faith become subjective? How does it grow in the heart to become a personal faith? When do common words become one's own? The faith of the Church, the faith of the Fathers comes alive only when it is my own.

* Kyprian (Borisevich), Archbishop, †1980—Rector of St Tikhon's Seminary, PA, and Archbishop of Philadelphia and Eastern PA.

## Saturday, May 25, 1974

Two days before I leave to meet Solzhenitsyn. I am quite emotional, wondering how the meeting will be. The phone has not stopped ringing: tell S., convince S., try to persuade S., ask S. etc. I am told that S. has a difficult time coping with exile, he is nervous, irritable, demanding. I feel quite peaceful, quiet. Whatever needs to be will be.

## Monday, June 17, 1974

Yesterday I came back from Europe. From May 28-31 with S. in the mountains—just the two of us. I will write down the little notes that I took every evening. Only much later will I be able to sum up what were these most significant days of my life.

"*Encounter on the Mountain*" (the title is from an inscription in a book given to me by S.) "To dear Father Alexander in the days of our mountain encounter, which we were approaching for a long time through a mutual recognition."

## FROM THE ZURICH NOTEBOOK

## Tuesday, May 28, 1974

We are beginning our descent to Zurich. It is pouring rain. In spite of a sleepless night on the plane, I feel wide-awake and strange: I am registering all the details. I see everything and everything comes to this, that I am going to be with Solzhenitsyn. Now I want to remember everything: I am waiting for my luggage; I am waiting for a taxi. Rainy streets, detours, and suddenly a little house, a closed gate, a neglected yard. I ring the bell and *voilà*: the door is opened by S. and right away one thing is clear: how simple everything is in him.

## Wednesday, May 29, 1974

It is 7:00 AM I hear S. fussing in the kitchen. All around—mountains and blue sky. Yesterday, in Zurich, the whole family came up to receive a blessing. We had tea. "I have the feeling that I know you all so well." And the wife, Natasha: "to be sure, how well we know you!"

My first impression of A. S. after his simplicity, his energy, his restlessness, his concern—immediately, "let's go." He is carrying little bundles of brown bags. A lovely smile. We drive for 40 minutes up a mountain road. A primitive cottage, rather chaotic. Things all over the kitchen and his desk. S. is obviously a Russian *intelligent*. No comfort, no armchair, no closet. Everything reduced to a strict minimum. His clothes are those he wore when he came out of Russia. Some sort of cap, officer's boots.

"I have so many questions"—our conversation is prepared, he has a list of questions.

About church, "I decided to popularize your ideas."?! About his book: "Read everything about the church—I will correct if necessary." About *Vestnik*, etc., etc.

## *Thursday, May 30, 1974*

Yesterday we spent the whole day together, taking a long walk, talking, an unforgettable day. When I lay in bed, I felt I was in a fairy tale. Only later will I be able to take it in, to understand it all.

A long conversation about many chapters of the book that he is writing. Some of my criticism he willingly accepts. Long talk about the Revolution.

New perspective about Russia and its history. The Russian *people*. All is new, elemental.

S. is very considerate, cares about little things, clumsily prepares dinner, cuts up something, fries it. He is enormously human and touching. Pressure and energy.

Of Russia, he says, "here." The West does not exist for him. No interest. Does not like Peter the Great. Pasternak "is not Russian." Wants to live in Canada, to establish there a little Russia. "Only that way will I be able to write."

Talks about his first marriage…

"I know that I will return." Complete faith that change is coming in Russia. Absolute denial of democracy. Yes to monarchy. Incredible moral health, simplicity, purposefulness. He is the carrier, not of Russian culture, but of Russia itself. The criterion of religion is the salvation of Russia.

S. is hearing, grabbing, choosing what he needs for his writing, the rest goes by.

Attentive to concrete details: make the bed, what will we eat? Take an apple.

A firm conviction of his mission—he is so convinced that it makes him humble.

Intuitive understanding, rather than knowledge. He passes over anything not essential, concentrates on what is required and important.

Having lived with him for two days, I feel small, tied down by well-being, unnecessary cares and interests. Next to me is a man who has taken upon himself the burden of service, who has totally given himself to it, who does not use anything for himself. It is extraordinary. Even a walk for him is not entertainment, but a sacred act. Such faith moves mountains! "Can you imagine? My lawyer is on vacation, resting all the time…"

"My wife and I have decided not to fear anything." No sentimentality, but his phone calls to his wife—so gentle, so caring.

I am sitting at his desk surrounded by incredible disorder. The mountains are coated with morning fog. The delicate sound of cowbells, of bleating sheep. The lilacs are in bloom. All this for him is not Switzerland, not the West; he is completely "there"; rather "here" as he says. Where he is, is the real Russia. For him it is so clear that it becomes true.

He instinctively and light-handedly rejects all that is not needed; that adds burdens.

No comfort, but he puts a nail in the wall so that I can hang my towel.

In understanding this phenomenon of a great man, mainly there is a sense of an elemental calamity. In that "calamity" everything is included (green onions, steamy milk, all the little details that surround us).

Not reaching out, but down and high up. A long walk over hills and through the woods. A long conversation about life, soul, faith.

Suddenly I have a disturbing thought: Will he burn out? How can one live in such a fire? While talking, he is gathering wild yellow tulips; at home he looks a long time for a glass—and the next day he does not forget to take them to his wife.

With pride, he shows me his little vegetable garden: dill, radishes, green onions.

At night—a long confession upstairs in his room—sunset behind the window.

"Let's take a last walk." So friendly, with such affection. Extraordinary with all their light and joy, truly "mountain" days.

Will I ever have in my life such days, such an encounter, in such complete simplicity, that not once did I wonder, what should I say? No falseness is possible while being with him.

## Wednesday, June 5, 1974

The last entry (May 30, 1974) was written on the eve of our departure from the mountain cottage. The next day, Friday, May 31, 1974, will remain unforgettable.

Early in the morning, Natasha's mother came to get us and we drove to Zurich. Preparation for the Liturgy. Confessions. After the Liturgy, A. S.: "How good it was, how everything reaches us, how close we are…"

Finally, after the awesome tension of these days, I am alone at the Zurich airport. Again, rain and fog. Again the usual Western crowd, essentially—my world, where I feel comfortable because I belong to it, because inside this world I am free and alone.

For the first time, I wonder whether it was a dream. Was it in the real world? Or in a dream, in an illusion created through immense effort? The illusion will inevitably be smashed against the immovable block of life. For the first time I feel fear and doubt, and a growing pity for S.

Zurich, Paris. A bath of reality. My mother, my brother Andrei. A few days of usual lectures, meetings, dinners with friends, a visit with N. Struve, with whom we discuss S. Will he be able to survive the pressure of his family, the West, his mission?

### Thursday, June 6, 1974

Today I received a short letter from S.: "We all love you!"

I feel that in Paris there is a growing irritation with S. His bursting into our lives does not promise anything but trouble and dissension.

In the evening, dinner at my mother's.

END OF THE ZURICH NOTEBOOK

### Saturday, September 7, 1974

The summer, like last year, interrupted these notes. We spent the whole summer in Labelle, a wonderful summer that stays in my memory as continuous light, sunshine, happiness.

### Monday, September 16, 1974

During these days I read and worked preparing for a new course—*the Liturgy of Death*. At first, it seemed rather easy and straightforward but then became complex and quite profound. Death is in the center of religion and of culture, and one's attitude toward death determines one's attitude toward life. Any denial of death only increases the neurosis (immortality) as does its acceptance (asceticism, denial of the flesh). Only victory over death is the answer, and it presupposes transcendence of both denial and acceptance—"death consumed by victory." The question is "What is this victory?" Quite

45

often the answer is forgotten. Therefore one is helpless in dealing with death. Death reveals—must reveal—the meaning not of death, but of life. Life must not be a preparation for death, but victory over death, so that, in Christ, death becomes the triumph of life. We teach about life without relation to death, and about death as unrelated to life. When it considers life only as a preparation for death, Christianity makes life meaningless, and reduces death to "the other world," which does not exist, because God has created only one world, one life. It makes Christianity and death meaningless as victory; it does not solve the neurosis of death. Interest about the fate of the dead beyond the grave makes Christian eschatology meaningless. The Church does not pray *about* the dead; it *is* (*must be*) their continuous Resurrection, because the Church *is* life in death, victory over death, the universal Resurrection.

"To come to terms with death..." At age 53, it is time to think about death, to include it as the crowning of the vision of life, as completing and giving meaning to everything. I feel this vision of life more than I can express in words, but it is a vision that I live by in the best moments of my life.

What disappears in death? The experience of the ugliness of this world, of evil, of the fluidity of time. What remains is the beauty that gladdens and in the same moment saddens the heart. "Peace." The peace of the Sabbath which opens the fullness and the perfection of Creation. God's peace. Not of death, but of life in its fullness, in its eternal possession.

### Friday, September 20, 1974

This morning I stayed in bed in a state of bliss—although with a nasty cold. I had time to think. I realized how difficult it is for me ever to be wholly in one camp. In all that I love and consider mine—the Church, religion, the world where I grew up and to which I belong, I often see deficiencies and lack of truth. In all that I do *not* like—radical ideas and convictions—I see what is right, even if relatively right. Within religion I feel stifled, and I feel myself a radical "challenger." But among challengers I feel myself a conservative and traditionalist. I cannot identify with any complete system with an integral view of the world or an ideology. It seems to me that anything finished, complete and not open to another dimension is heavy and self-destructive. I see the error of any dialectics that proceed with thesis, antithesis and synthesis, removing possible contradictions. I think that openness must always remain; it is faith, in it God is found, who is not a "synthesis," but life and fullness.

*Monday, September 23, 1974*

In connection with my new course at the seminary, I constantly think about death. The horror, the terror of death is one of the strongest existing feelings: regret about leaving this world, "the gentle kingdom of this earth." (G. Bernanos). But what if this "gentle kingdom," this open sky, these hills and woods flooded with the sun, this silent praise of colors, of beauty, of light, what if all this is finally nothing other than the revelation of what is behind death: a window of eternity? Yes, but this unique, grayish day, the lights suddenly coming on at dusk, all that the heart remembers so acutely—they are not anymore, they cannot be brought back... But the heart remembers, precisely because this gray day has shown us eternity. I will not remember that particular day in eternity, but that day was a breakthrough into eternity, a sort of remembrance of the eternity of God, of life everlasting.

All this has been said a thousand times. But when it reaches the heart and becomes a living experience...where from, why? Such peace, such joy, such a dissolution of fear, of grief, of depression, fills the heart. And one wish remains: to be able to carry that feeling without spilling it, to not let it dry out or lose its fragrance in our daily bustle. One almost starts to hear (but only almost), "For to me, to live is Christ and to die is gain" (Philippians 1:21). Then how should one live? Gather life for eternity, which means to live life as being eternal. To sow perishable goods so that "after" they would rise up indestructible. But one can also choose to live "gathering death," to live by "the lust of the flesh and the lust of the eyes and the pride of life" (1 John 2:16) which is already a torture, already death. One can choose to submit to daily bustle, to empty one's soul, to serve idols—a dead end—death...

*Wednesday, September 25, 1974*

To change the atmosphere of Orthodoxy, one has to learn to look at oneself in perspective, to repent, and, if needed, to accept change, conversion. In historic Orthodoxy, there is a total absence of criteria for self-criticism. Orthodoxy defined itself: against heresies, against the West, the East, the Turks, etc. Orthodoxy became woven with complexes of self-affirmation, an exaggerated triumphalism: to acknowledge errors is to destroy the foundations of true faith.

The tragedy of Orthodox history is always seen in the triumph of outside evil: either persecutions, or the Turkish yoke, Communism—never inside And so long as these convictions do not change, I am convinced that no Orthodox revival is possible. The many obstacles that make this revival so

47

difficult are not due to sinful people, but are rooted in what *appears* to be the essence of Orthodoxy: First—a kind of piety, full of superstitions and sweetness and absolutely impenetrable to any culture. A piety that has a pagan dimension, and dissolves Orthodoxy into a sentimental religiosity. Second—a Gnostic tendency in faith itself, which started as Hellenic influence and became a Western Cartesian intellectualism. Third—the dualism of piety and intellectual theology that replaced in the Christian vision of the world its primordial eschatology. Fourth—the surrender of Orthodoxy to nationalism in its worst pagan, authoritarian and negative aspects. This combination is offered as "pure Orthodoxy," and any attempt to look into it is immediately condemned as heresy. Nothing is as dangerous as the fanatical defense of Orthodoxy.

### Thursday, September 26, 1974

I spent two hours with N. who is interested in anthropology. He is unhappy, frustrated, offended. How can one explain to him that he is actually interested only in himself, his role in life, and that this interest is at the root of his unhappiness—it is always so, without exception. To be detached from the world is not to leave it, since to leave it can also be playing a role, searching for oneself and one's own; it is to liberate oneself from all this concern about "my" place, "my" role, and then to start a life that "passes all understanding."

"Unless it dies, it will not live." This applies to the past. In Christianity we deal not with the meaning of history, nor with the meaning of nature, but with death and resurrection as a continuous victory of Christ over history and over nature. In order to be our life, the past must die in us only as the past, nature only as nature, history only as history. This is the uniqueness of Christ and Christianity. The Kingdom of God transcends and conquers both nature and history, but it opens itself to us through nature and through history. The beginning and the end of everything: "Christ is the same today, yesterday and always." Everything is resolved only when the question of death is resolved.

### Friday, September 27, 1974

I asked myself this question: What makes a genuine work of art and where is the secret of its perfection? It seems to me that it is in the complete coincidence, the blending of law and grace. If, on a religious, spiritual level, grace is contrasted with law, it is because grace simply replaces and annihilates law. But without law, grace is not possible precisely because they are interrelated: like image and fulfillment, form and content, idea and reality. So grace is the same law, but law transformed into freedom, depleted of its lawfulness, i.e., negative, forbidding character. This is especially obvious in art. Art begins with "law," i.e., know-how, obedience and humility, acceptance of forms. But art is fulfilled in grace: When the form becomes the content it reveals the content, it is the content.

## *Monday, October 7, 1974*

On Saturday, the seminary held its annual Orthodox Education Day. One anticipates it with apprehension, but when it comes, when it starts—joy! A huge crowd, sunshine, festive tents. The Liturgy with hundreds of communicants. This is the church; one feels joyful to be dissolved in its life. I spent the whole day on my feet, greeting, hugging, welcoming—and somehow I didn't even feel tired. Although each one of us as an individual my be weak and inadequate, when there are many of us we feel the reflected light—unique in the world—of Christ's love. Russians, Arabs, Greeks, Ukrainians: where else do they meet but "in Christ?" This is the strength and the uniqueness of that day.

Yesterday we celebrated L.'s birthday. We drove to the Battery Park in Manhattan and enjoyed a warm, almost summery sunset. The Statue of Liberty and little islands in the golden light of the sea like in Venice. Some old men and women sitting on benches. Then quite by chance, out of curiosity, we had dinner at an Armenian restaurant. And we remembered Paris, Russian restaurant, Russian Paris—our childhood.

Reading the papers, we see the growing crash of the Western world. Crisis in Portugal, chaos in Italy, leftist victories in Paris elections. I am totally infuriated, not so much by the Left as by the huge bankruptcy of the "Right" that generated this crash, this dead end, with a complete absence of any dream, any ideal. Stifling boredom of capitalism, of consumerism, the moral baseness of the world that they created. What comes as a "replacement" is even worse. The guilty ones are those who, having power and opportunity, have led the world into that dead end.

Freedom? Capitalism is reducing it to the freedom of profit. The essential sin of democracy is its bond with capitalism. Capitalism needs the freedom guaranteed by democracy, but that freedom is there and then betrayed and distorted by capitalists. The vicious circle of the Western world is democracy without morality—at least so it seems to me.

The choice is frightening: a terrible "Right" or an even more terrible "Left"—they both have the same disdain for man and for life. There does not seem to be any third choice, which obviously should be the Christian one. But Christians themselves are divided into right and left, without any other idea.

Blessed Indian summer, wonderful beauty of the very beginning of autumn, of slightly yellowing leaves, of a golden light on God's creation.

## Tuesday, October 8, 1974

"It is difficult for the rich…" It is quite obvious that at the center of Christianity is the renunciation of wealth, any wealth. The beauty of poverty!—there is also, of course, the ugliness of poverty, but there is beauty. Christianity is enlightened only by humility, by an impoverished heart. Poverty does not consist always of lacking something—that is its ugliness—but in being content with what there is.

## Wednesday, October 9, 1974

Yesterday I met with a young man who came to talk about my book *For the Life of the World*—obviously read it through and through, underlined the text, made notes in the margin. He had questions about the symbolism of life, about reality, etc. I find it difficult to explain that Christianity—the Church—is the only possible and genuine encounter with the Reality of God, and therefore of everything. That's why Christianity is sacramental. The sacrament is the revelation, the encounter, the knowledge, the communion.

I heard on TV the President's speech about inflation. What nobody says, and obviously does not understand, is that "inflation" in our times is, above all, a spiritual, psychological condition, a form of consciousness. The whole world has become "inflation": inflation of words, of feelings, of relation with life. Inflation is the condition of the frog that starts to puff up and bursts (a fairy tale). When one starts calling the janitor in a store "maintenance engineer," it is inflation. And when the air that we breathe is full of inflation, life is destroyed. If everything is a lie, if everything is endlessly exaggerated, distorted, puffed up, there is no more measure or moderation in anything. Why should a price be increased by 3 cents when one could increase it by a dollar—and it will be accepted? One should start, not with an economic, but a spiritual struggle—a struggle with inflation—as a condition of the heart and of the mind.

I remember in the days of my youth when, walking to church in the golden morning light, there was a breakthrough, a touch with a mysterious bliss. And all my life, deep down, has been a search for this contact, this bliss. To feel it again! The rest is all relative, forced labor. One should be afraid of relativism. But because there is an absolute, everything in its light becomes relative. If there is God, *my* principles are not needed—God is sufficient. If not, then principles do not save us from anything, nor do they create anything.

## *Tuesday, October 22, 1974*

Yesterday we had a faculty meeting at our house. Rather peaceful, but, Lord, how difficult it is for people not only to agree with each other, but simply to hear the other. If it is the case with a small group of people who are essentially of one mind, what about the world at large? Division and alienation are the essence of the original sin. Unity can be restored only "in Christ."

Cool, transparent, sunny days. Slowly falling leaves. I am always impressed by the sad light of triumphant Fall.

## *Tuesday, October 29, 1974*

Today is Johnny Hopko's* birthday; he is ten. It seems like only yesterday that I flew to Boston to meet my son at Harvard where he was studying—and we learned by phone that my first grandson was born! Since then, years of my life went by and in my mind I can reconstruct its content. But that time, that whole long time and its reality, vanished, fell in some kind of abyss. Between then and today—a foggy morning and then a sunny autumn day—it seems that there was nothing. Time does not flow; it is spilled.

Behind my window, a morning fog, and, piercing it, bright yellow leaves. Squirrels rush from branch to branch. Everything is alive and moves in an absence of time. Extraordinary! In a spiritual life, this absence of time *is* reality, the only reality. A fallen life is a dissolution in this absence of time, a communion with death, whereas in a spiritual life, the absence of time is a communion with life.

## *Friday, November 1, 1974*

All Saints' Day—When I was a child in Paris, we went to the cemetery, drowning in an orgy of flowers, especially chrysanthemums. I remember the combination of a dark day, rainy and gloomy, and the brightly decorated graves. In 1935 on that day, I had peritonitis and almost died.

While at St Tikhon's Monastery, I read F. Jeanson's book about Sartre in a collection called *Writers Before God.*** I want to quote a passage that seems quite special:

> I was led to non-belief not out of a conflict with dogmas, but by my grandparents' indifference. Belief in God—at this time and in that milieu—was so self-assured that it had become peaceful, quiet and discreet, so that an atheist

* Hopko, Protodeacon John—Grandson of Father Schmemann, alumnus of St Vladimir's Seminary.
**Francis Jeanson, *Les Écrivains devant Dieu*, P. Desclée de Brouwer (1966).

looked like an original, insane, fanatic—a Sartre who was a maniac over God, who saw His absence everywhere and who couldn't open his mouth without pronouncing His name; in short, a man who had 'religious convictions.'

Good society had none; it believed in God so as not to talk about Him...

When I think about seminarians—ours and St Tikhon's—I see that one can love religion like anything else in life: sports, science, stamp collecting; one can love it for its own sake without relation to God or the world or life. Religion fascinates; it is entertaining. It has everything that is sought after by a certain type of person: esthetics, mystery, the sacred and a feeling of one's importance and exclusive depth, etc. That kind of religion is not necessarily faith. People expect and thirst after faith—and we offer them religion—a contradiction that can be quite deep and awesome.

### Monday, November 4, 1974

Twenty years since my ordination to the deaconate in Paris.

I do not have any more strength after last week's tension, after all the fuss. When I find myself alone, I get so discouraged. I feel nothing that I am doing is needed: the article which I am writing for the magazine *Kontinent* about the "crisis of Christianity," and all that I have to do—letters and papers that make a mess of my desk. Everybody around me seems to know so clearly what is needed; they are all goal-oriented, while I always have the feeling that I really do not know what, where, why... I am doing maintenance work so the pipes would be working, the water flowing, so there would be some light, some goodness. I do not act by conviction, but rather by reaching with something like a tuning fork in my heart.

### Friday, November 8, 1974

Forty-one years ago today the director of our Corps of Cadets school, General Rimsky-Korsakov, passed away. He was a man who played a huge role in my life. Through him I discovered Russian poetry and literature. He would read to me and let me read his handwritten notebook of poems and quotes from literature. All that in a military school where nobody went further than epaulets, regiments, and "Russian glory"! His death was my first conscious encounter with death. Because of a very narrow hallway, we—the older cadets, age 13—had to carry his body on a sheet from his bedroom to the church. It was the first time that I realized separation and the emptiness that follows the death of a close friend, the illusory aspect of life itself.

After his death, I became detached from the Cadets' school. Everything, including the epaulets, Russian glory, etc., became tasteless, futile, so that after a year I asked my parents to transfer me to a French lycée—the Lycée Carnot.

If I were to measure my life with decisive personal encounters, I would choose these four: General Rimsky-Korsakov; the school priest, Father Savva, who initiated me to church services and rituals; Professor W. Weidle, who was my mentor in pursuit of Russian literature and Italian art, and Professor Father Cyprian* [Kern], who "accompanied" me through my theological studies at the St Sergius Institute in Paris and was primarily a friend. Each one entered something into my consciousness, whereas others only influenced it. I am quite certain that each one of these friends not only gave to me, but also took something from me. They probably needed me in some way and certainly we loved each other very much. How much more important is a personal encounter, a mutual, personal love, than a purely intellectual influence.

Autumn. More and more open sky, more and more of this wonderful detached light.

### Tuesday, November 12, 1974

Last evening there was a seminar for our faculty. It was peaceful and friendly. Two papers by our historians M[eyendorff] and E[rickson] I keep thinking, again and again, about theological education in general, about history in particular. Ideally, the study of Church history should liberate people from enslavement to the past, which is rather typical for the Orthodox consciousness. This is only "ideally." I remember how slowly I became liberated from idealizing Byzantium, Old Russia, etc. and from fascination with that "game." A contemporary student who does not know any history, who knows no history at all, is even less able to find his own synthesis and holistic vision of the world. The Church does not have a sacred history, as does biblical history. Our teaching, which singles out church history, transforms it inescapably into sacred history and distorts the very teaching about the Church, the very perception of its essence. There is something there that needs to be corrected, but how? I do not know. On one hand, I agree with historians, since without a historical perspective there would be false absolutisms. On the other hand, I agree with those of the pastoral group who tend to limit history for the sake of a real, live, existing Church.

The basic formula is the same: eschatological. The Church is the presence

---

* Father Cyprian (Kern), †1960—Father Schmemann's confessor; Professor of Patristic Theology at St Sergius Institute in Paris.

in time, in history, of the saintly and the sacred. Everything in time and in history is related to the Kingdom of God and is evaluated by this relation. The life of the Church is always hidden with Christ in God. The Church lives not by history but by the Kingdom. The historical events of the Church—such as the Ecumenical Councils—are important inasmuch as they are an answer to the world, an affirmation of salvation and transfiguration. As soon as they are absolutized, as soon as they gain a value *per se*, and not as related to the world; in other words, as soon as we transform them into sacred history, we deprive them of their genuine value and meaning. Therefore, the prerequisite for the study of church history must be to liberate it from being a sacred absolute, and not to be enslaved by it—which is so often a burden on Orthodoxy.

### Thursday, November 14, 1974

Having read Solzhenitsyn's latest articles and letters, I keep thinking about the inherent danger of "ideologies." It seems to me that any ideology is bad because it is inevitably reductive and identifies any other ideology with evil, and itself with truth, whereas both truth and goodness are always transcendent. An ideology is always idolatry; thus it is evil and generates evil people.

I thought that Solzhenitsyn would preach a liberation from ideologies which poisoned Russian consciousness as well as the world in general. But, as is the case with many philosophers or writers, one is fatally drawn to crystallize one's own ideology—be it pro or con.

Yesterday I took my niece Natasha to show her New York, Broadway, our former home in New York across from Union Seminary,* where we spent eleven years. How much of that period of my life has ended, has become a faraway past—the decade of the fifties, before moving to Crestwood, when I was 30-40, still young and full of energy. Then the sixties in Crestwood, torn from New York life, I became involved in church work. So many of our New York friends died, drawing a line between then and now. Now the seventies, a decade of aging, or at any rate meeting old age. Maybe. Do I feel the beginning of an inner synthesis, of a clear vision? What is quite certain is the fullness of my family happiness: home, children, grandchildren. The presence of a secret joy.

When looking back, I see before anything else a midday sun filling all these years with light and clarity.

---

* From 1947 to 1962 St Vladimir's Seminary was located on West 121st Street in New York in a building owned by Union Theological Seminary.

I keep in my memory four distinctive and very different periods of my life: the thirties—my childhood in Paris, the golden years of the Russian emigration and the last rays of the European world; the forties—the war, the collapse of that world, theology, family, priesthood, youth; the fifties—creativity, happiness; the sixties—engagement, involvement in church affairs. And suddenly I have a strong feeling that there is more, much more past than future and everything from now on will be the summary, the opening of what already was a given.

## Sunday, November 17, 1974

After the Liturgy, enjoying Sunday peace at home (sunshine, bare trees), we listened to the *St Matthew's Passion* by Bach. Listening to it, I remembered my first "meeting" with this wonderful music in our little house in l'Etang la Ville, in France. It literally pierced and captivated me then. Since then, every time I listen to it, especially passages like the cry of the daughter of Zion and the final chorale, I come to the same conclusion: How is it possible, in a world where such music was born and heard, not to believe in God?

## Monday, November 18, 1974

We had dinner at the K[ishkovsky]'s home in Sea Cliff. They impressed me with their light, their simplicity, genuine goodness. We did not talk about anything important but I felt that I had been in touch with light.

Elections in Greece. War in the Middle East. Strikes in Paris. It is totally impossible to solve anything with the world's fixation on "rights." What is needed is a spiritual revolution, for which there is no hope, given the people's contemporary mentality. All that people know is self-assertion and condemnation of *others'* wrongdoing. We live in a kind of schizophrenia: on one hand, Christian morality is perceived only as an individual morality, but in relation to their people and their church, Christians are the first to live with pride, self-affirmation and the need to expand. Where can repentance come from, or self-limitation? "I" might give in, but "we" will never give in because "we" are right—always right; could not live a minute without our "right." Or people beat their chests like the liberals who crudely and superficially repent of their mistreatment of minorities, etc. Christianity consists in being right *and* of conceding, and in doing so letting victory triumph: Christ on the Cross *and* "truly, this is the Son of God."

On the eve of the Christmas fast, we are trying to preach to the students why the coming of God into the world in the form of a small child is not only a *kenosis*—a self-emptying of divinity—but the most adequate revelation of

God. In that Child, there is no need for strength, glory, "rights," self-affirmation, authority or power.

I just reread what I have written and stopped at the words: Etang la Ville, where we lived from 1945 to 1951. From there I went to be ordained, then to serve in a parish. From there I went to my first lecture as a teacher at the St Sergius Institute. L. went from there to give birth to Serge and Masha.

We were extraordinarily poor—so much so that, having fed the children, we often skipped dinner. But what incredibly happy years we spent there. We lived by a beautiful forest, in a drafty log cabin. We often went for walks in the woods. I remember many of these walks, the oak trees, birches, daffodils, lilies of the valley—somehow all of it stays in my memory, linked to the words: "Christ, a new and holy Pascha!"

## Tuesday, November 26, 1974

This morning, after Matins, I had a long conversation with N., a young student, about his friendship with an older student. What should one say about this eternal problem? How does one protect against emotion, sentimentality; against these "friendships" blooming under the unctuous cover of religious rhetoric and sensuality, where one already detects the dizziness preceding the fall? Scare people with hell? Quote the Apostle Paul? This is not a matter of "morality." I do not write this as a justification of "special friendships." I know that one can and needs to oppose it, but not with morality or a crude ban. The inspiration of purity, spiritual self-discipline, inner freedom, is a victory over all temptations.

## Friday, November 29, 1974

Yesterday—Thanksgiving—at Father Tom and Anya's in Wappingers Falls. The whole family: children, grandchildren, the Vino[gradov]s, and my niece Natasha. Nineteen people around the table—a glorious day! First a quiet, peaceful Liturgy. Then—it's already a tradition—a visit to Roosevelt's estate on the Hudson. A wintry, transparent sunshine, a windless day, the silence of these parks, these rooms where there used to be so much life. And again this wonderful light, somewhere across the river, the bright flash of the sun reflected from a window. In the evening the traditional turkey. The children sang, "Let All Mortal Flesh Keep Silent," "The Archangel's Voice," "Jacob's Ladder," "The Noble Joseph" and Christmas carols. Perfect happiness, fullness of life. Peace!

## *Saturday, November 30, 1974*

How often people have an innate fear of facing the Absolute, fear of losing one's freedom, of becoming involved. They take pleasure in a state of impulsiveness; they are afraid of any move toward more clarity, more choices. They shrink; they hide in themselves and passively resist.

Today is the 28th anniversary of my ordination to the priesthood. I remember that day so clearly. I walked with L. along the rue de Crimée to St Sergius Church. We were early so we went into the park for a quiet walk. It was a grayish, cloudy day. I remember seeing my father in church—quite unusual, this early—while I was censing, still as a deacon. The moment of ordination I don't remember. Only the joy of Father Cyprian, who took me around the altar table, many people in church, my new Greek cassock, my first vigil that evening, the good wishes pouring in from everyone. What remains is a vast feeling of gratitude for all that I have received in life, for all the undeserved happiness, so much happiness! And while I am writing, a bright red sun flows in my window lighting my books, so many of them acquired in those days, so many years ago.

I remember, among the many memories of my childhood, how we were taken to church every December 4th to attend a service for the Russian regiment in which my father served during the First World War. After the service, a few white-haired gentlemen, former officers, went to a restaurant to celebrate their annual reunion. Now nobody of the old guard is left, but my brother stands in church alone with a full choir and bright lights for the service. There is no more regiment, no more people, only a memory, a platonic idea. A memory of a memory, remembrance of remembrance.

I think that the goal of this journal, and the instinctive need I have to write in it, is to keep everything inside me and not to let myself be reduced to just one thing—"dean of St Vladimir's Seminary" or some such thing.

Never was that Russian regiment as alive as during those Parisian reunions and services, when memory cleansed it from distorting reality. This is the essence of a feast. "We celebrate your memory."

## *Friday, December 13, 1974*

Reflecting about the debates around Solzhenitsyn, I think that any debate is, before anything else, a debate about the hierarchy of values, about the treasure of the heart, about the "one thing needful."

Reflecting on my own life, how did the "one thing needful" get hold of my heart? —Through my mother, the church, friendships, the experience of "another" vision, of a secret light, a desire, joy in the very fabric of life. Then testing, deepening during the years at the St Sergius Institute, through the subsequent, fragmented experience of the Church; then a synthesis: cosmic, historical, ecclesiological. Then Russia: how did "meeting" Russia and its spirit and culture appear to an émigré child? Emigration: "if it does not die, it will not live..." The West: its truth and untruth, freedom, liberation, standing in freedom, the ultimate choice, service, sacrifice.

### Saturday, December 14, 1974

Yesterday at the Seminary we had a Christmas get-together—fun, witty, light. I am always surprised how students, so helpless in solving their own problems, can see so clearly and precisely the very essence of others (in this case, the professors).

### Thursday, December 19, 1974

Today (old calendar) is the parish feast of the Whitestone St Nicholas Church. As usual, I feel elated when I see eight young priests, a young choir, the parish full of movement and enthusiasm. I remember the same parish twenty years ago. How painful, how difficult was the breakthrough to renewed vision.

### Friday, December 20, 1974

It is the last day before vacations. At Matins, only a few students. Sun spots on the walls of the chapel. Yesterday, the first three-ode canon of the prefeast of Christmas. My favorite atmosphere of an "eve"—anticipation and joy.

Father Tom [Hopko] and Father Paul [Lazor*] are fascinated by the memoirs of Metropolitan Evlogy of Paris. We talked about Russian émigrés, about their specific characteristics in Father Paul's Americanized parish, about their vision of the Church. Father Tom's and Father Paul's question: Can one really build a parish "only on Christ"? Can one overcome the fusion of the Church with the "body and blood" of its people? That is the essential problem of American Orthodoxy and of Orthodoxy in the twentieth century, the test of its transcendence, truth, and universality. If its truth is only about this world (sanctification of life), it will fail. If Orthodoxy is the truth about the Kingdom of God, then it will be victorious. The early Church was victorious only through eschatological joy, the undoubted experience of the Kingdom, which comes in power, in the feeling and the vision of "the dawn of a

---

* Lazor, Father Paul—Rector of Holy Trinity Church, New Britain, CT, until appointed Dean of Students at St Vladimir's Seminary in 1977.

mysterious day." For the vast majority of Orthodox, it sounds bookish and abstract. For them, the only alternative to the "body and blood," to concrete Orthodox ways, to rationality, is in disembodied spirituality, quite individualistic. There is no other alternative.

While listening yesterday to the prefeast hymns—"Christ is born to recreate the fallen image," "the Mysterious garden," this whole collection of wonderful images and symbols—I thought again and again: the heart, the essence of everything in the Church is here, in the continuous surge towards the "ultimate" as already given, seen, sensed. The Church *is* the mystery of the Kingdom. The question is why Christians are forgetting it, and how can one come back to it? The essence of Orthodox revival and universal mission should be to bear witness to the Kingdom, to call people to the Kingdom. Everything is there: overcoming secularism, answers to contemporary problems of culture, history, religion, etc. Few people hear it, least of all theologians who are quite surprised that the world and the Church are so indifferent to their scientific research. Why do people prefer either to reduce the Church to Russian, Greek, or some other, or to throw themselves into (at times dubious) spiritual literature. We preach to people that Orthodox Christianity is not Russian, not Greek, not whatever. We tell them it enlightens the whole life. But people feel Russian, or whatever, and demand from the Church that it enlighten *their* lives, *their* reality. For the sake of what reality do we ask them to overcome their wish? "For the sake of the Church," we answer. But where *is* the reality of the Church? That is the question. In fact, the Church lives in and by the Kingdom; *this* is its reality, its life, truly its very own life. The mission of the Church is to carry to the world the experience of the Kingdom, not to reduce the Kingdom of God to anything in the world.

# CHAPTER III

# 1975

∾

*Monday, January 20, 1975*

Snow and cold. Yesterday I went to Wilmington, Delaware, for my annual lecture. After Paris, I feel quite acutely my ties with this culture and its people and enjoy being back *home*!

The rapport with Solzhenitsyn made obvious for me our essential difference. For him there is only Russia. For me, Russia could disappear, die, and nothing would change in my fundamental vision of the world. "The image of the world is passing." This tonality of Christianity is quite foreign to him.

*Tuesday, January 21, 1975*

I attended a seminar at the Union Theological Seminary, "The Liturgy and the Arts." I gave the introductory talk. After me, Ann Belford, a disciple of Jung, spoke about symbolism, the subconscious, etc. I sat there and thought, what an incredible confusion takes place in the consciousness or subconsciousness of Christians. It is difficult to imagine what Christians can offer to the contemporary world. Christianity (or rather Christ) is not geared to the contemporary world, but to the eternal and the unchanging in man. We commit a tragic sin when we agree with our contemporaries who deny the very existence of the eternal, or when we perceive everything in historical, changing categories.

*Monday, January 27, 1975*

Yesterday we went to Wappingers Falls to celebrate their parish feast. I enjoyed the early morning sunshine on bare trees, a spacious, bright, somehow washed-out sky. Joy from the feast itself, from the atmosphere of friendship, light, cordiality of that parish.

The attacks on Solzhenitsyn by an ever-increasing number of enemies is causing quite an uproar among his friends. People call me, try to enlist my help in his defense. I know that S. himself does not hesitate to offend people right and left in the rudest manner. I personally think that to defend him would be to tell him the truth. I really do not want to take part in that struggle. I see my role only in fighting for what is transcendent. I dislike "camps," whatever they may be. As for Solzhenitsyn, I will defend what I heard through his creative art, but I remain free of his ideology, which for me is quite foreign.

### Tuesday, January 28, 1975

I went to early Matins and walked home through frost and cold. Back to normal. How refreshing and peaceful is that "normality," the feeling that I have a clearly defined duty, which for me is simple and obvious.

### Friday, January 31, 1975

Our thirty-second wedding anniversary.

### Monday, February 3, 1975

Besides being in church, I spent the whole weekend at home. We celebrated the Meeting of the Lord, joyfully, solemnly, brightly. Yesterday I finally had time to work on my *Eucharist*. I want so much to go back to real work, to get away from the little articles, the little storms that lately fill my life. I want to write at least two or three pages each day...

### Tuesday, February 4, 1975

I spent yesterday morning working on my *Eucharist*. I have the feeling that I come back there to what is eternal, essential, unchanging. It gives me a joy that seems to be strongly rooted in my heart, despite unavoidable business.

### Thursday, February 6, 1975

Yesterday, because of a heavy snowfall, L. did not go to work and we spent a blissful, quiet day at home. I spent the day writing.

Behind our windows, incredible beauty of still branches covered with snow, white roofs and gardens.

### Friday, February 7, 1975

I am reading Chekhov—(how many times have I returned to him?) Besides the inherent fascination of his novels, they put in perspective the chaos in which I live. How important things seemed to be yesterday and how completely forgotten today!

ST. INNOCENT ORTHODOX CHURCH

## *Monday, February 10, 1975*

I spent Saturday writing my *Eucharist* (despite the noisy presence of all our grandchildren)—which made me so happy! What a joy to touch eternity, to have the possibility to live with what has been given us. How blessed is life!

## *Sunday, February 16, 1975*

I had lunch with two Anglican clergymen in the city. Conversations about the ordination of women. Suddenly, while we were talking, I thought, how not serious religion had become since it ceased being the essential form of life. Religion seems to be constantly reinventing itself, in order not to disappear completely, not to be discarded.

People have stopped believing not in God or gods, but in death, in eternal death, in its inevitability—hence, they stopped believing in salvation. The seriousness of religion was first of all in the serious choice that a person considered obvious, between death and salvation. People say that the disappearance of fear is good, although the essential experience of life is facing death. The saints did not become saints because of fear, but because they knew the fear of God. The contemporary understanding of religion as self-fulfillment is rather cheap. The devil is eliminated, then hell, then sin—and nothing is left except consumer goods. But there is much more fear, even religious fear in the world than ever before—but it is not at all the fear of God.

## *Saturday, February 22, 1975*

*Cornell University*

I am alone in my hotel on campus at Cornell where I had lectured five or six times in the sixties. I had dinner yesterday with a group of professors before my lecture. During dinner, listening to the conversations around me, I thought that the whole scene is exactly like the one described in *Pnin*, by Nabokov (who actually described Cornell, where he taught). The same sarcasm, a rather unnatural laughter, sophistication. There is something frightening in that profession—the power over young hearts and minds, power without limits, not human, but transcendental; the control that comes from conviction, integrity, vision. Of course there are many wonderful people in the profession, but the whole system imposes an interior apprehension and exterior cynicism.

Today I read in the *New York Times* an article about changes occurring in Russia. No more dissidents, no young people to carry on the opposition. Sakharov is quite alone. People want televisions, cars, ice cream, comfort. The tragic high note taken by Solzhenitsyn is lost in this decay. S. issues a call to "live without lies," but his opponents reply, "Does he not understand that people always and everywhere lived—and will live—by and with lies?" It is impossible to oppose society's lowest impersonal ways. The United States wants and needs to trade with Russia—and this is stronger than any potential protest. Russia wants a better material life and that's the strongest incentive. Religion is absolutely helpless, not because of the weakness and the fall of religion, but because religion has ceased to be the essential term of reference, the basis of a vision of the world, an evaluation of all these "wants." I felt it quite acutely today while attending a report of our church's committee on investment, including a discussion about what is better, more profitable, secure—some bonds or some stocks. Nobody felt the comical and demonic aspect of a discussion attended by bishops and priests who listened with genuine reverence and admiration to the financial experts: a banker and a broker. I saw for about an hour a true religious awe, which was completely absent when simple church affairs were discussed—in an atmosphere of petty mistrust, intrigue, and verification of every cent spent by the administration. The banker and the broker were listened to with hearty enjoyment, and questions were asked in the way that one used to ask elders, wise men and masters. They talked with the simplicity and the humility of people who know their business, their indispensable place in society. This is the way that religion does not express itself any more, because religion does not have such an indispensable place any more. What does it mean? It means that religion has accepted secular logic and does not see in that acceptance either its fall or even a "problem." For how could religion survive otherwise?

What I wrote is confirmed by two illustrations in a little pamphlet that was pushed under my door in the hotel:

Five years ago, in an enormous city hospital in Chicago, a crematorium was built to burn the corpses of the indigent. "There was no question," said the director, "that it would be cheaper to cremate the bodies than deal with private cemeteries." But the crematorium is still idle because of protests among the workers. One of them said, "We do have some people with a bit of religion left who don't buy this method for disposing of human bodies, and I guess I'm one of them." What is most remarkable is the fact that the construction of the crematorium had been decided after consulting religious leaders, and "there was absolutely no opposition." But of course! For leaders to resist the contemporary way? "A bit of religion left" is an attempt to resist, but not for long.

In the same issue, there was an announcement by a Catholic nun about the "new image" of nuns. "Sisters have become very serious ministers dealing with issues of social justice and with the Gospel in terms of the world today."

Was their "old image," of humble and obedient teachers, nurses, etc., untenable? "At present, the widespread attitude is that nuns are only cogs in institutions, either as teachers or nurses (!!), although actually they are increasingly moving away from simply staffing institutions such as schools and hospitals." What is awful is that neither this nun nor anyone else realized this extraordinary contempt for real and live work—children, sick people, the elderly (what could be higher, more saintly?) nor the ugliness of the conviction that "ministry" has to be an agency, an institution…What to do?

### Wednesday, February 26, 1975

Today we had an early Liturgy at the seminary. Walking to church, in the dark, but with a huge frosty moon, I thought with a great deal of repentance about my constant longing for freedom and some leisure from the fuss of my daily life. I felt quite sinful that I did not accept the reality of my life and was not faithful in little things. One has to accept each day and everything in it as a gift from God, and transform each day into joy. If all the details of my life (talks, students, meetings, correspondence) are not giving joy but are only a burden, then it is really my sin, my selfishness, my laziness.

Bright sunshine. Freezing. And some very tentative breath of spring.

A gift from God, a letter from B[ob] W[orth] which endlessly touched me: "I would like, in a very simple way, to thank you for a very memorable three years at St Vladimir's Seminary. Listening to you in class and serving with you both as deacon and priest has been a tremendous joy for me…"

### Thursday, February 27, 1975

Yesterday we had a distressing faculty meeting. Although the atmosphere was peaceful, even happy, two major obstacles make unity almost impossible. One is the deeply negative attitude, without any sense of reality, and the dangerous stubbornness of N. Another obstacle is when academic pursuit is seen as the main and major goal of our seminary. Then, with a group of wonderful people who understand the situation of the Church, its relationship with the world, with the culture, how can I coordinate all these tendencies and create some unity? This is my next problem, which I do not know how to approach…Why be so blind?

### Friday, February 28, 1975

After Matins, I talked with M. A. [Michael Meerson-Aksenov] about Solzhenitsyn: "He inspired us and educated us," says M., and that's why I am so frustrated when I see him ridiculing himself, dissipating his energy in trivialities. His blindness to culture, his horrible lack of comprehension about what is most needed for Russia, Europe, the West. They were torn away from them for fifty years and this is the result. Oversimplification, longing for oversimplification...

### Saturday, March 1, 1975

Yesterday and today in Pittsburgh. Last evening there was a meeting of our Foundation. Among those present were twelve of our priests and other alumni. It seems like yesterday they were sitting in our classrooms: Padlo, Leon, Steffaro, Lesko, Simerick, Stehnach, Ziatyk, Savich, Corey, Lukashonak, Soroka and Bishop Theodosius himself. Such a joyful feeling to see each of them full of fire and desire; to realize they are "mine," "ours." I remember my first trip to Pittsburgh in February 1952—so completely different.

Today from 10 to 3 in the Antiochian Church of [Father George] Corey,* a retreat, i.e., my two lectures and questions. Over one hundred people. I went there tired, uninspired, but as soon as I saw all these people, their attention—again I felt joy, enthusiasm. I even felt that I spoke easily and sincerely.

In Pittsburgh, in the morning, it was snowing and there was a blue sky and sunshine. At the airport, alone, I felt, as usual, a sudden moment of familiar bliss, hard to describe but full of blessed joy. The rays of the sun out of the huge windows of the airport, background music, flowing from everywhere and from nowhere, and suddenly a feeling of complete union with everything around, as if all things around were somehow becoming softer, turning a friendly close face to me. In such moments, out of time, my whole life is gathered, focused. Everything is here, nameless, but objective, everything from my early childhood. It is as if eternity touches the heart. There is no need for remembrance, since there is no gulf between the one who remembers and what is remembered, i.e., life itself.

In the evening, Vespers at the Seminary, I came in time to hear "By the waters of Babylon" and "Open to me the doors of repentance..." And again I felt the same piercing fullness and bliss. It is always there, right there, all around. How rare and fleeting is this gift which suddenly fills one's heart.

### Monday, March 3, 1975

It is the Sunday of the Prodigal Son. I served and preached. Beautiful mixed choir. Tchaikovsky's "Holy God," which reminds me of my father, who liked to play it on the piano at home.

---

* Corey, Father George—A priest in the Antiochian Archdiocese and former member of the board of trustees of the seminary.

In the evening, dinner at the Drillocks with the Ericksons. A feeling of closeness, family, complete trust, friendship. How many such gifts can one receive in just one day?

Yesterday I received as a gift, from a complete stranger, an older woman, an antique Russian pectoral cross. "Why for me? How do you know me?" "Oh, I know you well. I have been following you for a long time. I listen to you…"

It is a very special winter: through all February—a bright sun, a clear sky. Now March, and everywhere hints of spring.

### *Tuesday, March 4, 1975*

Yesterday I spent the day writing an article, "The Hierarchy of Values." Actually, I am thinking about Solzhenitsyn and his idolizing obsession with Russia. I am writing with great difficulty; not with the content, but with the tone of the article. After dinner I read the beginning to L. She said, "You managed to show, very convincingly, the truth of ecclesial nationalism." But I personally grew up in it; I can see the truth in it. I do not want to struggle with it by creating a caricature. "In this world but not of this world"—it is not a choice between two ways of living; it is always a Cross!

In the evening, I had a talk with students' wives about Lent. As all too often, I went without enthusiasm and with some inner resistance. I came back with joy from the communion with what is essential and vital.

### *Wednesday, March 5, 1975*

As much as I resist the tone of his writing, of his exaltation, exaggerations, I see that Leon Bloy is the "pilgrim of the Absolute."

Day after day a glorious sunshine, a triumphantly blue sky. In the peace and quiet of my home, I am writing "with fear and trembling" my "Hierarchy of Values." The morning Gospels of these pre-Lenten days tell of Christ's Passion. Again the same cycle, again everything comes to this *end,* without which no *beginning* is possible.

### *Thursday, March 6, 1975*

Leon Bloy:

> It seems to me that St Ignatius' *Exercises* correspond to the 'Method' of Descartes. Instead of looking at God, one looks at oneself (p. 181).

> …Psychology invented by Jesuits: a method consisting in continually looking at oneself in order to avoid sin. It is contemplating evil instead of

contemplating goodness. The devil substituting for God. This seems to be the genesis of modern Catholicism (p. 182).

*Exercises,* whence came the odious, abominable, depraving, contemporary psychology: always analyzing one's self; anxiously questioning oneself, contemplating 'one's own navel.' Flee from analysis as from the devil and trust God, being a lost man... (p. 184).

Yesterday I went to Radio Liberty to tape my radio broadcast to Russia.* I was given a report by Father Bordeaux about his trip to Russia. "The priest visited many private homes, talked to many people... The broadcasts of Western stations were appreciated. Father B. believes that A. Schmemann is the most popular broadcaster and one of the most popular foreign individuals in Russia. Solzhenitsyn is also highly regarded..." Funny, the "also"! Nice to hear that my work does reach someone there.

### Friday, March 7, 1975

Last evening we had *blini* with some Russian friends. Very nice, friendly. But what a gulf between our life—our vision of the Church, what we need, what is for us most important and what is only secondary—and their life. Coming home I thought about a certain type of Russian who is faithful not to Russia, which he never knew in the way his parents did, but to the emigration itself, its ideas, its way of life. Their consciousness is somehow in captivity, comparable to that of Orthodox Jews. Their childhood spent in émigré struggles and frustrations had a defining meaning for their entire lives.

### Tuesday, March 11, 1975

After Matins, I had a rather upsetting talk with N. about her husband, his rudeness, etc. She is crying... I know that I can help only by listening, by giving her the possibility to talk it out, but not in a Freudian way, but very simply: one needs to cry somewhere and complain a little and thus get some comfort. But, Lord! How false is all the talk about "spirituality," "truth," and the "Typikon" on one hand, and, on the other, the non-observance of the most elementary commandments.

On Sunday and yesterday, I reread heaps of my radio scripts. The overall impression is of a unity of vision, in spite of a hurried and disorganized presentation. If only I could have just a little freedom to put some order in all of that! But probably He knows better than I do what is needed and maybe this

---

* From 1952 and almost until his death, Father Schmemann made weekly broadcasts to Russia over Radio Liberty.

organizing, systematizing, is precisely what should not be done.

Wet snow. Very cold. Letters and phone calls.

### Wednesday, March 12, 1975

Last evening I lectured at Manhattanville College. Many people attended the lecture, which was about the Christian understanding of man, about the need to expose the man represented by science, reduced to total determinism, but somehow "free" and "having rights." I spoke about the rather poor apologetics built on the acknowledgment of science, then about man as the image of ineffable glory, created, fallen, restored.

Letter from a Swedish publisher asking permission to publish a Swedish translation of *For the Life of the World*. After the Russian (*samizdat*), French, Italian, Finnish and German, it will be the seventh translation. Hence my passionate wish to tear myself from the chaotic hassle of my daily life to start working and writing. Yesterday D. Drillock told me how much he was enjoying *Of Water and the Spirit*. "Write!" he says. And for three weeks I have not touched my *Eucharist*. On the other hand, isn't that wish ("my creativity") simply pride and ambition? Maybe the Lord is sending me this toil instead of "creativity."

My eternal question: How to draw a line between the pleasure given by "success" (pride), and the joy that something I considered important and true is reaching out (for God, not us, not me...)? How unattainable is genuine humility. Always, immediately, jumping to the surface is a small "I," whom one recognizes as nothingness, as common hope and fear. With what means will God cure this conceit?

### Tuesday, March 18, 1975

Radiant spring days! Yesterday, after dinner, we were baby-sitting Serge and Mania's children. Mania is in Washington taking care of her mother who had a massive stroke. We took the children to the St Patrick's Day Parade.

In the evening we read the Canon of St Andrew of Crete in a full church. I received a very nice letter from a totally unknown woman: "...your lucid descriptions of what was, ought to be, and is are very helpful to my own understanding of Orthodoxy. Were it not for writers and speakers such as you and Father Hopko, for instance, I might long ago have abandoned ship or what seemed to be a soulless dinosaur..."

### Thursday, March 20, 1975

Yesterday we celebrated the first Presanctified Liturgy of Lent, before it—two hours of confessions, All of it brings me to a truly blessed state and everything else begins to seem petty, unnecessary.

I tried to write an article in honor of Professor Weidle's jubilee. I thought about the very meaningful role he played in my life. We spent a summer in England together in 1935. He made me read *Le Grand Meaulnes* [by Alain-Fournier] and to read his article which I still keep for its inscription ("to Sasha with hopes of glory and goodness"—I was fifteen and he was an acknowledged literary and art critic). He was my professor of the history of philosophy at the Russian Lycée, then at the St Sergius Institute. Then I attended his courses on Russian poetry and Italian art. Every two weeks I had dinner at his house. For all of it, I feel a warm wave of gratitude, which I am trying to embody in my article in his honor.

## Monday, March 24, 1975

Awful news from Vietnam! The television reports are horrible—dead and dying, fleeing, abyss of human suffering. In Europe, Portugal is quickly drifting to communism. And in between those images of suffering, horror, treachery, we see images of "great values in appliances."

Essentially the West is frightful—frightful because of its Pharisaism, identifying freedom with profit. Once a rightist senator said: "We must remember that the basic principles of a free market—profit and freedom—are indivisible"—all that with a heroic tone of voice…the faces of farmers, deciding to reduce their crops, with faces lit up with moral pathos—while the whole world is clamoring about hunger. The West is frightful because of its baseness in everything. When did that fall begin? Where did the West renounce itself, renounce the flame that "lighted up the whole creation, then went into the night and cried…"?

All the lofty phrases about "freedom," "fairness," "equality," etc. (and their Christian rhetoric) sound unbearable, demonic, false. The devil is on the faces of the defenders of law and order and on the faces of revolutionaries.

## Tuesday, March 25, 1975

*Annunciation: "Archangel's Voice."*

I finished my article about W. Weidle. While writing it I remembered not only him, but also that whole period of my life, which was extremely happy. "You gave me youth without grief…"

I had a long conversation with David Drillock about the Seminary, about its future, its personnel problems. A small world, but how many undercurrents, potential conflicts, incompatible tendencies. I have to deal with it, although I am fainthearted, postponing the moment of truth. I really do not want to force my way onto any of it. Again and again, I am amazed and touched by David's simplicity, honesty and openness.

The TV news is awful: bloodbath in Vietnam, police corruption, terrorist bombs in Argentina, in Ireland, everywhere! Then sweet commercials about the softness of toilet paper! No fresh air left in the world. Only three days of solitude (L. is in Martinique) and I already feel its burden and begin to understand the pointless dramas of lonely people around me.

I spent the evening with some new immigrants from Russia. They cling to each other uprooted, emotionally strung out. I thought, what could I tell them from deep down, from the heart? What is most important? How to live? It is easier for those whose lives are filled with creative work: Solzhenitsyn, writers. The others are instinctively inventing some occupation, some way of life. I would love to tell them that the only meaningful thing in life is what conquers death, and not "what," but "who"—Christ. There is undoubtedly only one joy: to know Him and share Him with each other. Nothing else matters but faith, hope, love. But it would be "preaching," like a kind of platitude. But for me this is beyond all question, the rest—"in a way," "somehow," "sometime…".

## Monday, March 31, 1975

A quiet, peaceful Sunday at home with L. We went for a walk, then worked on taxes and had dinner. I tried to sort out the articles and lectures of the past fifteen years. Although there is an infinite variety of topics and themes, I was quite pleased by the unity of vision that is there. I accepted the idea advanced by David Drillock of a collection of articles, just to escape the pressure, but it turns out to be the reflection of a holistic vision of the world. I am quite surprised, because I always wrote to meet a deadline, in a hurry, often carelessly.

## Tuesday, April 1, 1975

From 7:30 to 4:30 at the seminary. Lectures, meetings, phone calls and appointments with students. And outside, a blinding, warm spring day after a whole week of freezing cold.

Yesterday, after such a day, I thought how grateful I should be to God for the atmosphere that surrounds me at the Seminary: David D[rillock], Father Cyril S[tavrevsky*], Ann Z[inzel**]—an atmosphere of friendship, essential understanding and total devotion.

* Stavrevsky, Father Cyril—Dean of Students at St Vladimir's Seminary, 1969–1976.
**Zinzel, Ann—former secretary in the Office of Records at St Vladimir's Seminary and personal secretary to Father Schmemann.

## Monday, April 7, 1975

Salt Lake City. Last night there was a very pleasant meeting in the Greek Church: interesting questions, an enormous thirst for more knowledge about the faith, the Church, etc. How little does the Church respond to that thirst, how little does she satisfy it.

This morning—breakfast with Jaroslav Pelikan in my hotel.

I looked through the Book of Mormon. I read the paper about their international conference. The Mormon religion is thriving, spreading, all the speeches reflect a deep conviction, joy. What is the matter? What is the attraction? Obviously not this strange book, rather hard to digest, nor the legends about Smith and the golden tabernacles. But then what? It is the eternal enigma of religion, which never ceases not only to surprise, but to scare me. Strange city with its wide avenues, heavy Mormon Temple that can be seen from everywhere, surrounded by mountains covered with snow.

## Tuesday, April 8, 1975

I spent yesterday attending the Salt Lake City Greek Church Conference. So many wonderful people. I was quite impressed by the irritation, even anger, against the Mormons—quite extraordinary coming from a usually cordial, well-disposed group of Americans, often inclined to pluralism.

## Wednesday, April 9, 1975

I arrived back at 2 o'clock in the morning after an endless flight. Before leaving, I went to the Mormon center, the new Visitors' Center. The style is that of a wealthy hotel, quite tasteless and luxurious. On the walls, paintings depicting the life of Christ and Mormon history, sickly sweet and simplified. Simplification, enthusiasm, and fanaticism. We flew over Rocky Mountains covered with snow and the Salt Lake. Strong contrast between greatness of water and triumphant lack of taste. Out of a fake world one enters a real temple. America: What a grandiose country!

## Thursday, April 10, 1975

The very principle of private property, as often and as much as it is distorted, is a Christian principle. The world, life itself, are given to us by God to be possessed, owned ("have dominion and rule over"). That is why Christianity is calling us to personally refuse private property in order to cure and restore the ownership of the world (personal, not collective) which man has betrayed and perverted. But Christianity does not call us to the annihilation of private property by replacing it with collective property. The call to give up everything is not a social program, but an eschatological principle, a way of transferring into another dimension.

### Friday, April 11, 1975

I served two Presanctified Liturgies—one yesterday and one on Wednesday. Yesterday in Syosset, confessions of the New York clergy. Pure joy from prayers and communion with those twelve priests: spiritual health of this growing American Orthodoxy.

### Sunday, April 13, 1975

Yesterday, Serge had his 30th Birthday. How unnoticeably my old age has really started. In my best moments, I feel almost free, able to freely breathe...In my worst moments, I feel irritated and grumpy at all that is "new." I know that it is just the law of nature, and nonetheless I comply with it.

### Tuesday, April 15, 1975

I am getting ready to leave for Munich, Germany, for a Radio Liberty conference.

I took part yesterday in a faculty seminar led by Kesich* and Verhovskoy** and lectured about Holy Scripture in worship. There was an atmosphere of friendship, joy and openness that made me very happy.

I am getting many phone calls and letters in answer to my letter to the editors of the *New York Times*—as if I discovered something! I realize any freedom of thought for people is difficult.

### Tuesday, April 22, 1975

Yesterday I came back from Europe. The conference in Munich was quite interesting. We listened to experts in radio broadcasting, a group of Russians, Muslims and Jews. Many useful insights. I was happy to hear about echoes of my scripts from Russia—quite pleasant for my self-esteem.

Then from Munich to Paris, to my mother, my brother Andrei and many friends. Trips into the past, walks through all my favorite spots in Paris, strength of family ties.

* Kesich, Veselin—Professor of New Testament at St Vladimir's Seminary, 1953–1991.
**Verhovskoy, Serge, †1986—Provost and Professor of Dogmatic Theology at St Vladimir's Seminary, 1952–1981.

## Friday, April 25, 1975

And finally we have come to the end of the sixth week of Lent: "Having completed the forty days of the fast…" rise up towards the Holy Week through the pre-Paschal light of Lazarus Saturday and Palm Sunday. This year, spring is late, so that at the seminary everything is in bloom: forsythias, purple azaleas, transparent greenery. From early childhood those are my favorite days of the year. And in the background, the nightmare, the bloody end of Indochina and Cambodia, arrests in Russia, elections in Portugal accompanied by assent from liberals of all kinds to the raging lies and evil (Mitterrand: "For us, the Soviet Union is an instrument of peace."!?)

## Holy Monday, April 28, 1975

Lazarus Saturday and Palm Sunday—two days of unqualified joy. Amazingly sunny days, beautiful services, the church overflowed with people. On Saturday, after the Liturgy, L. and I went to Roslyn Cemetery to clean up her parents' grave. Yesterday between services, we went to Wappingers Falls to visit our grandchildren. All the trees have transparent, barely green leaves. In the evening—"Thy Bridal Chamber…"

Late at night I had a somehow worrisome feeling that I often have: everything that impresses me in Orthodoxy, everything that gives me joy, inspires me, especially during these two deeply loved days of Lazarus and the Palms, is not what people look for and see in Orthodoxy. Yesterday's Epistle: "Rejoice, and again I say rejoice…!" and further: "Whatsoever things are true, whatsoever things are honest…" Everything speaks of the Kingdom of God and of joyful freedom which shines in the world through the Kingdom. Freedom, first of all, from religion, from the depressing religious "swarming." I had a dream yesterday about that: I was trying to convince someone of something essential, which to me seemed so simple.

Painful confessions, painful turning into oneself of religious people, painful lust for the "sacred." I keep thinking that if people would *see* that which was accomplished then in Jerusalem—in depth, for all eternity and onto ages of ages—they would be liberated from this "I" so painfully growing in the midst of religiousness.

## May 1, 1975

### Holy Thursday

Yesterday morning, a phone call from Solzhenitsyn. As usual, hearing his voice I become reconciled with him; all doubts, disagreements, perplexities disappear. He is so wholly in what he says and does. I will meet him in Canada on Pascha and then we will drive to Labelle.

Last evening, my very favorite Matins service: "Come, O faithful, let us enjoy the Master's hospitality: the banquet of immortality, in the upper chamber with uplifted minds…"

Again and again I *know* that everything in this world exists and bears a relation to this—"and I appoint unto you a Kingdom."

## May 2, 1975

*Holy Friday,*

Holy Thursday—with its double manifestation of the "red" Eucharist in the morning and the Twelve Gospels at night. Again and again, every year, comes the incarnation of the same day. Totally and essentially extra-temporal. The great and deep truth of tradition makes it possible for us to take part again in the immutable glory of the day, and nothing is expected from us except humbly, gratefully and joyfully to be part of it.

The law of the Church is to give oneself to what is given, not to seek one's own. All is already accomplished, all is fulfilled, all is given. The main mandate of the Church in the world is to reveal it and give it to us.

The danger is to love the Church somehow apart from Christ. There is more of that kind of love than one would think. But the Church *is* Christ, His life, His gift.

To seek in the Church anything besides Christ (and it means to seek oneself and one's own) inevitably leads to temptation, to distortion and finally to self-destruction.

## May 6, 1975

*Bright Tuesday,*

I am in Ompha-Plevna, Ontario, in a tiny hotel, in a Canadian wilderness with Solzhenitsyn. It is so unreal, so like a dream that I do not know what to say. The hard facts—I flew to Montreal on Pascha night after beautiful Paschal services of Holy Saturday and Sunday.

On Monday at 7:00 AM. we drove to Labelle, a hundred miles north from Montreal. Rain, fog, how strange to drive with S. along that road among these hills, through these towns. S. is in great humor, quite friendly. We spent a long day in Labelle, walking, the lake still frozen. S. likes Labelle! After dinner a bright sunset. Serge, my son, joins us for the day. Reporters somehow figured out where he was and S. was in total fury. Then we drove to Ottawa through country roads which S. enjoyed. Talks about everything. Lunch in Ottawa. Then off to the wild country and arrival in Ompha in the middle of nowhere. Trent Motel. Dinner. Deep red sunset.

## Bright Wednesday, May 7, 1975

We got up at 6:00 AM—a glorious morning, exploring the backcountry along lakes and woods. S. criticized the forest: the trees are too thin! His approach is practical and concrete—everything has to be put to use. His mood varies like a child's—"Where will I live?" S. thinks that at the end of our drive we will find him a place to live—how, where, when—quite irrelevant and unrealistic. He meets some people on the way: "We have to check: are they spies?" What spies? Spying what? His main fear: not to waste time: I have to work; no time for leisure, save Russia.

I feel as in a dream, quite out of reality, out of my own usual order and harmony, but fascinated. I have a sudden moment of total happiness, bliss, joy of life. In the middle of an impersonal crowd, in a strange motel room, I feel intensely alive—in this elemental immersion into Solzhenitsyn's whirlwind and at the same time in the divine bliss of life everlasting.

## Monday, May 12, 1975

So, again, after last year's mountain meeting in Zurich, four days with Solzhenitsyn, just the two of us away from people. This trip might be called a lake encounter—we passed by so many lakes!

Little by little my thoughts and impressions are put in order and I am asking myself: If I had to find a formula, what would it be? I think that during these days spent together, I felt quite strongly and acutely our basic difference—difference between the "treasures" that control our hearts. ("Where your treasure is, there is your heart.") His treasure is Russia and only Russia; mine is the Church. He is devoted to his treasure in a way that none of us is devoted to ours. His faith, I think, will move mountains, while ours—mine in any case—will not.

What image remains from these four days during which we spent every hour together?

A great man! In the obsession with his vocation, his mission, in the total identification with it—without a doubt, a great man. Truly, out of him flows strength!

When one remembers what and how much he has written, and in what circumstances, one is struck again and again. But (there starts the "but") what struck me during these days were:

1. A certain primitive elementary consciousness be it of people, events, view of nature, etc. Essentially he does not feel any nuances of complexity.

2. A curious lack of understanding about people, maybe even an unwillingness to think about them, to get to know them. He allocates them to ready-made categories; is quite utilitarian in his opinion of them.

3. No gentleness, pity, patience. On the contrary, immediate mistrust, suspicion, interpretation *in malem partem.*

4. Incredible self-assurance; infallibility.

5. Incredibly secretive.

I could continue, but I won't. I am quite certain that none of these defects that I am so sensitive to contradict in any way his greatness, his literary genius. I am sure that an artist's qualities (even purely human) can be in his creativity, that a writer in his life does not necessarily correspond to the writer in his creativity (see Dostoevsky *et al*).

On the contrary, one of the motive forces, one of the causes of creativity is precisely the intense contradiction between life and what the writer creates. What worries me, disturbs and frightens me, is not the difficulty of his life, not his personality, but the ultimate scheme to which he is totally, entirely committed, and which he serves without restriction.

In all these days spent with him, I had the feeling that I was the older brother dealing with a child, capricious and even spoiled, who will not "understand"—so better for me to give in ("you are older, give in!") for the sake of peace, agreement and in the hope that "he might grow up and understand." I am a student from a higher grade dealing with a younger one for whom one needs to simplify, with whom one has to speak "at his level."

## Wednesday, May 14, 1975

Yesterday I spent the whole day in the external trifles and tribulations of church life, all its difficulties, squabbles. I write it without any sense of depression because long ago it became clear to me that the humanity of the Church is a lesser temptation than a pan-spirituality, than all the attempts to disincarnate the Church. The Church is preserved in history precisely due to the endless rubbing of people against each other, like pebbles at the seashore, due to humility in accepting weekdays, working days and busy work. A genuine concern for the Church consists of never being led into temptation for the Church's sake. "Blessed is he who will not be led into temptation (scandalized) for My sake."

This morning during Matins I had a "jolt of happiness," of fullness of life, and at the same time the thought: I will have to die! But in such a fleeting breath of happiness, time usually "gathers" itself. In an instant, not only are all such breaths of happiness remembered but they are present and alive—that Holy Saturday in Paris when I was a very young man—and many such "breaks." It seems to me that eternity might be not the stopping of time, but precisely its resurrection and gathering. The fragmentation of time, its division, is the fall of eternity. Maybe the words of Christ are about time when He said: "…not to destroy anything but will raise it all on the last day."

The thirst for solitude, peace, freedom, is thirst for the liberation of time from cumbersome dead bodies, from hustle; thirst for the transformation of time into what it should be—the receptacle, the chalice of eternity. Liturgy is the conversion of time, its filling with eternity. There are two irreconcilable types of spirituality: one that strives to liberate man from time (Buddhism, Hinduism, Nirvana, etc.); the other that strives to liberate time. In genuine eternity, all is alive. The limit and the fullness: the whole of time, the whole of life is in each moment. But there is also the perpetual problem: What about the evil moments? Evil time? The terrible fear before dying of the drowning man, of the man falling from the tenth floor about to be crushed on the pavement? What about the tears of an abused child?

### Thursday, May 15, 1975

Last evening when I came back from the seminary, I tried to sit down to finish an article about relations in the Sacraments—and nothing happened. I reread that article as well as my article "Hierarchy of Values" and also my introductory chapter to *Eucharist*—"The Sacrament of Offering," and felt a total inability to work. It is a familiar feeling when everything seems unnecessary, superficial, when I have no inner conviction in what I write, in the need to write. A feeling of "what for?". When I immediately see all possible objections, and feel incapable of genuinely expressing what I want to say ("a thought once expressed is a lie"). I am always impressed by those who write and write without hesitation. One needs to write so that each fragment would shine and reflect the "whole"—that's the great difficulty that seems insurmountable.

### Monday, May 19, 1975

On Saturday, Serge Bouteneff was ordained to the Diaconate—a truly joyful and bright feast. Serge—so simple, serious, light, concentrated. At the reception in Scarsdale, everybody felt the clearly tangible light of that day.

On Sunday I went with L. first to the Hopkos (where we thoroughly enjoyed little Alexandra), then, following country lanes, we went to Kent. A sunny spring evening, beautiful flowering trees, still young and transparent greenery.

I talked at length with L. about Solzhenitsyn, about his dream of a Russian commune. However I turn it in my mind, the "dream" continues to seem unnecessary, false. This submission of his creativity to Russian life, artificially planted, is, in my opinion, a defect in Solzhenitsyn's view of the world. Somebody asked him in Montreal: "How do you like our Canada?" "I like *only* Russia." This "only" is a limitation, a "rottenness" in S.'s greatness. He thus denies what is best in Russia—its universality. I feel alienated by any "only"...

## Tuesday, May 20, 1975

There it is—a heavy, humid New York heat wave.

Early this morning I served my last Matins of this academic year, my twenty-fourth at the seminary. One more year and I will have spent a quarter of a century in America. I was thinking yesterday, has not the time come to sum up, to give up my place to others, to those younger?

All of culture and all in culture is about the Kingdom of God, for or against. Culture consists of bringing into real existence the treasures of one's heart—("where your treasure is...")

## Wednesday, May 21, 1975

Why did I always read everything pertaining to André Gide? I thought about it yesterday and then asked myself a further question, a broader one: what, in general, do I read, or have read; what is the principle of any choice and attraction? I do not mean the colossal amount of books that I read by chance or necessity (in school or for my lectures, as material for work or entertainment).

In Russian literature: (1) Tolstoy, which I read and re-read with sheer delight—*Anna Karenina* and *War and Peace*. Never re-read any of his other books. (2) Dostoevsky—I read it all, but never reread it, except *Brothers Karamazov*, never being tempted to re-read any more. (3) Chekhov—whom I can and always want to read and re-read. (4) Turgenev—I re-read some of it rather lazily and by chance. (5) Pushkin—read and endlessly re-read with the same pleasure. (6) Gogol—every time I re-read him, I find new enjoyment. (7) Nabokov—I like his writings with an almost physical pleasure because of the "perfection" of his writing, etc. Bunin, Lermontov, Rosanov, the poets—I like them all.

In French literature, I enjoy F. Mauriac, Green, Gide, Proust and many others.

I know English and German literature very scantily and have never been overly attracted by them—out of ignorance, I suppose.

I love biographies, diaries,

So there is my whole "baggage."

I do not like "ideological" literature: philosophy, theology. I do not like it because I have no need for it in my life and religious experience.

Rather than ideas and ideologies, I prefer the concrete, live, unique. When reading French contemporaries—Loisy and company—I am mainly interested in them as people, not so much in their ideas. What did the celebration of Mass mean to Loisy with all his ideas? What about wearing a *soutane*? I am convinced that no general ideas can explain reality, so they are unnecessary—for me, anyway.

### Sunday, May 25, 1975

Yesterday was the seminary's commencement, the end of the school year—twenty-four at the seminary, six at St Sergius Institute in Paris. All these days an endless chaotic turmoil and finally—"ouf"! All went well. A joyful Liturgy yesterday with Bishop Sylvester,* with the ordination of Mark Stevens. Hot. Sunny.

In three weeks—to Labelle. I have a passionate desire not only to rest, but to work. I have a dream—to finish my book about the *Eucharist* this summer.

### Friday, May 30, 1975

Another Solzhenitsyn petty scandal: he rudely refuses a TV interview, and "will never speak in the USA," because *Time* did not publish his letter to the editors. Narrow-mindedness, suspicion, fanaticism. How many more times will he be burned before he understands? Will he ever understand?

### Saturday, May 31, 1975

I had a long discussion with L. this morning about ideologies and the basic evil of the contemporary world. Marxism is in a way the crowning point of all ideologies, of "ideology" as such. Any ideology denies individual freedom; it sacrifices man to a utopia, to a truth torn away from life. Ideology is Christianity torn away from Christ, though it was born and reigns in the Christian world. Ideology is the denial of the present for the sake of the

* Sylvester, Bishop—Archbishop of the Diocese of Canada (OCA) from 1963-1981.

future; it is making the man into an instrument of its ideas. (How can man be used for "my" or "our" goals?)

It is a screen of abstract truths thrown over the world and over life, which makes impossible any normal communication. All becomes strategy or tactics. Ideology is the means distinct from the goal, while Christ eliminates the distinction between means and goal. In Christ the goal is the Kingdom of God revealed through the means: *He, Himself, His life.*

### Tuesday, June 17, 1975

*Labelle*

After many adventures along the way, we arrived in Labelle in the middle of a huge thunderstorm We put the house in order, organized my desk, went shopping and finally everything was ready: we could start! Start what? Take a leisurely walk, get reacquainted with Labelle, meet it again in the evening light.

I immediately started working with total delight on an article about Autocephaly.

Tomorrow, back to NY for meetings at the Chancery and the annual summer institute at the seminary. Last morning in bed without phone calls, without letters, just reading and living.

Yesterday I had a long talk with L. about Orthodoxy—Why is it the Truth? Because in Orthodoxy, none of the essential dimensions of creation are betrayed, neither the *world (cosmos)* nor *man* in his uniqueness (anthropology), nor *history*, nor *eschatology.* Everything comes together in the whole so that none of the parts are flawed. In Orthodoxy there is no less apostasy, no less betrayal than in Catholicism or Protestantism, maybe even more; but none of it is made dogma, or proclaimed to be the truth.

### Monday, June 23, 1975

A long series of radiant days. After a week of busy work in NY, I came back to Labelle to celebrate Pentecost with birch branches, flowers and sunshine.

I can't wait to start working. Unfortunately my summer and work will be interrupted by *nine* short meetings and conferences.

### Sunday, June 29, 1975

A whole week of sun, heat, light, bliss! I finished two chapters for the OCA's jubilee book and joyfully started working on "Offering" for my Eucharist. Today, after celebrating the All-Saints Sunday Liturgy and a leisurely brunch on our balcony, I rowed with L. across the lake. The lake is more beautiful than ever.

## Wednesday, July 9, 1975

Day after day—the same sun, the same happiness: the lake, the mountains, the greenery, the light. Nothing special happens. Mornings until lunch—work (a third draft of the chapter about "Offering"). After lunch, long walks with L., every day a new one—an unending delight. Almost every evening with friends and neighbors.

## Monday, July 14, 1975

I finished my chapter about "Offering." As usual, as I was rewriting and re-reading it, it seemed…not quite! I will let it sleep awhile in my drawer. I went to Montreal for the parish feast of Ss. Peter and Paul. I love parish feasts, community celebrations. During the Liturgy, I thought: What in my life gives me pure joy? Slanting rays of sun in church during a service.

## Sunday, August 10, 1975

All these days I miss Andrei and feel quite sad that he left.

Here, sunshine, bright light and a fierce heat wave. White birch trees lit up by the sun against a dark blue lake. Children on the beach. I feel all the time a sort of lyrical wave, a bright sorrow, contemplating what was and remains—not really remains, but fills the heart with a blissful heaviness.

I felt it quite strongly today going to church and then hearing confession outside behind the altar with a magnificent view of the lake, the forest, the hills around.

I read Jean-François Kahn, finished Claude Mauriac—feeling quite close to both.

I reread yesterday a photocopy of the chapter of *Eucharist*, the "Sacrament of Offering." I don't know at all, not at all, whether it is good or bad, necessary or not necessary. I know one thing: it is what I feel and think. It is a simple and liberating thought: if what I feel and think is not needed or already well known, or weak, or superficial—then all that writing will fall into nonexistence and that is the end of it. But I can and must write only what is my own…

I want to come back to "The Hierarchy of Values," which is my dialogue with Solzhenitsyn and many other people. If every Sunday I hold in my hand the Communion with eternal life, then to discuss problems as if this Communion was not there becomes impossible, unless something truly horrible has happened to our faith. "Opium for the people."

N. after his wife's death wants to talk only about religion, not God—

"that's too theoretical"—but death. And what is expected from the priest is to give immediate answers and consolation. In church, a candle on the memorial table, an *in memoriam* note with the wife's name—so little of it has anything to do with Christianity.

A conversation between two elderly ladies about a very interesting book dealing with afterlife: Total outrage. "It cannot be an Orthodox book," says one lady, "the author says that the dead are always with us, while the Church teaches that they remain with us for only forty days!"

While in Labelle, I feel more acutely than ever the gap between what I am and what people expect from a priest—mainly that nothing would change, that all would remain familiar. Sad.

## Tuesday, August 19, 1975

*Transfiguration!*

Clear and cold; a wonderful service. Many confessions. I have a clear feeling that all our sins and doubts come from an inner betrayal of light and joy, of the essence of this great feast.

"The earth trembled..." To feel that trembling in all things, in words, in nature, in ourselves, this is Christian life, or rather life itself given by Christ. As usual on this day, I remembered in the altar all those mentors who made me feel that trembling. My whole theology is about it. About joy that "no man taketh from you" (John 16:22).

## Friday, August 22, 1975

Yesterday I finished Theodore White's *Breach of Faith: The Fall of Richard Nixon.*

An extraordinary book! After only a year, White and the American people are trying to understand what happened and looking at it on a high level of intelligence, conscience, reason. Our Russian Revolution happened sixty years ago and didn't produce anything except passions, screams, emotions. All is narrow, partisan, passionate and partial.

I continue writing "Hierarchy of Values." It seems quite simple, but to embody my ideas is incredibly difficult, almost impossible.

## Saturday, August 23, 1975

I was quite discouraged and had decided to drop or put away my "Hierarchy of Values" but will try again...

During one of our walks, I talked with L. about old age and death. I told her that sometimes it seems to me that I have already received from life all that I wanted; learned all that I wanted to learn. That's the beginning of old age, and, I think, it should be the time to prepare for death. Not to focus on death, but, on the contrary, to purify one's reason, thought, heart, contemplation, and to concentrate on the essence of life, on the mysterious joy. Aside from that joy, one needs nothing else because "bright rays are rushing from that joy."

Youth does not know death unless one is hit by the neurotic, extreme fear of death. Death has no relation to "me" (when one is young), and if it touches me, it is outrageous, and my whole life is darkened. But little by little—not from outside, but from within, comes the knowledge of death. Then two ways are open: One consists of trying to stifle that knowledge, to cling to life ("I can still be useful") and to live as if death had no relation to me. Another, the only right one, I think, the only genuinely Christian one, consists of transforming the knowledge of death into the knowledge of life, and the knowledge of life into the knowledge of death.

Contemporary gerontology concentrates on the first way: making the old men and women feel needed and useful. But it is a fraud (they are really not needed) and self-deception (they know that they are not needed). On a different plane, however, they really are needed, but not for all the concerns that fragment our lives. Their freedom is needed, the beauty of old age, the reflection of the ray of light from it, the dying of the heart and the rising of the spirit. That's why one has to start early the asceticism of old age, the gathering of life everlasting.

I feel that my time has come. But immediately comes a flow of cares and concerns.

I want to add: Youth does not know death because it does not know life. This knowledge comes after "we have seen the evening light." "And the evening and the morning were the first day" (Genesis 1:5). The young live; they do not thank. And only those who thank truly live.

### Sunday, August 24, 1975

Today's Epistle—1 Cor. 3:18-19:

"...Let no man deceive himself. If any man among you seemeth to be wise in this world, let him become a fool, that he may be wise. For the wisdom of this world is foolishness with God."

*August 28, 1975*

*Feast of the Dormition*

Yesterday, before Dormition Vespers, I went with Liana to La Minerve—a village on a hilltop with the most magnificent view over fields, lakes and forests; a few red and yellow spots announcing autumn—and walked in the cemetery there. Peace, sunshine, eternity.

*Dormition Vespers*—the very special joy of that feast—all illumined by "the dawn of the mysterious day." I served the Liturgy with Father John M[eyendorff] and Father Leonid K[ishkovsky]. After the Liturgy, meeting with them and Father Thomas H[opko] about church affairs. I felt almost physically how quickly the feast was waning.

Yesterday, during dinner, we talked with one of the administrators of the Tolstoy nursing home about old age—the horror of these homes where old people are herded under the domination of social workers and all their theories—well meant, but so inadequate.

Last few days in Labelle. I already feel estranged; Labelle becomes the past. These first autumn days are incredibly clear and beautiful—bright red maple trees, a last flash of light. Obvious animation of nature, not pantheistic, but totally existing in the revelation of the Person. There is no nature by itself. It "becomes," comes into existence, when through nature, because of nature, one meets the Person and Epiphany occurs.

*Thursday, September 4, 1975*

Seminary—Chancery—A chaotic morning before the beginning of the school year, quite usual, even joyful.

*Friday, September 5, 1975*

Yesterday, while taping my script for Radio Liberty, N. listened; then said: "Great script, but why do you speak about biblical and not simply Christian sources of the teaching about personality?" Amazing how much resistance there is among many defenders of true Orthodoxy against the Old Testament.

*Sunday, September 7, 1975*

I spent two days in meetings with the Hartford Group.* This morning there

* The eighteen authors of the "Hartford Appeal for the Future of American Religion," of which Fr Schmemann was a participant, came together to repudiate "pervasive, false and debilitating" notions they believed were undermining contemporary Christianity and its influence in society. (*Against the World for the World* [Crossroads: New York, 1976], vii-viii).

85

was a Mass, at which all eighteen participants took communion, except me. Most of the eighteen are conservative Christians from other confessions. Then what is the division of churches and what other unity do they seek? In spite of a friendly atmosphere, I strongly felt my Orthodox alienation from all the debates, from their very spirit. Orthodoxy is often imprisoned by evil and sin. The Christian West is imprisoned by heresies—not one of them, in the long run, goes unpunished.

### Wednesday, September 10, 1975

The beginning of the school year. Slightly chaotic. Forty new students, meetings. Today—first lectures. Although it is my thirty-first year of teaching, I have a familiar and joyous feeling of enthusiasm, hope, that something good will come out of it, a breath of spiritual Presence.

Already—not a minute free! But I refuse to be upset by this prison of activity!

### Thursday, September 11, 1975

I had two painful conversations yesterday with two old former colleagues, both feeling frustrated and misunderstood—"Why don't people want me?" Both do not realize their absence of antennae, their misunderstanding of reality. They want something from me—probably to join the ranks of the accusers of the contemporary world. Perhaps a generation gap? But I feel a stranger in that kind of Russian tonality: dim and vague feelings, words and emotions under the cover of mysticism and theology, constant emotional strain. Sad…What can one do? In their writings, I fail to see depth, seriousness, inner responsibility. The Russian intelligentsia, be it with or without faith, lacks modesty and screams and loudly proclaims everything—unfittingly!

We celebrated my daughter Anya's namesday in Wappingers Falls. I thoroughly enjoyed the warmth of baby Alexandra on my lap.

Two invitations to lectures…urgent phone calls…theology: How often it is like a check with insufficient funds. In two days, I will be fifty-four.

### Friday, September 12, 1975

It is cloudy, humid, rainy. Autumn again. L. started work in her new assignment as dean of faculty. Alarm clock at 6:30, Matins in a darkish church. I always liked routine and rhythm. They help to recognize the gifts that, quite often, we fail to see as gifts because they seem dull and unimportant—essentially, life itself. Liberation occurs only through acceptance.

*Sunday, September 14, 1975*

Yesterday was my birthday. I phoned my twin brother Andrei in Paris.

In the evening, a festive, joyous Vigil of the Cross. Today a Liturgy with many communicants. I preached about the Cross. After the Liturgy, our house was full of well-wishers: children, friends. A beautiful, cool, sunny day.

*Saturday, September 20, 1975*

*Paris*

Night flight to Paris in an empty plane. Lunch at my brother's with his whole family, then a peaceful two-hour walk along my favorite places in the whole world: Pont Royal, Tuileries. A hint of autumn, but warm and sunny. An incredible light, everything seems to blissfully rest under the high Paris sky. Perfect!

Then, having picked up my brother, we go to Vigil. After the Vigil, a friendly cozy dinner on the Champs Elysées.

*Sunday, September 21, 1975*

Liturgy at the Russian Christian Center. Meeting friends there and later at the St Sergius Institute where I spent eleven years studying and teaching. Memories, recognition, the past is shining through every tree, window, path. Real and dear shadows seen through crowds of young new faces—people who have come to attend a wedding.

At night, my mother, Andrei and I walk to her house. And every time, the thought: for the last time?

*Monday, September 22, 1975*

Very early morning walk with Andrei and his daughter Natasha in the Bois de Boulogne. Wonderful, sunny morning and the same blissful Paris light. After our walk, I go to the Latin Quarter where I continue my communion with Paris, which has become a real need—this slow motion through the city where again and again I discover something new, not outside but inside of me—as if I were meeting myself deep down.

Rue Bonaparte, along the River Seine—and the sunny day is flaring up brighter and brighter. I stop at the Cathedral of Notre Dame—almost a ritual. A festive Mass is underway with organ music and devout singing by a huge group of German tourists. Then Île St Louis, Quai de Bourbon, Pont Marie, Quai Henri Quatre to the Gare de Lyon, where I have an appointment with

Mother Maria, a nun from Bussy. Then, again on foot, to the Sorbonne where I have lunch at the wonderful Café Balthazar with N. and M. Struve—(a real donkey—Balthazar—in the café). After a few more appointments, all over Paris, dinner at my mother's, with Andrei.

### Tuesday, September 23, 1975

I spent the whole day traveling—airport, change of planes in Hamburg, finally Helsinki, Finland. I really like these empty airplane days, this complete solitude in the middle of a crowd. Helsinki is cold, windy and dark. After a few encounters, lunch, dinner, I feel quite exhausted and happy to be alone in my room at the university. Tomorrow begins a very busy week.

I have a strange feeling being just half an hour away from Estonia, where I was born, and so close to Russia.

Each year, to be away from L. becomes more and more difficult and painful.

### Wednesday, September 24, 1975

After a busy day lecturing at the university, I find myself alone at last and thinking: What is there in Europe that is clearly absent in America? What is in America that is not in Europe? And, more personally, why am I drawn from America to Europe and from Europe back to America? I feel that the usual answer is, Europe is culture, roots, traditions. America is freedom and also lack of culture and rootlessness. This answer is incomplete, one-sided, simplified and incorrect. Tentatively, I would say that in America, one finds everything that Europe has, while in Europe there is hardly anything of what America is. One is drawn, not so much *to* Europe as *out* of America because in Europe one is spiritually more comfortable. There is always something to lean on, almost physically, whereas America is spiritually difficult. For years, people have rushed to America for an easier life, not realizing that deep down, life is much more difficult there. First of all, America is a country of great loneliness. Each one is alone with his own fate, under a huge sky, in the middle of a colossal country. Any culture, tradition, roots seem small there, but people strongly cling to them, knowing full well their illusory character. Secondly, this solitude in America demands from everyone an existential answer to the question, to be or not to be, and that requires effort. Hence so many personal crashes. In Europe anyone who falls, falls on some ground; in America he flies into an abyss. So much fear, such angst.

What draws a person to America is the possibility of having one's own individual fate. Once you have tasted it, it becomes impossible to be just a Finn or a Frenchman; in other words, to be determined once and for all. One is liberated from it. And although liberated, one is often drawn again to the illusory stability of Europe, to dreams and fantasy. But Europe's dream is ending; its ground is breaking. Europe is becoming a pitiful caricature of America, unable to become the "original," but an imitation denying its own originality. Our rather simple and slightly barbarian Gerald Ford is quite genuine when compared with the Giscards, Joberts and *tutti quanti* with their pseudo sophistication. While walking from Notre Dame to the Seine, to Place des Vosges, I realize that all that I like so much is illusory, not needed, that it has no relation with the France of Mitterrand and others. The real France wants to become America. America does not want to become Europe, therefore it is genuine, whereas Europe is steadily losing its genuine character.

New traditions are steadily generated in America; Europe's traditions, having lost their genuine character, are collapsing.

"If it does not die, it will not live." Europe gave birth to America out of its dream, and is dying in it as Europe. Out of that dying, America was born and is growing.

## *Thursday, September 25, 1975*

Two days spent discussing Orthodoxy and the West—Orthodoxy in the West—topics that I have struggled with all my life. I ask myself the question: "What is there that so clearly hinders Orthodoxy and distorts it?" That's what I always try to preach about, to defend. In other words, the question is: What is not relative, but *absolute*? I always come to the same conclusion: It is first of all a certain *vision*, an experience of God, the world, the man. The best in Orthodox theology is about that vision, although it does not simply coincide with it. (The Fathers are about it, but they often become the object of a dull intellectual cult. Liturgy is about it, as well as Church tradition, unless it becomes *pars pro toto* a recipe for a hopeless search for spirituality.)

Secondly, it is the Sacrament, in the deepest and comprehensive sense of the word, its key and criterion being in the Eucharist. Anything else is not only relative, but, by its very nature, passing. But Orthodox people love and absolutize almost only the "passing." Only *prophesy*, and, fatally bound with it, *martyrdom* (rejection, solitude, condemnation) can cure this crisis. What needs to be said is that Orthodox traditionalism is inversely proportional to faithfulness, to *Tradition*. This is neither a paradox nor an exaggeration. Orthodoxy became entangled in the past, which it worshipped as tradition. Orthodoxy is literally suffocating under its burden. Since genuine living and life-giving

Tradition comes to us from the past, through the past; since it is contained in it—and because the hungry and thirsty find bread and nourishment in it—the problem becomes quite complex. First of all, one has to be totally rooted in the *present*, whereas the first temptation of an Orthodox believer is to run way from the present, to turn back. But there, in the present, the past ceases to be Tradition—it becomes "dead weight and disappears." "No man, having put his hand to the plough, and looking back, is fit for the kingdom of God" (Luke 9:62). These words can be applied to the empirical Orthodox, which is either nostalgic and romantic or panicky and fearfully looking back.

Orthodoxy in our contemporary world is huddled in a cozy little corner. And from the rostrum of a Lutheran university, one affirms—quite sincerely—that without the Orthodox vision, the world's wounds cannot be healed and one is caught in a dead end.

A five hour drive with Bishop Paul* to Kuopio. A clear autumn day, pine trees, birches, lakes, quite deserted—very much like the Laurentians in Canada. The center of Finland's Orthodox Church, the seminary, is ultra modern, sparkling clean. Archbishop Paul is a great, transparent man, a gracious host. Vigil of the eve of St John. A classic Russian vigil, only in Finnish—a beautiful language quite adaptable to Russian chants. A friendly and warm reception after the service with the rector of the seminary (the translator of my *For the Life of the World*—our former student). One student plays the flute, another sings, all are young, blond, handsome.

### Friday, September 26, 1975

A festive and austere Liturgy that reflects Bishop Paul's discipline. All "mystical" prayers read aloud; everything is meaningful and thought through. A beautiful service. Then a whole day of lectures, quite tiring. The atmosphere is most friendly; the clergy are young and similar to ours in a most positive way. Nobody is putting on an Orthodox show; they are all at home in their own environment. No "showy" spirituality.

In the evening I visit with the local Lutheran bishop. Quite ceremonial and proper.

Then a Finnish steam bath with Bishop Paul. I wish I had a picture. I ended the day at Father Matti's.** Good and joyous.

---

* Paul of Finland, Archbishop, †1988—Head of the Orthodox Church of Finland, 1960–1988.
**Sidoroff, Father Matti—Graduate of St Vladimir's Seminary and a priest in the Orthodox Church in Finland.

## Saturday, September 27, 1975

I am completely squeezed out: lectures, discussions, tension, Vespers, parish reception with my talk, evening meeting with the Orthodox youth in some basement.

In the afternoon I heard a speech by Father N.—a "God's Fool," twelve children, an extraordinary face. One can see how much he is wounded by the rudeness surrounding him. He is clearly a failure—he speaks, people laugh— but what he said was unique, live, pure, and talented and refined. Like a few notes of Mozart among banging drums. One instantly felt the beauty and the nobility of such a failure.

Tomorrow a hierarchical Liturgy at the cathedral, a banquet, an ecumenical evening. I like Finland. I feel good in their church, but I irrepressibly want to go home...

## Sunday, September 28, 1975

Liturgy at the cathedral and again I have the impression of a great liturgical culture. Beautiful, strict singing without "concertizing." Without exaggeration, the best hierarchical Liturgy I have ever attended.

At some point during the Liturgy, I had a blissful feeling of eternity, of total joy. A white-haired bishop praying with ten priests and, behind the altar, golden autumn birches. Time stops, in touch with the highest, the eternal—when time is powerless.

Outside—low clouds, strong wind blowing off autumn leaves, Sunday emptiness in the streets and squares. I love the north and feel at home in it.

## Monday, September 29, 1975

A very special day. Early in the morning, we drive with Bishop Paul to the monastery of Valaam. The weather is clearing, It is a cold, sunny day, an empty road, golden birches and beautiful high pine trees. We cross the monastery gates and feel a hundred years back in time. Ancient monks, the abbot—Father Simforian [died in 1981 after 75 years in the monastic life]—is a copy of the portrait of St Seraphim of Sarov with his staff. He has been in Valaam since 1906. I can't even try to reproduce the story of his life, his tone, his expressions, his whole appearance, all out of an irrevocable, long-past time.

A thanksgiving service before the icon of the Virgin Mary, dinner with the monks, a tour of the monastery. I feel submerged in a storm of thoughts and impressions, which I will have to sort out.

Then through forests of the same golden birches—along large sleepy lakes—we arrive at the women's monastery—Lintula—and from there to the "cell" of Bishop Paul on a little island in the middle of a lake. What an extraordinary man.

Again a sauna with the bishop. The same light is flowing out of this fragile, transparent, radiant man. His memory will remain in my heart as a joyful festive gift.

Thinking about these days, especially about Bishop Paul, I want to end with "Glory to God for everything."

## Thursday, October 2, 1975

### Crestwood

I am home again. My Finnish experience has become the past and I need to integrate it in the whole perception of the fate of Orthodoxy.

Right now, my duty is quite simple—lectures, seminary, church. I always feel that all my fragmented experiences are not due to chance: emigration, America, Greece, Solzhenitsyn, Finland. Not chance because they force me to come to a synthesis, to overcome the fragmented character, the breaking to pieces of Orthodoxy in time and space; its running in many different little streams instead of one common flow. Just to mention my visit to the monastery Valaam—it was an immersion into another world. And the Dormition Vespers in Helsinki: pompous, imperial decorum, sophisticated choir, precious vestments... Once in a while, through it all, "there shines the Light..." The tragedy is that each fragment wants to be the whole—all of Orthodoxy—and passionately denies the others. Each one perceives Christ only through his own experience, his own vision. No one sees his limitations, his own relative character in Christ. I see my calling in trying—and praying—to overturn this approach, to unite all these fragments and to return them to life in and through Christ. I have to constantly repeat to myself: "Shout your enthusiasm in the name of Christ." I *must*, because it is the Truth, and I *can*, because I understand these fragments and can identify literally with each of them.

## Friday, October 3, 1975

In Valaam, as I already wrote, reigns Igumen Simforian, eighty-two years old and at the monastery since he was thirteen. Zealous, almost to the point of fanaticism and heroically preserving Tradition. What kind of tradition is this? A medley of pious, and some rather gaudy, icons, lithographs—characteristic of Russian Orthodoxy at the end of the 19th century. Seven hours of services in succession, beginning with a thanksgiving service at three in the morning. A deliberately primitive style. While talking with Father

Simforian, one feels that for him this style—as it has been for thousands of monks before him—is quite natural, salutary, that it is truly producing saints. Equally clear is the fact that to continue it is impossible, that after the disappearance of the last of the Mohicans, that style became artificial, a sort of emotional game. I felt the tragedy quite clearly in Valaam.

A break in external tradition, caused by revolution or the dying out of peasant monasticism, produced among the Orthodox an emotional pathos of restoration—from its very beginning, the Russian emigration was permeated with it, as well as Valaam, Mt. Athos *et al.* What used to be an organic, natural style became stylization, spiritually weak, harmful. The main problem of Orthodoxy is the constraint due to style, and its inability to revise it; a prevalent absence of self-criticism, of checking the tradition of the elders by Tradition, by love of Truth. A growing idolatry.

### Monday, October 6, 1975

Saturday was Orthodox Education Day. Large crowds attending. Beautiful weather. On my feet for eleven hours, enjoying the concrete reality of church life, of unity. Yesterday, Sunday, the church was overflowing with visitors.

Today I spent the day getting organized, trying to get into the rhythm of the new school year. Finland had interrupted it.

I eagerly want to start writing, especially after a few inspiring conversations during Education Day. One woman said, "I read *Of Water and the Spirit* and you answered all my questions." Quite an incentive. My dream is to write for the people, not for theologians. And when I find that it works—what joy!

Today L. is fifty-two. Beautiful weather—a transparent Indian summer day.

### Friday, October 10, 1975

Sakharov received the Nobel Peace Prize.

Yesterday I met with our new students, one after the other. Good impression and a feeling of enormous responsibility. How to avoid the dangers of religion and religiosity? "Do not let children play with the locks" says the sign on the doors of the train. The calling is quite genuine; idolatry is easy—just within their mind's reach.

### Thursday, October 16, 1975

Last evening I went to a memorial service for a cousin in the Synodal Church. I always feel self-conscious in that church since the priest and the deacon do not even say hello, but I mainly feel like a stranger in the midst of the typically Russian "cozy" atmosphere of the church: Russian piety, complete self-assurance, the absence of any anxiety, any doubt, any questioning. They serve well, sing well—but they would serve and sing anything well, as long as it was "traditional"! One word missing—and all would collapse. Russians accept as slaves, or deny as slaves—blindly and stubbornly. After the service, the priest announced a "memorial Matins," then "memorial Vespers," *then* of course, a *panikhida*—memorial service. What is the difference between these services? If one asked, one would be suspected of shaking the foundations of Orthodoxy. Everything has to be massive, blind, "according to rubrics"—that's the reassuring meaning of religion. One stands in a kind of solitude, feeling that if one would open up the meaning of the words of the services, people would be terrified. That's why the "Old Believers " feared any "book inquiry"—from lack of faith. To find Christ, the Russian believer comes out of the Church and joins a sect, transforming it into an "Old Believers' sect." But at the center of the Church is the *Eucharist*. The whole meaning of the Eucharist is to constantly blow everything up from inside by referring it not only to the transcendent, but to Christ and His Kingdom. It is not by chance that in order to "render harmless" the Eucharist, it has been first reduced to personal sanctification and personal piety, then separated even from that piety.

### Monday, October 27, 1975

Spent all of Saturday in heavy talks with N.—caught doing drugs with N., who hates her husband, etc. I feel quite discouraged when contemplating the muddy puddle in which we are immersed. Again and again I am convinced of the awful ambiguity of religion and the so-called religious experience. It sometimes seems fearfully obvious to me that everything in religion that is not from Christ—in Christ, through Him, to Him—is from the devil. According to the Gospel of St John, the Holy Spirit, when He comes, will teach the world about sin.*

Sin is not to believe in Christ. Nothing should be called sin other than not to transform religion into the knowledge, the love and the life of Christ.

Suddenly, in the middle of these weighty talks, a consolation: A little ten-year-old girl is being baptized. I felt a touch of the Holy Spirit, His beauty, purity, love, the experience of the love of God. I was even terrified by that experience—as if I had been in contact with a "chosen one."

---

* Cf: John 16:8-9: "And when he comes, he will convince the world concerning sin and righteousness and judgment concerning sin, because they do not believe in me."

I feel a sort of bad, "unkind" tiredness. Bad, because I want to run away from all the little passions, from the turbulent muddy waters where I have been floating for so many years. I want to leave, I am so tempted—and this temptation is so tiring!

## *Saturday, November 1, 1975*

November: and immediately the whole coloring of vision changes, the whole feeling of life. These feelings of the months come, of course, from childhood. November, in Paris, began with All Saints Day—no school! (My first—and only—poem written while sitting behind my desk in school was about Toussaint "Today, there are flowers on all tombs…" further, I absolutely don't remember.) Then Veterans' Day and finally the ascent toward pre-Christmas December. I see November as silver, black, sad, quiet. After the golden feast of October's fall comes this late November fall with its own particular secret joy, its own gifts to the heart.

While thinking yesterday about my last conversation with N. it seemed to me that in order to achieve some internal order and harmony, one could present a triune intuition of the following references (an intuition not of one's conscience, but rather one's heart):

A cosmic reference—it is the sense of life here and now, it is the safe-guarding of one's communion with the cosmos: nature, "this" time, light—one's own place in this scheme. It is the opposite of division, separation, isolation. The world as a continuously given and continuously accepted gift. Gratitude. Joy. And, in that sense, life itself as prayer.

A historic reference. This is the inner connection with one's work, place, calling. It is obedience, humility, readiness, knowledge of dangers, of temptations, of conflict ("Look carefully how you walk, not as unwise men but as wise" (Ephesians 5:15)). Here—prayer for help, prayer as exorcism, prayer as illumination ("give me strength to accept").

And finally, eschatological reference—with the ultimate, with the sought after, with the hoped for—"Your Kingdom come"!

I think that if one learned to really live with this tri-unity, one would find solutions to problems arising from falling out of those references or from their distortions. If our faith is cosmic, historic and eschatological, so must our spirituality be. Only Christ unites these three into one, since these references mean coming to know Christ in each gift of life—cosmic, historic and eschatological—the modus of His revelation to us and of His presence with us. To feel, to accept, to live everything as His icon (symbol, sign). And this is all confirmed by the Eucharist, by the Church.

All that is possible because it is how it truly is.

### Tuesday, November 4, 1975

Long, long day at the seminary. At night, I lectured about Chekhov's *The Bishop*—feeling an internal liberation and cleansing. I tried to communicate the striking melody of that story in the themes of the mother and childhood. Such high, pure art, where there is more inner essence of Christianity and Orthodoxy than in theological, triumphal "definitions." The mystery of Christianity: beauty of defeat; liberation from success. "Thou hast hid these things from the wise…" (Matthew 11:25-26). Everything in that story is a defeat and it is thoroughly illumined by a mysterious inexplicable victory, "Now is the Son of man glorified…" (John 13:31).

If theology is isolated from culture, which alone can reveal the beauty of defeat and the light of victory in it (*reveal,* not explain), then theology loses its salt and becomes empty words.

I couldn't sleep, plagued by strange dreams. Nervous exhaustion. But on my way to the seminary, there was over me such a high, pale, pale blue sky. And everything fell back in place.

### Thursday, November 6, 1975

Yesterday, my mother arrived from Paris. The plane was late and my daughter Anya and I spent two hours walking around the empty Arrivals building. I love these hours of waiting. On one hand, they somehow "fall out" of life and its rhythm (waste of time); on the other hand, they show better than anything else the mysterious essence of time: time measured ahead by expectancy and not back, time already lit up by anticipation, illumined from ahead…

Mother is in better shape than I expected. She is quite impressed by our wonderful weather, our golden leaves, blissful in the evening sunshine.

### Saturday, November 8, 1975

Funny how this journal, or rather contact with it, has gradually become a necessity. There is nothing noteworthy except the usual concerns: the illnesses of Serge's children, Mother's difficult character, the seminary's constant business, etc. All these, and more, consume me, my time. This journal is, in fact, an escape from it all; it fulfills the need to renounce it all and get in touch with something deeper in me. Hard to describe this contact with the only real, silent, unnoticeable in me, with the breath of eternity in this world. It might become needless and cheap lyrics. Silence.

Tomorrow I am leaving for Cleveland for the All-American Council. I have to acquire as much depth, as much detachment as possible, and prayer, not with words and prostrations, but with the attention of my whole being: vision, hearing, hidden knowledge of the Presence.

## *Thursday, November 13, 1975*

It is the beginning of the end, i.e., the last session of the Council. After four days of constant bustle, I still have a joyous feeling of the life and vitality of the Church, and mainly of her ability to turn from discussion about form (administration, rubrics, money) to discussion about the content of the Church. Moral problems were discussed with total seriousness. There is a large, creative group in the Church—actually the majority—that expresses the Church itself.

I decided to withdraw from church administration because I am convinced that what is badly needed is a clarification about the dead end where all administrative bodies are locked, in a total lack of confidence and trust. I do not want to be either a patch or a rubber stamp on this tragic discrepancy between the administrative powers and the people.

## *Friday, November 14, 1975*

### *Crestwood*

I still cannot believe it—I really declined to be nominated, and I am free. At first, although I dreamed about it, I was sad to be free, especially while the atmosphere of the Council still surrounded me. I am so accustomed to being in authority, in the center of things. I wanted out—but to suddenly find myself in the ranks and to return home out of it all was hard. Maybe my pride was touched: they did not hold on to me; they did not ask! But it did not last. While flying home with David D[rillock] and John E[rickson] I felt a new joy from being rank-and-file.

I came home quite tired. L. told me about her school events. I am always impressed by her tact, nobility, the truth of her decisions. At night, at 10:00 PM—general confession.

Today there was an early Liturgy. Mother took communion. While serving, I thought: my mother is in church, my whole childhood, all is enclosed in a sort of circle.

I came upon a quote from Saint Therese of Lisieux: "…and yet the soul seems to really be in a state where it receives no consolation, neither from heaven where it does not dwell yet, nor from earth where it does not dwell anymore and whence it does not want to receive any…"

## Monday, December 1, 1975

Coming back from Pittsfield after the Liturgy and a talk with the parishioners, I was trying to understand the very peculiar phenomenon of such a parish. Founded in 1905 by Galicians and Carpatho-Russians, the parish has worked ever since to maintain, to safeguard—what?—the old calendar, Slavonic, which no one can either read or understand—both the Epistle and the Gospel in Slavonic! An empty form, loyalty—to whom, to what? To childhood, to parents. An identity in the midst of American pluralism, with the B[obrovsky] family touchingly trying to do something in this total wilderness. My question is: What can one do? What should one do? Can one pour new wine in these old wineskins? On the other hand, this lovely white church with a cupola stood there for seventy years as if expecting something. How many liturgies have been served; how much faith and dedication went into the safeguarding of the Church? People, without even realizing it, kept the Presence.

I thought about it all while driving through empty hills and dales on a cloudy, dry, sad Sunday. I thought also that the whole life in the Church consists in continuously learning to have faith in Grace—"which heals the infirm and fulfills what is lacking."

Dean's conference at the Seminary

While answering questions, I was once again conscious of the two main dangers of the school: theology, tempted by nationalism, by wordiness, by smooth schemes; and piety, tempted by emotionalism and sentimentality.

## Tuesday, December 2, 1975

Last yellow leaves. Frost and sunshine. My favorite silver-lighted, festive, ceremonial December.

## Monday, December 8, 1975

I am staying home trying to sort out a pile of unanswered letters. While taking a shower, I thought about the dynamic of the fallen world—the law. The law is how society defends itself against the destructive chaos created by sin and the fall. Under the dominion of the law, everything—culture, religion, politics—serves the law and expresses it. It is *style* in art, *morality* in religion, *hierarchy* in society. Construction, creativity are under the law. But since the law is by essence limiting, it provokes opposition not only by evil and sin (criminality), but also by the undying thirst of man for "grace," freedom, unlimited space, Spirit.

Law (according to St Paul) inevitably provokes a desire to overcome it, to get beyond one's self. Then starts a crisis quite obvious in religion, in culture, in politics. The forces that are generated by law as a barrier and a guard against chaos begin to deny that barrier and destroy it in the name of what is higher than law. But the world remains fallen. The forces of law cannot create anything; they remain without grace, ambiguous, and even destructive (as can be seen in socialism, Freud, some new art). In the fallen world, there is no way out of these dynamics—the sublimation and overcoming of the law—there is none, and there cannot be. The law is the true reflection of the fall; therefore it is right. The "crisis" (the reaction against the law) reflects the truth of the search, the thirst, the freedom.

The truth of conservatism is sad and pessimistic. It is the knowledge of evil, its destructiveness, its power; the knowledge of the chaos behind each "barrier." But even sadder and more tragic is the joy produced by the "crisis" (between law and liberation), for it is a false joy that mistakes pseudo-grace and pseudo-freedom for grace and freedom. Conservatism is sad and heavy; revolution is scary and frightening: It is the Pentecost of the devil. There is only *one* crisis which is blessed and saving: *Christ*—because from Him flow grace and freedom. In Him the law is fulfilled, as well as revolution. It is quite frightening when Christianity itself turns into heavy law *or* becomes revolutionary. The whole meaning of Christianity is to soar upwards out of this rhythm, this course, these dynamics of the world. Christianity makes it possible to live by the truth of revolution inside the law and by the truth of the law inside the revolution. Christianity is the "*coincidentia oppositorum*," the synthesis of law and revolution, their fulfillment in each other—it is the Kingdom of God, truth itself, beauty itself for it is Life and Spirit.*

I see here the key to the Christian perception of culture, of politics, and, of course, of "religion" itself—a "holding it all together." Christianity is freedom from conservatism and from revolution. Hence, a "rightist" Christian is as frightening as a "leftist" one, and I know why I sway to the left when dealing with the rightists and to the right when I am with leftists.

More about the same. In the area of art, one can always find a law in the beauty of any genuine work of art. But the beauty is not born out of the law but is in its fulfillment. The beauty is born out of grace. Fulfilling the law, beauty overcomes it. When art remains under the law and is born in the law,

* Nicholas of Cusa (1401-1464), a Cardinal and Bishop of Bixen, generated the principle of *coincidentia oppositorum,* which "maintains that in God's being the various polarities holding sway in the world of actuality converge, or more precisely, exist in unity prior to any division."(Kitaro Nishida. *An Inquiry into the Good.* New Haven: Yale University Press, 1990, n2, p. 168).

(cf. contemporary iconographers, who are often copyists) it becomes stylization and dies, so that the law becomes the death of art.

### Wednesday, December 10, 1975

I am back from the airport. I took my mother there for her return to Paris. Her stay with us was difficult, but when saying good-bye I felt acute pity for her—lonely, helpless, old. Most important for her is her fight—helpless and hopeless—for her own place in life; for being someone, and not just a wreck. I feel ashamed of the times when I was irritated. What remains is all that she gave me, "a childhood without sorrow." Until now I lived in a world where I had a mother, but this morning when she was leaving me and walking through the narrow corridor to her plane, I knew that very soon my world will be without a mother—and at that point my own descent will begin.

### Thursday, December 11, 1975

I could not be a politician. In any discussion, I clearly see the truth in almost every point of view. The poet Georgy Ivanov said, "What is binding us all? A mutual lack of understanding..."

Annual meeting of the trustees of the seminary.

I have spent several hours working on my *Eucharist* and right away life is cheerful and good.

### Friday, December 12, 1975

The meeting went very well. I was touched once more by the readiness in America of so many busy people to give their time and their care.

I spent a few hours in New York. I really love the city—walked from Radio Liberty to Rizzoli (bookstore), along Fifth Avenue. Cold, dark, dry day and everywhere the lights of Christmas trees, the pre-festal excitement. Wonderful huge tree at Rockefeller Center. I sadly remembered mother's delight when I brought her to see that beautiful New York tradition.
Yesterday, after a little birthday party for Sasha Schmemann (3 years old), I walked with L. along Fifth Avenue to the Rockefeller Center tree. Lights everywhere. Christmas carols in the air. I love the city and its lively life.

### Friday, December 19, 1975

Last day before vacations. Soon the Feast! Last evening we celebrated L.'s last day of school at our favorite restaurant. L. asked me, "What do you like the most in your 'profession'?" I think, and said, it is the right and the obligation to be a witness (a poor and weak one, that's another question)—a witness of that which is the most important ("the one thing needful"), a witness to that which can never be limited either by emigration, by America, or by anything.

Yesterday, having finished my seminary business—vacation! L. and I went to the Hopkos with Serge's children, who are spending the weekend with us. Happy atmosphere at Anya's. I thoroughly enjoyed baby Alexandra (the "ultimate in the Hopkos").

I finished reading a two-volume biography of Simone Weil. I am always impressed by someone who is possessed by an idea, by any "possession." For me it is life without air. Of course those people become either *great* or *saints*. I realize with some sadness my own total inability to reach that kind of absolutism of mind and heart. I don't know.

First real snow. Worked at my desk at home, admiring behind my window dark branches heavy with snow. Total silence—only the ticking of our clock, total bliss. In the context of Weil's book (absolutism, possession)—is that bliss, fullness, happiness from God? Or is it from weakness (laziness, *farniente*...?).

## Tuesday, December 23, 1975

After two days of snowfall, frost and sunshine, L. and I, while waiting for the arrival of our daughter Masha, her husband, Father John, and little Vera, went to the city for a stroll along festive windows, street music and huge brightly lit building.

Decorated our tree with the Tkachuks.

# CHAPTER IV

# 1976

∾

*Thursday, January 1, 1976*

*Paris*

As always, we left New York for Paris right after our Christmas reception. Joyful, happy, wonderful services, huge choir, large crowds in church, fullness of the Feast. Family gathering around our tree. Tom took us to the airport. Snow falling and in every window bright Christmas lights. These are moments when life is so full! And suddenly, the quiet and emptiness of the airport. In Paris we were met by our Schmemann nieces. Cozy family lunch—Paris!

*Friday, January 2, 1976*

Breakfast on Place St Sulpice with our cousins from Germany and Switzerland. Then with Liana along the quays to our favorite restaurant with a view of Notre Dame. Then, friends, more friends, lunches, dinners, walks in between. Thanksgiving service, then New Year's dinner with all our cousins at my brother's.

*Sunday, January 4, 1976*

After the Liturgy, luncheon with my mother and brother, then a long walk with L. to the Place des Vosges—one of our very favorite places in Paris.

*Tuesday, January 6, 1976*

Christmas Eve, old calendar. I spent the days visiting all my childhood memories—where we lived, the local open market, my school, the last place where I saw my father waving to me from his sixth-floor terrace. Christmas Eve gathering at my brother's.

## Wednesday, January 7, 1976

Walk with L. to Place Vendôme, perfect in its glory and beauty. The elegant Paris: grayish, immobile. I felt Paris this winter in the perfect symphony and harmony of its windows.

## Thursday, January 8, 1976

I spent happy hours with my Paris friends discussing liturgical theology in an atmosphere of human warmth. Impossible to describe all the encounters and impressions. Then my friends return to their own lives and I return to mine. The whole point was: "Do you remember?" "Yes, I do."

## Friday, January 9, 1976

Departure. Early morning breakfast with Andrei at our hotel in total darkness. Goodbyes with my brother are always cheerful and merry, but deep down it's a painful rending since our closeness—for him and for me—is "beyond understanding." Mother, at the airport, a piercing sadness to watch her from the height of our fast moving magic carpet—old, unhappy, lonely, drowning in the decay, the ebbing of life.

And now—the sunshine and frost of home. We did not see the sun for fourteen days! Cheerful Tom, our warm home.

## Tuesday, January 20, 1976

### Austin, Texas

I am in Austin for three days of intensive lecturing about sacramental theology at the Episcopal Seminary.

Long flight that allowed me to finish Aries' book about death.* Very interesting, especially what he writes about the evolution of the perception of death since the Middle Ages. His historical scheme: first the acceptance of death by individuals and society, hence dying in public, becoming accustomed to seeing dead bodies, burial *ad sanctos*. No cult of graves (it's obvious that the dead being in and with the Church are considered to be part of life, with us.) Then, individualization of death (15th-16th centuries), personal judgment, etc. Then in the 18th century death becomes rupture. In the 19th century, the cult of graves appears, the idea of nationalism, of succession. And only in the 20th century, total removal of death from life (hospitals, nursing homes, funeral homes). I will have to reread and rethink it all.

* Philippe Aries' *Western Attitudes Toward Death.*

Today—lectures, luncheon with some professors, evening with the dean, cozy and interesting. During these conversations, one notes what in Orthodoxy is needed by everyone, and what has survived and needs "demythologizing."

Sunny, warm, beautiful Texan evergreen oak trees.

### Thursday, January 29, 1976

First day of lectures at the seminary and, after thirty years, I still have a feeling of newness. I think it's a sure sign that here is my true vocation—and in church services, of course. Everything else, I do under the whip—especially "spiritual" conversations.

### Monday, February 2, 1976

Feast of the Meeting of the Lord. Last evening I served and then lectured at the Church of Christ the Savior about Russian religious thought abroad. Many new Russian émigrés telling me about their divisions, fights and intrigues. Quite sad!

On Saturday, our 33rd wedding anniversary—cozy day at home; wonderful evening at Anya's.

Yesterday I heard three confessions—sad reality of unhappiness, or rather non-happiness; absence of any happiness, of anything that one desires; impossibility of having it—ever!

Perhaps only now, in my old age, am I beginning to "understand"—not with my mind, but my heart. I did not understand before, because all my life I myself was so happy, precisely by having what I wanted. I am even frightened when thinking that God never deprived me of anything. Nothing in my life of the fate of Job! Maybe God simply knows how weak I am. How can I teach others? How can I call them to be strong?

Freezing blizzard outside.

### Tuesday, February 10, 1976

I talked with L. and Tom [Hopko] about "counseling," in connection with two difficult visits and, also, an Anglican priest, psychotherapist, who wants to convert to Orthodoxy and "help" us in the field of psychotherapy. I need to sit down and carefully think through my instinctive aversion to this whole area with which others are becoming increasingly obsessed. What stands behind it? What is its attraction? Tentatively (but I might be quite wrong), it seems to me that the cult of psychotherapy is difficult to reconcile with

Christianity because it is often based on a monstrous egocentricity, on preoccupation with one's self. It's the ultimate expression and product of "I, myself," i.e., of the sin from which one must be saved. Psychotherapy reinforces that egocentricity, which is truly its basic principle. When psychotherapy penetrates religious consciousness, it distorts it. The result is often a search for "spirituality" as a distinct entity. Hence, the darkness and narrow-mindness of many spiritualists; hence the confusion of teaching, pastoral work, care of souls, with psychologizing. The principle on which Christianity is built—"Christ saves, revives, cures"—is opposed by "What saves and cures is understanding one's self." "To see one's self in the light of God and repent" is replaced by "to understand oneself and be cured."

### Wednesday, February 11, 1976

Why can't a woman be a priest? Long talk with Father Tom, who is being attacked by Orthodox women as well as many others, for his article in the *St Vladimir's Seminary Quarterly*. Since the beginning of the storm about the ordination of women, I am more and more surprised, not by the topic of the discussion, but by what comes to light about theology. It is impossible to find decisive arguments either for or against ordination—decisive in the sense of being objectively convincing for both sides. Each side is right for itself, i.e., inside its own perspectives, the logic of its own arguments. St John of Kronstadt said about the heresies of Leo Tolstoy: "Oh, demented Count! Don't you believe in the saintly Apostles?" But Tolstoy's heresies *begin* with his disbelief in the Apostles! So to find arguments *ex Traditione* is missing the target. A heresy is always "of one piece," integral, not made up; it is really a deep choice, rather than a reparable mistake in some details. Hence the hopelessness of theological dialogues. All theological arguments come *post factum*—after the fact. They are rooted in experience, but if the experience is different, they do not apply. What has become quite obvious in the discussion about ordination of women? Says Tom: "How can one explain that a woman can be the president of the United States but not a priest?" It seems to me (I say) that she should not be the president of the US. But nobody can say that nowadays, and to say it would be offensive. And one should not offend. So we are in a vicious circle—an unavoidable vicious circle, when an organic, primordial eternal experience is broken. Our contemporary culture consists in denying and breaking up that experience; its very essence is its denial. It is an experience of negativism, rebellion, protest. The whole concept of liberation is totally negative. The idea, "all people are equal," is one of the most erroneous roots *a priori*. Then follows: "all people are free," "love is always positive" (hence for instance, the justification for homosexuality), any limitation is oppressive. As long as Christians themselves accept all these "principles," as long as they accept the culture built on these principles, no arguments about the impossibility for women to become priests sound valid. They seem hypocritical and deceptive. If we start the discussion with an abstract, unreal, unnatural "equality" between men and women, no argument is possible. We have to start by exposing, unmasking this principle as false because it is an abstract invention. The whole contemporary culture must be rejected with its spiritual, false, even demonic, premises. There is deep falsehood in the principle of *comparison* which is the basis of the pathos for equality. One never achieves anything by comparison—the source of envy (why he, not I?), protest (we *must* be equal), then anger, rebellion and division. Actually, it is the genealogy of the devil. There is nothing positive; all is negative from beginning to end. In that sense, our culture is demonic, for at its basis is comparison. Since comparison always, mathematically, leads to the experience and the knowledge of inequality, it always leads to protest. Equality is based on the denial of any distinctions, but since they exist, the wish for equality calls to fight them, to force equalization on people, and, what is even worse, to refuse these distinctions, which are the essence of life. The person—man or woman—who hungers for equality is already emptied and impersonal because a personality is made of what distinguishes it from others and not submitted to the absurd law of equality.

To the demonic principle of comparison, Christianity opposes love. The essence of love is the total absence of "comparison." Equality cannot exist in this world because the world was created by love and not by principles. And the world thirsts for love and not equality. Nothing—and we know it—kills love, replaces it with hate, as much as the equality forced upon the world as a goal and a value.

And it is precisely in love, and nothing else, that the duality of man as male and female is rooted. It is *not* a mistake that humanity must rectify by "equality," not a flaw, not accident—it is the first and most ontological expression of the very essence of life. Here personal fulfillment is accomplished in self-sacrifice, here lies the victory over "law," here is the death of self-affirmation of the man as man, and the woman as woman, and so on. It all means that there is no equality but an ontological distinction making love possible, i.e., *unity, not equality.* Equality presupposes many equals, never turning into unity because the essence of equality consists of its careful safeguarding. In unity, distinctions do not disappear but become unity, life, creativity. The male and female are part of the nature of the world, but only a human being transforms them into the unity of the family. The aversion of our culture to family is based on the fact that the family is the last bastion to expose the evil of equality.

## Saturday, February 14, 1976

I received from my brother in Paris a package with all my childhood letters to my parents. Nothing interesting, really, except the realization how very happy our family was! While rereading those letters, I was thinking of the source of the drama of my three current young "spiritual" charges. No real tragedy, but something has been missing in their family lives. We had many tragedies in our family: my sister's death, acute poverty, sickness, but we always had a real family life: a home. The "family" transcends any relationships; it is not the goal but the source and the strength which feeds life.

Today, for the first time, I felt a breath of spring.

## Monday, February 16, 1976

Last night was the end of the Winter Olympics in Innsbruck. I think that we spent at least 12-14 hours glued to our television in admiration of the beauty, brightness, perfection and strong spirit of the participants.

## Tuesday, February 17, 1976

I am mentally and spiritually exhausted by trying to finish the first chapter of my *Eucharist: The Sacrament of Unity*. Exhausted because I try to discover and clarify for myself what I want to say—I try to justify every word.

And my work, which requires so much concentration, is always against a background of bustle and business which somehow dilutes my efforts.

A radiant, warm spring day.

## Wednesday, February 18, 1976

After yesterday—sunny and clear—today is damp, gray, dark. but the same breath of spring remains in the air.

I continue working, to the point of affliction, on my first chapter. My head hurts! Strange and mysterious is the working of thought—as if listening in on one's self to something or somebody else, as if recognizing something then trying to say it, express it adequately. But there is always the feeling of a hidden working which occurs without my knowledge. *What* I say does not come from me, only *how* I say it. All creativity is to make sure that the *how* corresponds to the *what*; that is the cooperation of man with God, the mystery of human freedom.

I slept today in the same room with little Alexandra [Hopko]. Very early in the morning she woke up and in total darkness sang for a good ten minutes—wonderful, real, creative singing.

I was writing about faith (in distinction to "religious feeling"). I felt quite inspired, full of joy, but, in reality, it was a judgment on myself.

Christ asked whether He will find faith on the earth when He returns. One thing is certain: He will find a great deal of religion and religious feelings. The Last Judgment is first of all the Judgment over religion. "For by your words you will be justified, and by your words you will be condemned" (Matthew 12:37).

Language is given to men to profess, praise, witness, pray. Whatever does not enter these categories is not only unnecessary, but can be harmful.

I gave myself a little time off while writing the above—but now back to working on a final concrete "embodiment."

### Monday, February 23, 1976

*Chicago*

I am writing late at night in Chicago where I came for eight days of lectures at a Lutheran seminary ("the Theology of Sacraments"). I was quite sad yesterday when having to part from L. for such a long time. I promised myself not to accept such invitations. Tomorrow, when work starts, it will be easier.

### Tuesday, February 24, 1976

Three lectures a day (too much), coffee breaks, lunch with three Orthodox priests—a Greek, a Serb, and OCA. Shop talk about church affairs. I am always amazed how we all agree about the crisis of Orthodoxy, about ethnicity, etc. What is also quite clear is that nobody will move a little finger… Conscience and being coexist, conscience does not define or influence the "being"—how things really are.

I have the feeling that I will have some rest here from the seminary's business.

### Wednesday, February 25, 1976

Again, a spring day. I am blissfully looking at the beautiful sunset (*tout est ailleurs*—all is elsewhere.) A break into some unbearable bliss, into the presence everywhere of some hidden knowledge, hidden light.

In all our conversations with students and professors I am struck by their unconscious tendency to follow fashion, to achieve success. They seem to need to "dress like everybody"—the same in theology.

Against that background, dinner with some Orthodox. We talked as we did in the fifties, as we will in the eighties. For the Western people, change is the obvious essence and form of life. For the Orthodox, an absolute immobility. Both make me discouraged, or, rather, bored.

I was invited to lecture at the Greek parish. Ten priests, a huge crowd, the warmest welcome and an enthusiastic response. All very pleasant.

### Thursday. February 26, 1976

Drive to Valparaiso, Indiana, for a final lecture at the Liturgical Institute. Wonderful drive by awesome, huge steel factories; a truly apocalyptic sight. Then humble rural Indiana, little villages. In Valparaiso, an enormous crowd listened with understanding and interest to "Eucharist and Prayer" and gave me a lovely welcome. I am quite sensitive to the provincial charm of America's heartland. My companion, Father S. G. nice, modest, genuine. has the radiance of real Orthodoxy. I thoroughly enjoy his company—everything is easy and light in his loving, open-minded, joyous presence. The weather is "playing along" my feeling of enjoyment, happiness in an apotheosis of sunshine, transparency, clarity.

But…I want to go home! I catch myself counting days on my fingers several times a day…!

### Friday, February 27, 1976

Last evening I met with the faculty for drinks and was immersed in talks about Orthodoxy, ecumenism, etc. And, as usual, I felt how far apart we are in the essential intuition, vision of the world, in the very perception of faith. Put simply: the Orthodox man begins with the "end," with the experience, the breakthrough, the very reality of God, the Kingdom, Life—and only afterwards does he clarify it, but in relation to the experience he has had. The Western man rationally arrives at and evokes the "end" from a series of premises. The Orthodox often expresses that "end" quite poorly in theology. For the Westerner, the end somehow disappears, is diluted in elaborate constructions. (I need to express this problem better…)

### Monday, March 1, 1976

Once more, while departing from Chicago, I was amazed by the quantity of enormous churches built at the end of the last century by all sorts of immigrants. How much sacrifice, religious feeling went into these buildings! An almost pathological religiosity mixed with an almost total secularism.

In Portland I was met by three priests and their wives—OCA, Greek, Antiochian—all serious, dedicated, enthusiastic. Saturday, lecturing to the point of becoming hoarse! Everybody considerate, welcoming; quite touching.

Then Seattle—old Russian parish, slow pace, warm welcome. Russian cozy atmosphere. Such a joyous reception that I feel quite encouraged and realized that "The harvest is plentiful…" (Matthew 9:37).

At night, flight to San Francisco where I meet with Father Tom [Hopko] from New York for some business meetings.

Back to Chicago, to my cozy hotel which has become my home. Cold, rain, gray. Outside my window, a lace of black branches against a gray sky. Warm, cozy. Phone call from L.—All is well, so I feel even cozier!

Three more days in Chicago, then homeward. In spite of the fact that I am counting hours until I get home, I know that this whole week and the busy weekend on the West Coast will remain in my memory as "full of light."

## *Wednesday, March 3, 1976*

Eve of my departure. As usual, the order, the rhythm of this past week are beginning to break up, to show the end and the sadness that accompanies any end. Encounter, separation. Beginning, end.

In this world, nothing can ever be final, definitive; there is a promise in everything that is never totally fulfilled. These twenty students who listened to so many of my lectures this past week have hardly ceased being anonymous. We just genuinely met each other, we just became conscious of each other's uniqueness, then separation occurs. Hence the saying, "love is strong as death" (Song of Songs 8:16).

I had these thoughts while returning to the hotel. A white windy day. I am quite tired, I count hours until my departure for the airport, but I feel that sorrow of separation, the same experience of the irreparable fragmentation of life.

Western Ash Wednesday—A short service at the seminary chapel. Everything in that service is good: the singing, the preaching (about prayer as "Abba," "Amen," and "Alleluia.") I deeply feel the words of the prayers and the hymns. I have always loved Western hymns since my trip to England in 1937. But then the question: Why is Christianity so weak, so powerless; why is life continuing as if there was no Christianity?

Last evening, dinner at the N's. The happy reality of a family, its beauty, its goodness. We did not have any important or serious discussions. The children played the piano. Everybody felt "good" quite genuinely. The family does not have a goal, is not pragmatic. The family is a source, it is life, and out of life appear goals. I came home after that evening somehow bathed in that joy, that "goodness."

### Monday, March 8, 1976

Great Lent! As usual, during these days, going back deep into my childhood, I remember a long series of Forgiveness Sundays.

I am reading the third volume of Solzhenitsyn's *Gulag Archipelago* and *Winter Sun* by Vladimir Weidle. Again I plunge into the nightmarish world of the Gulag; the strength, range, deep water of S.'s talent. Every page is startling. The language is precise, pliant, rich and melodious, whereas from Weidle's book flows, literally flows, light. The book is about light, about gathering life and its memory *in* light. I need that music and love it—like air and food.

### Tuesday, March 9, 1976

Yesterday, I spent the whole day in church—five services—deep into Lent. I listened to and heard the Psalms in a new way: the striking collision of human despair and faith. They show the conventional, illusory character of the whole evolution of man. There he is on the surface. What is fundamental is eternal; hence, truly contemporary. Byzantinism is, at least partly, obsolete. I always feel it when reading the Canon of St Andrew of Crete, but never when reading the Psalms.

We talked yesterday with L. and Tom about homosexuality. Tom was telling us about his conversation with N. who defended homosexuality and was leaving his wife. Why do all arguments condemning homosexuality consistently seem weak, as weak as the obvious (to me) impossibility of ordaining women? Is it not because everything that is evident in religion cannot be proven, since the evidence is rooted in "bright knowledge," in communion with the "mind of Christ"? And proofs, in order to be proofs, must operate in a dark knowledge, in the logic of this world. According to logic, this world is always stronger, since this world fashioned logic to justify itself. Christ tells us about sin. Without Christ, sin is only a problem, which this world is solving, and the solution is always liberal, positive, tolerant, loving... The horror of contemporary Christianity consists of accepting this logic and in measuring faith by its laws.

So the light in us becomes darkness! (Matthew 6:23).

## *Wednesday, March 10, 1976*

Three points that are often found, in different degrees, in our culture and in particular, in American culture:

(1) the denial of the very possibility of having any axiological ethical conviction; the denial of the presence in this world of black and white, good and evil, not only of God, but of the devil. Hence, an addiction to meetings, dialogues, mutual deepening; hence a deep relativism.

(2) a typical, cheap self-identification with suffering people, particularly among American liberals. A rather cheap cult of Chavez, of the Indians, of any minority. An attitude, a posture of righteous indignation directed always, dogmatically, *a priori* to the right, never to the left. An urge to castigate oneself

(3) The confusion of "religion" and "faith." Pseudo-spirituality, pseudomysticism, pseudo-asceticism. As in any religiosity—idolatry.

Yesterday, confession of N. He is totally happy. Well, "What should I do?" Maybe Christ would answer, "Give away everything…" But I cannot. I have the same happiness, the same well-being, but covered up, justified by my church activity (which I constantly curse and find heavily burdening). I did not "give away" anything. So I told him: "Be happy, be grateful to God for that happiness, and, mainly, stand before Him so that you will hear Him when He calls…"

Students' confessions. Always sex. I am beginning to think that this sin is useful; otherwise they would consider themselves saintly and plunge into guruism. As it is, they are half convinced of it. So this sting in the flesh is useful. It cuts us down to size!

## *Friday, March 12 1976*

Yesterday was the last reading of the Canon of St Andrew of Crete, the last massive liturgical concentration of the first days of Lent. And Lent became light, which is its main essence and goal. This morning—a light Matins service, somehow understated, all illumined and resounding with the "bright sadness" of Lent.

Sunshine again. Although it's cold, everything is filled with the promise of spring. I was in the city and walked at five o'clock for twenty blocks. The usual bustle of the city—everybody rushing home! —and of life, living life, and everything lit up by the bright rays of this evening sun.

## Monday, March 15, 1976

A long Sunday! In the morning I served in an old Russian parish in New York, then a banquet and a lecture. It is the last little piece, or rather shred of the first Russian emigration. One can see the principle governing it: totally out of time and immobile. Really amazing. I lost the habit of the Russian way of serving the Liturgy, which I was used to in my childhood. During the service, everything which *could* reach the consciousness of the faithful is carefully *hidden* from them; any semblance of meaning. No prayers out loud, the singing is all concert pieces, no way of catching the words of the Epistle and the Gospel, etc. All of it is embellished, curtained off by every sort of heartfelt sentimentality. During the litany for the repose of the dead, a real flood not only of names (the tsar, etc., ) but also of every possible category of names (those who were killed for their faith, for their tsar and their motherland, those who…, etc.) Before communion (two communicants—and this the first Sunday of Lent) an old deacon, the obvious heart and soul of the parish and the keeper of traditions, made announcements for at least ten minutes: a concert by a talented pianist; a call to show moral support for the parish by enlisting and paying one dollar a month, etc. One feels that the deacon lives for those ten minutes—his mission. Unconsciously, subconsciously, this style hides, slurs the meaning of the Liturgy, of Church, of faith, and replaces it with a sort of generalized "feeling." One does not have to *do* anything except have this "feeling," which probably helps to cope with life, like a tribal rite.

In all of this there is a thin sense of pride: We Russians have a soul, a heart. We know how to feel. We kept the true…what? We still keep it! There are few of us, but we stand firm. Even the many, many wonderful lenten cakes that the deacon mentioned, saying that they are "at your service" after the Liturgy, even they become a heroic testimony, a confession of faith! Terror if any change is mentioned (language, calendar, etc.) If one would try to touch anything, they would leave. "We are used to what we have." A panicky, though unconscious, fear of any "meaning."

Then evening at the N.'s—new émigrés from Russia. Another little world—but I feel helpless and too tired to try to "enter" it. So, in one day, I traveled through whole continents, tightly enclosed in themselves, isolated, living only by their own thing, which has become "the only thing needful"! I sometimes have the feeling that most of the people, unknown to themselves, really live by hiding from reality (not only of death) and find this hiding to be the essential function of religion. "In this drowsiness, do not disturb." In this church, where walls are "drowsily" covered with very dark icons, one hears sweet and soul-nurturing words: "for the Tsar, the Motherland, the Faith";

"do not wait for the end of Lent to come to confession." I hear the argument (heard it since I was sixteen): "What's wrong with this? It really helps to cope!" I answer: "What is wrong is that this drowsiness so easily changes into hate and blood." (Ireland, Lebanon, the inner discord between Orthodox *et al*) No consideration for truth, for canons; only hatred for all those who disturb and destroy that "drowsiness."

### Wednesday, March 17, 1976

I received the Dutch translation of my *Great Lent* and also a few letters of appreciation from a Catholic nun, and from a pregnant woman in Maine. Joy from these letters: "it has reached"! I always thought that theology books for theologians are unnecessary. The criterion of theology is to write without simplification, but so that it would reach the normal faithful (or unfaithful).

This is one of those days when in spite of intense cold (snow yesterday) nature is rejoicing in the coming spring. When traveling to Long Island I drove along the edge of the water. Bright blue and, far away, haze over the shore. Festive, triumphant clouds. Deep down, indestructible joy of life.

### Monday, March 22, 1976

Sunday (21st), I was in Campbell, Ohio, in Father John P[sinka]'s parish. Solemn Liturgy, great choir, a banquet with my lecture, then a second lecture in the evening. Endless talks about the Church, the bishops, dinner in a restaurant in the middle of the woods—everything as usual down to the smallest details, like playing from music. I have "done" this for 25 years! I leave home quite unwillingly, but always end up encouraged, happy. When I look back from the altar and see one more crowd, many young people, lots of children, my faith in the Church, in Orthodoxy, and in the purpose of all my efforts is revived.

This morning we left at dawn under falling snow—in Crestwood, sunshine and spring. Masha and Vera are here [daughter and granddaughter].

### Tuesday, March 23, 1976

I really would like, before I die, to write *Holy Week, Pascha, Pentecost;* also *The Virgin Mary, The Liturgy of Death,* and *Christmas and Epiphany*—to embrace and cover the whole cycle. I know the value of writings, but I also know that my approach to liturgical tradition, right now, in any case, is only mine; therefore, I must proclaim it.

The question in every life: How to truthfully discern what is from God, what is obedience to Him (Lord, what do You want from me?) and what is from "this world" (and from the one behind it)? Questions about one's calling. My own life is that of a churchman. But every year I feel more and more burdened—from weakness. Or is my real calling something different? I truly suffer from constantly asking myself this question. I live a double life—one is consuming the other. Does God want this? Is this the condition of my salvation? When I ask this question, I have no answer. And I am 55!

### Wednesday, March 24, 1976

Yesterday I drove to Bryn Mawr. Lecture about Dostoevsky. A blinding spring day, joy from these copses, still transparent but ready for spring; from a touch of God's world. It was 130 miles each way, but I come home not tired, but actually restored.

### Thursday, March 25, 1976

Spent the morning at the Cathedral of St John the Divine—debate about the ordination of women. A large crowd of Anglican women, priests, laypeople. Some women wearing collars. For me, this was a heavy atmosphere, since I know that I have no proof, no arguments, nothing that can be demonstrated. So I said there are two musical renditions, two tonalities, and the choice is made not by one's mind, but one's heart—and then to that choice some proofs are affixed.

At noon, Annunciation Vespers and Liturgy—supremely inspiring after this morning's simplification and chaos.

I was quite stunned by the anger provoked by my remark that Christ was a man. Once more I see that the word "Christ" is used in our days as a symbolic name of what *we* consider to be our main treasure!

### Friday, April 2, 1976

While finishing a course on the Eucharist, I was thinking about what "piety" (religion) has done to the Liturgy. Without actually changing it, it has distorted everything.

Religion and ideology make slaves; only faith is liberating. Religion and ideology speak of freedom. Faith speaks of obedience, but only in faith is there freedom (obedience to God is the only freedom in this world and the only source of freedom).

The world lies in evil. But how many good people there are in this evil world! I was thinking about this while talking with Father N. and his wife, and lovingly admiring them.

*Monday, April 5, 1976*

Spent two days in Washington lecturing and visiting with friends, preaching, lecturing again. Finally, this morning back to LaGuardia where L. met me. And again a radiant day which raises the spirit and fills the heart.

On one hand, I am very tired; on the other I feel fulfilled because I am doing what I know how to do and what I am called to do, other than the endless administrative sweat at the seminary.

I get such joy from being with friends with whom I can be myself.

*Wednesday, April 7, 1976*

Yesterday I went to Amherst and Smith College—two lectures. Mainly joy from the drive through New England and the absence of phones and fuss.

While looking yesterday at all these eyes fixed upon me during the lecture, I thought (and thought again while driving home) about what is education, upbringing. What fills the life of these huge luxurious colleges, exuding such well-being, nobility, power, surrounded by parks, reflected in the water of its pools? "We teach to think, we teach to question..." analysis, criticism, reflection. But talking to some students, I realized that before criticism, maybe even before any facts of knowledge consciously or subconsciously, they expect something else. Inspiration? Truth? Meaning of life? Those are clichés, but they are it—denied with fear and contempt by contemporary academic psychology and ideology. They deny any inspiration, any vision. These youths rush with total delight to any imitation of religion, radicalism, transcendental meditation, communes. Nothing, nobody educates, directs them, nurtures them. That which created these colleges, which they still externally reflect, has been thrown away—i.e., an image, a vision. Education used to be based on a vision, concentrated on service. Life was important, beautiful, and the light of life as service was nurturing. Poor are the youth who are offered only "critical approaches," Freudian introspection and petty success.

*Friday, April 9, 1976*

Today—Praises of the Theotokos—in my life, one of the days that brought God to me, when I walked as a young boy to church for the Praises service and ...there was no fire, no "cries of joy," but a contact, a touch that later slowly began to illumine my whole life. "Rejoice, O dawn of the mysterious day..." Illumined with that dawn. Here is the source and the focus of everything in my better theological self.

## Monday, April 12, 1976

On Friday evening, the singing during the "Praises" was done almost exclusively by our seminary women—which made it even more fitting, closer to the Virgin Mary. How could one convert the contemporary world to that feeling of life?

Afternoon spent at Anya Hopko's with her children. It seems to me that I don't know a happier home, a happier family.

Yesterday, the last Sunday of Lent. Confessions. Full church!

Our son Serge is 31 today. It seems like yesterday that we rejoiced in the quick and easy birth of a son!

I talked with L. today about belonging to the Church. We grew up in it, but we feel more and more that the way that we knew, the Orthodox aesthetics, are drying out, that it is the culture of the past. So—what should we transmit, what should we hand down? One can transmit only living life, whereas nowadays one transmits some archaism that takes one away from the world. We already perceive some Byzantine or Russian music as romantic, so what do we do now?

## Friday, April 16, 1976

"...Having fulfilled the forty days of Lent..." Were they really enriching, saving? I wasted so many days in trips, talks, fuss. My heart is so heavy! I am so discouraged by the level of some meetings and concerns and cares.

Suddenly, a gift: Bach's *St Matthew's Passion* on television. Then, Mrs. N. sent me a portrait of the late Metropolitan Vladimir from Paris—all in white, so peaceful in a beautiful garden. A reminder, a stern warning after yesterday's despondency.

## Lazarus Saturday, April 17, 1976

My favorite feast of all feasts. A full church! Children's procession. A very warm sunshine. I could not work in the afternoon, but spent the time just thinking. I feel such joy that all of us here are today in the same high spirit, all sharing the feast without needless words. Of one mind, of one heart: here is the center of everything; justification, life.

I formed in my mind a presentation that I will make in Paris at a youth rally about tradition and freedom in the Church.

## Holy Monday, April 19, 1976

A record heat wave—95-100 degrees; the sun is hot even at 6:00 AM! Palm Sunday Vespers and Liturgy surpassed all expectations. This is the feast of the Kingdom of God, its affirmation here on this earth. "Rejoice…and again I say: Rejoice!"

Afternoon lecture in New York about Holy Week. I thought that nobody would come because of the heat, but fifty people came and I felt that they heard.

First Matins with the "Bridegroom" and "Thy Bridal Chamber…" Of course it's all from childhood, it is the life of childhood in my heart. Holy Week tightly linked to blooming chestnut trees in Paris. But is that all? Yesterday I tried to depict an image of Holy Week to my listeners, to show its growth, its rhythm, its logic. Yes, one can analyze and reflect. It nurtures the heart and the soul and the mind. Nothing more beautiful, more perfect has been created by men, more beautiful in the deepest sense of the word: a coming together of all needs, an answer surpassing the question.

It has not been so much "created" as seen, lived—in answer to the gift and the revelation. To create it would have been impossible. All is from the sober, absolute, full words of the Gospel, of Christ Himself.

What else is needed? Look—all of you who rush about in vain. Do not think that something else is needed. See the fight of light with darkness, the descent into death. It is at the same time the revelation of the power of evil and its destruction. That is where one would find the answer which everyone is seeking and often finding in pitiful idols. Lazarus and Palms: "Rejoice, and again I say rejoice…"at the very beginning of Holy Week and at the same time, the onslaught of darkness. ("I am deeply grieved, even to death…" and "My God, my God, why have you forsaken me?") and of light ("Now the Son of Man has been glorified and God has been glorified in Him…") up to the bright silence of Holy Saturday. Where else should one search for the solution to problems? Where else can one see, feel the only ray of light which illumines and solves everything?

## Holy Wednesday, April 21, 1976

I just came back from the last Presanctified Liturgy. I did not serve but I stood in church thinking how grateful I am that God let me live in a liturgical paradise! The church is flooded with sunshine. Wonderful choir. Wonderful service. Without it all, any explanation of Orthodoxy is impossible, unconvincing and needless because the revelation, the epiphany of Orthodoxy is only here.

Evening Matins of Holy Thursday: "Come all you faithful; let us enjoy the Master's hospitality, the banquet of immortality…" and the "bond of love" of the Apostles!

## Holy Friday, April 23, 1976

I spent almost all of Holy Thursday trying to keep intact the fullness of the day. After my beloved "red" Liturgy, I drove to the city to get a haircut, thus keeping silence and peace.

During the service of the Twelve Gospel readings, I was struck quite strongly by the lack of correspondence between the Gospels and the hymns, the antiphons. Friday is indeed the revelation of evil and sin in their full horror, in their utmost greatness. But Byzantine hymnographers are engrossed with beating and blaming the guilty ones. We are the witnesses, we are the judges! We feel pity for Christ and condemn the guilty. How dared they? Our conscience is clear because we, supposedly, know and stand on the right side. What is lost, what is not felt is the very meaning of Holy Friday: everybody betrays Christ. The whole creation, the Apostles ("then all the disciples deserted Him and fled...").

He is betrayed and crucified by the blindness and darkness of distorted love (Judas); by religion (the High Priests); by power (Pilate), by society (people). Then, turning around, they all accept Him— "Truly He is the Son of God..." —the guard and the Apostle at the Cross and those who, beating their chest, left this infamy.

There is nothing about it in the hymns; they concentrate on who was guilty, excluding from that guilt all others, and depriving the service of its meaning: the summit of Evil, the judgment and the victory over it—now, here, in us. Thank God the Gospel remains and dominates over rather weak and unnecessary rhetoric.

Yesterday, coming back from the city, I was thinking that I should write "Religion and Faith," showing that religion without faith is idolatry. "Little children, keep yourselves from idols" (1 John 5:21).

I feel so grateful that, without deserving anything, we receive the gift of Pascha, freely, every year! Holy Friday, the Hours, the Holy Shroud, the evening Praises, the Bones, then Great and Holy Saturday and the Paschal Night. A liturgical banquet.

On Monday all our grandchildren came to church then to our house. Noise and so joyful. Then L. took me to the airport for my flight to Paris where I was met by mother and Andrei. Then a walk around familiar libraries, streets, cafés and dinner with friends. Next day, my secret lunch with Andrei at the Café Lipp, then...impossible to write about all the places, people, about the very air of Paris.

### *Thursday, April 29, 1976*

*Paris*

Early morning at my brother's apartment!

### *Sunday, May 2, 1976*

Yesterday I spent the day at a youth rally outside Paris at which I was to lecture. I feel somehow alienated from the interests of these young people—many of them French. I feel that I would like to pass on a vision, which I feel is right, but do not find any "receiving line." As long as Christianity tries to answer or wants to answer the problems of this world, created by this world, it does not "sound" right. A lot is just empty chatter. Where is the treasure of your heart? That is the only question!

### *Tuesday, May 4, 1976*

Radiant days, sunshine on Paris roofs. Another circle is closed—coming, leaving. One more piece of life transformed into memory. I am finishing writing this in Crestwood, my own life, my seminary!

### *Wednesday, May 5, 1976*

May is so beautiful this year. I enjoyed Paschal Matins, sunshine, blooming azaleas, thin, light air. How to keep and preserve that joy, guard it from fuss, words, bustle?

### *Friday, May 7, 1976*

"Grandparents' Day" at the nursery school of our little Anya, Serge's daughter.

I read a rather surprising article about Jimmy Carter in the *National Review:* "The other candidates speak to problems out of context; Carter deals with the context itself. And that context is nothing less than the Christian religion…" When I read it, I thought—What if? What if in the desert of secularism something came from God? If it's true, what an enormous joy in the midst of "the rotten West," of "materialistic America…"!

### *Saturday, June 5, 1976*

I haven't written here in a long time. Not that there wasn't anything worthwhile, but because of the chaos and disorder of these days. I could not begin to write down all the thoughts that come to mind, the constant revery that is truly the meaning of this journal. Now it's too late!

Leavetaking of Pascha and Ascension—beautiful services. I live in a liturgical paradise and once again I felt how truly essential is this liturgical "other" life for our normal life; it gives it terms of reference.

Yesterday I was in Evanston, Illinois, as the commencement speaker at the Seabury Western Seminary. Cozy old-fashioned hotel, a familiar feeling of being away from home—alone in a strange city, on a cool summer night. An Episcopal ceremony, my favorite hymns accompanied by a powerful organ, always inspiring. Following the service—traditional, festive—I thought about the deeply rooted, hopeless well-being of the Christian West, maybe even the irreparable bourgeois state of Western Christianity. All the words, the rites, the prayers presuppose, reveal, make you feel some great tragedy, but tragedy in the Greek sense of the word.

What God reveals to people is unheard, impossible, and the tragedy consists of this deafness. And this revelation can no longer penetrate Western life without ripping it apart. What is revealed surpasses and therefore tears apart life—the gift of joy "which nobody will take away from you." Genuine Christianity is bound to disturb the heart with this tearing—that is the force of eschatology. But one does not feel it in these smooth ceremonies where everything is neat, right, but without eschatological "other worldliness." This is, maybe, the basic spiritual quality of any bourgeois state of mind. It is closed to the sense of tragedy to which the very existence of God condemns us.

Maybe it is the absence of the poor and the suffering, but then I realized that this was not the reason. In Byzantium, in St Sophia, there probably was a thousand times more gold and riches, but Byzantium was not bourgeois. There always should remain a feeling of absolute, incommensurability; it is the knowledge that there is but one sadness, which is not to be a saint; it is the hearing of the call, the breath, that cannot be reduced to "social problems" nor to "the place of the church in the contemporary world," nor to a debate about ministry.

Maybe poverty is the central symbol, not the economic factor of poverty, but the approach to it. The West has decided that Christianity is calling us to fight against poverty, or to replace it with relative riches, or at least economic equality, etc. The Christian appeal is quite, quite different: poverty as freedom, poverty as a sign that the heart has accepted the impossible (hence tragic) call to the Kingdom of God.

I don't know. It's so difficult to express it, but I clearly feel that here is a different perception of life, and the bourgeois state (religious, theological, spiritual, pious, cultured, etc.) is blind to something essential in Christianity.

## *Tuesday, June 8, 1976*

Twenty-five years ago, around noon, we left Paris for Cherbourg, where we boarded the Queen Mary on our way to the United States. When I woke up, I thought: why did we leave? Surprising how the most fateful, the most important decisions are taken not by the mind, not by convincing arguments, but in some other way. Yesterday, by some coincidence, I wrote a radio script about "Revelation," trying to explain what happened, for instance, to Abraham. What appeal did he hear ("rise and go") and how? The whole of life, deep down, is a chain of such revelations. We had weighty reasons to go: three children, no house except a crumbling log cabin, no income…But we were going to a total uncertainty—for 160 dollars a month! I had a call from Professor Florovsky,* and the atmosphere at the St Sergius Institute in Paris was stifling. But these were not the reasons. There was a kind of inner vibration, not choice, which we followed almost unconsciously. A sort of "rise and go"!

## *Wednesday, June 16, 1976*

### *Labelle*

We are in Labelle, our twenty-fifth summer. It seems that the interval between our leaving here in the fall and coming back in the summer gets shorter and shorter. We just left! Old age? I don't know. I only know that every year our gratitude for the lake, the birch trees, the pace and happiness is growing.

Before arriving here we spent a very hot and humid day in Montreal to celebrate Father John Tkachuk's (our son-in-law's) nameday. He was receiving the Gold Cross. Standing in church, listening to the choir, looking at the evening rays through multi-colored windows, I thought: the Church is, before anything else, a flood, an uninterrupted flow of sound, of melody. One really must rise above a meaningless understanding of this flow in one's piety and consciousness.

But there is that flow, that stream which one must feel and understand. It can be sullied by pagan piety, by little committees, by heavy theology, but neither the truth nor the strength of this flow is weakened. "If any man thirst, let him come unto me, and drink…" (John 7:37). I feel gratitude, joy and strength.

We arrived in Labelle in the middle of the night. Thunderstorms, stuffy and humid. But the house is welcoming, neat and happy, just as we left it. I organized my books and papers—and am writing here!

* Florovsky, Father Georges (†1979)—Professor at St Sergius Institute in Paris; subsequently Dean of St Vladimir's Seminary, 1949-55.

## Saturday, August 21, 1976

*Mexico City*

I am sitting in front of my window overlooking the main square in Mexico. On my left a huge baroque cathedral, across—a palace. Rain.

I am here for three days for a friendly visit.

## Sunday, August 22, 1976

Yesterday I walked around the city without Bishop Dmitri.* I was sorry that I do not know more about the history of this country, a whole world. I am not a good tourist, but whenever I find myself in a strange land, I want to understand it, to feel it.

I did not like the city with its messy American modernism. Behind the mess, one feels the presence of a recently living soul. The rhythm, the crowd, the long streets with street lamps are not American.

I was surprised how young the crowd was. The people are very attractive, beautiful eyes. Each has his own face, his own way of walking, and everybody has nobility. There is not that feeling of solitude in the middle of a crowd that one has in New York. There is no conventional laughter, artificial tone of the type "for he is a jolly good fellow." One feels human warmth and an innate dignity. Beautiful children with such huge black eyes!

At 2:30 we drove to the banquet in our honor. The banquet was in a small house, about twenty Orthodox Mexicans. I could never have imagined such cordial simplicity with dignity and genuine nobility. A four-musician "orchestra," lots of food, drink and everything in a delightful tone. A young deacon read a poem about Jesus Christ; the host sings, a young woman dances— a delightful mixture of passion and purity and in everything real joy, subconscious joy, and mainly—kindness.

I am worried about Mexican Orthodoxy—so naive, childish, trustful and wholesome. Everything is poor and radiant and everywhere these dark-eyed children who come to you with angelic beauty and light.

Finally at ten at night I return to my hotel, exhausted but completely happy.

This morning for the first time, sunshine and blue sky. A long hierarchical Liturgy. Standing at the altar, I thought: I am the only native Orthodox! Looking at the faces of old women, beautifully severe and humane, I repeated to myself: "You hid it from the proud and revealed it to infants."

* Dmitri (Royster), Bishop—Now Archbishop of the Diocese of the South (OCA), 1978–present.

Fullness of joy!

I am sitting now at my window looking out on Constitution Square. The street lights are reflected in the wet pavement…

## *Monday, August 23, 1976*

My third and last day in Mexico. Dinner with Bishop D[mitri] talking about church, Mexico, *et al.* Later at night I walked around the square and some other streets. I was trying to get a feeling for the very peculiar atmosphere of this city compared to the States. Here and there one can see European roots, but the difference is striking. I think (tentatively!) that the difference is of a religious order. Mexican roots are Catholic, the U.S. roots are Protestant. The difference is in the approach to life, in its acceptance and vision.

The Protestant builds a useful, comfortable earthly life. In none of its aspects does it remind one of paradise, does it open it, or reveal it. The Protestant lives in the fallen world, not referred any more to the primordial, joyous, divine world. He is bound with the world by his reason, knowledge, analysis, but not faith, not a sacramental intuition.

The Catholic, even secularized, remembers. In all these gilded, sometimes tastelessly heavily decorated churches, there is longing for paradise and there are pieces of paradise, of joy—"…and it was good…" (Genesis). And the remembrance is constantly in their culture, cities, life.

Communism, utopianism are victorious or at least are attractive to people in Catholic countries because they can dream. And they are powerless in Protestant countries because they have no dream, but a diligent, durable reform.

Protestantism is the denial of the Church as paradise—it is its sin and heresy.

Lately, Catholicism is trying to follow suit with a dull social message and service to the world.

It is more comfortable to live in the Protestant world, although life in it is hard and full of psychological afflictions. Man cannot live without remembering paradise. He becomes engulfed in fear, in a search for security, in depression. He loses *himself.*

I started writing at 8 AM and continue at 10 PM. Went to visit Indian pyramids and I was quite impressed by their grandiose cosmic design: the pyramids of the sun, of the moon, a temple, and everywhere human sacrifices. On the way back, the "portico of three cultures," where in 1521 Cortez defeated the last Aztecs.

No tue triunfo ni derrota
Fue el doloroso nacimento
Del pueblo mestizo qui es
El Mexico de hoy.

A late walk in the city. Tomorrow, departure for New York.

### Tuesday, September 7, 1976

*Crestwood*

Last day of summer vacation; tomorrow first day of school. We came back from Labelle a week ago and I tried to organize my life—courses, meetings, business. The weather is superb:—light, sunny, cool.

I joyfully anticipate lectures, the revival of seminary routine. Back in June it seemed frightening!

I pray to keep peace deep in my heart; not to yield to all sorts of concerns.

### Friday, September 10, 1976

Mao has died.

There is a real possibility that L. will be offered the post of headmistress of Spence.

About Mao: a few pages in the *Times,* and in spite of the flow of information, it is quite difficult to really understand how mysterious and unreal is our history. One characteristic of Mao, often repeated, struck me: "he saw far…" In other words, the winner is the one who sees ahead, who does not let himself be diluted in the present.

### Saturday, September 11, 1976

A cool sunny day. Yesterday I spent the day meeting new students. Almost all of them, when asked about their religious roots, i.e., family, parents, answered: "no roots." Parents are without religion. I am amazed how groundless, how lacking in foundations is contemporary America. All the more surprising is the progress of *grace* in the youth. One could write a book out of these meetings with students!

### Friday, September 17, 1976

I am about to leave for St Louis and Kansas City.

Yesterday the Episcopal Convention adopted a ruling on women's ordination to the priesthood. Two thirds of the bishops voted for; one third against. Clergy and laity—51 percent for; the rest against.

I received a telephone call from Minneapolis to join some kind of protest rally, but decided that it's unnecessary. It would be awful to exploit such a huge essentially mystical tragedy.

A low-level egalitarianism, cowardice before the contemporary world. Nothing deep or genuine. The fact alone that there was a *vote*…! But the opponents of the ruling seem as petty and as shallow—so I don't want to go.

Heavy, humid and stifling.

## Monday, September 20, 1976

A long and rather tiring trip to the Midwest. First a retreat in St Louis. Spent the whole day with people. Then off to Kansas City for a celebration of a new parish with Father Joseph Hirsh—all converts. I was afraid of the convert's maximalism and raptures, but was happily struck by the firmness and the tranquillity of the whole group.

Though quite tired, I am so happy to find in the center of nowhere a few young priests : Father Homiak in St Louis; Father Lecko in Madison; Father Madison in Kansas, and now Father Hirsh. They struggle, work, and something begins to grow, to bloom. A wonderful Liturgy in the small church, just built. And as a background to it all, the expanse of America.

Friday night I had a phone call from a friend in Minneapolis, from the Episcopal Convention. In spite of the shock, the majority will reconcile themselves with what happened. In any case, the scope of the crisis is considerable. I am so glad that I did not have to plunge into that atmosphere.

## Wednesday, September 22, 1976

Yesterday, for the first time after many weeks, I spent time at my desk working on the latest chapter of the *Eucharist*. Immediately I am in an entirely different mood, a feeling of inner order.

## Friday, September 24, 1976

At the seminary, thank God, all is well. I almost finished meeting the new students (forty of them!). It is really amazing: in the fifties and sixties we had students from church families. Now most of the students have no church affiliation through their families. They are children of a lost generation which left everything for the notion of American success that flourished after the war.

Beautiful cool days. Yesterday walking home after Vespers in the midst of the splendid beauty of sparkling trees, I thought: how much undeserved happiness God has given us.

Today, at Matins I gave a little talk about the "hardening of the heart"! (The Gospel was about the disciples who were surprised when Christ walked on the water) "…And they were utterly astounded, for they did not understand about the loaves, but their hearts were hardened" (Mark 6:51-52). The main sin, the main obstacle on the way to the Lord is this "hardening of the heart."

### Monday, September 27, 1976

I reread, by chance, a few pages of my 1973 journal. Deep down, it is all about the same thing: about that which shines through life, through the world, about the time of grief (grieving for God) and the time of joy, in their utmost purity—and their blending into one.

All these days I worked and wrote a great deal with no substantive results. But the fact of working itself brings me joy and peace.

### Thursday, September 30, 1976

Talk yesterday, before my evening lecture, with Andrei and Galya Tregubov, recently from Moscow. He is not yet baptized, but attends all our evening lectures. Thirst for the Church, for knowledge, truth, light.

I read a book about Bishop Pike (*The Death and Life of Bishop Pike*, by William Stringfellow) and was horrified. I knew Pike when he was at Columbia and at St John the Divine. Tragic life: two divorces, son's suicide, lover's suicide, alcoholism, leaving the Church. In the book, all of it presented as a testimony, a feat. It is not a question of judgment; only God judges; but it seems that the contemporary conscience is pathologically distorted in its tragic choice and affirmation: black as white; white as black. And all that for the sake of some self-fulfillment and of some horrible blind hatred of all values…

### Tuesday, October 5, 1976

I had a talk yesterday with Tom about prayer, or rather about the contemporary obsession with the "problem of prayer." I am sure that this contemporary prayer is rooted in the same old pride. The essential in it is missing—one's submersion into God. A person praying like this is affirming himself in prayer, is searching for himself, is loving himself, is proving something to himself. Then he becomes interested in prayer and studies its technique. O Lord, how much in religion makes me…sick!

## *Wednesday, October 6, 1976*

L. is 53 today. How and where did all these years slip by from that Vespers service at the St Sergius Institute in 1940 when we *really* met for the first time? Before that we had met briefly at the Sorbonne while taking the Baccalaureate exams in 1939. On that day in 1940, I told a friend of mine, "Today, I met my future wife."

## *Saturday, October 9, 1976*

"Religious experience." While listening to others—(I had meetings with quite a few students, each with his own problem)—and trying to understand them, I became convinced how varied that experience is, how different for each—and this is among people of the same faith, the same Orthodoxy. What about other religions?!

## *Tuesday, October 12, 1976*

Meetings, talks, phone calls. I am tired of complaining, but the fact remains : in this constant pressure and haste, it's impossible to work. "Father, when can I see you?" No way out, that's the way it is. Today's Gospel: "By your endurance you will gain your lives" (Luke 21:19).

Clear, radiant cold days.

The source of false religion is the inability to rejoice, or, rather, the refusal of joy, whereas joy is absolutely essential because it is without any doubt the fruit of God's presence. One cannot know that God exists and not rejoice. Only in relation to joy are the fear of God and humility correct, genuine, fruitful. Outside of joy, they become demonic, the deepest distortion of any religious experience. A religion of fear. Religion of pseudo-humility. Religion of guilt: They are all temptations, traps—very strong indeed, not only in the world, but inside the Church. Somehow "religious" people often look on joy with suspicion.

The first, the main source of everything is "my soul rejoices in the Lord..." The fear of sin does not save from sin. Joy in the Lord saves. A feeling of guilt or moralism does not liberate from the world and its temptations. Joy is the foundation of freedom, where we are called to stand. Where, how, when has this tonality of Christianity become distorted, dull—or rather, where, how, why have Christians become deaf to joy? How, when and why, instead of freeing suffering people, did the Church come to sadistically intimidate and frighten them?

People continuously come and ask for advice (today since 7:30 AM, confession, talk, talk, talk, four people with problems, not counting appointments for later). And some weakness or false shame keeps me from telling each of them, "I don't have any advice to give you. I have only weak, shaky, but, for me, unremitting joy. Do you want it?" No they do not. They want to talk about "problems" and chat about "solutions." No, there was no greater victory of the devil in the world than this "psychologized" religion. There is anything and everything in psychology. One thing is unthinkable, impossible: Joy!

## Wednesday, October 13, 1976

Faculty meeting with the reports of our delegates about the conference of Orthodox theologians held in Athens and I thought, what a strange time, how much is simply invented—the reduction of everything in Orthodoxy to the "Fathers" and "Spirituality"! They are made into a kind of caricature, idols, a panacea, a remedy for all evils. The triumph nowadays of a sectarian "only"! Only the Fathers, only "Dobrotolubie," only *typikon*. Boredom, mediocrity and lack of seriousness and talent in it all.

This morning while walking to church I thought about foolishness. I thought that it is the most frightening fruit of original sin. The devil is intelligent, they always say. No, the truth is that the devil is exceedingly foolish, and his foolishness is the source of his strength. If he was intelligent, he would not be the devil; he would have long ago repented and "covered himself with ashes." To rise against God is, before anything else, very foolish. The essence of evil: pride, envy, hatred, longing for freedom ("be like the gods") comes from foolishness. Stalin was foolish; Lenin, Mao were foolish. Only a metaphysical fool can be so totally possessed by one idea, one passion. But then foolishness, by being a simplification, is very powerful. The whole fallen world is foolishness, skillful in inventiveness. Foolishness is a fraud, a self-deception. The devil is a liar from time immemorial. He eternally lies to himself and to others. And his intoxicated lies seem intelligent, mainly because they give quick satisfaction. Foolishness is always content and contentment is impressive. What can be funnier now than the idiotic, conventional self-satisfaction of communism? But then, it works. One can say that in the fallen world foolishness is successful because it has declared once and for all that it is intelligent, it has vested itself in intelligence. That is why Christianity and the Gospel begin with *metanoia*—with the conversion, the transposition of intelligence, literally with becoming intelligent. That is why, finally, it is quite frightening when religion, revived by Christ, having been filled again with the light of reason and having become a verbal service—*logiki latreia*—reverts to foolishness. The most frightening aspect of contemporary religion is the new rebellion against the Logos. A great deal in it serves the Devil!

The essence of faith is not the denial of intelligence ("because it is from the devil..."). The denial of intelligence is the highest and ultimate victory of the devil, the triumph of foolishness. The essence of faith is to heal intelligence and liberate it from victorious foolishness.

## Monday, October 18, 1976

Spent two days in Richmond, Virginia. A retreat in the new mission of Father DeTrana. Many Anglicans and at the center of all discussions the question of women's ordination. Little by little, I begin to feel the outlines of a genuine answer. Father and Mary Ann DeTrana show me the city, which I had visited before. I admire the fall, the gardens, the columns and classical proportions of the Capitol, built by Jefferson.

As soon as I came back from Richmond we had a reception at home for the seminary's women students. "The Church must find a place for us." We must "reeducate the Church." Rather hopeless approach. Thank God quite a few of them feel it but they live at a time when all is defined by struggle.

The height of autumn, really golden, really crimson and bright. This morning, early frost, immobile, transparent. In this light, this beauty, petty news and commercials on television seem blasphemous and shocking!

## Wednesday, October 20, 1976

Yesterday, lecture about prayer and liturgy. Lecture against pseudo-religion, pseudo-spirituality, with their frightening flooding "Hear and hear, but do not understand; see and see, but do not perceive" (Isaiah 6:9). It refers quite accurately to contemporary Orthodox people: the majority want something different, see and hear something different, different from what the Church offers to see, offers to hear, from what the Church calls us to love.

## Thursday, October 28, 1976

Identification of faith, Christianity, Church with piety, with some sentimental and fanatical religiosity. I am so tired of talks about statutes, spirituality, all this fear, slavery, boredom. Life in abundance, the Kingdom of God lowered to the level of pious dullness. Behind it all, an endless interest in one's self, one's own spirituality. Why is it so attractive to so many people?

I think about the words of a Russian poet: "But then the words: a flower, a child, a beast..." while looking at the golden trees pierced by an afternoon sun behind my window, at a wandering cat, at children, rather disheveled,

returning home from school. It turns me to God so much more than theological and religious talks. One more question comes to mind: "Who said
that man had to do something on this earth?"—epigraph to Henry de
Montherlant's book, *Service inutile* (*Useless Service*), which I read when I was
13 and which impressed me forever.

The Gospel is quite clear: both saints and sinners love God. "Religious"
people do not love Him and, whenever they can, they crucify Him.

I spent two hours in the city. Radio scripts, shopping. New York under a
bright blue cool sky. Human faces, mostly worried...

### Wednesday, November 3, 1976

Carter has won the election. Spent most of the night watching returns. It
seems to me that all those who voted for Carter were those who want a
change; all those who really have a poor life within the system (blacks); those
who want a guaranteed well-being (unions); those who believe in those guar-
antees and changes and professionally advocate them (intellectuals); and
finally those who look at everything through colored glasses (utopians)!
Carter's majority was quite minute; he actually received only a quarter of the
votes of people who have the right to vote. It remains to follow his career.
How does the messiah act once he gets power?

After so many hours spent watching television, I am quite impressed by
this system that purges politics of that which would make it evil: hatred! This
is the American miracle, whereas America's lie, its original sin, is in its cult of
riches and its denial of poverty. More precisely: happiness without wealth is
impossible; happiness is identified with success. Thus, whatever is rhetori-
cally said, in reality America does not respect the poor man, for his existence
is shameful, fearful, like a secret disease. The very first basic myth, therefore,
is the faith that each poor man *can* attain riches, "make himself rich." Now
that this myth has collapsed, another myth has replaced the first: that society
must make the poor wealthy, must provide for them, and the debate between
Republicans and Democrats consists only in *how* to do it.

The leftists always fight against private property, seeing in it the root of all
evil, not understanding that the feeling of property is the only way to safeguard people from the absolute, demonic power of money. Money, in the
capitalistic system, is not property. People do not control money, but money
controls them. In the jargon of "the American way of life," a house is not my
home, my life, my breathing, my warmth. It is an abstract value, an investment. If its value grows, one can and should sell it. It is foolish not to sell it,
just as it is foolish not to invest money so that it grows!

Property is what one can love. And love is always giving and possessing. Man *gives* in order to possess more and more. Only the one who has his own property can attain the depth and the power of giving. Love is giving freely. I can give only what belongs to me, my possession. And the gift does not annihilate possession, but enhances it a thousand times.

People, Christians too, do not see this because they see in everything a problem that must be solved. God, when creating the world, did not solve problems or pose them. He created what He could call "very good." God created the world, but the devil transformed the world and man and life into a "problem." And a legion of specialists solve it. That is why in the world it is so dark, so cold, so joyless.

### Thursday, November 4, 1976

After almost freezing temperatures, the day is summery warm. Today is the thirtieth anniversary of my ordination to the deaconate. I remember it all as in a fog. I remember that on the eve of my ordination, I was close to despair. We left Vespers before the end. No prayer, no joy, nothing, real emptiness. The ordination took place on a weekday; there were not many people in church. I absolutely can not remember the Liturgy, myself in it. I know who took me around the altar. I remember standing in a corner, next to a table with a priest's vestments, in total isolation. Something was happening to me but I was passive. After the Liturgy we returned home and I slept for many hours, then went to serve my first Vespers at St Sergius Institute.

Thinking about it all, I ask myself: Does not what is most important in our life, the divine, happen to us, so to say, not without our knowledge, no, but when we completely give ourselves up, almost die for a while? It's strange. I just wrote these lines and quite by chance picked up André Froissard's book—*Il y a un autre monde* (*There Is Another World*)—which I bought today and I read how he prayed alone, with his cat, in some Italian church!

> ...apparently we both pray in the same way, Lord, with the same innocent pleasure in gently drifting into the shade, in submitting without the slightest thought to the secret fascination that you exercise on all that exists and in being carried towards You by the force of inertia, in our silent cell...

### Tuesday, November 9, 1976

#### Mount Manresa, Staten Island, NY

I am spending three days in a Jesuit retreat house where I lecture about the theology of sacraments. I rest between lectures and try to climb out of the disorder in my life these past days.

Troubled days because, since the beginning of the school year, I feel more acutely than ever the terrible confusion of the religious situation. On one hand, the book by Froissard, a meeting with youth in the city last Sunday, the Liturgy—all are like drinks of "living water" that bring inner joy and satisfaction. On the other hand, a foolish conflict at the seminary, the denunciation by some students of other students' heresies (they do not kiss icons, etc.) and not enough piety, and more—a student who wishes to exorcise another, etc. A dull wave of pseudo-religiosity, the whole atmosphere saturated with self-affirmation, spiritual hostility, tension and unhealthy stress. Everybody has problems, everything is burning hot, distorted, caricaturized, and in everything one pushes "God" and "Orthodoxy." It seems that nobody around us is happy—happy with the happiness that should be flowing out of Liturgy, prayer, theology, etc. We all firmly proclaim that one cannot be happy without God. But then why is man so unhappy *with* God? It seems that religion amplifies all that is petty and low in man: pride, self-glorification, fear! For years I have been asking myself this question. It seems that in the world there is no longer a peaceful, humble, joyful and free standing before God, walking to Him; no more: "Serve the Lord with fear and rejoice in Him with trembling..." (Psalms 2:11). So, I rejoice in every hour of solitude, of autumn sunshine on golden trees, of total calm and silence.

### Thursday, November 18, 1976

Tomorrow I leave for Alaska.

### Friday, November 19, 1976

Busy morning at the seminary because of my departure. Confessions, talks, lecture, letters, phone calls. I open this notebook like a mirror, to make sure that I still exist.

### Saturday, November 20, 1976

### Sitka

Now I am in Sitka, the old capital of Russian Alaska, in Bishop Gregory's house. A three-hour flight. On the plane I sat next to a Catholic archbishop also going to the Sitka celebrations. Landing in Sitka: snowy mountains, a low sky, strong wind, and everywhere—water. Bishop Gregory met me and took me to his house. I have not seen anything yet besides the new cathedral. Long Vespers, many people, many priests, great enthusiasm. The children looked adorable. An enormous choir—all young people.

## *Sunday, November 21, 1976*

*Sitka*

A long, full day. I rose at 7:30 and went to church at 8:00: the night is still dark, rain, empty streets. I went by the old Russian cemetery, down the street and to the cathedral. From all sides a flow of people. The service starts with a procession of the clergy: three bishops, sixteen priests, among them Aleuts, Indians, Eskimos. The service lasted four and a half hours! At times, especially during the first part of the blessing of the church and the altar, I was irritated by the deliberate complexity of the ritual: all these endless litanies, the roping off of the altar, the pouring of rose water, etc. What for? But then, while meditating on it, I thought that my irritation came from the loss of an essential sense of time. Why should one hurry? In this slow, ceremonial, unquestioned fulfilling of all these details of this solemn performance, there is a wonderful victory over fragmented, empty time, a filling of it with what is needful. At the end, after four hours, the old Adam is humbled and he accepts and rejoices. There was a striking moment after the blessing of the church, when the Liturgy was just starting, when a bright ray of sunshine suddenly struck the windows through what seemed to be hopeless clouds.

After the Liturgy, in the Centennial Hall, a five-hour banquet. Behind the windows, snowy mountains. This small fishing village used to be the easternmost part of the Russian empire. In the evening, an endless reception at the bishop's residence. Right now, while I write, young people in the next room are singing the Russian "Kalinka," and "Let my prayer arise," and the American "Goodnight Irene"! The singing is poor but quite enthusiastic. In the middle of the noise, a long talk with B[arbara] Smith, professor of Russian history in Anchorage. Right away we talk about what is most important...He is thirsty and full of longing...

## *Monday, November 22, 1976*

*Sitka*

Rain, rain, and more rain. At 9:30 in the morning it is still dark. At the cathedral, a newly ordained Indian priest is serving his first Liturgy. A choir of Aleuts and Eskimos. Joyful feeling from this obvious life of the Church.

On my way to Anchorage where I will lecture about Solzhenitsyn at the University of Alaska. I am staying with the wonderful family of Father Nicholas Harris.

## Wednesday, November 24, 1976

*Crestwood*

Home after a long night on the plane: Kodiak, Anchorage, Seattle, Chicago, New York.

Yesterday we went to Kodiak Island and stayed at Father J[oseph] Kreta's,* visited the school. I feel that these four days have been an "immersion in grace." I rejoice about "the church never aging, but eternally younger…"

Now, Thanksgiving and three days of vacation.

## Tuesday, November 30, 1976

Thirty years since my ordination to the priesthood at St Sergius Institute. I served an early Liturgy today with Father John M[eyendorff] and Father Tom. How fast life is going by; how fast life went by!

## Wednesday, December 1, 1976

I was told by Alexis V[inogradov**] that Solzhenitsyn wants to see me tomorrow morning.

## Thursday, December 2, 1976

I just took S. to the station, having spent over an hour with him. He came to Matins, stood at the door, in the same outfit that he wore in Zurich; tall, stately, handsome. He obviously wanted to be nice, almost affectionate, and just as obviously was not interested in the seminary, my work, etc. He is totally engrossed in himself, in his projects, in his mission; he is possessed by it. He wants to start a new series of publications about recent Russian history:

"We will soon go back to Russia—my boys are anticipating it…"

"American schools are only a shell…"

Everything passionate, fast, not a single question, no consideration. He is completely alone. People bother him, he does not need anybody. He is "practical"—his world, his Russia, his mission. He reminds me of Balzac, who told someone who had announced the death of a friend: "Well, now, let's go back to life…" and talked about his own novel. He—S.—does not have any real antennas. He is writing from "inside"—describing a world which is

---

* Kreta, Father Joseph—First Dean of St Herman's Seminary, Alaska, and Chancellor of the Diocese of Alaska (OCA), 1973-1995.

**Vinogradov, Father Alexis—Rector of St Gregory Orthodox Church in Wappingers Falls, NY. Architect and seminary alumnus.

constantly alive inside him, so that his writings are really autobiographical.

This was our fourth meeting: Zurich, May 1974; Paris, December 1974; Canada, May 1975; Crestwood, 1976.

## *Friday, December 3, 1976*

Had lunch with the former editor of the Soviet journal *Science and Religion*—a philosopher, as he introduced himself. I really did not like him. Although I am not obsessed by suspicion, I was wondering whether he was sent from Russia. S. told me yesterday, "This whole third emigration is suspicious and undependable…"

From there, arrived wet (it is snowing) and bedraggled to City College to an ethnic Russian conference, in connection with the Bicentennial, where I willy-nilly agreed to read a short paper about the seminary. When will we see the end of the emigration's mediocrity, self-praise, lectures in poor English (in the hall 35 old Russian people, not counting 12 speakers, who have to listen to each other) about our contributions to America? How pitiful! "In order to make our contribution to America, we must mainly remain Russian. If we were not Russian, we could not make our contribution…" What is unclear is, what contribution? The level, the shallowness are rather appalling. What remains of the emigration is a huge old-age home where some people read needless papers to each other about their own mission.

What a day! In the morning, Solzhenitsyn, then lunch with a very suspicious man from the Soviet Union, finally afternoon with the emigration in its purest form!

Today: Matins, confessions, lectures, appointments from 7:00 to 2:00! I think God will forgive everything except lack of joy; when we forget that God created the world and saved it. Joy is not one of the "components" of Christianity, it's the *tonality* of Christianity that penetrates *everything*—faith and vision. Where there is no joy, Christianity becomes fear and therefore torture. We know about the fallen state of the world only because we know about its glorious creation and its salvation by Christ. The knowledge of the fallen world does not kill joy, which emanates in this world, always, constantly, as a bright sorrow.

This world is having fun; nevertheless it's joyless because joy (different from what is called "fun") can be only from God, only from on high—not only joy of salvation, but salvation as joy. To think—every Sunday we have a banquet with Christ, at His table, in His Kingdom; then we sink into our problems, into fear and suffering. God saved the world through joy: "…you will have pain, but your pain will turn into joy..." (John 16:21: "When a woman is in travail she has sorrow, because her hour has come; but when she is delivered of the child, she no longer remembers the anguish, for joy that a child is born into the world").

### Wednesday, December 15, 1976

On Monday, L. and I drove to New York under an exceptionally cold, windy and sunny sky. The view of Manhattan from Brooklyn, coming out of the tunnel, is absolutely wonderful. On Fifth Avenue everything is gloriously "Christmassy"!

For many weeks I haven't sat at my desk. Meetings, conferences, "busyness."

Yesterday I visited Matushka Telep in Fairlawn, New Jersey. She is 84, was born in Osceola Mills, spent her life in Pennsylvania parishes. Joyful, wise, speaks good Russian. I was thinking about the contempt that the self-satisfied Russian emigration has for these people, the Carpatho-Russians...

Lunch with Metropolitan Philip,* who has just come back from Russia and is deeply impressed by the services, the people, the faith.

### Friday, December 17, 1976

Yesterday, while reading the Paris Russian daily, *Russkaya Mysl'* (Russian Thought), I was strangely irritated. Russia, the emigration, all these arrogant discussions, rhetoric, idle talk, against a background of announcements for memorial services, cheap trips to USSR, the "Rasputin" nightclub advertising for experienced balalaika players—all of it suddenly made me nauseous, as at the sight of food after a big meal. While walking to Vespers yesterday, I asked myself, "Then what do I want? What is my life? If everything is unnecessary and fussy, then what; sit at home, in comfort, with money, write a little, watch television?" I am well on my way to doing just that. I come home every day from the seminary, deafened by phone calls, a pile of seminary concerns, unending problems, and sit—like a dead body—in front of the television, watching some Carol Burnett show! I don't know; these thoughts were quite real. I should ask myself: "What does Christ want from me? Am I doing, at least partially, what He wants?"

Tuesday, I read the latest *Vestnik (Messenger)* from Paris. It seems that so many words are said and printed without any need, any justification. So

---

* Philip, Metropolitan—Head of the Antiochian Orthodox Archdiocese of North America, 1966–present. Alumnus and Vice-President of St Vladimir's Seminary.

much is diluted, weakened by an empty chattering, and all the more painful because it's about God, religion, Church. While reading, I wonder what of all these writings can still be effective; what will remain and will live? Almost nothing. It's like an itch—the more you scratch, the more it itches. With Western intellectuals, a refined sharpening of ideas, of concepts which take on a life of their own. Here the Paris *Vestnik* is prophesying even when talking about the simplest matters. There—all is about words, semantics. Here—indifference to words, which, as a result, are often emotional and subjective. Russians do not understand each other because they do not agree on words. Western intellectuals see their goal in clarification of terms, which end up not meaning anything real. Both, however, are quite content, despise "the others" and consider their own talks as exceptionally meaningful.

We decorated our tree with little Vera. Frost and sunshine outside our windows. Peace in our home, blissful contact with the "one thing needful."

### Thursday, December 23, 1976

Services, confessions, prefeast preparations at home. But the situation at the seminary is worrying me. I have the feeling that we are not doing what we should; not heading where we should; something is wrong! We had a three-hour faculty meeting about it, but without a consensus, neither about an analysis of the situation, nor how to deal with it. My point of view is that a good half of our students are dangerous for the church—their psychology, their tendencies, a sort of constant obsession with something. Orthodoxy takes on a different, ugly aspect, something important is missing, and the Orthodoxy that these students consciously or subconsciously favor is distorted, narrow, emotional—in the end, pseudo-Orthodoxy. Not only at the seminary, but everywhere, I acutely sense the spread of a strange Orthodoxy. I see it in Russia (*The Messenger*) and in the Church at large. Everywhere some anxiety, an unbalanced search, as if there was no joy from God's presence, joy from faith. What is missing is "joy and peace in the Holy Spirit" and the whole attention goes to something else—pride, self-affirmation, desire to save and teach, absence of humility.

### Sunday, December 26, 1976

Christmas: A full measure of joy. Church services, Christmas tree with all our grandchildren, and today—a miracle! When we woke up, everything was covered with snow, bright sunshine. The sky is radiant and in my heart—the Feast!

Confessions, conversations. The power of sin is not in being tempted by obvious evil, but in the imprisonment of the heart in all sorts of little passions and in the impossibility to freely breathe and live. To fight this prison, it is not enough to advocate to piety and prayer. Piety can be, and often is, petty, and prayer—self-centered. The same question arises, about the treasure of the heart, about joy. Without joy, piety and prayer are without grace, since their power is in joy. Religion has become the synonym of a seriousness not compatible with joy. So it is weak. People want answers, peace, meaning from religion, and the meaning is *joy*. That is *the* answer, including in it *all* answers.

## Thursday, December 30, 1976

College student retreat at the seminary. Over fifty participants—a comforting and joyful impression—to see that during Christmas vacations they are spending two days listening about prayer, attending services, etc. I remember myself at their age. I loved the Church, but would not have gone to a retreat, would not have done without a worldly Christmas season, dances, Christmas parties, etc. All these kids are healthy, happy, down to earth. Lord, I only hope that they will not be drawn into "religious exaltation" or some "spirituality"!

## Friday, December 31, 1976

Last day of the year! Again, frost and bright sunshine. Yesterday, dinner at C[onnie] T[arasar]'s.*

During these festive days, I very specially feel sorry for all the lonely people, left out of life, wallowing in their loneliness. How many of them all around! We have not been in New York for a New Year celebration for years; always in Paris. I am so happy that we will stay home this year in this peace, full of sunshine, that surrounds my desk while I work. I am happy also that there will be an evening Liturgy, that we will meet the New Year in "the Lord's time."

---

* Tarasar, Constance—Lecturer in Religious Education at St Vladimir's Seminary 1970–present, and first woman graduate of the seminary.

# CHAPTER V

# 1977

∾

*Saturday, January 1, 1977*

Evening Liturgy at the seminary. Many people, wonderful choir, two deacons. A clear feeling that one must meet the year here at His Table, in His Kingdom.

The rest of the night we spent with relatives, all L.'s brothers and sisters with spouses, cousins, etc. All slightly older!—but a strong feeling of kinship that unites us through all our lives.

*Wednesday, January 4, 1977*

Letter from Struve: "I am very glad that Solzhenitsyn visited the seminary, but what you write about him is so right. His going to America is turning into self-isolation, partially forced by the need to work, partially voluntary—'you are a King, you live alone…'"

Yesterday, the first service of the Prefeast of Epiphany.

*Tuesday, January 11, 1977*

*Paris*

Visiting and spending the day with Nikita Struve and his wife: a vast survey of everything that happened this year. First of all Solzhenitsyn and his rushing around in a stifling atmosphere of impulsive and inconsiderate decisions. We (Nikita and I) fully understand each other and I thoroughly enjoy being with them. In the evening—far back into my childhood—a delightful dinner with my classmates from the thirties!

*Wednesday, January 12, 1977*

With every day in Paris, it becomes clearer that the honeymoon with the new wave of dissidents from Russia is over. There is a fight for acquiring or retaining positions of authority, added to a total lack of accord—different wave-lengths, different styles, different tonalities.

### Sunday, January 16, 1977

Last Liturgy in my brother's church. Last visits, appointments, two hours with Mother—always a subconscious feeling: is it for the last time?—and it hurts…

### Tuesday, January 18, 1977

*Crestwood*

Arrived yesterday in New York in an incredible cold. Festive, white America from the plane. Thoroughly delighted to be back, warm, at home. A very cozy evening with L. Now, I am going to the seminary—one more "recess" has ended, once more my Paris becomes memory!

### Wednesday, January 19, 1977

I read in Paris, and finished on the plane the latest volume of Julien Green's diary—*La bouteille à la mer: 1972-1976,* with less interest and less pleasure than usual. I can't seem to be quite convinced by this 100 percent total Christianity, mystical, but also requiring life to be comfortable, beautiful, peaceful, refined, requiring the Church to be as "I loved it when I was 15," expecting to go to Vienna, to Italy, to Sweden to delight in golden ornaments, etc. God knows that I am irritated by leftist Christianity and the surrounding farce no less than Green. But this narcissism is tiring, despite the perfection of his language.

I think a book should be written entitled, "The Realism of Orthodoxy and the Romanticism of the Orthodox People." I think it while remembering church services in Paris—in all the churches. There is an absolute (I am not exaggerating) rupture between content (what is read, sung, accomplished) and its perception by the praying people. An unconscious—or rather subconscious—fear of suddenly finding that it all has a meaning. But fortunately, everything is covered with a thick layer of *Slavonic,* closed by the doors and the walls and the curtains of the *iconostasis*; diluted and domesticated by harmless customs and tradition, full of pride that "we have kept and are guarding it all" (what?). All this is presented to the West as having "a sense of mystery," the "mystery of *theandric life*," etc. One can understand the pathos of some rebels who suffocate in the midst of this brocade, this romantic nominalism. As a result, we do not actualize the life, the service, and the teaching of Christ in our Liturgy, including "and He began to be greatly distressed and troubled. And he said to them, 'My soul is very sorrowful, even to death...' " (Mark 14:33-34) but, on the contrary, we transform the tragedy of this life and service into a beautiful and smooth liturgical mystery.

### *Thursday, January 20, 1977*

Two hours in front of the television watching Carter's inauguration. He is my sixth president since we came to this country. I am impressed by America and I am genuinely delighted by the simplicity of the whole ceremony, which makes it truly symbolic. Here is what makes America truly great. What impresses me the most is the transfer of power when enmity and partisanship disappear. An ovation for former President Ford, and Carter's simple words of thanks, "from me and our whole nation," the flag, sunshine. "America the Beautiful." A prayer, a hymn. All that is grandiose and absolutely simple. As I am watching, Carter—hand in hand with his wife—is walking to the White House. I am sure that this walk will always be remembered. But his speech seemed to me to be rather weak. And he himself does not strike me as very likable. He smiles all the time, but his eyes remain cold. But what delights me is America, its deep essence, America which has found—alone in the whole world—a formula, almost miraculous, of government and society not turned into idols, but combining living tradition with life. I thought again about Solzhenitsyn: here is what he should look at, research, humbly learn. But no! only *they* can teach the world from under the rubble, only *they* know! Neither S. nor, in general, Europeans will ever try to understand!

### *Saturday, January 22, 1977*

Today, at 5:00 AM, Mania gave birth to Natasha, our ninth grandchild! Spent the whole morning in a happy fuss, forcing myself to write my weekly radio scripts. Yesterday at the Hopkos, I thoroughly enjoyed little Alexandra!

Winter beauty, snow, huge white spaces.

I continue reading the book about Marx. What a degradation took place in the nineteeth century! Fall of perspective, of level, of focus, of interest and attention. Marx lived his whole life in a spiritual swamp and infected the whole world with it, the whole human conscience. Paradox of that era: in the same time, the reduction of man (Feuerbach) *and* a passionate desire to liberate him. The Christian era lifts man to heaven (anthropological maximalism) but is reconciled with his enslavement on earth. The anti-Christian era is quite minimalistic, but wants to be of service to man. Quite smooth—still not explainable, still a paradox.

*Monday, January 24, 1977*

Painful thoughts about the Church, about the destiny of Orthodoxy. Essentially there are two positions. One—quite clear, the position of the Russian Church in Exile and of the Old Believers. To keep, to guard, to protect the Church not only from evil, but from the world as such, from the contemporary world. No checking, no verification—everything, every *stikhera* is equally important. The other position is ours. But what is it? In practice, in life, what does the *meaning* that we find behind the *form* demand of us? What is to be done? In the former position, the world is included in the Church, not our world, not the contemporary world, but the "past" (customs, tradition, etc.). In our position, the world is not included in the Church because we want reality. But how should we act in this real world? What do we offer when we say; here is the wonderful design of God for the world, for man, for life. Go and live by it! But how? Little by little, Orthodoxy becomes neurotic, people are rushing around searching for answers, and there are *no* answers, or rather, the answer is so general that people do not know how to apply it to their lives. This is the painful background which is almost always deep in my conscience!

*Thursday, January 27, 1977*

Sunshine again, snow and frost. Every morning a triumphant sunrise. Yesterday Father Leonid K[ishkovsky] told me about the large number of children of his parishioners who disappeared from church life—the majority. But their parents insist on *Russian* Orthodoxy—same as in Paris. It seems that the Orthodox Church in the whole world is like an ostrich hiding its head in the sand not to face reality. Everywhere, everybody playing childish games.

Yesterday, on television, an interview with Artur Rubenstein to celebrate his 90th birthday. He plays the Grieg piano concerto. What a beautiful old age; one can endlessly admire his face—fully illumined by his spirit.

Rubenstein spoke about the uniqueness of every gift: to be great is to be wholly one's self. Why is so much of what is true, liberating, genuinely Christian, experienced outside the Church, while inside Christianity we hear something weak, repetitive, and often unkind. When Christians were chased out of history, they started from the opposite side of the road to shake their fists and quarrel with each other—and to show each other pictures of Hagia Sophia, of St Basil in Moscow, of monasteries on Mt. Athos, and real German reproductions of Orthodox icons.

## *Monday, January 31, 1977*

Our 34th wedding anniversary. I remember so well this windy gray January day in Paris and my walk to the cathedral with my parents. And the eve of our wedding, when I came to get L.'s bag and waited forever for a bus. Gratitude!

## *Saturday, February 5, 1977*

### *San Francisco*

Lecture at the Russian Center. Diocesan meeting with the bishop; familiar discussions, but I thoroughly enjoy the presence and dedication of all these young priests (and laypeople). "He who is faithful in a very little..." (Luke 16:10). Friendly gathering until late in the night. Drive around San Francisco—without a doubt the most beautiful city in America. I always enjoy plunging into its charm.

Tomorrow I fly home—already counting the hours.

## *Tuesday, February 8, 1977*

### *Crestwood*

Same intense cold which is becoming rather tiring. Yesterday we went to Goshen for the funeral of Kit Wallace's father. A severe Presbyterian service. Two beautiful hymns (one of them "Just As I Am"). Bare walls, no service, no *leiturgia*—it is very strong in its simplicity and barrenness. Our funerals are full of concern about the future life—"have mercy, forgive, accept..." Here, total trust, faith in God's promise; not only faith in God but trust in Him. This severe religion has created an extraordinary type of people—humble, strong-willed, with self-control in everything, including religion. Goshen is also that way, like Boston. The beauty of these little houses, the village square surrounded by trees, also beauty on our drive back—cold sunset over snowy fields.

The most frightening aspects of the contemporary decline of culture is the drying up, the failing of modesty, of the hierarchical intuition, of a sense of proportion. There is a cheap pride in everything, including the Church, a total impossibility, inability to discern what is fake (be it in literature, in art, *et al.*) It seems that everyone stands on a roof and shouts his own ...what? But since he's on a roof, people listen!

## Thursday, February 10, 1977

General assembly of all students. I told them all the things that I believe in my heart to be right and necessary. Did it reach them? I do not know. They are so armored in their cassocks, so convinced that they know and can do anything in their youthful self-assurance.

## Monday, February 14, 1977

### Hillsdale College, Michigan

"Alone with you, my friend..." I constantly quote it to myself while, in the midst of the bustle of the last days, I turn to this journal. I am writing at 10:00 PM in my room at Hillsdale College, near Detroit. I came to give two lectures, today and tomorrow. I just finished the first one, went to the reception and am trying to regain my senses.

I want to write about:

Friday night—I lectured to our students' wives about "the woman." I thought about it and prepared for the lecture very carefully. I wanted to say, as simply and truthfully as possible, first—what I feel, and second—what I think. It seems that they appreciated the food for thought and were inspired to continue their search. "I never heard the like..." said N.

On Saturday, I served the Memorial Liturgy (Cheesefare). I felt the reality and actuality of the remembrance of the dead. I feel more and more its power, importance and mainly, joy.

On Sunday, I spent the day at the seminary—St Vladimir's Theological Foundation Day. I was very tired, when Father N. came to tell me about his troubles in his very Russian parish. No meekness, no humility, no thirst in this "very Russian" parish—only self-adulation, stifling anything alive. When will we finally repent of this ever-flowing Russian boasting about everything, religion and everything else?

I realize how spiritually tired I am of all this "Orthodoxism," of all the fuss with Byzantium, Russia, way of life, spirituality, church affairs, piety, of all these rattles. I do not like any of them, and the more I think about the meaning of Christianity, the more it all seems alien to me. It all literally obscures Christ, pushes Him into the background. Maybe it is my pride? I don't know. I think not. All of it appears to me to have no common measure with Christ and His commandment: "But seek first his kingdom and his righteousness, and all these things shall be yours as well" (Matthew.6:33). I can't find words to express what is most important, what Christianity means to me, what *is* its design, its gift, its call, its challenge.

## Saturday, February 19, 1977

I talked with L. about talent and intelligence. I compare intelligence with the gall bladder whose function it is to "regulate." It is quite rare and fortunate when talent and intelligence fully coincide. For example Pushkin, who had both. Tolstoy is a genius but not intelligent (his philosophical works). Solzhenitsyn's intelligence does not serve his talent, but undermines it. I think that Russians (what a generalization!) are mainly talented but not always intelligent (i.e., rational).

Quote from Balzac:

"Create and you will die persecuted as a criminal; copy and you will live happily as a foolish man."

## Monday, February 21, 1977

*Great Lent*

Yesterday, because of a snow storm, we spent the night in Wappingers Falls at the Hopkos. I was substituting for Father Tom in the morning. As a result I missed Forgiveness Vespers at the seminary and served it in Wappingers in an empty church with L., Anya and her daughters. When Anya sang alone the *prokimenon*—"Turn not away Thy face from Thy child, for I am afflicted. Hear me speedily, draw near unto my soul and deliver it"—so simply, so purely, I felt the whole piercing fullness, the blessed joy that one is sometimes given to feel. We ended with Paschal *stikheras*. This morning I drove back with L.—a radiant sunny day in the midst of a fairytalish world, joyfully decorated with snow. Two great days with Anya and our grandchildren.

## Tuesday, February 22, 1977

With passing years, I am conscious more and more of the feeling of *time*, of its flow, its changing. Thus, for instance, those two days at Anya's in the coziness, the light of her family, of her home: while living those days, I begin to remember them, to convert them into the happiness which is given in them and through them, as a nourishment absolutely free and absolutely needed. Gifts, which we do not appreciate because they seem so little—they are the only genuine ones—like walking home after a beautiful Vespers service through deep mounds of snow. All of that together: snow sparsely illumined by street lights, windows with cozy light behind them, little Alexandra, like a little ball rolling on that snow. All of these are gifts from God!—All from God; all about Him.

There is difficulty in any beginning, for instance the beginning of Great Lent. "I don't feel like it." What is absolutely necessary at the very beginning is to have *patience.* "By your endurance you will gain your lives" (Luke 21:19). To be patient is to accept the "don't feel like it," to stifle it—not by forcing one's self to "want" it, which would be impossible and false, but simply by accepting, submitting, obeying. And patience is sooner or later transformed into desire. And what one did not want becomes happiness, fullness, a gift. And one is sorry that it will soon be over.

I am listening to the prayers, the hymns. And again, I see the obvious, incomparable superiority of the Psalms and, in general, the Scriptures, to any hymnography.

### Thursday, February 24, 1977

Yesterday, the first Presanctified Liturgy—with enthusiasm and joy. Between services, I was home writing "Unity of Faith"—which seems to be finally crystallizing. Sunshine and thaw.

At night, I read Chekhov's letters written during the last years of his life. I always liked and like more and more Chekhov the man, not only the author—the quality of his consistency, restraint, and at the same time his deep, secret kindness. Among all the great Russian writers, he is the closest to Christianity in his sobriety, his absence of cheap feelings. But what a sad, tragic life with tuberculosis at the age of thirty!

### Friday, February 25, 1977

Strange how what I am working on, sometimes seemingly fruitless, begins to "work" in me in a hidden way. As if I were sleeping, but my heart and mind are awake: this is what is happening with my "Unity of Faith." I am in total darkness—and suddenly the light is on. It's rather amazing how I can live all my life repeating someone else's words as if they were mine. But everything changes when the words that I used all my life suddenly become "mine."

Yesterday, last reading of the Canon. A crowd of priests. A Greek bishop. I hope that Lent will now become lighter, will become what it is calling us to be: light, free from the sinful weight of the soul.

### Sunday, February 27, 1977

*Sunday—Triumph of Orthodoxy*

As usual at the beginning of Lent, I have an acute sense of my past, my childhood, of everything that literally has "submerged into eternity." It is so important to remember—even some casual evening at my old aunt's and the sunset of that day, and the leaves in the little yard.

## *Tuesday, March 1, 1977*

I am reading Henri Bremond with enormous interest. I am always interested in people like Bremond, Loisy, and Laberthonniere, who lived through doctrinal crises. I am interested in the personal, internal aspect of their religious dramas. I feel somehow, *mutatis mutandis*, related to them—totally belonging to the church. This is obvious to me like the air we breathe, like life itself, but at the same time completely free inside the church. I am endlessly distressed by the enslavement to something or somebody that I see happening all around, distressed by the idolatry, so often triumphant in the church. A rebellion against the church, always cheap, is equally wrong, as well as mutiny, or spiritual sectarianism with its false pathos, unctuous sweetness, self-satisfaction, narrow vision. I can say in all conscience that the church has always been for me higher than anything, without any doubt an unseen, unquestionable—not authority—but *Light.* Everything lives in that Light; everything *is* that Light! The church in its essence, in its light, must not narrow but widen, not submit but liberate. This essence of the church, this Light is our life.

Church people—how should I say it—do not like to be faithful to the Church. They want the Church to be faithful to them, to fulfill their needs, so that those who love the essence of the Church are bound to suffer from the Church. In the life of "modernists" (and later Teilhard de Chardin) what is interesting is not their "leaving." To leave is to betray, it is dull, it is spiritual "vulgarity"; whereas loyalty is a cross, it is victory. One suffers from misunderstanding, solitude, feeling walled off. The victory comes from a gradually growing clear evidence inside one that this *is* Christianity. That is why the books about these people, dead long ago and now forgotten, disturb me so much. "Then all the disciples forsook him and fled" (Matthew 26:56). I think that every man who believes in Christ must go through that; it is the test of his testimony.

March. Although one walks to church in the early morning in intense cold, the light of the sun, the color of the sky, the lightness of air are—Spring!

## *Wednesday, March 2, 1977*

Yesterday I had hardly finished writing in my journal when I received an unfair, malicious letter which distressed me, irritated and poisoned my heart. And what remains of my "nice" words yesterday? Nothing. I thought that at least on that level, I had achieved a certain detachment!

149

Book about Henri Bremond: Did he believe? Pages about his not being able to pray, about God's silence: "all those whom I see and ask, tell me without hesitation that, in some beautiful hours of their lives, they have met You. To all of them, You said something. All of them, at a certain moment, were unable to doubt Your presence and Your love…And I, never, never!" (p. 78) What is it? Unbelief or the failure of a definite, almost technically organized spirituality (the Exercises of Ignatius and their development by Jesuit confessors)? What is prayer? and this Western choice, either-or? Either pure transcendence or pure immanence (humanism, etc.). Is the reason for Bremond's tragedy in this false choice, as well as that of many others?! To pray to God—determined, defined by philosophers? Bremond is striving for a religious feeling, i.e., experience. But experience also is precisely described, defined, classified. The whole West functions on such classifications, in these false and absolute dilemmas and dichotomies.

### Thursday, March 3, 1977

Continuing triumphant spring.

Spent the morning at the Spence School, where our little granddaughter Anya was performing. All the time while the girls were walking to the assembly hall, I held Sasha on my knees, with a lump in my throat from the joyful perfection of childhood.

### Saturday, March 5, 1977

Saturday Lenten Liturgy—I have loved it since I was a child. Such a clear answer to all the discouragement and doubts of the last days: "take heart." The Church is, above all, higher than everything—"at my table in my kingdom" (Luke 22:30). The Eucharist… How can one not see it, agree with it? I am on my way to Sea Cliff where I am going to talk precisely about that.

Warm, sunny, spring

### Monday, March 7, 1977

On Saturday I went to Sea Cliff. Before my lecture, I visited Professor Arseniev,* who has been asking, demanding, threatening (he talked to L. on the phone) for a whole week, that I visit him. In fact, there was nothing urgent, no reason at all for our meeting besides solitude, besides the awful immersion of living life into death. He shows me some family albums, his estate in Russia

---

* Arseniev, Nicholas, †1977—Professor of New Testament and Apologetics at St Vladimir's Seminary, 1948–1969.

(1910), those beautiful linden alleys, his whole Arseniev world. I feel for him the power of this remembrance. He probably thinks that if only *they* would understand how beautiful, wonderful, profound that world was, they would know where salvation is. For him, everything—including poetry, books and religion itself—are a hopeless attempt to resuscitate it. I came to him irritated (by the tone of his phone calls). I left not only pacified, but with an acute feeling of pity *and* repentance.

### Thursday, March 10, 1977

Speaking of church activity: announcement yesterday at the Synod meeting in Syosset by Metropolitan Ireney* of his retirement. For the sake of history, some little details: It was 3:00 PM and I was ready to go home, since the Synod was about to discuss awards, when Serge Troubetzkoy** told me: "It seems to me that the Metropolitan would agree to leave; he is constantly talking about it." I went to him and said: "*Vladyko*: you cannot do it any more; you are tired. We will take care of you..."And he agreed. In ten minutes I typed (with one finger) a resignation and he signed it. The resignation will become official in October at the Council, which will choose a successor. *Sic transit gloria mundi*! Strange how in one instant the impossible becomes possible. Deep down we cannot understand events in which we do not participate, but which we somehow provoke.

At night I wrote the communiqué of Bishop Sylvester (temporary head) to the Church. And there started a new era.

I ask myself (I do it after each Synod): What constitutes the impossibility of replacing the bishops, the necessity to have bishops; why are they needed, useful, yet on a special, much deeper level which alone is important and makes the Church to be the Church? I know, I always knew that it is so, but how to express it, how to explain it?

When I was thinking about this, while walking home from the station, I suddenly heard these words in my mind: "on an immovable rock..." The bishops are "an immovable rock" in two meanings of the word. In the negative, a "rock," blind authority, fear, self-affirmation, etc., and hence comes the difficulty for them to deal with the living Church. In the positive: yesterday, for example, they refused the candidacy of a priest because he was an innovator. At first I became quite incensed: we "innovators" are trying to go

* Ireney, Metropolitan, †1981—Primate of the "Metropolia"/OCA, 1965-1977.
**Serge Troubetzkoy—Secretary to both Metropolitans Ireney and Theodosius and worked as the church archivist, 1971–1984.

back to genuine tradition etc. Then, having cooled off, I realized that if they are slow in accepting a good "innovator," they will not allow a bad one! Whatever is good, if it is genuine, true, the Church will sooner or later let grow and bloom, while what is bad will be kept back. They—the bishops—are needed as "rocks." The bishops' function is to be the bearers of "conservatism" in the Church in the deepest sense of the word, the belief that at its depth the *Church* does not change because the *Church* is an "immovable rock." Since in the Church, more than anywhere else, the Spirit is breathing—but also "spirits"—this conservatism is absolutely necessary. To work with bishops is almost always difficult, but, in our better moments, we know that in the Church, "difficult" is good. Having spent my life with this difficulty, I believe in bishops with the same faith that I believe in the Church.

### Monday, March 14, 1977

I am sick, have no voice, coughing—so I stayed home. The trip to Minneapolis-Chicago finished me off: two lectures, questions lasting three and a half hours.

Baptism at home of our little Natasha.

It is one of those days when I very well know that I am incapable of doing any work. I am simply stretched thin and probably rather sick.

The political events in Paris pose a question: Does the mystical, national feeling of a "nation" make it into a "transcendental personality?" The Bible, it seems, says yes: "My beloved son, Israel," etc. Does it remain so after Christ? After the revelation of the Church? It seems questionable from a Christian point of view. Questionable, because nothing, nothing at all has harmed Christianity and the Church as much as the merging of Christianity with nationalism, of the Church with a natural order of things.

Just had a long telephone conversation with Father N. about who will be chosen as Metropolitan, how to choose, etc. This will last seven months! Nobody can believe that I am really not concerned, not out of cynicism ("who cares?") but because I *believe* and I *know* that the faultless and slightly frightening logic of Christianity and of the Church consists in the fact that a defeat turns into victory, and victory into defeat. It is the divine logic, and against it, all our reasoning and plots are quite powerless.

### Tuesday, March 15, 1977

Yesterday, I read Gogol's *The Inspector General* and *The Marriage*. I was struck by the insignificance of *The Marriage*. Why is it good? Why did Gogol write it? Before his death, Gogol was accused of having created caricatures, and he became afraid of the revolutionary influence he had on his readers. Something frightening and dark and even demonic was in him, some bottomless pride, and, as a result, a lack of any self-confidence.

In the Sunday *New York Times* there is an article about shrinking church attendance and the decline of faith, the rejection of dogmas, of any doctrine. A young Catholic: "I don't see how the acceptance of this or that dogma can change anything in my vision of life." This makes me think of the success of subjective religiosity. Faith decreases, religion becomes stronger. I am afraid that faith basically began declining long ago. Churches were held together in the last centuries not by faith but by religion, as long as religion corresponded socially to something in culture, in society, etc. and also as long as freedom and secularism did not penetrate through the thickness of the world's consciousness and civilization. Now it has happened and the first victim is the Church. Protestantism was the "de-churching" of Christianity or, at any rate, its beginning. The post-Vatican Church is now leaning toward Protestantism (denial of authority, of the concept of heresy, of objectivity). Orthodoxy is held together by holding on to the Church as a natural society—ethnic, national, etc. The foundation of the Church is faith. Faith eternally gives birth to the Church and fulfills it, and faith sees the Church as "the assurance of things hoped for, and the conviction of things not seen..." (Hebrews 11:1). The Church is needed as the sacrament of the age to come. Religion needs a temple, not the Church. The temple's origin is religion. Thus, in the Gospel: "I will destroy this temple..." The Church has a Christian origin. However our Church has identified itself long ago with the "temple," has dissolved itself in the temple, and (this means) has returned to the pagan temple as its religious sanction. Protestantism was an attempt to save the faith, to purify it from its religious reduction. But the Protestants have paid a heavy price for denying eschatology and replacing it with personal individual salvation; and therefore, essentially, denying the Church. The greatest anachronism, on a natural level, was to be found in the Catholic Church. Catholicism was possible only while one was able to deny and limit the freedom of the person, the basic dogma of the new times. While trying to change its course, to merge with freedom, Catholicism simply collapsed, and I do not see how its revival could be possible (unless fascism can get hold of the human race and deny the explosive synthesis of freedom and the person).

"People who listen to us sincerely do not understand what it is that we want from them." Ultimately, "we" (a tiny group) want the Church. But in Christianity, for a very long time, there has not been any experience of the

Church; it was replaced by the experience of a temple, plus individual religion, deprived inside of any faith such as "the assurance of things hoped for, the conviction of things not seen." Hope of what? What—not seen? Something divine in us, *per se*, transcendent, after life, not of this world, something that helps to live. But all of that, finally, is a matter of taste, of individual choice, of habit. And one cannot argue with taste.

I just reread what I wrote and I want to define more precisely faith, Church and freedom. They say: "freedom for each to have his or her own faith…" Good. So be it: a religious coercion of one's conscience is indeed the worst thing that can happen. They say: accept the faith of the Church (the authority of the Church, etc.). No, that is not it, not so. When I am saying that faith gives birth to the Church, I am talking about the ontology of faith itself, because faith and Church are not two different realities, with one of them the keeper and guardian of other. *No.* Faith is to possess the Kingdom (the assurance of things hoped for—and the conviction of things not seen—the Kingdom). This possession *is* the Church as a sacrament, as unity, as new life. The Church is the *presence* of the hoped for and the unseen. Thus to speak of some freedom of faith within the Church is as meaningless as to speak of freedom within a multiplication table. The acceptance of the Kingdom is the fruit of freedom, its fulfillment and its crowning. In that sense, as this constant, continually renewed acceptance, faith *is* freedom, the only genuine freedom, and as such the Church must be the fulfillment of faith.

### Thursday, March 17, 1977

Early this morning a phone call from the Spence School that L. has been chosen as the next headmistress. The "American dream" is still real. We came in 1952; L. did not know a word of English—and now headmistress of one of the very best schools in the States!

Yesterday, a wonderful Presanctified Liturgy.

I am in Little Rock. Long flight with stops in Washington and Memphis. I am now sitting at the window of my hotel room on the 9th floor. A huge view of the Arkansas River and far, far beyond. Gray and cloudy, but trees are turning green. The South: this is the city where, in 1955, began the recognition of blacks. Eisenhower brought in troops when the whites refused to integrate their schools.

On the plane, I read Morris Dickstein's *Gates of Eden: American Culture in the Sixties.* Quite interesting in general, and in particular as an obvious attempt to create myths: the play of the fifties, sixties, seventies is slightly irritating. The analysis of cultural change is focused on an ever-changing intelligentsia which is continually changing its gods, burning what it bowed to and is bowing before what it burned. Actually, deep down, the changes are very slow—for instance, the Orthodox mentality in America—so that I read all this sophistication *cum grano salis.*

## Saturday, March 19, 1977

*Montreal*

I am writing in Montreal at Father John's and my daughter Masha's. I flew in early in the morning for an all-day retreat; two lectures about the Cross and the Theotokos. Many people. I was happy with what I said. It was *what* I think and *how* I think. English Vespers. Again I am touched by these young voices, by the youth in the Church. And I fear for them—let them not "go off the rails."

While flying many hours from Arkansas, I finished reading *Gates of Eden.* I came to the conclusion that one of the characteristics of our time is to attach great importance to completely unimportant things. Hundreds of pages dedicated to the analysis of totally forgotten articles, novels, trends—all of it endlessly "deep" as if talking about world events. Nobody wrote about Tolstoy and Dostoyevsky as this Dickstein writes about Mailer, Updike, *et al* and about some minor magazines. There is so much pettiness dealing with pettiness.

## Tuesday, March 22, 1977

On Sunday, in Montreal, while standing in church during the English-language, early Liturgy, I was thinking: Is it possible that someday the Orthodox will understand that to serve, to sing, to stand in church has to be done *like this,* and *only* like this. After this, the Russian hierarchical Liturgy—in which I took part—appears as a real slump. These arrogant subdeacons, throwing around the *orletz,* the special performances of the choir, the roaring of the Epistle—all so familiar from my childhood—strikes me as a betrayal. Why do I hush it all up? From fear? No, rather from being realistic, from an aversion to any rebellion in the Church, from a feeling that partial corrections will not help if there is not, at first, a conversion to a different vision of the Church and to a different perception of the Liturgy.

Conversion is difficult if one is in love with one's self, completely content and satisfied. And how close beneath the skin lies genuine hatred!

## Thursday, March 24, 1977

Yesterday, the coziest, happiest evening with our two *matushki*—my daughters Anya and Masha. Delight in their spiritual health, light, transparency.

I am about to leave for the Annunciation Vigil: "The Archangel's Voice..."

## Friday, March 25 1977

*Feast of the Annunciation*—my most loved of all loved feasts! Standing in the sanctuary during the Vigil listening to these exultant hymns: "...proclaim, O Earth, the news of a great joy; sing, O Heavens, the glory of the Lord," I thought: How could there be problems? Doesn't our whole life consist in accepting and assimilating this joy from on high, in making it ours, in seeing and accepting this joy as eternally new?

## Saturday, March 26, 1977

Yesterday, the Akathist, and this morning a quiet, *blue* Liturgy of the *Praises of the Virgin.*

Pure, undiluted joy of this day since childhood, when, sitting at my desk at the Lycée Carnot and being bored, I would tell myself: "Tonight, the Praises to the Theotokos..." Flowering chestnut trees on my way to church.

I thought today about the debates concerning "the place of the Theotokos" in our salvation—its definition, etc., and about the mediocrity and the weakness of theology that is understood in this way. One cannot understand anything without first accepting it all: "Rejoice, for through you joy shall shine forth...," without first being lightly touched with wonder and gratitude for this purest Image. How can one define it all in the "scientific" language that theology has chosen?

In everything feminine, even made profane, there are shreds of this image. In *Her,* they are fully gathered.

Absence of negative women's images in the New Testament (like Judas, the Pharisees, etc.). Christ denounces the Pharisees, but forgives the loose woman and speaks with the Samaritan woman.

Definitions, i.e., the essence: Mother, Virgin, Bride, The Woman clothed in the Sun, Queen.

## Holy Wednesday, April 6, 1977

I just finished *Gates of Eden* by Dickstein and thought that alongside popular courses like "Great Western Ideas," it would be useful to teach a course entitled "Great Western Errors," following approximately this plan: Rousseau and "Nature," with a capital N; The Enlightenment and "Reason," capital R; Hegel and "History," capital H; Marx and "Revolution," capital R; and finally, Freud and "Sex," capital S—realizing that the main error of each is precisely the capital letter, which transforms these words into an idol, into a tragic "*pars pro toto.*" Show all of these as a fragmented Christianity and show the awful guilt of Christians in that fragmentation. The guilt is not only ideological, but before anything else, spiritual (spirituality) and practical (merging with the world, accepting the functions of a natural religion, denying eschatology on one hand, the *hic et nunc* on the other).

Sin has been dissolved in a petty focus on little details. One does not realize that pettiness—even moral—is sin; is the aversion to God, the rejection of God; but pettiness is easier, religion is easier.

A question remains unsolved (insoluble, perhaps?): What to call people to? What to teach them? I think that one should start with the *body*. In the body, everything is given for communication, knowledge, communion: feelings, eyes to see (what?), ears to listen and to hear (what?), etc. A terrible mistake is made when everything is reduced either to reason or to emotion. Reason prevents us from seeing and hearing, because it transforms the "other"—given, seen, speaking—into a rational object. Emotions: they focus on themselves, transforming everything into narcissism. In both, reason and emotion, a deviation, solitude, sin. Quite important, of course, is what to hear and see—this is the *hic and nunc* (here and now) that reveals eternity *now*. It is the realization of "the Kingdom of God is in you…"

## *Holy Thursday, April 7, 1977*

I am more and more convinced that nothing, absolutely nothing is achieved or solved through discussions, arguments, debates—an aberration of our times. It's hard to imagine Tolstoy, Rembrandt, or Shakespeare at some colloquium, dedicated to the ways of contemporary art. Anything that convinces, or converts others, grows in solitude, in creative quiet, never in chatter. It does not mean that a creator should not have a universal vision—he must have. The error of our times is the belief in words, leading to their complete devaluation. People will tell me: "What about Plato's dialogues?" But they support precisely what I am saying. These dialogues are not just a recording of a particular debate, but the demonstration of an ideal debate in which every word has its full weight, *and,* in which everything is built on hearing what the other one is saying.

A real discussion has become impossible because the topics have become accidental, arbitrary, not justified in any way. A genuine conversation pre-supposes the justification, the necessity of the topic. The topic is objective and everything becomes organized around it organically. Finally: in this world everything that is not related to "the one thing needful," that is cut off from it, is empty, unnecessary, harmful. "But seek first His Kingdom and His righteousness, and all these things shall be yours as well" (Matthew 6:33) is the basic methodological principle, the only one possible.

## Holy Friday, April 8, 1977

Everything as it should be—as always—on these high days. In the best mo-ments, one is painfully pierced by *what* is remembered and celebrated. Im-possible, unheard of, when one thinks about it. The Holy Week is somehow "gathering" one's whole life. One thing is clear: these days are a merciless judgment over everything. It is Sin and Evil in their purest form. And Ju-das—who "did not want to understand"—he is me, us, the whole world.

It seems that a circle is closing in the history of religion—it is a time for judgment. What will remain depends on what will be accepted, acknowl-edged and seen as the meaning of this judgment.

## Bright Friday, April 15, 1977

Seminary, church. Lunch with Father D[aniel Hubiak*] discussing church affairs. How many little passions, little obstacles! Of course it is all unimpor-tant, but it poisons and darkens one's life. But then how much joy comes from people like Father D.!

## Thursday, April 21, 1977

I woke up in the middle of the night, and, as happens quite often, could not fall back asleep for a long time, pursued by an awful thought: Life has gone by and nothing has been done. All my time is spent on petty little affairs, semi-nary "tragedies," radio scripts, etc. In the morning, only a vague memory re-mains, but in the middle of the night, it seemed absolutely horrible. Still, what remains is the question: Is this total waste of time needed? Is writing needed? Should there be a change? Is this total giving of self to minute details needed, should one accept life as is—and is that its Christian meaning?

This morning I was talking with L. about going from one rhetoric to an-other—the rhetoric of the French Left, of the Russian dissident emigration,

* Hubiak, Father Daniel—Chancellor of the OCA from 1973-1988. Currently representative of the OCA to the Patriarchate of Moscow and rector of St Catherine's Church, Moscow.

the rhetoric of Orthodoxy. What is awfully disconcerting in each is its total enclosure in itself, the self-sufficiency, complacency. Each one is enclosed in itself and quite worthless because of that. I feel so weary of this pettiness. I have a passionate desire to get away from *all* rhetoric. But then, what is needed?

### Friday, April 22, 1977

The following is a letter to the editor of *Le Messager* in Paris from a reader in Soviet Russia (a well-known author):

> …I especially want to tell you my thoughts about the discussion in your publication between A. Solzhenitsyn and Father Alexander Schmemann. I totally share the high evaluation that Father A. gives of our great author, whom he very accurately calls the exorcist of the Russian soul. Indeed, the service of S. is undoubtedly prophetic. His life—a rare miracle. This man found himself so many times at the edge of death—on the front, in a concentration camp, in a hospital with cancer, protected by God, in order to become the best known preacher of truth in the second half of the 20th century. We often have to hear reproaches of Solzhenitsyn for his harshness, for his words being strange, etc., even from people who, on the whole, sympathize with him. One can answer with total assurance that all of that does not matter in evaluating a man who was the first to force the world to hear the truth about the Soviet Union, with its secret police, its camps; to hear the truth about the many millions of innocent, tortured people, about its antihuman essence. The strength of the rightness in A.S. is in his uncompromising striving for truth and his call to "live not by lies," addressed to the whole humanity, already heard by many, and bringing a noticeable change in the political climate.
>
> At the same time, as we well know, every prophet is only human, and, as a human being, can, in some instances, be carried away and get lost. Solzhenitsyn is, at times, carried away, for instance in his "letter from America" (p. 116). It's gratifying to see with what brilliant erudition and with what tact these human aberrations "come off" in Schmemann's article, 'Answer to Solzhenitsyn.' Here, as in most of his other articles, the opinions of Father A., for many of us, are a sort of standard in evaluating many ideas and happenings. His judicious, lively, churchly position on the pages of your magazine adds brilliantly to and corrects Solzhenitsyn's passionate appeals…

### Wednesday, April 29, 1977

In East Hampton, I read a few issues of the Israeli paper *Time and Us*. It is the paper of the Jewish Russian intelligentsia in Israel, trying to find some meaning for its fate. Very strong and very strange impression, before anything else, of a dead-end pathos penetrating the whole paper. Those are all

Russian people, Russian intelligentsia, for whom Russian culture, Russian language is *their own.*

And, at the same time, deeply offended by Russia, not only by the Soviet element in Russia, but by an intrinsic Russian anti-Semitism. Offended, wounded by this rejection, and unable to tear themselves away from the Russian theme, in spite of their departure from Russia, their repatriation in Israel and their Jewishness, which they cultivate with passion. The tone is essentially this: We love Russia, but Russia never loved us or recognized us. What is needed is a delineation of each group (Russians and Russian Jews) but for such a delineation there must be mutual recognition—and it does not exist, in any case on the Russian side. A dead-end, a real tragedy. While reading, I thought once more that Jewishness demonstrates the horror of any nationalism (whose driving force is almost unavoidably anti-Semitic), but while demonstrating it, it does not seem to realize that Jewishness *is* nationalistic in its essence; that it is the substance of nationalism, not only colored, but determined by religion. Precisely *because* their religion is totally directed at themselves, at their people, at their being the Chosen People, at their special mission, at their standing apart, their religion is a source and an internal measure of any nationalism. It is quite clear that this problem disappears only in Christ (but it is easy to say!). The paradox of Jewishness: It requires that everybody deny their own nationalism, but recognize that the only legitimate nationalism is theirs, the Jewish one. What they denounce and condemn deserves condemnation and denunciation. But their *reason* for condemning is the same as *what* they condemn. A vicious circle! Their only "regal" greatness would be in total self-renunciation—and it happened in Christ. But they live by self-affirmation which does not have, never had, either greatness or truth. And since Jewishness refused to die and become alive again and receive "all that is promised" in Christianity, Christianity became poisoned by pseudo-Jewishness: self-affirmation, the messianism of Christian nations, nationalism, etc. Deep down one thing is clear: Jewishness is about Christ, but the Jews want to convince us that Christianity is only for Christians. And how wrong are those Christians who, out of pity, sense of guilt, etc., think that the Jews are right, that they have their own covenant with God separate from ours. Everything genuine in Christianity comes from Judaism; the whole of Christianity is "…glory to Thy people Israel," (Luke 2:32) but the Jews want us to recognize that it does not concern them.

*Thursday, April 28, 1977*

In connection with the recruitment crisis at the seminary, I was thinking:

Why do people so often simply destroy their life, harm themselves, as if they were possessed by some *amor fati*. It would seem that simple selfishness and instinct of self-preservation would guard them, but no, even this instinct stops working. One can clearly see some kind of madness, a real passion for destruction. This passion is "I"—i.e., *pride*. Pride has transformed "the angel of light" into the devil, and now pride alone has the power to destroy people. Therefore, anything, one way or the other, even in a microscopic dose, connected with pride, is connected with the devil and with the diabolical. Religion also is a ready-made field of action for the devil's forces. Everything, absolutely everything in religion is ambiguous, and this ambiguity can be cleared only by humility, so that the whole spiritual life is or must be directed at seeking humility. The signs of humility: *joy*! Pride excludes joy. Then: *simplicity*, i.e., the absence of any turn into one's self. Finally, *trust*, as the main directive in life, applied to everything (purity of heart, when man can *see* God). The signs of pride are: the absence of joy; complexity and fear. All this can be verified every day, every hour, by watching one's self and contemplating life around.

It is frightening to think that in some sense, the Church also lives with pride—"the rights of the churches," "the rights of the Ecumenical Throne," "the dignity of the Russian Church," etc., and a flood of joyless complicated and fearful "spirituality." It is a continuous self-destruction. We try to protect the "Truth," we fight with something and for something without understanding that Truth appears and conquers only where it is alive: "…humble yourself, be like a slave," and you will have a liberating joy and simplicity, where humility is radiant in its divine beauty; where God is revealed in creation and salvation. How can I myself live by this? How can I convince others?

I lectured today about Sundays after Pascha (Thomas, the Myrrhbearers, the Paralytic, the Samaritan, the Blind Man)—about the meaning of these Gospel readings and the whole time of Pentecost, as an answer to the question, What is this new life of the new creation which we received with Christ in the baptismal death of the old Adam? On one hand, it is a time of joy, of communion with a new resurrected life, with a day without evening (each Sunday liturgically lasts the whole week). On the other, it is the revelation of how to live this life in this world and in its ancient time. Does this message reach anyone? I can only hope!

Yesterday, I had a long conversation with Father Paul L[azor] whom I am trying to persuade to accept the post of Dean of Students. I really do admire this man and enjoy being with him. I hope so much that it will work!

I continue yesterday's notes about pride, about self-centeredness, as source of sin, as the content of sin and its destructive, deadly strength. I thought today about the connection of sin, flesh and lust. Lust is essentially the same self-seeking, the same pride, turning the body toward itself, toward its own self-affirmation and self-satisfaction. Thus, genuine humility is impossible without victory over the flesh and consists in the end, in the spiritualization of the body. But the fight with the flesh can easily become pride, and a source of pride if it is not rooted in seeking humility, in its pursuit. Asceticism can be bliss in itself, and not in God. The signs are clear. Bright asceticism—joyful, simple, trusting. False asceticism lives, without exception, by abhorring the flesh, the world, life; it is nurtured by contempt, takes part in the devil's blasphemy about creation. For such an ascetic, sin—as well as temptation and danger—seems to be everywhere; while victory over the flesh never becomes aversion, and always leads to a "pure eye." "If your eye is not sound, your whole body will be full of darkness." (Matthew 6:23).

## Wednesday, May 4, 1977

### Early Liturgy

I received two letters—one from a Greek priest asking for permission to translate *Great Lent* into Greek. Another letter from I. Hoening, from Munich, asking for the same thing into German.

> "…Your books, concise, simple in the beautiful way of being represented by a person who knows his subject so well that he is able to offer it so clearly that it sounds simple and not complicated… Your books would fill the vast gap which is felt here…"

Why hide this sinful truth! It is always pleasant to be praised. In this case I am happy for *what* they are praising—the "simplicity." I am glad when I know that my books reach simple believers, even if there are only a few of them. Without it, I do not know of anything more useless than theology. The fact that students are "stuffed" for three years with scientific theology is, in my opinion, quite unfortunate for the Church. Some students are transformed into snobs, others into half-educated people; others into angry anti-intellectuals.

What is my calling? To lecture, to preach, *maybe* to write—as a continuation of lectures and sermons (not research).

What is *not* my calling? Spiritual guidance. "Scholarly" guidance. Spiritual conversations. Education and discussions.

Question: Not called? Or am I escaping something through indifference, laziness, lack of effort? I think and think—and it seems to me (maybe only "seems")—that, no, it is not indifference towards people. On the contrary, I am rather drawn to the person, to a personality, to its uniqueness and peculiarity—certainly much more than its social aspect. I think (rather than indifference) that I distrust the whole area of "guidance" because I am not too sure that, in general, it is needed, justified or useful. In my own life, I firmly know that I have never been guided by anyone in this specific sense. It does not mean that I was immune to influences. On the contrary, I know quite well how much I owe, and how grateful I am, to Father Sava (in my cadet years, early childhood); to Father Cyprian and other professors at St Sergius Institute in Paris; to Professor Weidle, General Rimsky-Korsakov, Metropolitan Evlogy and so many more. But never, not once in my whole life, did I feel any need to "talk" with someone about myself, about my problems, to ask for spiritual guidance, to devote attention to *me*. When such attempts were made from outside, I ran away. Many people influenced me, to whom I am eternally grateful. Their influence consisted in giving me themselves, their own, that which I admired in them. The more I admired them, the less I felt the need for a specifically personal contact, personal guidance. The truth, the vision, the image of kindness that I received from them *was* their guidance, their influence, their help; then it was up to me to *apply* it to my life, to my problems. I always considered that salvation does not consist of focusing on one's self, but in being liberated from one's self by turning to what is real, to God, the world, etc. Looking around myself, I seldom saw many convincing examples of the success of all this spiritual guidance. I saw many hysterical people—of both sexes—insatiably pouring out their souls to all kinds of *startsy* and spiritual guides without seeing much improvement. On the contrary. In Christianity itself, and, mainly, when I am with Christ, I do not see any basis for "treatment of the soul" in the sense used by the lovers of spiritual guidance. I don't know. Maybe I do not see something that is obvious to others—do not see, do not feel! Whereas I sometimes feel quite strongly that what attracts others to Church, to Christianity, is quite foreign to me. And what interests me—captures, gladdens and convinces me—is often foreign to many around me.

### *Friday, May 6, 1977*

Growing political crisis in France. A leftist victory is unavoidable. The question remains the same: Where does this unrestrained striving for the left come from? Why? For socialism, in spite of all that has come to light these last years? Nazism, fascism were enough to break the rightist myth into little pieces; but neither Lenin nor Stalin, nor the Gulag were enough to even question the "leftist dream." Yesterday, Eric Sevareid, CBS correspondent, spoke about this, about the link between the highest possible level of living reached in Western Europe and the general drift of young people to the left. "In these young people," said Sevareid, "the imagination is stronger than reality…" True. The fact is, however, that in pushing aside the world, the culture, for the sake of what they "imagine," the young have rejected (and that is their fall) any imagination, any dream; they have reduced everything to *reality*, which they supposedly know. This is the root of what is happening. There was a "Christian dream"; for the sake of that dream the best people went into "service." Let's admit it: there is no such dream any more. But nature abhors a vacuum; so there appears, on the ruins of one dream, another one. The Christian dream died when it became "bourgeois," because the spiritual essence of the bourgeoisie is precisely the rejection of a dream. To fight the left in the name of the right is as meaningless as to fight the beginning of fall or spring. Therefore, most frightening in the contemporary world is the weakness of Christianity, its own self-reduction—to the right, to the left, to religion—its romanticism and its inferiority complex. Frightening, but perhaps unavoidable, because until Christianity overcomes all these reductions, it will not resurrect.

### Saturday, May 7, 1977

All these days, I continue mulling over this growing French crisis, over the "ways" of Christianity in the world, over the only real crisis, the source of all other crises, over Christianity itself. I just received the newspaper, *The Orthodox Church,* and feel quite discouraged by the level of questions, of interest of the Church and church people. But what *is* needed? The Orthodox world scares me with its provincialism, narrow-mindedness, deadening of thought and vision, growing decline of culture. The West is collapsing. If prophecy is needed, then what? About what? I feel so tired spiritually, almost apathetic.

Yesterday, while driving to Serge and Mania's for dinner, we went down the northern part of Lexington Avenue. Stifling, stormy evening and this swarming crowd, half black, half Hispanic. A totally different world, which lives its own very special life, right next to us.

The Spence School's *Bulletin* has on its cover Liana with the reproduction of a few notes of her speech of acceptance: "Joy of living (gratitude), of learning (discovery), of being together (community)." There is something inexpressibly inspiring in her success, so full of light, so pure.

I thought again about crisis and prophecy. Prophecy must be about *Christ;* not about Jesus, not about a religious revival, not about prayer and spirituality, but about *Christ*, as He is revealed in the genuinely Catholic, genuinely Orthodox faith. It means, of course, the disclosure of the faith. Not return to the Fathers or Hellenism, but, in a way, the overcoming of the whole "shell" of tradition—the opening, the rediscovery of *Truth* itself, of life itself, as given to us in Christ. One cannot expound any more about transfiguration and the deification in some ancient Byzantine or Athonite or any other "key."

### Monday, May 9, 1977

Yesterday, during the Liturgy (week of the Samaritan woman)—such a bright, firm sense of the presence, of truth, of light. Here, in the Liturgy, is *everything,* the "Spirit and Truth" which give birth to true disciples of the Father. Here is the *reality* of the Church, and here is where one must start its prophecy in the world.

Last lecture this year: "*The Eucharist and Eschatology.*" My whole heart is there.

### Tuesday, May 10, 1977

Long discussion with N. and NN.—long hair, vegetarians, endlessly in love with themselves. Why go to church? They speak of "levels of consciousness," etc. Not an iota of modesty, no questions, only affirmations. Contempt towards everything that is not their immediate concern. I pity them so much, pity them for their inner poverty, limited vision. N. is an artist. The house is full of his paintings; helpless, provocative, endlessly unnecessary. The other is studying some strange music. Talk about identity. Not interested in diplomas or salaries. What went wrong? And where? These two boys are interesting because they are not original and accurately reflect what's in the air. Their clinical diagnosis could be that they are "children of the century." The characteristics of "the child of the century"—an inordinate narcissism, occupation with self, with the "I," excessive importance attributed to their ideas.

Conviction that this egocentricity coincides with "love," that all the others do not have conviction, that he himself somehow, *is* genuine religion.

Denial, added to total ignorance, of culture, tradition, continuity, responsibility, etc. Denial *a priori,* based on contempt. Total lack of a desire to even try to get to know what one is denying. Denial, rooted in the subconscious certainty that such knowledge would limit their freedom, i.e., narcissism. Self-admiration and, to that effect, selection of pseudo-absolutes:

vegetarianism, rejection of diplomas, of the very idea of work and salary, judgment of all those who do not recognize their pseudo-absolutes. In short, feeling of cheap superiority. Selection, as authority, of something on the margin of basic tradition, be it of culture or religion. Selection of some "wonderful little books" (rather *book*, because there is no energy to deal with more than one). "Wonderful" because it promises a short-cut to the "Truth," to perfection, to knowledge, to happiness. A sense of "mission" in relation to parents who do not understand, added to a total absence of pity, love, sympathy, etc. "We want to save them," i.e., "We love them." Total conviction that their success is guaranteed, that they will be—are—recognized as artists, thinkers, carriers of salvation. Use of words and expressions, supposedly explaining and justifying it all, some undigested shreds of psychology: "level of consciousness," etc.

It all creates something in any case impervious to Christianity, to its basic "triune intuition"—creation, fall, salvation; to its basic historical meaning. In fact, it is, of course, anti-Christianity, moreover a hidden anti-Christianity because of the constant use of the word "love."

Now if one would translate it into the language of common sense (coinciding with a spiritual evaluation), what emerges is laziness, pride, self-deception, self-justification, selfishness. As simple as that. But our culture does not accept "common-sense language"; it runs away from it as from the devil. Thus it leads to the death of human souls.

### Wednesday, May 11, 1977

Yesterday was my last lecture for this year—my thirty-first year!

Phone call this morning from a mysterious Pennsylvanian, the same who three years ago called me at 3:00 AM promising to kill me. Today he asked for my forgiveness. He said, "You told me then that God is stronger than the devil. Since then I have been thinking about it, and it helped me…" But the whole logic of our time (including that of the anti-Communists) is infused with the unconscious conviction that the devil is stronger than God, that one can destroy evil only with evil, even if it is called anti-evil. How understandable and needful becomes Christ's silence about all the things that so passionately interest us: government, religion, history, even morality. He always talks to me and about me—only that is of interest to Him. But in me, for Him, is the whole world, the whole of life, the whole of history. Therefore He saves me, not Russia, not the government, nothing else. So that any fight, any "anti"—always has and carries in it the most awful "spiritual" defeat. Christ saves the world in me. "All creation rejoices…"

*Thursday, May 12, 1977*

I leafed through and reread this journal. It seems that everything that really, genuinely interests me flows into it, never occupying me outside it. Who said—Bergson?—that every philosopher has really only one *idea* (insight? intuition?) and is really concerned only with it. Lord knows I do not consider myself a philosopher. But if I apply this appellation to myself in the most general meaning of the word—applied to anyone who thinks, be it a little—then I have to recognize that my one main idea is the idea of "reference"—*the reference of everything* to the Kingdom of God as the revelation and the content of Christianity. The "new life" starts with this relation and is fulfilled in it. The sin of many Christians is their limited horizon—the interruption, the breach of that relation, broken by idols and idolaters. The depth and the newness of that sin is that the idol is the Church, the services, theology, piety, religion itself. It sounds like a cheap paradox, but the Church is most harmed and hindered by the Church itself, Orthodoxy by Orthodoxy, Christian life by piety, etc. When Christ says that we should not call anyone on this earth "father" or "teacher," that is what He means (I think). The Church is a point of reference, so that we know to *what* everything is related, what reveals the truth about everything, what is the content of our life. As soon as the Church becomes one of the components of the world (Church, government, culture, ethics, *et tutti quanti*) as soon as the Church ceases to be a point of reference, which means to reveal and to judge by this revelation, to convert and transform, it becomes itself an idol. Here starts and here must end any teaching about the Church. This is addressed to the Church: "be the image…" But the Church has for a long time begun to live by itself, is growing into itself, not in God, is arguing about its mission, is discussing its calling—therefore reflecting this world, and not relating everything to the Kingdom of God—thus saving the world. The difficulty is this: we get our knowledge of the Kingdom of God from the Church, we get to know the Church through the knowledge of the Kingdom, received only from the Church. Here is the essential understanding of the Church as Sacrament.

*Saturday, May 14, 1977*

In Los Angeles at Father Dimitri G[isetti]. Flew in with Father Tom and C[onnie] T[arasar] for an Orthodox Institute. Lecture at the Russian parish. Long conversation with Father D. and his wife about the Church, the parish, emigration, etc. A familiar conversation, somehow continuous, wherever I go—Montreal, San Francisco, Detroit, Paris. Many years, many efforts, all the same.

What is quite obvious in such conversations, first of all, is the sad fact of a final failure. I think of all the attempts to unite in one life—moreover in one prayer, in one Liturgy—"Russian" and "American," or rather Russians and Americans. Neither of them accept it. At the seminary, N. and many with him become hysterical when they hear one hymn in Russian.

In Montreal, here, everywhere, Russians become even more irritated with any word of English. All appeals, exhortations, explanations are powerless. "We don't want it"—that's all! Deep, innate, instinctive understanding of the Church as "our own." Lack of understanding of the Church as love, readiness not only to give, but to suffer for the other. Selfishness of religion, emotional and narrow-minded.

Late at night, in bed, I read, or rather glanced through a brochure from the Valaam Monastery about the Jesus Prayer. Strange feeling—as if I were reading about some other religion. The words are the same, the same general goal—communion with God, the Kingdom, joy; but, at the same time, it is as if deep down I was reading about something different. I will have to clarify for my-self—precisely deep down—what in me is alienated by all this. Is it fear of the maximalism of that appeal, or is it a justified question? So I thought: It says be like children! Children do not know the difference between external and inter-nal—the basis on which this "appeal" is built, the whole mechanism (Theophan the Recluse). A continuous memory of God. Yes, *there* is the content and the goal of everything. *There* is life. But doesn't that memory consist of, and is it not fulfilled in the referral, the relation that I mentioned earlier? The world also, i.e., the external, is given to us to make possible the memory, to transform everything into communion with God. They write that this mechanism (of the Jesus Prayer) is impossible without love and without the fulfillment of all the other commandments of Christ. But it sounds almost like an excuse: Is not love get-ting out of one's self, a giving of self, and not an enclosure in a cage? I do not know. I always want to find time to think it all through, to think about it deep inside, with God's help. And I always postpone it. The point of departure, agreed upon, is obvious to me—"pray without ceasing" (1 Thessalonians 5:17). But as I think further about the understanding, the realization of the "without ceasing"— something becomes entangled in my mind...

### *Thursday, May 19, 1977*

*Ascension*

The best of all *kontakia:* "When Thou didst fulfill Thy dispensation for our sake..." The whole of Christianity is essentially about that "...uniting things on earth with the Heavens…" I preached about it: everything is decided, so to say, in relation to the Resurrection. Christianity can be downward or upward. The same words, the same rites, but the treasures of the heart are different.

## Tuesday, May 24, 1977

Yesterday, having come home after the unbelievable chaos of all the celebrations of Commencement, I was troubled by what is so evident in the Orthodox experience: fear to face the truth, fear of a true prophetic word, or, rather, a lot of prophetic words—about unity, about the mission of Orthodoxy in the world, etc. (Patriarch of Antioch's speech yesterday), but these words are known to be in vain, like checks without funds. It is the most frightening aspect of contemporary Orthodoxy: words do not bind, they are inconsequential, they are part of the ritual. And the reason is simple: Orthodoxy refuses to recognize the fact of the collapse and the breakup of the Orthodox world; it has decided to live in its illusion; it has turned the Church into that illusion (yesterday we heard again and again about the "Patriarch of the great city of Antioch and of all the East"); it made the Church into a nonexistent world. I feel more and more strongly that I must devote the rest of my life to trying to dispel this illusion.

Letter to L. from Natasha Solzhenitsyn, congratulating her on her Spence appointment. "…let these changes in your way of life be beneficial to Father A., I constantly and gratefully feel his presence in our life."

## Saturday, May 28, 1977

On Thursday night, L.'s installation as head of Spence. Garden party. Many people. I had to greet endless guests. Anya, Masha (my daughters) and Mania (Serge's wife) were with us. At the very end, Serge flew in from London. L. gave a wonderful speech. The whole atmosphere was quite friendly. Sunny May evening, not too warm, with a very high and very blue sky over New York roofs.

Today, memorial Liturgy, eve of Pentecost. While serving a memorial service for people I never met, I felt quite strongly the wall separating the service from the people. "A lovely service!" For non-Orthodox, it is understandable, but the same wall is there for the Orthodox: I am afraid that the search for any kind of meaning has fallen out of Russian Orthodoxy. This wall used to be hidden under a way of life, which was like ivy growing on stone. When the way of life changes, the wall becomes visible. But the conviction that an Orthodox way of life is quite sufficient is one of the reasons for the loss of Church understanding and total belonging to it.

After the Liturgy, I cleaned the church and prepared it for Pentecost. I always have such joy when preparing for a feast! How, with what theology, can one express and convey that joy?

### Sunday, May 29, 1977

*Pentecost*

One of my very favorite feasts. Beautiful services yesterday and today. "O Heavenly King…" "We have seen the True Light…" The inexpressible genius of the service, where everything is opened, all is revealed. Theology, by putting it in smooth categories, essentially annihilates it all.

Many confessions. Wonderful, sunny, cool day. God, the world, overabundant life. What else do people need? What can one thirst for? "We have seen the True Light…" Sufficient for us.

### Tuesday, May 31, 1977

Yesterday, on Monday of the Holy Spirit, I went with L. to St Tikhon's for their Memorial Day celebration. Liturgy with six bishops in the open air, crowds of people, sunny spring day in all its glory. Standing during the Liturgy in the liturgical turmoil of a hierarchical service—so familiar in its every detail—I thought again that I am *at home* in the Church, although so often in doubt about churchly details. A blue window and a flowing light out of it—and an immediate contact with the joy and peace of the Holy Spirit. As ailing as the Church is, as coarse, as worldly as church life has become; no matter how much the solely human, too human, triumphs in the Church—only through the Church can one see the light of the Kingdom of God. But one can see that light and rejoice in it only inasmuch as one denies one's self, liberates one's self from pride, from narrowness and constraint.

### Friday, June 3, 1977

Yesterday, a letter from Solzhenitsyn, begging me to find time to write about Russian history, to "correct the world's view about Russia—there is a huge Russian emigration, but no energy, no force…"

I am tempted to write him about what I think is the key to correct the West's view, etc. One has to write about:

1. The origin and the meaning of this negative Western Russian "myth." The guilt for that myth is with the Russians, at least partial guilt. Russian historiography creates "myths." The history of each nation is tragic. So, first of all, one needs to formulate that tragedy, etc. etc.

2. The meaning of the irrepressible tendency toward the Left in the world, in spite of all the Gulags, in spite of the obvious bloody crash of the leftist experience literally everywhere. Reason: The Right has no dream; it is pessimism, mistrust, passion for the *status quo*, and, in fact, it is power and profit.

## *Saturday, June 18, 1977*

Betty Friedan about women. She starts with an analysis of the women's "malaise." But all that I read so far can also be attributed to men. Her whole theory, that the woman must catch up with the man, does not seem serious to me. What seems important is not to "catch up" but to find out where this running is leading. The feminists do not seem to think about that. It's like the "we must change our life" of the Leftist movement, but how and where is never explained.

That explanation will remain impossible as long as mankind, while keeping eschatology, denies God. Here, in this paradox, is the whole absurdity of contemporary civilization, its internal dead end. Contemporary civilization speaks a religious language, and, at the same time, hates religion. To a totally meaningless—without God—world, it announces "meaning." Where would that meaning come from? The real demonic mystery of our civilization is not in the search for a meaning, but in why it so passionately searches for a meaning *without God*? Why is civilization so metaphysically foolish? The name of that foolishness is *pride*: be like gods. The Fall of Adam and Eve is happening, continuing, acting always, and the place of that continuing Fall is not an abstract nature which we inherited from Adam; the place is civilization—the tempting serpent!

Civilization opens to men endless possibilities and hides from them their ontological limits. It tells them: be like gods. It is rather amazing that every genuine "creator" is humble, but the civilization created by those creators is full of pride. A little man, climbing out of a tourist bus, looks at a painting by Michelangelo and says: that's what we are able to do, that is what we created! What made an artist humble (and every creator creates only as much as he humbles himself before his creating gift) becomes a source of pride for mankind.

## *Wednesday, June 22, 1977*

Gray, cool, rainy days. I am working on the preface to *Church, World, Mission*. Infinitely hard work that seems to give birth to more and more difficulties, so that after hours of writing and rewriting, all that is left are a few lines. To write is always real torture for me and I do not understand how others manage to write so fast, finding right away how to express their thoughts...!

## Wednesday, September 14, 1977

Yesterday, my fifty-sixth birthday. Long solemn vigil of the Cross. Spoke to my twin brother in Paris.

Started lectures. And, as always, I have the feeling that in Orthodoxy, (i.e., in Christianity) two religions coexist in many ways opposites of each other. The religion of Christ—fulfilled in the Church, and the religion of the Church, or simply religion. In the first one, everything is understood and measured by Christ. In the second, Christ is, so to say, created, defined, seen, heard only inasmuch as He is Himself submitted to a "religious feeling," to "churchliness," etc. And people—students, for instance—are divided in these categories. Someone who belongs to the second type—"religious, churchly"—can study theology for three years, but his treasure is not in the truth about Christ, but in something else. Such a person is "impenetrable."

## Monday, September 26, 1977

St John Chrysostom. Early Liturgy. Epistle: "There is no fear in love, but perfect love casts out fear..." (1 John 4:18) The opposite of love is not hate, but fear. How deep and how true. Fear is, first of all, the absence of love, or, rather, it is what grows like weeds where there is no love—therefore, *angst, angoisse,* anxiety—which all kinds of therapies try to overcome but which, in fact, is quite normal in this world; is its substance. The fall of the world is its alienation from God, who is love—hence, darkness and shadows of death.

## Tuesday, September 27, 1977

One never knows where consolation will come from—like yesterday, before my lecture, a student told me: "I almost called you last night...While reading *Of Water and the Spirit,* I understood for the first time what the Cross means..." So something that is most treasured has reached, *is* reaching.

Course about the Theotokos in Orthodox services. The inadequacy of words, the poverty and even vanity of our modern, scientific theology is exposed nowhere as obviously as here, where everything is mystery, everything is knowledge from inside, not from outside—not from evidence or data.

## Friday, September 30, 1977

Last night, while turning off my bedside lamp and being quite close to it, I was, for a second, completely blinded, could not see anything in total darkness, although there was light coming from the next room. I thought: thus is man, he saw God, he saw His light—this is why the darkness that began after his rupture with God is so total. And in that darkness, the man gropingly searches, learns to understand, to guess the meaning of a mysterious light that he still sees, still feels. Science, culture, philosophy—efforts in total darkness.

My Serge, told us yesterday that his transfer to South Africa is definitely decided.

L.'s inconsolable grief.

Conversation this morning with L. about the tension in our lives: school, seminary, everywhere; about how exhausting that tension is. I am quite convinced that the fundamental error of the contemporary man is his belief that thanks to technology— (telephone, Xerox, etc.)—he can squeeze into a given time much more than before, whereas it's really impossible. Man becomes the slave of his always growing work. There is a need for rhythm, detachment, slowness. Why can't students grasp all they're taught? Because they do not have time to become conscious of, to come back to, what they heard, to let it really enter their minds. A contemporary student registers knowledge, but does not assimilate it; therefore that knowledge does not "produce" anything. A downpour of rain is immeasurably less useful for a drought than a thin, constant drizzle! But we are all the time under a thunderous downpour—of information, reports, knowledge, discussions, etc. And all of these flow around us, never sticking to us, immediately pushed away by the next deluge.

Tomorrow, Orthodox Education Day, one of the busiest days of the year.

## Wednesday, October 5, 1977

Our service to God; service to *our* God. How easily, how unnoticeably the first becomes the second, and, while keeping a Christian appearance, becomes idolatry. "For freedom Christ has set us free; stand fast therefore, and do not submit again to a yoke of slavery" (Galatians 5:1). These words, more and more, strongly and forcefully, become for me the keys to everything in life.

## Thursday, October 13, 1977

I spent the day at my desk in New York writing radio scripts, preparing my *Church, World, Mission* for publication. After all these years of continuous strain from phone calls, meetings, conversations, I have to make an effort to get accustomed to these "empty" days in the city, this working leisure, this peace.

While rereading my articles, I realized that "theologically," I have one idea—the eschatological content of Christianity, and of the Church as the presence in *this* world of the Kingdom, of the age to come—this presence as the salvation *of* the world and not escape *from* it. The "world beyond the grave" cannot be loved, cannot be looked for, cannot be lived by. Whereas the Kingdom of God, if one tastes it, be it a little, cannot be not loved! Once you love it, you cannot avoid loving all creation, created to reveal and announce the Kingdom. This love is already transfigured. Without the Kingdom of God being both the beginning and the end, the world is a frightening and evil absurdity. But without the world, the Kingdom of God is incomprehensible, abstract and in some way absurd. "Today the fragrance of Spring, and the joy of new creation are with us...."

What a tedious torture to reread one's self. All that is written seems awful, unnecessary, totally invalid. Maybe God is being greatly merciful by not giving me time to write! But I do not want to talk about myself.

"Once in a while, there is such a sky, such a play of solar rays..." When even the greatest poets and writers seem so absolutely superfluous—unnecessary; when you feel so clearly: For what?

Today, on my way from Radio Liberty, I went to Bloomingdale's to buy a frame for my father's picture and a pair of scissors. I was almost frightened by the abundance, the bacchanalia of all kinds of goods, by the "liturgy of consumerism." Mirrors, lights, flowers and crowds of shoppers. After five minutes, one feels like having eaten too much of something heavy and one longs to have some fresh air.

On a shelf over my desk I arranged the pictures of Bishop Vladimir (who ordained me); Father Cyprian (professor of Liturgics, friend); in a beautiful blooming garden, my father—our last picture together, at the Schmemann gravesite, where he is buried now, my father and his five sisters. When I die, nobody will know any longer what huge layers of my life are reflected in these pictures. And a picture of Solzhenitsyn and me, the day of his confession and communion in Zurich.

### Wednesday, October 19, 1977

Two very full days at the seminary with the usual problems. First year students want to gather together to pray, to study the Gospel, etc. Religious excitement, maximalism. Older students point to them as being heretics. All of this is quite innocuous, but has to be seriously talked about, we have to hold a meeting, etc. Each year the same thing happens—and I always think that essentially, "seminary," i.e., the very idea and principle of a seminary (*as inherited from the*

*West*), is ambiguous. It is precisely in seminaries that developed, on the one hand, the clericalization of theology, and, on the other, the religious fixation of Christianity.

Dinner yesterday with two couples—one a lawyer, one a doctor—L.'s trustees. A certain image of America, a specific American mixture of good nature, idealism, materialism, activism, psychological "keep smiling." Pleasantly at ease with them, but one realizes why, as soon as a sort of superficial harmony is broken, a frightening collapse occurs (depression), because in this mixture there is no room for genuine grief, tragedy, and, perhaps, genuine joy. The American obsession with psychotherapy comes from that—from the necessity to maintain this equilibrium, from a subconscious fear that it might break down, and then, right away—an abyss. And the essence, the function of therapy is that it explains and explains and explains that essentially there is not, and cannot be, grief, tragedy, etc., but there is only some defect in the mechanism, like a garage whose only importance is to make a car run well.

Religion can be, and much too often is, an "exercise in demythologizing." In a civilization without God and without religion, speculation on reduction becomes not a vice, not a defect, but the norm, the essence. In that sense, whoever defined Sartre (who was it?) as a fundamentally contemporary man—was right.

Homosexuality. The question is not at all whether it is natural or unnatural, since this question is generally inapplicable to fallen nature, in which—and this is the point—everything is distorted, everything, in a sense, has become unnatural. Is it natural for man to devote himself totally to money or Russia or anything else? Created to give himself to God, man perverts his nature, his essence, by giving himself to some other thing, by transforming this "other" thing into an idol. Therefore, the point is not in making homosexuals "normal," or liberating them by agreeing that theirs is a different "life style." The point is, must be, in the acceptance by a homosexual, as well as by any other human being, of a total appeal, and of an appeal to integrity, addressed by God to each man. Homosexuality is a manifestation of the "thorn in the flesh" which tortures in various ways, but tortures every one. In the fallen world nothing can be "normalized," but everything can be saved.

## Saturday, October 22, 1977

Crestwood. Sunshine. Golden trees. Peace. Just had a call from my brother Andrei. Mother is in the hospital, very weak.

Putting my desk in order before going to Montreal for a week for the Church Sobor—the All-American Council.

## Saturday, October 29, 1977

I am home after five days at the Council in Montreal. I have the feeling that I am coming down from a mountain, so strong was the feeling of a *Presence* at the Sobor.

*The Church*—as much as we are given to see it and experience its presence in this world. Wonderful Liturgies every morning, with hundreds of communicants. The transfiguration of the lay people (remembering the Sobors in the Fifties), a feeling of the fundamental strength of life. In the rare moments when I managed to pop out of the hotel, radiant light of late fall, like a blessing flowing from on high. I cannot describe the details, but the active presence of the Holy Spirit was evident, most of all in the election of Bishop Theodosius as Metropolitan* by the bishops. The wisdom of the Church, of the protective, rather than prophetic function of bishops; wisdom of acceptance by the Church. Really—a living experience of the Church. Quite difficult, therefore, to come back and get busy with daily affairs.

## Wednesday, November 2, 1977

Yesterday I had lunch with Andrew Tregubov,** who works with Solzhenitsyn: archives, preparation of a canonical text of S.'s work. T.'s analysis seems to me quite sober and intuitive. The tense, super-human work of S. is, before anything else, salvation from himself. His instinctive search for isolation, estrangement, separation from any community are elements, thinks A.T., of real psychosis. Solzhenitsyn's Russia is his idol, his strain and psychosis.

I wrote yesterday to Father J[ames] M[orton], dean of the Cathedral of St John the Divine and a great friend, asking him to remove my name from the list of honorary canons of his cathedral. On that list: women, rabbis and Zen Buddhists; highly respectable, but not a place for me. I hope that it will not reflect on our friendship. I don't know, but in my conscience, I cannot be part of that group.

Yesterday, meeting with all students about the Sobor. Delighted by their understanding, interest, participation. Total joy from the group of our young ones: Father Tom, Father Paul, J[ohn] Erickson,*** David D[rillock].

Phone call from Paris: mother still in the hospital, very weak. She will be

---

* Theodosius, Metropolitan—Primate of the OCA, 1977–present. President and alumnus of St Vladimir's Seminary.

** Tregubov, Father Andrew—Graduate of St Vladimir's Seminary and Rector of Holy Trinity Church, Claremont, NH.

***Erickson, John—Lecturer in Church History and Canon Law at St Vladimir's Seminary. Subsequently appointed Professor, 1973–present.

transferred for one or two months to a convalescent home. Maybe it is not the end yet. But, clearly, life is finished and existence is starting. Deep down, I constantly "carry" her in my conscience.

### Thursday, November 3, 1977

Lunch in the city yesterday with N. He complains about his heart, his diabetes; pitiful beginning of the end. I thought about the frightening burden of homosexuality: Proust, Gide, Julien Green, etc. So many people all around are saying: this burden, this trauma, this neurosis comes from being rejected as outcasts by society, from the necessity to hide, to lie, etc. It is probably partly true. But only partly—and it's not what really matters. Gide, for example, overcame this denial and forced people to accept him. I think what matters most is the sense of a dead end, of insatiable thirst which cannot be transformed into life. At the end, always, there is not only a wall but a mirror. In the fallen world, everything strictly sexual is ugly, distorted, base. In a "normal" human being, there is at least the possibility of transforming the ugliness and thus eliminating it. For homosexuals, this possibility, this promise, this appeal, this door—do not exist!

But if homosexuality is a deviation, a distortion, where does it come from, how does it happen and why can't it be changed? I do not know any scientific theories, but I suppose that they all reduce the problem to biology, or society, i.e., to external causes. It seems to me that the root is spiritual: it is the essential ambiguity of *everything* in the fallen world. One abnormality generates another in this world of crooked mirrors—in this case, the fall of the family, the fall of the very image of sex, i.e., of relations between man and woman. The fall, also, of motherhood, the fall, finally, of love itself in its bodily and, therefore, sexual expression. On one level, homosexuality is a mixture of fear and pride; on another, of eros and auto-eroticism. It is not by chance that a common trait of homosexuals is their egocentricity (not necessarily selfishness), an excessive concern about self, even if this egocentricity is combined with a boundless curiosity and openness to life (as was the case with Gide).

### Saturday, November 5, 1977

In connection with St Vladimir's Women's Conference, I talked with L. yesterday about the feminine question in the Church. I do not have in my head, in my mind, any clarity nor conviction, and what I feel does not fit into words, into a clear outline. I feel, however, that there is, close by, in the Church, a simple, light and really self-evident Truth, true to the spirit, the logos and faith. How can one see and express it?

*Monday, November 7, 1977*

Yesterday, Sunday (except for a quick trip to Wappingers to see Anya and the children—mainly to enjoy a gray November day, bare trees, rust and the peace of the fall)—I spent almost the whole afternoon working on a regular lecture on Mariology—this time on Dormition. How utterly comforting and spiritually useful is this work, as if the light and the power of that feast were flowing into my heart.

*Tuesday, November 8, 1977*

Second day of pouring rain. Today the Liturgy of Michael the Archangel. Old calendar, it is the day of St Dimitri of Thessalonika, my father's saint's day and the anniversary of the death of General Rimsky-Korsakov, the director of the Cadets' School where I spent many years of my childhood, a man who opened for me the whole world of poetry in general, and of Russian poetry in particular. I vividly remember the handwritten notebooks he put together by himself—actually an anthology of Russian poetry. If I hadn't met him when I was nine, if I hadn't been his favorite student (because of poetry) in those formative years, from 9 to 14, I think my life would have taken a different course. With the opening to poetry began a liberation of the spirit, an intuition of something "other." The death of the general was my first encounter with death, since I hardly remember my sister Elena's death, when I was five.

*Thursday, November 10, 1977*

Had lunch yesterday with my son Serge in the United Nations' restaurant. A mixed crowd of delegates, all performing, so to say, some ritual, and all part of that ritual. Huge halls, like temples, flooded with sunshine. A strange way of walking up and down with each other, politely conversing. All dressed up. And I thought that however weak and inflated is the United Nations, as a group these delegates are useful and needed and justified, precisely as a ritual. A ritual performed by us in a sense that defies us. A ritual incarnates a dream, a vision, an ideal; all that probably cannot be fully incarnated.

At the entrance, in the sun, stood four Soviet citizens—not diplomats, but, as it seemed, observers, or guards, or agents. I don't know. But looking at them I was awed: scary faces with prominent cheek bones, arrogant, and, at the same time, dead eyes. The system breeding such anthropoids is demonic.

Both magazines—*l'Express* and *Nouvel Observateur*—are dedicated this week to the Sixtieth Anniversary of the October Revolution in Russia. What week to the Sixtieth Anniversary of the October Revolution in Russia. What is the most impressive in this horrible event is how long, despite everything, the world passionately and enthusiastically believed in it. I think that in the whole history of the world, there was nothing either more tragic or more funny than this belief, this decision to believe, this tense self-blinding. It is the proof, however, that in this world only a dream is that strong and that effective. If the divine dream in man is dying, he rushes into a diabolical dream. That is why one can fight a diabolical dream, a diabolical deception *only* with the *divine* dream, the dream of God. But this dream has disappeared in the wind, it has lost its savor in historical Christianity, it has turned into piety, into a religious way of life, a frightened curiosity about "eternal life," etc. This degenerating Communism continues to talk over and over about revolution, changing. But Christianity has not been true even to its essence as "Good News"—the Kingdom of God is near, seek first the Kingdom of God. All this is common knowledge; one gets tired of repeating it; however, here and only here, in this betrayal of eschatology, is the cause of the historical breakdown of Christianity! The world's fire, fanned by a very dull Communism (the "masses" etc.)—what a terrible judgment of Christianity!

### Thursday, November 17, 1977

Had dinner yesterday with Metropolitan Theodosius, Father Daniel [Hubiak] and Father Leonid [Kishkovsky*] near Syosset. A feeling of mutual trust, so precious and rare in the Church, of brotherhood, simplicity. Thank God the Metropolitan is giving us so much hope.

### Tuesday, December 6, 1977

Just came back from Paris. Spent ten days there. I flew with my daughter, Anya, on Icelandic Airline, arrived in Luxembourg after stopping in Iceland. Andrei met us in Luxembourg and for five hours we drove to Paris under pouring rain. I remember these five hours through fields and little French villages as pure happiness. Anya spent all these days with me; L. came separately on Air France and left after just a few days. To have Anya with me was my main joy during these Paris days. I walked with her all over Paris, went to l'Etang la Ville where I spent the first six years of my married life. Her clearness, modesty, wholeness are truly touching—I can't find a word that would describe it better!

* Kishkovksy, Father Leonid—Rector of Our Lady of Kazan Church in Sea Cliff, NY. Currently the Ecumenical Officer of the OCA.

## Wednesday, December 7, 1977

On Saturday and Sunday (November 26 and 27) wedding celebrations of my niece and goddaughter Elena, Andrei's daughter. At the reception at the Hotel Georges V, how many friends and old acquaintances!—sometimes hard to recognize.

Daily visits to mother. Walks. Visits. And the whole time, dry frosty days, sunshine and a wonderful blue sky. It seems to me that I have enjoyed Paris more than ever, enjoyed a physical contact with Paris during this trip. On Wednesday, the 30th of November (my ordination thirty-one years ago) I served at St Sergius, then a festive dinner with the Institute's professors. Sometimes I had a feeling of total alienation and sometimes a very powerful feeling of unmoving time ("temps immobile").

## Saturday, December 10, 1977

Today the sky is blue and everything is lighted by a frosty pale sun.

I can't work or concentrate on anything, probably because of my recent trip to Paris, where, as it happens every time, the past welled up in me, the past not of events, but of a child's vision of life, its perception, a perception which was the beginning of everything in me.

I remember my visit with Anya to the Lyceé Carnot (my school)—nothing, absolutely nothing has changed; a rather decrepit school yard surrounded and darkened by two stories of classrooms. How often did I dream in this yard, in these classrooms. What a double life I was leading when I felt—precisely then, with extraordinary force and reality—that "all is elsewhere" ("*tout est ailleurs*"). A late night walk with Anya in the gardens of the Palais Royal and its rows of trees; in the Tuileries garden lit up by the setting sun—a very cold frosty night. Paris is always, for me, the light of those years when my soul was truly being born, my true self—which cannot be expressed even to myself, but which is present everywhere. Because of that presence, I always feel quite strongly the sadness and the happiness of life. When I go to Paris, I truly meet myself again; I meet the image of myself as a wondering child.

Maybe I am just under stress, tired and exhausted by the pressure of life.

I just reread what I wrote—and I think that the Russian poet Khodasevich expressed it better than anyone:

Amidst the cares of every day
I live—and my soul, under a heavy bushel,
By some fiery miracle,

Is alive in spite of me.
And often, hurrying to the streetcar,
Or over a book bending my head,
Suddenly I hear a grumbling fire—
And I close my eyes.

## Tuesday, December 13, 1977

Day of St Herman of Alaska. Early Liturgy which I served with my sons-in-law—Father Tom [Hopko] and Father John [Tkachuk]. Father Alexis Vinogradov, my niece's husband, was late and took communion at the altar. Feeling—no, not of pride—but of grateful joy.

Double personality! I always feel it, always (or almost always) see things from outside. Like yesterday's meeting at the seminary. I was at the same time participant and observer, almost spectator. While observing, I also see myself from outside, so to speak, and I see the "me" that is observing and *not* participating in the meeting, but looking at the window and beyond it, to bare trees, winter dusk and the silence of the huge park.

## Thursday, December 15, 1977

Last evening, Christmas concert at L.'s Spence School. While looking at these singing girls, I thought:

1. There are no girls who are not good looking, when they give themselves, be it in a choir, to something higher and better.

2. Every human face is actually beautiful, and each one reveals, proves the existence of God.

3. There is in America, in Americans, an inherent goodness, a desire that all would be well, an ability to give of themselves.

After yesterday's storm and downpour, sunshine again and pure blue sky. The semester is finished. On Sunday—Serge and his family leave for South Africa.

## Friday, December 16, 1977

Yesterday, the last meeting of the Board of Trustees this year. How much the church has changed these past years! An atmosphere of service, benevolence, a genuine desire to help the seminary. How far we have come from the epoch when plebeian anger and pettiness, envy and intrigues reigned.

Christianity requires, absolutely requires, simplicity; it requires a "clear eye," a "seeing love." Christianity is distorted everywhere—where there is strain, where it relies on howling and wailing. Our times are saturated with it; our whole civilization is permeated with it to an impossible degree. Man has lost the ability to admire, to wonder, and everything has become for him a problem. One must leave, come out of these problems; this means purifying one's sight, purifying the heart from all unhealthy excitement.

### Monday, December 19, 1977

Yesterday, saw Serge and Mania with their children off to South Africa—a very difficult moment, especially for L.

Late at night, phone call from Father Leonid. Professor Arseniev has died. He called me three days ago, and I thought then that it was his last call—so weak was his voice!

### Tuesday, December 20, 1977

Memorial service for Professor Arseniev in a Synodal Church in Sea Cliff. A whole group of us American priests, headed by the Metropolitan. Quite surprisingly, I was asked by the priest to say a few words at the end of the service.

### Saturday, December 24, 1977

Christmas Eve. Just came back after a long service. Beautiful sunny day. Masha and her family are with us these days.

Festive peace. Tomorrow, after our Christmas reception, we leave for New Orleans for a few days.

### Friday, December 30, 1977

Three days in New Orleans, in the Hotel St Louis in the center of the French Quarter. A great number of artificial tourist attractions, jazz, dancing, bars, taverns. But beautiful old streets with wrought iron fences and balconies. A huge cathedral. We drove along the Mississippi River to spacious old plantations. Visited old cemeteries where the graves are above ground because of the swampy soil. Left there a piece of my heart, as if I somehow became connected.

Two contradictory experiences in such cities: time flying on one hand; unmoving time ("temps immobile") on the other. Little side streets next to the cathedral, huge, green, oak trees, silence, presence, victory over chaos.

I started reading Rollo May's *The Meaning of Anxiety.* I really want to understand the whole world of psychotherapy which obsesses so many people nowadays. I *honestly* want to verify my instinctive aversion, my conviction that it is incompatible with Christianity, with faith. I remember my only crisis of 1935-36 (when I was 14-15). Was it anxiety? And if it was, what cured it? In any case, it was not psychotherapy, which pushes people to "talk it out," whereas for months, with incredible effort, I did not show anything to anybody, never discussed it. Everything was hidden. Even now I see it this way: God left me, God came back! Sometimes I have the feeling that I *really* prayed only then. Since then, I have not had such a crisis. Today I had a frightening, incomprehensible dream: I am eating, and behind the window are three gallows, and from each one, one by one, all three people fall down. One of them is crawling threateningly. What is it? From where? But when I woke up, no trace was left, no fear. Sun on roofs, sun in an empty apartment, and, in everything, the presence, and from that presence—joy of life. Sometimes (often) I think that maybe I am a very cold, indifferent and superficial man who only wants peace. Is it wrong to want peace and quiet? Is it wrong to have an inner aversion to "religious" conversations, to "religious" fuss, to the organization of "religious life"? At the same time, aversion to any spiritualism, Buddhism, to departure from history. I would like so much to honestly, simply, clearly express what is my faith—but I find it impossible to do so! First of all, it is not clear to me, in my mind and conscience. One thing seems clear: the basic coordinates of this faith are on the one hand, an acute love for the world, for all that is given (nature, city, history, culture); on the other, the conviction, as acute and as evident, that this love itself is directed at "the other" (the "all is elsewhere") that this world reveals. In this revelation is the world's essence, calling, beauty. But these are just coordinates, and the main and only question remains: what to do, how to live *in* the world—*with* God and *in* God—*with* the world, i.e., *with love?* What is the essence of man's creativity? For with God, man creates his life and thus his Kingdom of God.

### Saturday, December 31, 1977

Father Tom gave me a circular Christmas letter from some Trappist in Massachusetts. In his monastery, all traditions meet (West, East, Buddhism), all rites, all experiences. Sounds rather barbarian. It is as if traditions were some sort of clothing. Dress as a Buddhist—and right away an "experience." This cheap, murky wave of spirituality, this petty syncretism, these exclamation marks—upset me. "I celebrate once a week the Divine Liturgy in the rite of Chrysostom in the joy..." Shamelessness of this contemporary religion. "Culture cannot be improvised," notes Julien Green. *Nor can religion.* In the midst of all the excitement where one has to live, one literally loses courage.

183

One wants to leave. A cup of coffee and a hamburger in a simple diner are more genuine, more real, than all this religious chatter. As the sacrament is impossible without bread, wine and water, so religion requires peace, true daily peace. Without it, religion becomes a neurosis, a self-deception, a delusion.

Last day of the year. How quickly time runs!

# CHAPTER VI

# 1978

∾

## Tuesday, January 3, 1978

The New Year met us with frost, snow, sun. All these days at home, lazy and idle—which is torturing my conscience.

## Wednesday, January 11, 1978

I finished Bishop John [Shahovskoy's*] book, *Biography of Youth*. Professor [Konstantin] Mochulsky wrote the author a letter, which Bishop John quotes:

> …You are telling me that about certain things one cannot speak simply and clearly. I will answer you: in that case, I would prefer not to say anything out loud. Hints and reticence—I don't like. Complexity always seems to me arbitrary, but simplicity is the most difficult achievement and its lack is either a failure or a mistake. The more I read your letter, the more I am perplexed. Where does this complex tangled phraseology come from? Why don't you fight it? Why do you enjoy what you yourself call your confused way of speaking and thinking? Symbolism is essential as a step, but one can not stop there. A genuine mystical experience does not know symbols because it is most purely and fully *real*. There are no two worlds for the believer; there is only one world—in God—and it is simple and real. Why speak in riddles? Also in the style of German idealistic philosophy?

My dear Konstantin Vasilievich! For these lines I want to kiss his hand! But he is not with us a long time now, and now, having read his letter, I recall him so clearly—at the St Sergius Institute, at Mother Maria's on rue Lourmel, small, fragile, joyous…

* John (Shahovskoy), Archbishop, †1989—Member of the faculty during the early years of St Vladimir's Seminary and Bishop of the Diocese of the West (OCA).

## Saturday, January 21, 1978

At home, in New York. The city is covered with snow. No traffic whatsoever and children everywhere on skis and sleds in the middle of the street. A feast in the air.

I just went outside to dig out our car. On my way back, across from our apartment, I saw police cars, an ambulance, a big crowd. A hold-up: they carry out an old man, the owner of the store, covered with blood, with a shot through his face. And the feast of a sunny snow day grows dark in the horror of senseless cruelty and brutality!

## Wednesday, January 25, 1978

Dinner yesterday with Metropolitan Theodosius at Metropolitan Philip's residence in Englewood. Very friendly and decorous.

Snow, rain, thaw. Huge puddles, a deluge! It is hard to drive. I am always surprised how simple things, such as weather for example, reduce to nothing our fragile well-being, the polished life which we have carefully organized for ourselves.

## Friday, January 27, 1978

First lecture of the semester and immediately a feeling of being back to "normal," doing my primary duty.

I just accompanied Metropolitan Theodosius to Archbishop Iakovos. He says that in Constantinople there are only 5,000-7,000 Greeks left. Will we be witnesses to the end of Constantinople? The myth of Constantinople, the myth of some Patriarchates, the myth of Mount Athos, of the Holy Land? Everybody is betting on "spirituality," but what is most important for *Christianity*—the *Church*—is dying. The *spiritual* people are the ones who shake the foundations of the Church. They rejected the Eucharist as the Sacrament of the Church ("we are not worthy!"). They reduced the Church to religion, and religion to themselves. And the world remains without Church, or rather with some of its remnants—national, ethnic, ritual, etc.

Letter from Mother. She is moving to a nursing home in Cormeilles en Parisis.

## Friday, February 10, 1978

### Cairo

First morning in Cairo. I have not seen anything yet except the hotel. Yesterday I spent five hours in Rome between flights. After New York's snow drifts, a gentle, cool, sunny day, in a light haze. Everything is genuinely radiant. I arrived at about 11:00 AM. at St Peter's from there started wandering. Over the Tiber by the Ponte degli Angeli to my beloved Piazza Navona, then little streets to Piazza di Spagna. Had lunch in a dark little tavern. And further, all on foot across the city, back to the station. Stood by the Forum of Trajan, the Aventine Hill. Like in a fairy tale: suddenly, out of nowhere, five hours in Rome.

Very ugly surroundings of Rome—everything that is not the past is rather awful! Unrestrained growth of some cancer, something deadly. Suddenly, in the middle of that ugliness—a huge old church, which seems tear-stained, hopelessly unnecessary in its decaying beauty. The faces of old or older people—a stamp of humanness, of human sadness, concern. Noisy crowds of young people. On Piazza Navona, two of these *"homunculi" demand*—don't ask, but *demand*—a hundred liras.

At 10:00 PM arrival in Cairo. All around—ragged, slovenly soldiers with light machine guns. In the air, a mixture of uneasiness and carelessness. The impression is that if somebody would suddenly be caught and shot in the middle of the crowd, it would be in the order of things. Rather chaotic, dirty, some new and decaying buildings. All quite poor—the hotel, the furniture, the sheets. But the Arab waiters are cordial and friendly.

I just went out for a walk while waiting for my Coptic hosts. How to describe it? A depressing filth, dust, poverty. Half the people (hurrying somewhere in an unending flow) in burnooses, the other half clothed in poor and cheap western outfits. How very poor! In the shop windows, pitiful, tasteless West in the midst of the poverty-stricken East. Some rickety old buses rush with piles of people. But everything is lit up by the sun. In Cairo, I am told by the Coptic Bishop Samuel, who met me, there are eight million inhabitants. Of course they can be fed only by Western technology. But while feeding them, it kills their soul, transforms them into this shapeless swarming crowd—and wants them to be a democracy!

I have a strange feeling that, sooner or later, all of this is bound to start destroying the West as the deceived dream. The old immobile East is dying—simply because of its quantity. It can be replaced, in the minds of people, only by utopia. And utopia is deception. Frightening!

How absurd, after a ten-minute walk around Cairo, seem the discourses of American liberals about the "poor" and the "minorities" in America, and of French Leftists about an "unbearable" life and the urgent necessity to change it!

If socialism were not a faith turned to itself as if it were the Kingdom of God, it could be a solution. The truth of socialism is its hatred of "profit" as the main motive force of life. The falsehood is the idea of collective profit, the materialistic aspect of the ultimate goal, its alienation from eternity.

## Saturday, February 11, 1978

Immersion yesterday and today in a totally unknown (to me) world of Coptic Christianity. Right away I must express my main impression: it is edifying and it is alive. I remember my trip to the Middle East in 1971 and my impression of something outlived, nominal, dying, chained to the past—the existence of a non-existent world. Lifeless Hierarchs. Fear. Lies. Corruption.

And then, last year in Los Angeles, I met His Holiness Pope Shenouda III, the Patriarch of the Coptic Church. Right away—an impression of genuine life, spiritual openness. And now, in Cairo, I am meeting the very Coptic reality. There are about seven million Copts in Egypt! And this church, despite persecutions (Byzantine, Arab, Turkish), despite the surrounding sea of Islam, despite its isolation and loneliness, and the whole spiritual and political chaos of the Middle East, is revived and alive!

In the morning, a long reception at the Patriarch's residence. Right away, we talk about the essential—the Church, ways to unify, mission, Africa, youth. Visit to the grandiose new cathedral, the seminary, the press, the half-built patriarchal palace. A great deal is rather tasteless, due to centuries of ghetto existence.

In the evening, I witnessed something truly amazing. In the packed cathedral, seven thousand people listen—as they do every Friday—to the Patriarch. In front of him, on a little table, hundreds of little pieces of paper with questions. He chooses five or six and answers them so simply, and at the same time so deeply (about the meaning of "Lord have mercy"; about the death of a mother—"where is she now?"; about a fifteen-year-old girl—"should she go to a monastery now?"; about somebody who promised to work in the church school if he passed his exam and has not kept his promise, etc.). Then he lectures about the temptations of Christ in the desert, and again—genuine, lively, pastoral, nurturing. Where in the Orthodox world can one see and experience this, a patriarch with the people, in a live dialogue?

In the afternoon, a visit to the pyramids. I am glad that I went; one can not visit Cairo and not see them. Somehow, they did not impress me. In my mind, I understand why they are interesting, grandiose, of a special beauty. But for me it is so dead; not mine; it is the past, torn away for tourists. Only the desert is alive and genuine, whereas the pyramids and the Sphinx are dead memorials to a dead pride.

But then today I had an extraordinary day: a visit in the desert to three monasteries with an uninterrupted tradition from Anthony the Great, Makarios, etc. In one of them is the sarcophagus of Ephrem of Syria. And the most amazing, of course, is how very much alive it all is: Real monks! In my whole life, I have seen only imitations, only playing at monastic life, false, stylized; and mostly unrestrained idle talk about monasticism and spirituality. And here are *they*, in a *real* desert. A real, heroic feat.

So many young monks. No advertisements, no brochures about spirituality. Nobody knows anything about them and they do not mind it. I am simply stunned. I have a thousand questions, and I will have to gradually start sorting it all out. Right now, this trip to the desert remains in my memory as something radiant.

### *Sunday, February 12, 1978*

In the morning—Old Cairo. Liturgy in the Coptic Church. The impression is somewhat confused. On the one hand, it is undoubtedly Alexandrian—everything is under cover, seen only through covers. Tiny royal doors, and there, at the altar, the priest performs something belonging to another world. He performs very slowly, accompanied by one very long, inimitable, prayerful melody. On the other hand, a refreshing absence of any Byzantinism.

The Coptic block in Old Cairo is a ghetto, with hidden entrances to the church. One feels a habit of hiding, of always being suspected, of living inside one's self. The women's monastery is peaceful, sunny, joyful.

All around is Old Cairo, which is impossible to describe. It is swarming with people, endlessly lively, but also congealed in this swarming and unchanging chaos.

After dinner, a long walk under a very warm sun. The filth, the noise, the overcrowded streets are difficult to describe. And poverty, terrible poverty. Everyone is selling something, but somehow hopelessly, apathetically. They might buy it, they might not. No projection into the future (improve one's way of life), for there is no hope. Fatalism: of usual poverty? of Islam? Survive one more day, sit down, smoke, chat a bit. The poverty of their clothes! Everywhere some old Arabs squat on the ground as in some kind of stupor. But if one asks directions, they are quite friendly.

A different, completely different world. One wonders: should one try to change them to a Western, civilized way of life? If they remain as they are, they will die of hunger.

No future—for Arabs, for Copts. Reality consists of trying to survive.

One can understand why people prefer to join a monastery. The world is survival. How far are we from "cosmic universe," "eschatology," "action," "mission"... I am thinking about Islam, about its fateful significance in history in general, in the history of Christianity in particular.

### Monday, February 13, 1978

Last evening, last sunset in Cairo. And as usual, in my heart a haze of sadness. When I arrive, I count the days until my departure. And then, it is as if all of it—the city with its indescribable atmosphere, the people, the light—become part of the heart. I would not like to live here. I do not like the East. Here I feel quite strongly that the West is my native land, my air. Rome, not to mention Paris, are closer to me than Athens, Istanbul, Palestine or, now, Cairo and Egypt. I do not believe in Eastern wisdom, supposedly inaccessible to the West. But here I feel a connection with something important and deep. Maybe it's the combination of endless antiquity with a childlike perception of "now," which is quite absent in the Western man. Time exists here. Here man is enslaved from outside, but freer inside. In the West, man is free, but enslaved by an always pressing concern inside. Here—it is politically frightening, but not so with people. In the West, there is political security, but people are fragmented, lonely and not at ease with each other. I am afraid that these are hurried generalizations. I don't know...maybe. But I have the feeling that a beggarly old woman in black rags is not isolated—as in the West—from other people. She remains a member, a part of society. In the West, where society is not organic (especially in America), everybody makes inhuman efforts to remain on the surface, not to drown. Money is needed, it means success; money is success!

But what will happen to the East, which already gave in to the West? Today I visited a bourgeois milieu—doctors, professors; one feels how much they are already a Western caricature.

Tomorrow I fly to Paris.

### Thursday, February 23, 1978

Returned to New York last Friday after two and a half days in Paris. Mother is in a nursing home—such piercing sadness and pity, although objectively she is well. Saw my brother Andrei, Nikita Struve and his wife on the Place du Pantheon. The Tuileries under snow. The usual, necessary outing from my life, immersion in a kind of other existence. Here, immersion in boiling activity.

Heard the news of the death of my very good friend V. S. Varshavsky in France.

*Monday, February 27, 1978*

All these days since last Thursday I "live" with Varshavsky. I reread his two books: *Expectations* and *The Insignificant Generation* (first emigration). Since he left for Europe, we saw each other once a year; we did not correspond, but I feel his death as a real loss. Yesterday I was thinking that I have very *few friends*, but V. was undoubtedly one of them, somebody who was part of my life. In my mind I am composing an article about him for the *Vestnik*. While rereading his *Expectations*, I was thinking what a good book it is, but can I demonstrate and prove this? "I can't play in a world where everybody is cheating!" (Who said it?) But this is Varshavsky, full defenseless honesty, "strength nurtured in weakness." Nothing artificial, no loud cries, no self-glorification.

L. left for three days for Charleston, South Carolina, and right away I feel lonely, almost depressed. Last evening I couldn't work.

On Saturday evening, in church, the choir sang "By the waters of Babylon…" Does one really *hear* that sigh? There is so much mistrust, concentration on one's own, so much murky and pitiful "religion."

I am constantly trying to solve a question in my heart: I want to leave. Is it escape from the field of battle, or, on the contrary, a step that I can't take out of cowardice?

How well I felt these days with Varshavsky!

*Sunday, March 5, 1978*

One thing is clear to me: Only failure is beautiful in this world, only poverty, pity, compassion, vulnerability. "The lot of the poor   vicissitudes of fate" and also no protection—children. Everything that is fat, loud, successful is awful. The most talented symbol of Dostoevsky: "the little tear of a child." It is never a part of the music of the Right, and maybe generated the music of the Left!

The Right is incompatible with today's Gospel: "…sick and in prison and you did not visit Me…"(Mathew 25:43). The Left is incompatible with the prayer of thanks: "Great are You, O Lord…"

*Thursday, March 9, 1978*

All these days, I feel depressed, deeply unhappy with myself. What am I really doing in life? Actually, I am sarcastically grumbling about all those who don't understand, who don't do what they should. But I myself don't do "what I should." I live in a continuous daydream, but passive, not active.

Neither prayer, nor heroism. Search for peace. Laziness...When I feel this, as I do these days, I don't want to write because of the obvious falsehood of my life. "Arise, why are you sleeping?" Because really, "the end is near...!"

### Thursday, March 16, 1978

First Presanctified Liturgy after three days of confessions and services. All is going quite well and during the services several times I felt the presence of a total "fullness," impossible to express or explain, but the only one that is convincing.

Failure of the Left in France, in spite of all the polls, all the predictions.

Israeli attack on Lebanon.

How insane all this seems when one is in the depth of the prayers of a Presanctified Liturgy! But somehow these prayers are not effective; they have no effect on those who safeguard them in the world. These days, I feel quite strongly that the expressions in the Gospel, "this world," "not of this world," are quite concrete. I write: "are not effective"—they really are not effective, inasmuch as the Church and Christians live and act according to the logic of "this world." So everything that is said according to the logic—"not of this world"—is completely neutralized. This is true, in one's personal life and in the history of the Church. As long as the Church becomes one of the factors, one of the parts of "this world" (politics, nationalism, even religion), its message, at best, does not ring true, and at worst, sounds like a deception. What is "this world?" Before anything else, a reckoning and *faith in this reckoning*, and this is always "the logic of power."

### Monday, April 10, 1978

Sad parish troubles: in Montreal, Father John T[kachuk]; in New York City, Father Alexis V[inogradov]; in Sea Cliff, Father Leonid K[ishkovsky]. The same everywhere—a mean, irrational hatred by Russians, not only of the English language in church—a single word in English!—but of the very fact that they are called somewhere, asked to reconsider, asked to understand... It is a frightening self-infatuation. The denial of any reason, logos, analysis.

Father D[mitry] G[rigorieff], in Washington, tells me about Russia, where he goes quite often. The same mean nationalism, anti-Semitism. Always "we," "ours," or abuse and humiliation. "We repent better than anyone else..." "We have a spiritual revival, purification through suffering." In reality, what is crawling out of there is quite awful. Sometimes, I confess, listening to the tales of Fathers John, Alexis, Leonid and others about their parish meetings, about screams such as "where it concerns nationalism, our being Russian, there ends our love and patience!" (verbatim), I feel like turning my back to it all…!

The bishops' advice to these young fathers: "slowly, lovingly, gradually…"

I feel no desire to fight. (Where? In the Russian daily paper?), only a desire to leave as far as possible. Not out of cowardice, but out of a conviction that it is impossible to even hint at what would be the goal of such a fight. To hint at the joy—mysterious, never loud; at the beauty and humility—secret, never showy; at the goodness, never extolling itself.

"Come to Me…and I will give you peace"—How can this be reconciled with a never ending, thunderous "_we_ declare, _we_ demand, _we_ protest…"

As a result, I feel weak, lazy, undisciplined—I realize that, "who am I to talk?" I feel a kind of fear when faced with activism (of the young at the seminary) who passionately want to be pastors, to guide. It always seems to me that it's not needed—for if man would _see_ what I call joy, or if man would simply love Christ—just a little, would come to Him, nothing else would be needed. If not, nothing will help. All begins with a _miracle_, not with conversations. I feel tired of the noise and the petty intrigues that surround the Church, of the absence of breathing space, of silence, of rhythm, of all that is present in the Gospel. Maybe that is why I love an empty church, where the _Church_ speaks through _silence_. I love it before the service and after the service. I love everything that usually seems to be "in between" (to walk on a sunny morning to work, to look at a sunset, to quietly sit a while), that which may not be important, but which alone, it seems to me, is that chink through which a mysterious ray of light shines. Only in these instances do I feel alive, turned to God; only in them is there the beating of a completely "other" life. I felt it most acutely when standing on Second Avenue changing a tire in a garage. I contemplated people on the street who were going home from work with shopping bags; and earlier, a mother with two little boys, all three in poor but obviously festive clothes, all three lit up by the setting sun. Why do I like it _so_ much? I, the most non-sentimental and indifferent man (L. said!), want to cry. Why do I know with such certitude that I am in contact with the "ultimate," that which gives total joy and faith, the rock against which all problems crash?

## _Monday, April 17, 1978_

I reread _The Life of Turgenev_ by Zaitsev. I love the 19th century, both Russian and Western. It is the period when, on the one hand, began to appear the experience, the idea, the wish for "abundance" (the fruit of Christianity), and when, on the other hand, this completeness began to crack and break up.

Our century lives by denying this completeness, by affirming *pars pro toto*, by each one running into one's own, a limited and negative "reduction." The pathos of our era is the fight with evil, with a total absence of any idea and vision of the good for which one fights. So, the fight becomes an end in itself, whereas a fight as end in itself unavoidably becomes evil. The world is full of fighters with evil. What a diabolical caricature. Non-believers—like Turgenev, Chekhov—still knew "good," its light and power, whereas now, even believers, maybe especially believers, know only evil. They do not understand that the terrorists of all kinds about whom we read every day in the paper are the product of such a belief: the declaration of a fight is the goal and the content of their life. They completely lack any convincing experience of goodness. Terrorists, from that point of view, are consistent. If everything is evil, one has to destroy it!

I am writing this at 8:00 AM and behind my window a lot of clean little boys and girls are going to school. In what kind of world will they live? If at least they were reading Turgenev, Chekhov and such, but, no, some enthusiastic nuns will teach them to "fight evil" and will point out an enemy whom one must hate. Who will share with them the knowledge of goodness, will let them hear the sounds of heaven? Such sounds are without words, but alive. They are the only ones that give depth to our classics.

*Thursday, April 20, 1978*

An unexpected gift—the silence and solitude of our New York apartment. On Tuesday, I went to Bethlehem, Pa., to Moravian College. Lecture, cozy evening with a professor and his family, with whom I spent the night. All our conversations revealed the deep malaise of the school, of universities in general. It is not clear anymore why they exist and what is their goal. A school used to exist, must exist, to bring new generations into a live inheritance of culture, and also, of course, into real freedom, into a critical search for truth. It seems to me that contemporary schools do not fulfill these functions. They are not interested in the search for truth. Everything seems to be turned toward a profession or toward an ideology which the school nurtures. The small amount of required knowledge, crowned with diplomas, makes the student pretentious; the discussions make him self-assured, and his enthusiasm and disappointments make him shallow and fragmented. Schools without depth prepare people who become certain that they can undertake anything.

## *Holy Monday, April 24, 1978*

Lazarus Saturday, Palm Sunday. Enthusiasm, joy, connection, communion with the only thing needed. As a special grace, an exceptional radiance, sunshine, light of these two days, blooming trees. Paschal and joyful yellow forsythias. On Saturday, after the Liturgy, we went to the cemetery. Lazarus Saturday more than any other day is made for the cemetery because it is "the assurance of the universal resurrection." Leisurely walk with L. along the Bronx River. In the evening, the first Bridegroom Matins. The only thing that keeps me from totally giving myself to the service is the feeling of responsibility for all the details. During these days, one needs to be completely carefree, or at least there has to be a lightening of life's burdens—and it is impossible! I understand so well Chekhov's Bishop who, in a dream before he dies, becomes again little Paul, a free child... But this temptation is not Christian because "real Christianity" would consist of giving the burden a spiritual meaning, not an irritated desire to escape it...!

Many confessions. Why can't people resist almost systematically spoiling each other's lives? That is the essence of evil. The spoiling of each other's life is the contrary, the "inside out," of the love for which man has been created.

## *Holy Tuesday, April 25, 1978*

There is in America some kind of latent violence, along with childish simplicity. Fear? Self-preservation in rivalry? Silence does not come easily: "let us live a quiet and silent life." If a person takes a walk, it is because the doctor prescribed it or he read about it in the paper. There is little enjoyment of life for its own sake, no stopping of time, no feeling of the presence of the eternal. An average, "regular" person is afraid to trust life: the sun, the sky, peace. He or she must have everything under control. Hence this edginess in the air and the constant attention directed at others, a sort of shadowing of others.

## *Holy Friday, April 28, 1978*

Expectation and Fulfillment. It seems that Lent will never end, these endless forty days will never get moving...then, Lazarus Saturday. It seems that Pascha will never happen, but then it always comes and always finds you unaware. Really: "Behold, the Bridegroom comes at midnight." I have the feeling that I am not prepared, I did not expect it; I am hopelessly out of "the Chamber."

Yesterday, Holy Thursday—Time does not exist. It is the same Holy Thursday when we walked with brother Andrei along the rue Legendre, then through blooming chestnut trees to the cathedral on rue Daru; or maybe even an earlier Thursday—Holy Thursday does not come to us; we come back to it, we again immerse ourselves in it. Holy Thursday is again a gift to us—"…and I assign to you, as my Father assigned to me, a kingdom …" (Luke 22: 29). The whole "liturgy" of the Church is there; it makes the return, the immersion possible. Spiritual life is *to be there*, not only to touch it once in awhile symbolically. "In the upper chamber, with uplifted minds…"

I saw today an announcement about a huge building conceived by Dali and built in Paris—all made of cubes and such. A simple thought came to my mind: What is the horror of new art, new architecture, painting, literature? Any building of the past—the most vulgar, Victorian, sugary, adorned with columns and little baby love statues—was symbolic. Even vulgarity was related to something else; it was a caricature of something other. Everything was related to "the other." New art wants one thing: to destroy that referral, that symbolism of the other; rather, to denounce it. It says, "Look! There is nothing behind this!" Surrealism started it: Although it spoke a lot about the dream, in fact it exposed the dream as absurd or meaningless, as a sort of dull itch. Any vulgar, sweet novel conceals some potential. It describes a human world. There is no way anywhere from the cubic buildings. That is why I think of them in connection with yesterday's conversations with my poor unhappy friends. The dead end of their unhappiness is the fact that the victim, the unhappy victim, can explain everything and analyze it with the help of psychotherapy. But this analysis, this dead knowledge of live suffering and of real evil, makes the cure impossible. Where would the cure lead to? Religion itself has closed access to the old, eternal, living and healing symbols. Holy Week has become a discourse about what happened to Christ two thousand years ago, and not the revelation what is happening to us *today*. This Byzantine, rhetorical settling of accounts with Judas, with the Jews, our righteous pious anger… How pitiful it all sounds after the first Gospel on Thursday night. Holy Friday exposes evil as evil, but the destruction of evil and the victory over it has become a day of our human delight—how noble and pious and triumphant we are! We don't even know that we finally abolish Christ's Cross.

### Bright Monday, May 1, 1978

Pascha. I can't remember such a Paschal Day; sunny, cool, light, airy!

Talked with my son Serge in South Africa.

## *Monday, May 8, 1978*

Yesterday, the sudden death of Mrs. Verhovskoy. When I arrived, two medical orderlies were trying to revive her by giving her artificial respiration. The ugliness, disgrace of death. The body spread on the floor and the room with all the belongings; all that is needed for life and that becomes horrible in its needlessness, senselessness when next to death. And then a slow, victorious transformation of this ugliness by prayer, its rhythm, its power to transform, to transfigure, to show so clearly that the last word is God's and not the devil's; not a breaking into the world of non-existence, Sheol, and evil. In the evening, the church was packed for the memorial service.

## *Thursday, October 5, 1978*

*Rome.* It is strange and quite sad, that this "Pope of the smile"—*le pape du sourire*—has died.* The three days I spent in Rome from the second to the fifth of September remain in my memory as especially intense. Above all the very special light of the evening that I spent with Metropolitan Theodosius at the enthronement. Golden and so gentle. I remember as a dream the endless procession of Cardinals to the Pope, the singing—extraordinary—of Latin hymns (the often repeated *Tu es Petrus!*, then the simplicity of the Mass, especially when the Pope started giving Communion to his immediate entourage while two or three hundred priests moved with their chalices down to the people. Even then it seemed so fragile, despite the huge size of St Peter's and the presence of centuries and centuries of tradition.

On Monday, lunch with the Russian Metropolitan Nikodim in Russicum. He had 18 hours left to live, but no premonition. Fragility. I felt it most acutely on Tuesday morning in the Pope's palace. First—thunderstorm and pouring rain, the darkness of that morning. Metropolitan Nikodim getting into the car: "We'll see you at the Pope's." One can not see anything through the pouring rain! In the palace, in spite of all the chandeliers, it is quite dark. Nothing left from the bright light of two days ago. We are waiting in a huge reception hall. Then someone comes for Metropolitan Nikodim. After five minutes, Father Leo, Nicodim's aide, runs somewhere through the halls. Something is obviously wrong; nobody *runs* around here. Somebody says: "Probably Metropolitan Nikodim forgot his gift for the Pope." Someone else: "I know the Metropolitan; he never forgets anything." The monk, Leo, runs back with a black satchel. N.'s medicine. After five minutes, Monsignor Arrighi: "He has died." The monsignors of the court, who are taking care of us, are slightly

* Pope John Paul I who died in 1978.

197

tense; everything must go according to protocol! We are led to the room where the Pope is waiting for us. Metropolitan Theodosius reads his greetings. I am looking at the Pope and feel his frailty. Much older than his picture. He exudes gentleness, almost tenderness. While answering Theodosius, he holds my hand. Three-four minutes. Picture taking, and we leave for the airport to New York.

In Crestwood, the beginning of a school year. Meetings, services. Feasts: Nativity of the Theotokos and the Elevation of the Cross.

On September 22nd, flight to Helsinki—five days in Finland. On Sunday, Liturgy with Archbishop Paul in New Valaam. Drive there and back through crimson forests.

Two days in Kuopio, meetings, celebrations. Air France is on strike, so I have to spend two extra days in Helsinki. I had a delightful time with Father Tapani Reno—lunch with him and his son in an old fashioned Russian restaurant in a grand yellow Empire building. "Time immobile." Behind the high windows, a gray autumn day. Then drive to his *dacha* (villa)—lakes, pines, birches. Silence, gratitude. Wonderful evening! Finnish bath. Immersion in friendship, trust, genuineness. Affection of the son to his father, who has cancer. Contact with real life!

Then, stopover in Paris—visit to Mother. I spent three days in Paris and visited her three times. Didn't have time to really feel Paris because of endless meetings, discussions, et al.

Last, but certainly not least, all these months L.'s sickness: continuous loud noise in her head, attacks of discouragement. So much pity! Simple lesson about the meaning of suffering in our life. I am ready to get sick myself, to suffer, if only she could be better. Liberation—though temporary and partial—from selfishness.

### Tuesday, October 10, 1978

I started meeting new students yesterday, wrote some letters. Checked the translation into Russian of my *Great Lent!* And immediately, by fulfilling my immediate duty, I feel better and stronger. Cool, clear, sunny autumn days are helping!

Joy from the realization, more and more often, that my books reach out, that they are needed by some people. For example, I received the manuscript of a full Russian translation of my *Of Water and the Spirit* from Russia in a *samizdat,* hand-written form. One woman on Education Day: "I lived for so long with your books that I can hardly believe that I see you...live!" Yes, of course, quite pleasant. But not only. These testimonies come, I noticed, always in moments or periods of doubt, of horror that life is almost over and nothing is being done and time passes by...!

### Wednesday, October 11, 1978

Had lunch today with N. who wants to bring Solzhenitsyn together with a leader of American Indians. I do not cease being surprised by this American passion for service, for utopia. She firmly believes that the world will be saved by Solzhenitsyn and the Indian!

### Monday, October 23, 1978

Andrei, my brother, called from Paris: Mother is in the hospital with pneumonia and a kidney infection. She is delirious, does not seem to recognize people. Beginning of the end!

On Saturday, retreat in Richmond at the DeTranas.

Spent two hours on Sunday watching on television the enthronement of the new Pope. I was there eight weeks ago, going through exactly the same procedure. Again the hymn that never ceases to move me—"*Adoro Te, devote, latens Deitas*"—the slow procession of Cardinals, St Peter's Square packed, the illumined faces of nuns... I liked the Pope's speech: "You are Christ, the Son of the Living God..."without clichés, friendship of all people, peace of the world. Faith, God, Christ, Man. It is not quite clear why he was elected, and where Rome will be moving now. Two-three sentences in Ukrainian. I recognized Bishop Sylvester and Father Leonid [Kishkovsky].

Phone call from N.: "What is going on at the parish on 71st Street in New York? Something *must* be done..." Another: "G. S. has beaten up a policeman by mistake! We must help him!" Then Bishop Alexander from Paris: "My nephew just came back from Australia; he is not happy with the parish there. What can we do?" I am not exaggerating; it's like this every day!

Beautiful golden days. Call from my brother: Mother is better!

I just met with one of our students who is interested in Dostoevsky, Solzhenitsyn, Russian history. How rare in our clerical little world, usually stifling in its "Orthodoxism." I never cease being surprised: Why don't the Orthodox "hear" the melody of Orthodoxy, precisely never stifling, but joyful, light, free? "But people prefer darkness," even in religion.

### Tuesday, October 24, 1978

Last Thursday, I drove to Vermont to see Solzhenitsyn. We talked for three hours—very friendly. I feel his interest, his affection for me, but I cannot rid myself of a feeling of estrangement. What so passionately occupies him, what he is immersed in, is alien to me. His defense of Russia from those who abuse it, his settling of accounts with the intelligentsia, the Jews, the Soviet republics, the Kerenskys, et al. is fruitless. I agree with many of his ideas about the Revolution in Russia, in my mind and my reason, but I can not share his passion because I do not love Russia "more than anything else." My heart's treasure is not in Russia, whereas for S.—his love is obvious, complete.

The next day, a long drive to Burlington where I lectured at St Michael's College. Long trip there and back in the sunny fire of autumn.

Yesterday, I went with Father Tom to New Skete Monastery, visiting with monks who are about to become Orthodox. Again a whole day of sunshine, woods, fields, Indian summer.

### Monday, November 6, 1978

I am reading—very slowly—Zinoviev's *Yawning Heights*. A wonderful book, extremely intelligent, on the verge of some vision. Something from Jonathan Swift's *Gulliver's Travels*—merciless, implacable, logical.

These days I'm working slowly and painfully on the "Sacrament of Thanksgiving." And right away I feel so much better!

Today, I walked along Broadway from 96th to 120th Street. How many memories! We lived there for ten years.

Torturing pity for L., the uncertainty of her illness—a constant background of our life. But then, how wonderfully sickness purifies everything—sometimes it seems to me that I was never more blissfully happy with her than in these few months.

### Monday, November 13, 1978

Ivan Morozov has died! A whole era of my life—the Student Christian Movement; St Sergius Institute, where we studied together; his growing persecution complex and poisonous suspicions, the tragic crisis of YMCA Press.

Three days of traveling: On Saturday in Chicago for the consecration of Bishop Boris Geeza. A celebration full of light. His own congregation, his own cathedral. The loud people's *"AXIOS."* The Church is alive. Yesterday, Sunday, I went to the Parma parish for their anniversary. And again rejoicing at their growth, genuineness.

Went today with my daughter Anya to Sea Cliff to visit my mother's brother [Alexander Tikhonovich Shishkov], his wife, his daughter's family. How cozy these visits to my very close blood relative could be if it were not for our accursed differences in Church affiliations—they are violently against our OCA.

Early Liturgy, which I served with eight priests! St John Chrysostom.

On our way to Sea Cliff, last leaves, all is transparent behind the bare trees. A light gray sky. How I love this time of year, the mysterious testimony of these transparent trees, this slow immersion into the cold and the darkness in which Christmas lights will soon appear.

## *Sunday, November 19, 1978*

Just came back from LaGuardia Airport after three days in Wichita, Kansas. Retreat, interviews, church services, lectures. I am quite tired, but also joyful from the attentiveness, the interest of the people; from close contact with people of God. I am always deeply impressed by the American plains, by the enormity of this country, by "soul-rending" sunsets, by this huge sky. A strange and joyful feeling—it's my country: America the beautiful!

All these days, I live under the dark weight of the awful news of Morozov's death. He hanged himself! Ivan Morozov hung himself! These words are so impossible that every time I say them they strike me with their horror, their nonsense! Contact with the prince of this world!

This whole week, under the impression of the frightful tragedy in Jonestown: religious suicide of nine hundred people, ordered by the head of the sect, Jim Jones. How thin, how fragile our rational, comfortable, consumer civilization. I look at the faces of those who were saved from this voluntary slaughter—the same as the faces of men on the street; the same clean shirts, blue jeans, style. *Why* do nine hundred people throw away everything and follow, in the middle of the jungle, a man who affirms that he is the incarnation, at the same time, of Christ and of Lenin! And when he orders them to stand in line and drink poison—they stand and drink? And the guards with guns kill those who resist, before killing themselves. The horror is that this is not a phenomenon *outside* our civilization, but *within*, although in protest against it. Within, our civilization lives in utopia, with faith in recipes for final happiness, with denial, disregard of suffering, death, discomfort. So that from within, it generates fear, insecurity, thirst for an even more complete utopia. Thus the Jonestown event is not a *falling out* of civilization, but the final product, the outcome of the content of civilization, the content of life. It is also the product of the decay of Christianity, its polarization between social utopia and philanthropy on the one hand, and on the other, dark apocalypticism. In other words, the same tragic ambiguity of religion; the price to pay for the liquidation of "theology" in the deepest sense of the word. People do not ask anymore who and what is Jesus, but call what *they* believe—"in Jesus."

## Thursday, November 30, 1978

Thirty-two years since my ordination to the Priesthood!

In connection with F. Giroud's book and what was /is being written about the tragedy in Guyana (excerpts from letters of some sect members to Jim Jones, as well as some conclusions drawn by the magazine *Nouvel Observateur*), I was thinking, What is the fatal mistake of Christian history? Is it not that logically, methodologically, one derives Christianity from religion, as the "particular" from the "general," which means that Christianity is reduced to religion, even when it is affirmed as fulfillment, as the accomplishment of religion. Whereas Christianity, in its essence, is not so much the fulfillment as the denial and destruction of religion, the revelation about it as the fall, as the result and the main expression of original sin. Now our times are returning to religion, but not to Christianity, and Guyana, Moon, etc., are some of the symptoms. One will ask, "Is it not the denial of religion, i.e., of sacredness and meditation, the quintessence of Reformation from Luther to Calvin to Karl Barth?" No. And the proof of this "no" is that radical sects (like Jones') are invariably born from within, from the depths of Protestantism. Why? Because, I think, Protestantism, intending to purify Christianity from pagan contagion, in fact was the annihilation of the eschatology of Christianity. Christ did not eliminate death and suffering, but trampled them, i.e., radically changed them from within, made victory out of defeat, "converted" them; in so doing, He "converted" religion, but did not destroy it. Converted it, not only by filling it with an eschatological content, but by revealing religion, making it the sacrament of the Kingdom of God. The sin of religion—more exactly, religion as a sin—is not in the feeling and experience of the sacred, but in the immanentization of the sacred, in identifying it with the created world. The world is created as communion with God, as ascent to God; it is created for spiritualization, but it is not 'god' and therefore spiritualization is always also the overcoming of the world, the liberation from it. Thus, the world is a "sacrament." The fatal mistake of Protestantism is that having justifiably rebelled against the immanentization of Christianity during the Middle Ages of Catholicism, it rejected the "sacrament," not only religion as sin and fall, but also the religious nature of creation itself. The mistake consists in saying that the Church is the totality of the "saved ones," but saved individually ("I am saved"!), so that each salvation does not mean anything for the world, does not accomplish anything in the world; the salvation of the world is not accomplished in the salvation of each man. The Church, in other words, becomes a sect—a sect obsessed with salvation as such, without relation either to the world or to the Kingdom of God. By renouncing cosmology, Protestantism actually renounces eschatology, since man has no other symbol, no other sacrament, i.e., no other knowledge of the Kingdom of God, than the world; so a man's salvation is always also the salvation of the world, the knowledge of the Church as the presence of "new creation." This experience of "being saved"—since in fact it has no content except "being saved"—is unavoidably being filled with any content. *The one who is saved must "save."* A sect is always active and always maximalistic, a sect lives in the excitement of being saved and of saving. Since either being saved or being a savior has no cosmic or eschatological horizon, no spiritual depth, no spiritual knowledge of the world or of the Kingdom of God, the goal, the object of salvation becomes the evil or the sin that one has to be saved from, whose annihilation will produce salvation. It can be alcohol or tobacco, or capitalism, or Communism; it can be literally anything! On that level, a sect leads to morality, social gospel, or "prayer breakfasts" for bankers, who, if they feel that if they are saved, will become better bankers, better capitalists, etc. "The Cause!" Finally, on that level, a sect is transformed into an agency (churches, synagogues, other agencies)—philanthropic, humanitarian, anti-racist, etc. Even on that level, a sect carries the foundation for radicalism. While identifying evil with something concrete, tangible and usually very evil, while absolutizing this concrete evil, a sect easily mobilizes people *against* and not *for*. The experience itself of being saved, of tracing a clear line between the saved ones, i.e., the good ones, and the not-saved ones, i.e., the evil ones, makes the life of a sect, so to say, negative, directed at accusing and condemning. Even a continuous feeling of guilt, characteristic of contemporary Protestantism; a continuous public repentance offered to the third world, or to minorities, or to the poor, is born of the need to have a clear conscience—the basic sign of "being saved." By denouncing not one's self, but the Church or white society or something else, the one who is saved feels that he is good.

On a low level, this radicalism comes out into the open and is the logical conclusion of the sect. If Protestantism is individualizing salvation, and making it a personal salvation by emptying it of any cosmic and eschatological content, it makes man endlessly lonely, torn apart, separated from the world, from history, from the kingdom of God. Thus, paradoxically, the sect becomes a rescue from solitude, but at the cost of diluting one's personality *in* the sect, *in* the cult. A sect is united around a savior, around the leader. His power is rooted in the sect's weakness. He determines the "Cause," he leads the fight, he knows. Turn your will to him! So, in a world totally secularized, i.e., totally desacramentalized, totally "de-eschatologized," saviors appear: Moon, Jones, etc. And nine hundred people obediently stand in line next to a barrel of arsenic, to die! All is tied together, all leads to all. "Beware how dangerously you walk."

### Thursday, December 14, 1978

*Baltimore*

It is the eve of Liana's brain surgery (tumor on the ear nerve). We have been here for ten days, she at the Johns Hopkins Hospital and I across the street at the Sheraton. The darkness and the light of these days cannot be described. I only know that I have never, never, in my life lived through such days.

### Monday, December 18, 1978

*Baltimore*

Third day after the operation. I do not want to ever forget how I sat with my daughter Anya, thinking that we would have to live in that tension for four or five hours and suddenly—the appearance of Dr. Nager and joyful news. Immediately the whole tone of life changes, the perception of the blue sky, of skyscrapers sparkling far away in the bright sun, the time of waiting receded, the time of constant inner effort to a *sursum corda*. Life becomes banal. One begins to understand why God sends such ordeals.

I *know* that I am simplifying, but I cannot repress the strong conviction, which has matured in me for a very long time, almost since childhood, that the essence of Christianity is eschatological. Any deviation from it, which began quite early, is a substitute for Christianity, an apostasy. "Eschatological" means that Christianity is directed, at the same time and totally, both on "Now" *and* on the Kingdom to come—that the experience of the Kingdom is completely dependent on the experience of "Now." One feels this with special force in a hospital, where I have been wandering for the past two weeks, whose atmosphere and rhythm has become, for a while, my whole life. This world is busy with tomorrow, passionately busy, busy with something that does not exist; whereas Christianity is "busy," or, rather, should be busy with today, which alone gives us the experience of the Kingdom. Does it mean leaving history? or indifference to practical action, to responsibility, to involvement? No, inasmuch as all of it is part of our today, of our "duty"—the duty of Christians, not of the Church as such. The Church is here so that not one action of this world, not one "tomorrow" would become an idol, a goal in itself.

Letter from Nikita Struve about Ivan Morozov's death—intelligent and, I think, right. We felt a wave of love, attention, prayer with almost physical force these last days. The Kingdom…

More about the hospital: It is a microcosm, a thousand times more real than the normal and healthy world surrounding it. Here everybody is busy with the essential, and the essential is now, in the light of the end, of eternity. That's why everything, every detail is so important; there are no cheap emotions, no rhetoric, no idle talk. Each word is important. There is no room for facade, for showing off, for demagogy. While walking on the street, one *knows* what is awaiting each of these smiling, professional, optimistic, conventional, healthy people.

## Tuesday, December 19, 1978

*Baltimore*

I read many newspapers. I remember Emmanuel Mounier writing somewhere that one should not read newspapers. It's not true. For me, reading newspapers (especially here in forced idleness), is always a source of thought, of contact with the reality in which we live, of the necessary calibration by reality. Without the background of reality all the ideas and solutions to problems are abstract and groundless. What is the content of man's life now, today? How did he reach this life and why? To think about these questions, a newspaper is a treasure, although a frightening one.

I had dinner yesterday with the local priest. Wonderful, pure, young man, charming wife. What strikes me is the fact that he has been in Baltimore for five years and does not know anything about the city. I know, and knew about it even before coming here, a hundred times more than he does. No interest in the past. He is interested only in his parish. The rootless character of most Americans always surprises me.

## Wednesday, December 20, 1978

*Baltimore*

Last evening I read in the Science section of the *New York Times* an article by two women about the position of contemporary science on the differences between men and women. All rather inconsistent, unclear, with hasty generalizations. But mainly, a prejudiced desire to prove that the difference is biologically accidental and socially determined. Monstrous foolishness and obsession with egalitarianism. We live under such pressure! One consolation: most women do not even notice this frenzy. Another idol of our times—the polls—confirms these scientific findings.

I am leaving Baltimore today. I know that these two weeks were for L. and me the most decisive days of our lives.

### Friday, December 22, 1978

#### Crestwood

I came back from Baltimore on Wednesday and drove there and back today. I walk around the hospital as if it were my home, but this world of the hospital—so special, painful, heavy, but also full of light—is torn away from me and is receding, although L. is still there.

Everything is behind us, and how fast one gets used to what is, in fact, a miracle and God's mercy! But the normal and healthy world still seems unreal. What remains quite clear is that a real fight, real victories and defeats come only in this—inexplicable, but so real—suffering.

Life became completely unsettled during these past weeks. I don't know how and what to start. On Wednesday, I served the first pre-feast Vespers. Yesterday I checked our apartment in the city. I feel that I must again get used to living!

### Saturday, December 23, 1978

Home alone. Sunshine. Cold. I am writing to get back into the habit of writing. This morning, Liturgy of Saturday before Christmas. I am beginning to feel the rising of the Feast.

### Monday, December 25, 1978

#### Christmas

Beautiful services; better than ever! Three days of confessions. All the time in touch with L. But Anya is right here, next to me, and that makes my life very cozy.

# CHAPTER VII

# 1979

∾

## Monday, February 5, 1979

Eric Hoffer: *Before the Sabbath*. I agree with almost every line of the book. I feel more and more alienated by the rhetoric of social environment, the poor, etc. Before that, I read Theodore White's *Search for History* with enormous interest. Behind all this, the ultimate question is, Does the West still have spiritual and moral strength, or was it destroyed by anti-Christian pseudo-goodness, which has penetrated civilization, psychiatry and narcissism? All these days, while watching on television the raging crowd on the streets of Teheran, with the astounding idolization of Ayatollah Khomeini, I felt that despite all its technocracy, the West is bankrupt. The West has nothing to offer to the Third, Fourth or other worlds that are just awakening. The reason, it seems to me, is quite simple: the First world never had any other "dream" than Christianity—maybe better to say—than Christ! Only around Christ did "freedom," "culture," "technocracy" have any meaning. But the West renounced Christ and Christianity; renounced them for the sake of the freedoms that Christianity had planted. Marx, Engels, Freud are stages of that renunciation. And with that renunciation, the soul was lost. Everything started to decay and into everything entered death. It was the renunciation of Christianity, of its vision, but mainly the renunciation of Christianity by *Christians themselves*. And thousands of people now clamor about the mysterious Islamic Republic.

The uniqueness of Christianity is the "immanent character of the transcendent," and the "transcendent character of the immanent." Christ is not *for* political freedom, not *for* culture, not *for* creativity; He is transcendent over them, from within, and thus makes them (freedom, culture, creativity) a way towards the transcendent. Islam is the return to the dichotomy of the transcendent and the immanent; it is, above all, the denial of the Incarnation of God. Law, reward, punishment. Static. Amazing hatred of America by the world. Groveling of America before China—sad sight!

Pope John Paul II is in Mexico. Will he succeed in what seems to me the paradox of his program; to return the Church to spirituality, to continue its service to the poor? Does Christianity have any answer to the problem of poverty other than a personal appeal to the rich: "...give everything that you have and follow Me.."? The problem is a spiritual one before it is economic.

Painful writing of my *Eucharist*. I write devoured by doubt: does one need to write it? to write it this way? For the theologian, it is not theology because it is not scientific. For simply religious people, who like services, it is probably strange because it is directed against religiosity. And finally, do I have the *right* to write this and write it this way? I have a painful feeling of unworthiness: "not to touch..." But everything else (including theology and religiosity) seems to me not only unnecessary, but also harmful.

## Thursday, February 8, 1979

Yesterday, a whole day of snowfall. Today New York City under snow in a bright sunshine. Evenings at home with L. in our very cozy New York apartment.

Reading Philippe Ariès, *L'Homme devant la mort* (*Man Before Death*). While reading such a book, and the newspapers following events in Iran, passionately hoping for Ayatollah Khomeini's failure, I feel a growing need for a synthesis—a clear Christian answer to everything, to our entire crisis. Christianity remains hopelessly "Constantinian"; hence its shameful weakness. Its only chance is eschatology. I continually think about this, that precisely this "eschatology" of Christianity contains in itself the explanation of everything: of life and of death; of the horror in Guyana; of the decay of the developed world; of the scary revival of Islam; of the mystery of Russia; of ecology; of psychology; of everything. This eschatological synthesis could be revealed by Orthodoxy, but the Orthodox themselves neither see it nor want it, from theologians and "spirit-carriers" to pious little old ladies...!

## Friday, February 9, 1979

I am writing on a flight to California.

A quote from *Time* magazine from the German mathematician C. F. Ganss: "The meaningless precision in numerical studies." It explains my constant dislike of all statistics, polls, etc.

In the same issue of *Time* there are pictures of huge crowds of humanity: in Teheran, the Ayatollah Khomeini; in Mexico, Pope John Paul II. So at the end of the 20th century, here is the power of religion! What else could mobilize so many (millions!) of people; provoke such expectation, such enthusiasm? The power, and, at the same time, the ambiguity of the Ayatollah; not one word about love, peace, the transcendence in God of all petty divisions. And the threat of a holy war. The Pope, in a sense, speaks only about love. Frightening face of Islam…hence, this Khomeini, in the end, will give nothing to his people (who are so happy with him) except grief, hate and suffering. Whereas from the Pope's visit, only joy, only hope—even if nothing comes of it.

I am flying over huge, snow-covered America.

Meeting last week with the sculptor, Ernst N[eizvestny] in his studio. A very kind, intimate conversation. The studio is full of grandiose, disturbing sculptures; one of them I remember: a huge human foot with toes separated and directed upward! All the other items were of the same type. N. explained his project of a grandiose symbol—cosmic, religious, etc.—that will reveal and explain something to humanity. I don't know… I only know that I am absolutely blind and deaf to that art, in which I literally don't see anything and don't understand anything. So that I feel painfully awkward, especially since he turns to me with some expectation…!

## Sunday, February 11, 1979

### San Francisco

San Francisco, this time, is gray, foggy, without the feeling of a feast which I usually have here. Between services, meetings, conversations with friends. I am reading a book about the early years of T. S. Eliot, about his path to religion. Eliot interests me because in his religious search he never seeks personal gratification or personal religious experience, but the restoration of the reality of the world and of life, i.e., of the Church, of Catholicity. He is, in this sense, the opposite of contemporary narcissistic and, therefore, destructive spirituality. The *experience* of the *Church—this* is what needs theological clarification; this is what is so difficult, because scientific theology says (in the textbooks) that the "Church believes" and that this belief is relegated to the realm of the authority of dogmas. In other words, the word "belief" itself does not have the notion or the reality of experience, so that the word "experience" sounds like some subjective moods, emotions, feelings.

## Wednesday, February 14, 1979

Growing dissatisfaction with my lectures, courses, all the *academia* of my life. I don't believe in any theological science; it's time for me to admit it. But I do not have to deal with it (I don't remember when I read my last theological book) so much as to pretend that I deal with it (for example, guide master's dissertations) and inspire our poor students, creating in their minds utter confusion. From all of that, I have a painful and unpleasant aftertaste in my heart and in my mind!

Long letter from my friend Father Igor from Paris. Horrible, painful atmosphere in Paris (following Ivan Morozov's suicide); a terrible dead end: everyone accuses everyone else.

### Thursday, February 15, 1979

Same frost, same life congealed in icy cold.

I spent several hours yesterday writing an answer to Father Igor's letter. How easily mutual understanding is destroyed and disappears when something as frightening, as outrageous and as extraordinary as Ivan's death occurs. People who literally spent their life together, who know each other since childhood, become deaf and blind to each other, like Leibniz monads. Half of these people (who accuse each other of Ivan's suicide) are priests, live in the Church. And where does everything disappear that for years was so good, so eloquently explained in lectures, in conferences, in sermons? Hatred for the sake of truth and fairness is the most awful of all.

### Wednesday, February 21, 2979

I feel depressed and disgusted by the news. In Iran—executions; in China—war; in Africa—terrorism; in Baltimore—the mob, using the cover of a huge snow storm, smashes stores. I have the feeling of a total disintegration of the very fiber of life. "The whole world is in the power of the evil one" (1 John 5:19). I really should not be surprised that I am depressed; not because of all these events, but because of the terrible weakness and baseness of the developed and the Christian world. All that this world knows is how to sell its technology and advance weaponry; its Western way of life, i.e., with appliances and skyscrapers. Where Third World people cease to digest and accept this technology, everything crumbles down, falls; what's left are thousands of these screaming people with raised fists. Blood. Revolution. "Islam and its revival" they say. I don't believe in that revival. It is not without reason that the same Ayatollah, although he pronounces the word "Islam" every instant, gained success not in Islam nor through Islam, but through the revolution. The righteous man, the ascetic, is guiding the revolution... And the revolution will destroy him and Islam. The only thing that this righteous man has done is to shoot twenty generals and open the frightening valves of revenge, blood and destruction.

In China, it is the opposite process. In Iran, it is the idolization of the righteous; in China it is technology and appliances. Great progress, says the *New York Times*! Chinese women have been allowed to curl their hair, and Chinese men to drink Coca-Cola—a triumph of freedom and democracy!

Sad and contemptible. If this Islam did not have oil, nobody would have paid much attention and there would not be any revival. But oil is the nemesis of these nations. They will end up choking on it!

On Sunday, annual meeting of the St Vladimir's Theological Foundation. A large check, great success and well deserved. These are the best people of our Church. But how fragile that success; how weak and barely glimmering is Orthodoxy; how many winds of pettiness, provincialism, simply evil envy and other small passions blow from all sides.

Letter from Russia. People reading my *Introduction to Liturgical Theology* are demanding immediate reforms of the Church, of the Liturgy, quickly, now...!

I leave all this in order to write, in snatches, my *Eucharist*. While I write—joy! Then—doubts. In all my writings, I never had as many doubts, as much difficulty: sixteen pages since summer!

## *Thursday, February 22, 1979*

Passionate interest in Iran's events. The papers are filled with the war between China and Vietnam, but I seem to be completely bewitched by this Ayatollah. I know why, of course: because of religion, because in Iran, right now, is the focus of what is happening with Christianity; its weakening, its dying away as a power in history. Today on a back page of the *New York Times*: "the Pope spoke in favor of social justice..." Big deal! Even at home, in Italy, he is powerless against abortion, against terrorism, against debauchery. What remains are clichés... I do not even mention the Orthodox who join, through cowardice, any strong leadership. In Iran, the power of Islam flared up in that old man. It will probably be defeated and crushed by the same West with its other power: the frightening mysticism of the revolution of the masses, of Marxism, Leninism; but the West, as Christianity, is dying. It poses so many deep questions about the essence of Christianity. Islam, to sum it up, is anti-Christian. It seems that:

—the West—secular, hedonistic, technological etc., lives by its renunciation of Christianity. I emphasize, not by indifference to Christianity, but precisely renunciation (happiness, economics, sex, abortion...)

—the revolutionary West lives by its fight with Christianity, with the Christian man, the *homo Christianus*

—the East is divided between Western renunciation (Japan, maybe now China, their dream to modernize) and the fight with the West under the sign of either revolution or Islam.

The "death of Christianity"! It sounds horrible. But is it so? It constantly seems to me (and gives me inner light and joy) that the death of Christianity is needed, so that *Christ would be resurrected*. The deadly weakness of Christianity lies in only one thing—forgetting and neglecting *Christ*. In the Gospel, Christ always says "I"—He says about Himself that He will come back in glory, as a King. One must love Him, expect Him, rejoice in Him and about Him. When nothing of Christianity will remain, only Christ will be visible; and neither revolution, nor Islam, nor hedonism will have any power left. Now is the time for the prayer, "Come, Lord Jesus...!"*

### Friday, February 23, 1979

*New Skete, Cambridge, NY*

I am writing just before the rite of acceptance into Orthodoxy of the monks and nuns of New Skete. I flew in yesterday with the Metropolitan. It is my third visit—and I have the same impression of light, simplicity, joy. Nothing forced, ostentatious. All around, snowy mountains, frost (I have a miserable cold).

### Monday, February 26, 1979

On Friday night, after returning from New Skete and the joy that I felt there, we had dinner at N.'s and heard many stories about the quarrels and conflicts in Nyack. Total absurdity. I thought once more about the Russian emigration in general. As any living organism, the emigration lived and lives mainly with an instinct of self-preservation. And for self-preservation, quarrels, for example, are no less needed than a feeling of comradeship, of like-mindedness, etc. So as strange as it may seem, although quite logical, the reason for quarreling is not really that important. The reasons, the pretexts for the quarrels quickly become a "myth," something elusive. The function of a quarrel is in allowing people to feel principled, to serve the cause, i.e., to feel alive. This is so because the main quarrel, the constituting principle of the emigration—the Bolsheviks—is abstract, and cannot be incarnated in daily life. And free time can be filled with a quarrel. The law of émigré life: those who don't like to quarrel organize balls and can also keep busy—endlessly—reconciling those

---

* "He who testifies to these things says, 'Surely I am coming soon.' Amen. Come, Lord Jesus!" Revelation 22:20

who quarrel. And those who enjoy quarrels—quarrel! But the function of both is the same.

Yesterday, after dinner, a drive to the hospital in Derby, Conn., to visit Tanya L[opukhin] who had a terrible car accident. Her parents' joy: "Thank God! It could have been so much worse." And in the light of that joy, of that contact with real life—aversion to fuss, to superficial daily concerns.

## Tuesday, February 27, 1979

I read yesterday R. Bornert's book, *Byzantine Liturgical Commentaries.* (I am preparing a lecture for Dumbarton Oaks). Once more, I am convinced that I am quite alienated from Byzantium, and even hostile to it. In the Bible, there is space and air; in Byzantium the air is always stuffy. All is heavy, static, petrified. What is surprising is that the Byzantine *Liturgy* basically withstood and endured this stuffiness and did not let it into the "Holy of Holies."

My intuition remains the same: the transposition of the experience of the Church from an eschatological to a mysteriological key. Here Plato turns out to be stronger than the Bible; Plato and the Christian empire, the Christian world. People do not understand that eschatology is interest in the world, whereas mysteriology is indifference to the world. Byzantium's complete indifference to the world is astounding. The drama of Orthodoxy: we did not have a Renaissance, sinful but liberating from the sacred. So we live in nonexistent worlds: in Byzantium, in Rus, wherever, but not in our own time.

Rain, wet snow. The whole day a gray twilight behind my window. And a feeling of fatigue from the approaching Lent, which means for me a great deal of traveling, lectures, added tension.

## Friday, March 2 1979

Progress brought to man the desire *to live* fully, but did not tell him, nor can it tell him, what life is and what it is for. Hence, the insane acceptance of ideas—a substitute for meaning in life; or of a fight, not quite clear for what, but useful because one can stop thinking.

## Tuesday, March 6, 1979

Great Lent! Yesterday and today—long services. Between the services, I am home alone, working on a lecture for Dumbarton Oaks ("Symbols and Symbolism in the Byzantine Liturgy"). I started, as usual, unwillingly. But, as almost always happens, while working quite blindly at first (I first "hear" separate sentences, "see" an unclear appearance of something yet unknown), there comes a kind of revelation: *This* is what happened; what was...

Three layers of symbolism. A representative symbolism, i.e., the last one, the contemporary (which started already in Byzantium), torn away from theology and from piety. Then, under it, a spiritual symbolism (mysteriological): Dionysius, Maximos, Theoria: contemplation, gnosis. And then, under it, an eschatological symbolism, the Kingdom—*this* world. And then, what remains is to express it all…quite painful!

### Thursday, March 8, 1979

French weekly papers. Amazingly empty! Emptiness of a country which has ceased to play any role in the world. In the *National Review*, an analysis of England's decay. I have a strong feeling that we are seeing the end of the Western world, the last carrier, not of Christian culture, but of a culture vaguely marked by Christianity.

I forgot to note a two hour conversation last week with Father George Grabbe (the senior priest at the Synod). Peaceful conversation, even benevolent, but rather amazing: the fact that somewhere in some basement in Jerusalem, "they" are in the process of bringing up a messiah, i.e., anti-Christ; some signs, and the need to be insured against "it"! I am always surprised at the localization of evil, of dark forces; at the belief in some esoteric history with total lack of a simple understanding of history. Stifling, dull world, without joy, without light.

In the *New York Times* today, a picture of the shooting in Teheran of eight homosexuals. There it is!—the "moral restoration of health" in Iran with Islam's help. The French bookstore in New York City is densely packed with books about magic, masonry, astrology. The saleswoman tells me that there is great demand for these books. There is in the air an attraction towards extremism, the irrational, perhaps because the rational is so pitiful! "If then the light in you is darkness, how great is the darkness!" (Matthew 6:23)

### Thursday, March 15, 1979

*Vancouver, British Columbia*

Early morning. I am in Vancouver, where I have come to give two lectures at the Faculty Club of the University of British Columbia. Beautiful view of the bay and the islands. Cloudy, but all the bushes are blooming.

Busy week. Last Sunday in Montreal for the Triumph of Orthodoxy. Monday, meeting with church archivists at the Chancery. Tuesday, seminary lectures, talks, students. Yesterday, long flight across America.

On the plane, I read religious magazines, which I usually do not have time to read: the British Catholic magazine, *The Tablet;* the American magazine, *The Oxford Review*—Episcopalian dissidents, i.e. extreme Right. I can't accept either position, neither Right nor Left. The Right one is depressing because of its superficial lack of seriousness. Everything is treated with cheap irony and with tiring clericalism. The Left one is tiring with its "social concern" (something like "the theology of workers' strikes").

I also read the Synodal (Russian Church outside of Russia) magazine, *The Orthodox Monitor*, created for the defense of persecuted Orthodox people. While reading, I asked myself, "What is the clearly tangible falseness of everything in that magazine?" An article by the Greek Bishop Panteleimon from Boston about prayers in his monastery to *each* of the miraculous icons of the Virgin Mary. Is it this unctuous rhetorical tone which irritates me, or something else? No, I feel in all of it some self-adulation, self-righteousness, concern with one's self. Persecutions, martyrs, etc., are the confirmation of their right, their high quality, and it is completely unbearable. The exploitation of martyrs. A primitive approach: not reality, but myth. Besides that, a false myth.

In the morning, I drove with Professor D. Conomos around Vancouver. Such a beautiful city, clean, festive. Bright blue water in the bay; snowy mountains all around. Then my two lectures, and lunch with the Slavic Department. At night, a lecture at the local Russian parish. Everywhere a dual experience: feebleness, distressing feebleness of Orthodoxy, and its power. Tomorrow, back to New York.

### Friday, March 16, 1979

Vancouver, before my return flight to New York. I had tea at the local priest's house. Such good people, everywhere, in the Church; my guide in Vancouver, Professor Conomos, Deacon Somov and his wife. Presence of such good people, such goodness everywhere. But few people see that goodness—and the world appears as hell!

### Tuesday, March 27, 1979

Ordination to the priesthood of Father Andrew Tregubov. Beautiful Annunciation with the celebration of the Cross.

L. going back to Baltimore for tests.

### Thursday, March 29, 1979

On Monday, the 26th, the signing of the treaty between Israel and Egypt. James Reston underlines in yesterday's *New York Times* the religious dimension of the three "creators" of this world: Carter, Sadat and Begin. "Belief in believing" says he. Even if there is a partial truth in this, the main factor is different: the part of gain, of mistrust, of endless mental reservations is much too strong. In politics, it cannot be otherwise, but that is why a religious interpretation of this event, and of its main protagonists, seems dangerous. If it were not for a hopeless Western dependency on oil; if it were not for the newly appearing power of the Arab world; if it were not for the dependency of the U.S. on the Jewish contingent; if it were not for the fear of the USSR; if it were not etc. etc.—I am afraid that there would not be much left of this "religious inspiration."

## Sunday, April 1, 1979

Long phone conversations with Nikita S[truve] and Natasha Solzhenitsyn (about the crisis in Paris over Ivan Morozov's suicide, ascribed to the two above). I feel saddened by their irreconcilable attitude, by their desire to finish off their enemies, even to avenge themselves. Once more I am convinced that it is impossible for me to be in any one camp, party, clique.

## Monday, April 2, 1979

### Los Gatos Motel

Yesterday, on the plane, I read a volume of stories by the Soviet writer Vladimir Voinovich. While reading, I forgot at times that I was reading a Soviet author and not, say, Chekhov. Chekhovian people, situations. Same small life, foolishness, fear and kindness.

Conventionalism and, also, small inside "feasts." One more image of Russia. A feeling of a real gap between the "people" and the intelligentsia: Voinovich is a man of the people. He has no "plan," but life is shown in its daily routine, and, as such, strangely enough, it seems less hopeless. A man from the intelligentsia is usually egocentric, occupied with himself; he emphasizes his ideas and thus simplifies them.

Read the letters of Father Dmitri Dudko* (arrested then freed in Moscow), "Letter from the Russian Golgotha" and "Letter to Philaret." Quite strong and truthful, but, in my opinion, why is it necessary to indulge in emotional rhetoric, to create an atmosphere where even truth sounds like an exaggeration and generates mistrust?

All these days, the papers are filled with news about a serious nuclear

---

* Dudko, Father Dimitri—Priest of the Russian Orthodox Church, and author of *Our Hope* (Crestwood, NY: SVS Press, 1982).

malfunction near Harrisburg, PA. Immediately a collective hysteria begins, fanned by the press and television, without which, evidently, people can't live. Huge crowds of students with posters, loud screams, like we saw against Vietnam, against Watergate. There appears to be an amazing *need* for a holy anger, for creating an enemy; and fanning it; an enormous feeling of self-righteousness, of self-adulation.

An Islamic Republic has been proclaimed in Iran: 99 percent of the voters voted for it! The vote was open for everybody to see, in an enthusiastic atmosphere. How absolutely familiar and repulsive. How foolish—always and everywhere—are the masses. Nobody knows, nobody told anybody *what* this Islamic Republic will be. Everything is taken on trust. Maybe this is what is essential to understand in our times: a radical turn from politics in the usual sense to a massive thirst for a charismatic leader. People do not believe what the leader is *saying,* but believe *in* him. He says: "Islamic Republic," and nobody except "rotten and Westernizing" people ask, "What is it?" Really, people only want and look for someone to whom they can surrender their hated and unbearable freedom.

But is not Christ also a charismatic leader? Does not trust in Him, belief in Him, come before the acceptance of His commandments? Where is the fundamental difference that contemporary people feel and sense less and less? Does the difference, before anything else, consist in the fact that Christ does not want, nor does He seek, any power *over* people; that He declines every time the temptation of changing individual people into a crowd, a collective, a blind obedience? Is not the difference in the refusal to identify His "concern" for the world with any earthly "project," in a constant affirmation of the transcendence of that "concern"—an appeal to the heavenly, to the Kingdom which is not of this world? Only two poles: a concrete love for one's neighbor here and now (cure, feed, etc.), and search for the Kingdom of God and eternal life. Total indifference to daily cares, a sort of contempt for them—give to Caesar the things that are Caesar's. Your service to the world, says Christ, is in complete freedom *from* the world, and in this freedom—your victory over the world.

## *Wednesday, April 4, 1979*

Acute need for solitude, peace, silence, concentration.

Yesterday, an unexpected joy: the Serbian translation of *For the Life of the World.* The book is very nicely published, and in the preface, Father Amphilokhy [Radovovic] speaks of me as the heir to Bulgakov, Berdyaev, Shestov and someone else! I never quite understand the success of that book.

Appointments, like every Tuesday, with students. It would be so profitable to spend a lot of time with each of them to fashion them, to form them...But I have neither the talent, nor the time. Maybe laziness...??

## Friday, April 6, 1979

A letter yesterday from N. who complains that her priest has forbidden her to participate in a group of Christian students at Manhattanville College (prayers, Bible study, etc.). "He told me that it's a sin, that I pray there to a different God, not to the real God...that the Protestant Christ is not the same Christ as the Orthodox one..." O Lord, what a mess, what mediocrity—our empirical Orthodoxy. I answered as well as I could, but I do not know whether what I tried to say will reach her.

Yesterday morning, the Canon of Saint Andrew; today, Akathist to the Theotokos—and a very bright, cold sun. I went to the French bookstore where the saleswoman confirmed massive sales of books about magic. It seems to me that nobody in this world wants to breathe fresh air—freely, joyfully, lovingly. Only old New York workers, sales people, who joyously greet me, "Hi Father!"; and it is clear that they simply like meeting a priest; that, in general, they are open to something "good" in life. An old black waitress in Chock Full O' Nuts, where I stopped for a sandwich, called me "darling"! "Hidden from the wise, revealed to the humble"—and they are happy! But this happiness shocks all wise men, all specialists in religion. For them, everything is a "problem," a difficulty. At the seminary, our priests are overtired because of constant talks with the students about their problems. And to the seminary come so many tortured people, torturing themselves, obsessed with heavy maximalism. I think about that while anticipating today's beloved Akathist: "Rejoice..." If only I could let this joy not die in my soul...Please, Lord!

## Wednesday, April 11, 1979

Saturday and Sunday in Toronto. In two Churches—OCA and Antiochian. Two lectures, two sermons, common confession, talks with the priests. Sunday night—snowstorm.

Today, I woke up quite early. I am alone in Crestwood, and reread two stories by Ivan Bunin which I know by heart. Fear of death in a radiant world with sun, greenery, fragrance...

Flow of letters from Paris. A feeling that a dam is broken, everything is flooded by a wake of insanity, hatred, disintegration. I am trying to answer the letters, but, essentially, I do not know what to do.

Executions in Iran. Signs of beginning persecutions of Christians in India. Hatred of Sadat by Arabs. How can the world, bursting with these dark passions, avoid exploding?

The Pope has reaffirmed the rule of priests' celibacy. The *New York Times* writes that every year three thousand Catholics leave the priesthood. Nervous breakdown of Christianity, total confusion. The Church literally does not know what to do in the world. Perhaps it is the price to pay for the centuries'-old substitution of Christ—by Christians!

### Holy Wednesday, April 18, 1979

For the first time this year I feel quite old. Never before. I always thought that my most important, my main time was ahead. And suddenly I noticed that my memory is weakening—especially names. In my subconscious, I feel that "the day is leaning towards evening..."

### Holy Friday, April 20, 1979

Time immobile...Three hours standing before the Cross, reading the twelve Gospels. And so—every year, "always, now and ever..." While listening (there were six priests), I thought that this was my fifty-first or fifty-second time, without ever missing one. In the morning, the *Red* Liturgy of Great and Holy Thursday. I will say it again: It is *not* Holy Week that is *coming back*; we are *returning to it*, touching it, communing with it. There—all is already eternity. As a special blessing and grace—blindingly bright days.

### Wednesday, May 2, 1979

Pascha—joyous and bright, more than ever. Then, on Pascha evening, to Paris. Three hours in Luxembourg, then a four-hour train ride to Paris. My brother Andrei—always the same acute joy to see him!

Six days in Paris. Six days of rain, of wetness. Daily visits with mother in her "home." And the rest of the time, tense, painful search for ways toward a reconciliation in the little world of the Orthodox Christian Movement, literally collapsed and living in intense mutual hate. I am torn between hope and distress.

### Thursday, May 3, 1979

Recurrent, yearly, already habitual crisis at the seminary. I always wonder: Where does that tension come from, these seething passions, these radical disagreements—wherever there is religion? It is as if professional religiosity was creating an immunity against its own basic requirements: love, mercy, patience, etc. It's enough to join the seminary for smoldering, basic passions to flare up with a bright flame, as if some fuel had been added.

## Thursday, May 10, 1979

*Washington, D.C.*

Spent two days in Oklahoma with Antiochian priests. Humid, hot and a very strong, quite restless and unpleasant wind. Whole day, debates, talks, "ecclesiastics." This morning in Washington, D.C., attending a symposium in Dumbarton Oaks dedicated to Byzantine Liturgy. For a long time I had quite a dislike for Byzantinism—and what I heard so far confirms my opinion. One seeks small exciting details—exotic and mysterious…!

While flying from Hartford, Connecticut (funeral of Kunett) to Oklahoma, I read *The Heroic Feat* by Nabokov—one of his earlier novels, which I read long ago. The most humane of his novels, not yet spoiled by deadening irony, as in *Despair.*

Inspiring reading of Levy's *God's Testament.* I have the feeling that something is being purified, is rising above life's confusion and pettiness. Levy, with a joyous and religious inspiration, glorifies Jewish monotheism. It is still far from Christianity, but it is already the God of Abraham, Isaac and Jacob, and not Hegelianism. The whole book is permeated with, "I sought your commandments…"

I am reading Nabokov as if I am settling some personal score with him. Maybe because I always read him with a sort of physical enjoyment. Endlessly "tasty." But this reading feels almost as if I am taking part in something "bad"—so that I need some catharsis, some clarification: What is "bad"? I never had that feeling while reading other Russian writers. Nabokov is always stuck in total emptiness. His *Despair* concerns the despair of a creator who has come to the conclusion that his whole creativity was inevitably a failure, obvious to everybody except him (but how much effort, how many details to kill this Felix, to commit the "perfect crime").

## Friday, May 11, 1979

*Dumbarton Oaks, Washington, D.C.*

Continuing heat wave. I read my report ("Symbols and Symbolism") right after R. Taft, who had praised a horrible commentary of Germanus of Constantinople. There followed a sort of argument, which slightly enlivened the terrible boredom of such symposia. Most of those attending were art connoisseurs of a Byzantine vintage. They could talk for hours about icons and curtains and temples and narthexes, but had never become interested in the only thing that could have added *some* interest to the discussion. But all this took place in a very elegant Dumbarton Oaks, with excellent dinners and cocktails, so it was bearable.

Talks about symbols: I don't know of any more aimless talks. Down deep, they are a substitute for "life in abundance."

### Friday, May 18, 1979

A kind person—a virtuous person. Between them, there is a big difference. A kind person is kind because he or she accepts people as they are, covers them with kindness. Kindness is beautiful, the most beautiful thing on this earth. Virtuous people are activists, obsessed with the desire to impose their principles and goodness and easily condemning, destroying, hating. Turgenev, Chekhov are kind people. In this world there is a lot of virtue, and so little kindness.

### Wednesday, May 23, 1979

Spent the day at Solzhenitsyn's Vermont retreat. First, coffee with his wife, Nikita Struve and Alexander Ginsburg. Then an hour conversation with Solzhenitsyn. The general impression...

### Friday, May 25, 1979

...is that he has settled down. In any case at this stage of his life, he knows what he wants to write and do; he has control of his topic. Hence, a polite indifference to any other opinion; absence of interest, of curiosity. He put aside some time for me, for a personal talk, but the talk was about nothing—friendly, but for him quite unnecessary. He has already found his course of action, his question (about the revolution, about Russia), and his answer. He is developing this answer in a novel; others must corroborate his research. The elements of this answer, as I see them: Russia did not accept Bolshevism and resisted it (a revision of all the explanations of the Civil War). Russia was conquered from outside, but remained healthy at its core (e.g. peasant writers, who are now rising). The victory of Bolshevism was helped by those who turned their backs on the essence of Russia—the authorities (Peter the Great, Petersburg, the Empire) and the intelligentsia (Westernizers). Bolshevism was a plot against the Russian people. No Western ideas nor values ("rights," "freedom," "democracy") can fit Russia, nor can be applied to Russia. Western goodness is not Russian goodness: the crime of the dissidents from Russia is that they do not understand this.

Therefore, he is working with a frightening inhuman tension on a "novel with a thesis." The question: Will he, Solzhenitsyn, conquer the thesis, or will the thesis conquer him? This "thesis " is for him absolutely essential because he lives by what he writes; on the other hand, it is dangerous because it is constricting for the writer in him. It is the eternal gamble of Russian literature. Without a thesis, there would not be any literature. But there is a Russian literature that is successful as literature only to the extent that it overcomes not only the "thesis," but the full dependence on it.

It seems that the only one who is free from the conflict of "thesis vs. writer" is Pushkin—and in all its soaring, Russian poetry.

### Thursday, June 28, 1979

This whole week—Summer Institute—seminar about death, funerals, etc. I lecture (quite inspired, with conviction). I listen, discuss—and all the time have a stronger and stronger question in my mind: What about you yourself? What about your death? How are things in that area?

L.'s medical checkup went well; all is in order. These past two weeks we lived under that threat.

### Monday, August 13, 1979

I am in Crestwood, where I came from Labelle for Father Georges Florovsky's funeral.

The same day I heard about Professor Weidle's death. All my professors at St Sergius Institute have died; now it's our generation's turn!

Wonderful summer! Two weeks with Andrei. Then, three weeks of Serge, Mania and their children in Labelle: this was an enormous joy!

I worked, first on death (*The Celebration of Death*); then editing the Russian translation of my *Great Lent* (it's not *my* Russian language, it's the translator's, but, thank God, it's done). Finally, started working (again) on my *Eucharist*. Every day, our walks—with ever-increasing, almost painful, joy—about fields, sky, woods, about God's world. And almost all the time, sunshine and warmth.

Read *Albert Camus*—a huge biography by Luttman. Rather disappointing. Camus does not appear as a great man, in all that French glitter, as the author tried to present him.

I noticed that when I work ("create") I not only read less, but I don't feel like reading anything too serious. Maybe not to disturb the inner working of my thought, of "contemplation"...

Continuous interest in the Khomeini phenomenon in Iran, and also the "fall" of Carter—rather his extraordinary failure. I unite these two names because here and there religion is mixed in, and here and there, religion is one of the main factors of the failure, the collapse, the tragedy.

## Monday, August 27, 1979

*Crestwood*

Last evening L. and I drove back from Vermont where we spent two days with the Solzhenitsyns. Sunday Liturgy, everybody took part. Solzhenitsyn himself is somewhat absent, though friendly. He is obsessed with his writing and his fights against enemies—those who doubt the grand resurrection of Russia ("our" people, "our" tendencies, "they"…). And as background, a simplified condemnation of the evil West. On Saturday night, his three boys played the piano, recited long poems—without any affectation. What will they become in this airless space? Amazing lack of interest in anything that we do. They are completely bound in themselves.

Professor Florovsky's funeral was quite sad; very few people, no choir, messy service.

In Labelle, I read the rather extraordinary *Letters* of Flannery O'Connor (*The Habit of Being: Letters of Flannery O'Connor*).

## Tuesday, August 28, 1979

*Feast of the Dormition*

First contact with the seminary. How many years? All is in order, familiar; it's all mine, part of me. But precisely this habit is frightening: I know that nothing consumes time as unnoticeably, but totally, as this habit does.

Yesterday we heard the news of Serge's appointment to the Moscow Bureau.

## Tuesday, September 4, 1979

From Thursday to Saturday, in East Hampton at the seashore. Blessed plunge in a sunny feast.

Labor Day at home. Putting my office, my desk, books, in order. Such a pleasure—as after a cleansing bath! How many letters and documents, which seemed so important—and now, nothing is left of what all these papers were about. What remains of life? So little. Recently, I thought with great surprise, almost horror, that for three years, as I walked in Paris from home to school, I can't remember once leaving home, not a single morning. How did I get up? What happened every day? It's as if these three years simply did not exist.

Last week, two interviews: in *Nouvel Observateur* with Maurice Clavel, who passionately rejects as the devil's inspiration a spirituality without God; where he sees a new and frightening substitution for faith. Another interview with Mircea Eliade, who speaks with great inspiration about the sacred, the holy, cosmic time, saved history, etc., without a word about God. Really, it seems that Eliade's "optimism" is confirmed: we are seized, swamped by this troubled wave of spiritualism, the highest, hence the most frightening form of pride.

All these days, I am reading Flannery O'Connor's *Letters*; extraordinary in their sobriety, depth, absence of anything false.

In the Dominican Republic, hurricane David destroyed a church where 400 people had taken shelter. Everyone died! What a horrible symbol; what a terrible fate!

Father Tom Hopko was telling me about his trip to Europe, to Taizé. Hundreds of young men and women. About the Syndesmos conference in Montgeron, near Paris. One gets the impression that the Church and Christianity are somehow busily bustling, but "without sails or wheels." They discuss and discuss without taking time to pause for a breath.

I reflect, while writing my *Eucharist*, about Communion, on the strange, mysterious alienation from it in the Church (on Mt. Athos—they don't regularly take Communion; in our churches, those who seek frequent Communion are held in suspicion). Mystically—it is the central question. The transformation of communion into the "sacred," the taboo, and, thus, a paradoxical naturalization (as awesome, demanding purification, etc.). Deafness to the absolute simplicity of "Take, eat..."—simplicity and humility, which alone correspond to the absolute transcendence of the Eucharist.

## Friday, September 7, 1979

I read a little book by Bishop Paul Moore [Episcopalian bishop of New York]—the explanation of his ordination of a lesbian to the priesthood. In a way, it is an extraordinary book, extraordinary as a witness to the radical transformation of Christian love into something quite different, literally quite opposite. The author does not see, does not understand that if Christian love were what he makes it to be, the whole Christian teaching, the whole Gospel would be totally meaningless. The question is essentially about the earthly happiness of man, i.e., not about man's denial of self for the sake of a new life, but on the contrary, about Christianity as a method of self-acceptance. Even the enemies of Bishop Moore do not see it. For them, there is good sex and bad sex (homosexuality). They do not understand that in the area of sex, we deal with the fallen world, so that Moore seems to be defending love against moralists and Pharisees. People do not understand that grace liberates us, before anything else, from ourselves, from our en-slavement by flesh and blood ("It is no longer I who live, but Christ who lives in me" Galatians 2:20). Here, Christianity is the affirmation of the natural man with all his lust... Amazing that people of Moore's type, educated, theologians, simply do not see this radical substitution.

## *Sunday, September 9, 1979*

This whole week was the beginning of the school year. Students' arrival, old and new, meeting them, registration, and, finally the crowning Feast of the Nativity of the Theotokos. A feeling of joyful excitement, for which I am endlessly grateful. Truly: *Grace.*

I finished Flannery O'Connor—also with gratitude—for the purity, clar-ity, simplicity of her testimony. Almost at the end, a year before her death, she writes:

> I do pray for you, but in my fashion which is not a very good one. I am not a good prayer. I don't have a gift for it. My type of spirituality is almost com-pletely shut-mouth. I really dislike books on piety most of all. They do noth-ing for me and they corrupt most people's ear if nothing else... (p. 572).

And this quote from Braque:

> ...I like the rule that corrects the emotion... (p. 486).

I spent almost the whole day reflecting on a course which I must give this semester: "The Church in Russian Thought and Literature." The topic of this course, or rather, its perspective for me, is Christian culture and its col-lapse. The significance of Russian literature in this perspective lies in the fact that it is both a testimony, one can even say, a prophecy about this collapse, and its last, maybe its brightest incarnation. But I don't quite know how to put it all together.

Christianity is not *about* culture, but it cannot avoid giving birth to cul-ture, inasmuch as culture is a holistic vision of God, man and the world. By tearing itself away from culture, Christianity either becomes "clerical" (reli-gion, not life) or betrays itself, "surrenders" to culture. About this there are testimonies in books that I read by chance (without planning any research): Berger's *The Heretical Imperative* and P. Moore's—*Take a Bishop Like Me*.

The mediocrity of the understanding of Church these days: either little parish affairs, or secular activism, falsehood.

### Monday, September 10, 1979

First days of lectures. Five hours: three in the morning; two at night! At the lecture about Russian literature, lots of people. I think that it was good. While preparing for the lecture, I glanced through Nabokov's *Gogol* and Billington's *The Icon and the Axe*. There is a strange desire to explain Russian culture, not *ad malem partem*, but from "below." Some strange resistance to anything that comes from above. Denial of a "gift." A large group of Russian dissidents attended the lecture.

Once more I was convinced today that such a lecture is addressed also to me and that I learn a great deal while lecturing. A sort of consolation—only while talking to others do I understand and fully take in what I am saying.

### Friday, September 14, 1979

*Exaltation of the Cross*

Last evening, at the Vigil (concelebrated by Metropolitan Theodosius), the church was packed. Beautiful choir. And for an instant, with all my heart, I felt the *truth* of this ritual. The Cross is lowered, as if disappearing, and then is slowly raised—victoriously, joyously. Like an answer to the sort of depression of these last days that comes from contemplating the world's collapse, the triumph in the world of evil and absurdity.

### Monday, September 17, 1979

Quiet, working weekend, with wonderful sunny and cool weather. I was struggling, if one can say so, with "The Sacrament of Repentance"—with its historical, theological, psychological metamorphoses. As always, I wonder: it seems that theology simply has not said anything sensible about the question of repentance. *How* and *why* has the sacrament of reconciliation with the Church been transformed into our contemporary three-minute confession? *How* and *why* was all laity transformed into excommunicated individuals. There are no answers. Nobody ever bothered to deal with it, whereas for the Church, for its daily life, there is no more vital, urgent problem. What is the "absolution of sins"? In what lies the power to bind and to absolve? It seems that whenever one tries to deal with real "live" questions, one always faces virgin territory and one must start from the beginning, while even this beginning is not clear.

I do not doubt that in spite of all the changes, there is in the sacrament of repentance a progression, some essential, deep basic point, reality itself, the essence of repentance, inseparable from the essence of Christianity. Christianity *is* repentance; that is why the Church *is* the Sacrament of Repentance, and thus the Sacrament of Repentance is *in* the Church. But to comprehend, to uncover the genuine meaning and content of this "Tri-unity" is not easy because everything becomes ambiguous. Repentance is *not* longing for righteousness, but longing for God: "…cast me not away from your presence, and take not your holy Spirit from me" (Psalm 51). In isolation from this theocentricity, repentance becomes anthropocentric and unavoidably slides either to a juridical or a psychological approach. But how can this sacrament be restored if the faithful themselves accept this reduction which permeates our whole culture?

I started working on "The Sacrament of Remembrance" and see right away how difficult it is going to be.

### *Tuesday, September 18, 1979*

Letter from Mother…repetition, erasures—So sad!

A few quiet hours yesterday, and a gradual plunge into the "Sacrament of Remembrance." As usual, only when really starting to write do I realize what I *want*, or rather, what I *need* to write. Whether I will succeed is another matter.

### *Thursday, September 20, 1979*

I spent time today with three very different people. One—obsessed with Russia, torture, blood, camps, persecution. Tense, intense, excited, burning…! Then, with a young man whose only interest is his painting. Should he continue? should he not? And his whole vision of life rests on it. Finally, a short meeting with a Radio Liberty writer, whose interests revolve around his success, practical, tangible.

Three extremely personal worlds. If these three people would meet, they would not know what to talk about, since each one is totally occupied with himself and would consider the other's interest irrelevant, not worthy of his attention, a waste of time. *My* role—certainly not chosen by me and always a burden—is to listen. While I listen, I feel, alive in me, an interest in what they say, or rather in *them*. But when the conversation ends, nothing remains. And again I ask myself, what is it: self-defense? unwillingness to get involved? indifference? Then it's my sin! Yes, probably that too, but not only. I feel pity that such a bright flame is burning and burning out in each of them, somehow, in vain, it seems to me wasted, spent to no purpose. When spending all our time in even the most important, the most positive occupation, there is no time left simply for life, to meet life, or to experience and to understand *for the sake of what* one is thus occupied. Again, I remember Julien Green's: "All is elsewhere." I don't really know. Maybe I am making an "impious" mistake, but I hear something of this in the words of Christ: "…how long am I to be with you? How long am I to bear with you?" (Matthew 17:17). It does not contradict at all the total love and gift of self to this "you." It is sad that people do not see what is most important, which is not one's occupation, but its transformation, its crowning in life and in the fullness of life. In this world, any endeavor in some sense is cursed and saved *only* when it exists for the sake of life, for the sake of communing with life. Without this connection, any occupation, any endeavor becomes an idol and a torture. What would these words mean for any occupation, "…in the heavens, triumphant and beautiful, in a blue radiance, the world is resting…" And of what use is this bright dream with "a cool source of water, flowing down the ravine"? Meanwhile, everything, almost everything in our life depends on these breakthroughs because in them we get the experience of *life*.

## Monday, September 24, 1979

Is there a common past for Russians? Each—Solzhenitsyn and others—sees it differently. To seek and restore the truth about the past—any past—is impossible, unless one sees it in the light of God. If there is not a desire to see it in God, not humility in facing truth, each one will see the past in the light of his heart's treasure, and also will thrust his own present on those who listen to him, who even in history saw and spoke the truth about Russia. Prophecy is needed (love, humility and hatred for idols).

## Monday, October 1, 1979

### Feast of the Protection of the Holy Virgin

During the early morning Liturgy, I preached about the rejection of suffering by our world, by the contemporary man. The symbol of our age—the painkiller.

Everything is directed at fighting suffering, so that religion is also perceived as a pain killer. Quite a difference between this truly demonic approach to life and the one revealed in the Feast of the Protection, in the whole image of the Mother of God. Yes, here also we find "help us," "have mercy," but with the knowledge of life's depth and of suffering as the inescapable fate of man in this world. To stand at the Cross…

Yesterday, in the *New York Times,* articles about tomorrow's arrival of the Pope. The point of these articles is the fear that the Pope does not understand the contemporary world, especially America with its pluralism; does not understand the depth and greatness of the sexual revolution, abortion, denial of dogmatism, etc. Not for a minute does it occur to the authors that all of it can be evaluated differently, from inside faith itself. In the same article, they write that the main religions—liberal and moderate, Presbyterians, Methodists, Lutherans, Catholics—are losing people to conservatives. "It's awful! It's a breach with culture!"—and culture is abortion, adogmatism, etc. Truly: intellectuals are the blind leading the blind…

## Tuesday, October 2, 1979

Yesterday, faculty seminar about pastoral theology. Very scientific, with Greek and psychological terminology and diagrams. All of it might well be formally right. But the knowledge of these rules does not help, will never create pastors. Scholarly theologians do not understand, do not see it. The sum of scientifically stated truths does not discover nor reveal *Truth.* The sum of theories about God, does not give the knowledge of God. There is something pitiful in those debates, agreements, disagreements, corrections, definitions. I feel it with special intensity right now, having just painfully expelled one of our students. Always the same, absolute "apart from Me, you can do nothing" (John 15:5).

## Wednesday, October 3, 1979

The Pope of Rome is in New York. We watched him on television in Yankee Stadium. A mixed impression. On one hand, an unquestionably good man and full of light. Wonderful smile. Very genuine—a man of God. But, on the other hand, there are some "buts"! First of all, the Mass itself. The first impression is how liturgically impoverished the Catholic Church has become. In 1965, I watched the service performed by Pope Paul VI in the same Yankee Stadium. Despite everything, it was the presence, the appearance on earth of the eternal, the "super earthly." Whereas yesterday, I had the feeling that the main thing was the "message." This message is, again and again, "peace and justice," "human family," "social work," etc. An opportunity was given, a fantastic chance to tell millions and millions of people about God, to reveal to them that more than anything else they need God! But here, on the contrary, the whole goal, it seemed, consisted in proving that the Church *also* can speak the jargon of the United Nations. All the symbols point the same way: the reading of the Scriptures by some lay people with bright ties, etc.

And a horrible translation: I never suspected that a translation could be a heresy: Grace—"abiding love"!

Crowds—their joy and excitement. Quite genuine, but at the same time, it is clear that there is an element of mass psychosis. "Peoples' Pope..." What does this really mean? I don't know. I am not sure. Does one have to serve Mass in Yankee Stadium? But if it's possible and needed, shouldn't the Mass be, so to say, "super earthly," separated from the secular world, in order to show *in the world*—the Kingdom of God?

### Thursday, October 4, 1979

The Pope's days in New York are accompanied by extreme excitement and rapture. What remains is that one can see something quite genuine (man's longing for goodness) and something obviously connected with our civilization: television, "media," etc. What worries me is this: this popularity will recede as soon as the Pope concretely expresses his faith. Then the euphoria will end... And then will begin: "crucify Him" and "we have no King, but Caesar..."—i.e., a return to the present. (Mark 15:13-14, John 19:15)

### Friday, October 5, 1979

The prophecy did not take long to become reality. Yesterday the Pope spoke in Philadelphia against abortion, against ordination of women, etc. And today the tone in the *New York Times* changed significantly and the *Washington Post* came down on the Pope because he did not mention Israel by name. *Sic transit gloria mundi.*

### Saturday, October 6, 1979

*Mayflower Hotel in Washington, D.C.*

I came here after the incredible but joyful bustle of Education Day. Glorious Liturgy in a huge tent. Beautiful, cool, sunny day. Once more, *immersion in the Church*, and the feeling: What would we be, what would I be, without the Church? Communion from four chalices. I preached about "...no eye has seen, nor ear heard, nor the heart of man conceived, what God has prepared for those who love him."(1 Cor 2:9)

The Pope continues—yesterday against homosexuality. Therefore, a new "tune" in the press: "...he did not understand American pluralism." While flying here for a meeting with the Pope (tomorrow morning), I thought about this pluralism, which by its very essence consists of rejecting (cannot *not* reject) the concept of *Truth*. Pluralism is an *a priori* affirmation that there are different points of view about everything and the "operative" principle of pluralism is affirming that one must not, need not, ever question them. These points of view exist—and that's all. One must respect them, and, as far as possible, share them. And the poor Pope did not understand it! The deadly foolishness of all that magniloquence!

The Catholics in America—if not all, then many—plunged with naive delight in this pluralism, so that it will be interesting to see whether or not the Pope will succeed in turning the tide. Father Tom [Hopko] predicts that there will be a schism. I don't know. I only know that this pluralism—for religion—is death and decay.

## Tuesday, October 9, 1979

We had to wait a very long time to see the Pope in the reception room of Catholic University. He was two hours late. A huge auditorium packed with academics in multi-colored doctoral gowns and clergy. An orchestra continuously playing some noisy marches, which made the waiting rather painful. The Pope was actually next door—at the Shrine of the Immaculate Conception—where, as was announced later, some nuns were holding a protest.

Finally he appeared. A paroxysm of total rapture—never, nowhere have I seen the like. I don't think that the people assembled there were particularly "papist." No, rather typical American intellectuals, with a touch of cynicism. But they also screamed and threw their caps high in the air—for a long, long time. While he walked slowly through the auditorium, the choir and the orchestra were roaring Liszt's *Tu es Petrus*.

And I felt—not only on that Sunday morning, in the physical presence of the Pope, but also before that, when I followed him on television—that people, crowds, who go into rapture when with him, do so *not* because they see in him Peter or Christ, but on the contrary, they "believe" in *him*, while they accept Peter and Christ, and Christianity in general, without too much interest. Only *he* is needed, the Pope, needed as manna, as a physical presence of the supernatural. Like the unfortunate nuns who pathologically seek priesthood, those who resist this psychosis and are relatively free from it are already obsessed by something else. Again, a thirst for the sacred. And I fear, for religion.

Another temptation of religion—which was made clear to me in conversations about some priests—is *piety*. Looking at some of our priests, walking around the seminary on Education Day, one can physically feel their worship of cassocks, clerical hats, all that constitutes this visible piety. And then one hears that almost all of them are condemning all others for lack of spirituality, lack of piety.

People are torturing each other. After a few conversations yesterday, I felt the essence and the heaviness of evil as well as its painful and irrational strength.

## Saturday, October 13, 1979

Two days in Chicago: meeting with Orthodox clergy, then lecture at a cluster of theological schools, lunch and dinner with theologians. All of that, in an extremely friendly, brotherly atmosphere, a gift of joy and happiness against the background of my beloved Chicago, sunny and already autumnal. Like a respite, since next week, there will be a bishops' assembly and I am worried. There seems to be little unity and many passions and mistrust. But my long-life experience is reassuring: the grace of the Holy Spirit never leaves the Church!

In Chicago, yesterday morning, long interview with Roy Larson, the religion editor of the *Chicago Sun-Times*. Talk about the Pope and the tumultuous days of his trip to America. I told Roy I am convinced that this phenomenal success will not make even one nun go back to wearing a robe. And I have an almost immediate proof: during lunch, five Jesuits and one Franciscan, professors at the Catholic Union, are wearing elaborate lay clothes, almost glaring with their multi-colored ties, light suits, colored vests. Jesuits and Franciscans! Two nuns (one assistant dean, the other a professor) also, not only in civilian clothes, but in a very deliberate, carefully thought out civilian apparel. I do *not* write this in condemnation, *not at all*, but only as proof of my affirmation: the Pope will not succeed in turning back Catholicism. Maybe he will not succeed because he is trying to achieve this turning back seeing not only the salvation of the Church, but its very essence in the restoration of the monolithic character of the Church of Rome. The tragic paradox of Catholicism is that without an absolute obedience to the Pope, without the cult of the Pope, Catholicism falls apart. But *with* this cult and obedience, it reaches a dead end. And the question—as I understand it—is: Will the Pope be willing to pay for the restoration of the monolithic structure of the Church, with the loss of many of its incurable members, as the Papacy had to pay the price for the infallibility of the Pope in 1870, by the schism of Old Catholics? But, at that time, the great majority of theologians were ultra-Montane and the schism was hardly noticed. Whereas *now*, it is not just a majority, but theology as a whole, the whole *thought* in Catholicism that is against the monolith, against Papacy as it is now. After only a week of the unheard of triumph of the Pope and the Papacy, these Jesuits and nuns look and behave as if "nothing was the matter," as if all of it had nothing to do with them. They are not even angry, or sad, or hopeless. This triumph, says Roy Larson, my interviewer, might have some influence on the young people who might join the seminaries. Will it be better? Will they be narrow clerics and "religious" people? I agree with that fear.

Yesterday, during a very friendly and genuinely disturbed discussion after my lecture (about the Holy Spirit, the Liturgy, Eschatology) these same Jesuits in bright ties ask: "…yes, but the world; where is the world? Where does it connect with the world?" And I answer: Yes, maybe, there is a frightening, devilish perception of the Church: faith *in* the Church, replacing faith in God and simply excluding the world. Whereas the Church is needed only because the Church is not a third element—between God and the world—but a new life (i.e., life with God and in God) of creation itself, of the world itself. The Catholic idolization of the Church—is it out of fear of that temptation which is alive mainly in Catholicism, almost identified with Catholicism, that these Jesuits take off their collars and cassocks? Maybe their fear *has to be* understood, has to be heard. No, it is *not* simply liberalism, it is also the knowledge of sin inherent in a certain type of churchliness. It is not by chance that our own young churchly people turn back with such enthusiasm to cassocks, to clerical hats, to the whole clerical apparatus. I may be wrong, but it seems to me that if they loved above all God and their neighbors, it all would not be so necessary. But they often love the Church *in se*; its triumph, albeit symbolic, is their triumph. "And God?"

In any case, the crisis of Catholicism which, I am certain, is not being solved, but is deepening with this monolithic Pope, is our common crisis, in which, whether we want it or not, we are included. If the Pope is successful, clericalism will become stronger for all Christians. If the Pope is not successful, clericalism will, in any case, become stronger in *our* Church because we will be the last truly apocalyptic carriers and worshippers of the *typikon*, of canonical law and of clerical triumphalism. One must pray for the Church!

## *Sunday, October 14, 1979*

The 19th century—Hegel and Co.—worshipped history. Now, disappointed by history, the majority of thinkers, as well as all sorts of spiritualists, are "dethroning" history. Some affirm that only in history, only serving history and its meaning, can man find meaning in his own life. Others, with as much passion, affirm that only in being liberated from history can one find this meaning. The Christians have accepted this "either-or" and submitted themselves to it. This is the tragedy of contemporary Christianity—tragedy because ultimately the whole novelty of Christianity consisted (consists) in destroying this choice, this polarization. *This* is the essence of Christianity as Eschatology. The Kingdom of God is the goal of history, and the Kingdom of God is already now *among us, within us.* Christianity is a unique historical event, and Christianity is the presence of that event as the completion of all events and of history itself. And only in order that it be so, only for that, only in that, is the Church, its essence, its meaning.

This all seems like elementary truths. But then why are they not effective? Is it not because Christianity started being, on the one hand, "perceived" (piety), and on the other hand "interpreted," "explained," (theology)—according to the views of this world and not *in Christ.*

Here is, for me, *the whole meaning of liturgical theology.* The Liturgy: the joining, revelation, actualization of the historicity of Christianity (remembrance) and of its transcendence over that historicity ("*Today,* the Son of God...") The joining of the end with the beginning, but the joining today, here...

Hence, the link of the Church with the world, the Church *for the world,* but as its beginning and its end, as the affirmation that the world is *for the Church,* since the Church is the presence of the Kingdom of God.

Here is the eternal antinomy of Christianity and the essence of all contemporary discussions about Christianity. The task of theology is to be faithful to the antinomy, which disappears in the experience of the Church as *Pascha*: a *continuous* (not only historical) passage of the world to the Kingdom. All the time one must leave the world and all the time one must remain in it.

The temptation of piety is to reduce Christianity to piety; the temptation of theology—to reduce it totally to history.

### Wednesday, October 17, 1979

"Freedom." I read recently a few lines from the Koran and I felt what it is that moves the Ayatollah, why he hates freedom, which in its Western understanding and perception is directly connected with moral and ideological relativism. Both the Ayatollah *and* Solzhenitsyn deeply hate relativism, since they consider their vision of the world to be absolute. The combination, one can even say the coincidence, of Truth and Freedom is possible only in Christ, but it is already breaking up in Christianity inasmuch as Christianity is not Christ Himself, but *about* Him, the conclusion *from* Him, the keeping of His teaching.

*Thursday, October 18, 1979*

Tired! Not physically; differently. Tired from all that consumes—little by little—all my time. Today—my only day in New York City. It is my constant dream to sit at my desk and work on my *Eucharist*. But I wake up and remember that in the morning I have to go to Radio Liberty to deliver a radio script; at noon, a memorial service; then lunch with Father Lutge, followed by a counseling meeting with N. and his fiancee. The whole day is already eaten up and I am so discouraged! I know that depression is always sinful. But the reason is that except for Radio Liberty, the rest is quite unnecessary; rather, I am not needed. But the day is killed, and not for the first time.

For weeks I don't do anything really needful. Thus I am always depressed and trying to tell myself that perhaps, in God's eyes, what *I* need for myself is not needed and I must humble myself and accept life as is! L. always tells me: "You don't know how to say 'no'!" It would be possible and good to do so, only if I could do it out of love, out of something like: "I am defeated by them all, and only in that is my victory!" But I don't really feel love; on the contrary, irritation. Soon I will be 60, and I continue to flutter around, on and on. Besides, I don't really know who I would be *if* God had given me the longed-for solitude and freedom! Having said that, I have to start my day.

Quote from an article about Solzhenitsyn in *l'Express*: "Solzhenitsyn confirms quite clearly what Ionesco recently wrote, 'Utopians hate happiness, which they consider a kind of vice'."

Another quote from the Pope's speech to a group of theologians in Rome: "an authentic theological involvement can only start and end on your knees... There is today the risk for theologians to belong to the cohort of chattering arguers."

An article by Hans Küng: "*Jean Paul II—An Interrogation.*" It is clear that Hans Küng is dissatisfied with a Pope who is "a defender of old bastions" (*Le Monde* 17/10/79). What Küng does not realize and does not feel is how impossible it is for the Catholic Church to accept his program, his theological method, his understanding of the Church, etc. Küng is essentially preaching and preparing a new Reformation and the Pope cannot allow it. Such is the dead end of Catholicism. The only thing that Catholicism can do is to periodically purge itself of any Reformation: in the 16th century, Martin Luther; in the 19th, Lamennais, then the Old Catholics; in the 20th, the modernists, and now, the Küngs and Co. How can one not understand that infallibility, i.e., the absolute authority *ex sese, non ex consensu Ecclesiae*, is not a deviation, a change, but the *norm;* denying it, the Roman Church begins to collapse. In the same issue of *Le Monde,* a different bell is ringing. A certain Jean R. Armogathe, a Parisian priest, writes, "…for the first time, I saw people acclaim a man who spoke about fidelity, true love, control of one's body, respect for life. A man who fearlessly said that enjoyment is not the ultimate goal of life, that the visible does not coincide with the real. Those are new words: the true sense of the human is a new idea in this world. These novelties disturb and perplex; could this Pope, who comes from nowhere, be a dissident, dissident against our consumer society, dissident against our inhuman liberalism?"

"Inhuman liberalism"—well put! And compared to this short note of a young priest, Küng's article and another by some pastor (who is indignant at the Pope's return to Mariology) seem repetitive, boring, precisely the product of "inhuman liberalism."

## Tuesday, October 23, 1979

Reading C. S. Lewis' letters to his friend. The years 1917-18, time of the Revolution in Russia. In the letters, not a word about it, only England, English literature, Oxford. . . Worlds torn apart, each totally self-sufficient.

Lecturing always gives me joy. Last evening about Tolstoy. Today, a course on liturgics, about the Holy Spirit. Why can I speak rather easily and while speaking give birth to thought, yet find it so difficult to write?

What is the most frightening aspect of social work, administration, power? It is the gradually growing indifference, a certain passive cruelty. In order to satisfy *everybody,* one way or another, one must limit each, reduce one's rapport with each to a minimum, until it becomes impersonal. Each person demands everything. The mystery of Christ: giving Himself totally to each one.

## Monday, October 29, 1979

Spent Friday and Saturday attending the Canadian Diocesan Assembly in Moose Jaw, Saskatchewan. So far! Strongly impressed by the enormous prairies, the grain basket of Canada.

At the assembly, I spoke about the Church. In Canada, there is hardly a spark left in our Church, and an absence of any leadership. But then, some young priests appear, and, Lord willing, the flame will become brighter. Looking at these young people, listening to them, I thought: "the gates of hell will not prevail…" The flame is almost dying and lives again.

Read with infinite pleasure R. Emmet Tyrrel's *Public Nuisances,* about the vulgarity of contemporary politics.

I reread for my evening lecture Turgenev's life and his story, *The Living Relic*. I want to show it as an example of "the Mysterious Light," which is the title of my lecture.

### Tuesday, October 30, 1979

Yesterday, during my lecture, I read the whole story, *The Living Relic*. Surprising how even in English it reaches out. And I thought: This, as well as thousands of other enlightening testimonies, has been written, but unfortunately our contemporary culture rejects them, simply does not see, nor hear, nor perceive them. The awesome words of the Gospel come to mind: "and men loved darkness rather than light…" (John 3:19). Precisely: loved more. It is not lack of knowledge; it is a choice, an act of preference!

### Thursday, November 1, 1979

November: one of my favorite months; full of childhood memories. In Paris, this day—All Saints Day—was a school holiday and we, as a family, went to have lunch with my aunts, then to the family plot at the cemetery. It was on this day that I fell gravely ill with peritonitis, requiring immediate surgery. I remember so well wet bare trees behind my window at the hospital. This was the beginning of the deepest crisis of my life: horrible screaming, fear of death. I am sure that at the time, death touched me. In the hospital (age 15) I read (how? and why?) a journal called *Numbers*—the quintessence of a slightly decadent Parisian tonality, which I remember to this day. Since then, since that dual crisis, spiritual and literary, the world has become for me in some way transparent, two-dimensional, enabling me, while living in it, to look at it from the side, and also to see, from within, something "other"(the "all is elsewhere"of Julien Green). That's why I remember not so much "events"—what happened—as the air, light, coloring by sun, rain, clouds when the events happened. All of the things that make the poem of Innokenty Annensky so close and so clear to me:

> What is happiness? …
> Is it an autumn rain,
> the return of the day, the closing of the eyes,
> the good things never treasured,
> clad as they are in unsightly apparel…?

Yesterday, a phone call from Serge from Johannesburg, South Africa. They received visas and the whole family is moving to Moscow! To Moscow, which I feel, is off limits for me. And Serge and his family will live there;

Moscow, Russia will be his profession. How strange life is. And what is the mysterious meaning (there must be one) in all these whims of life?

### Thursday, November 8, 1979

Humiliation of America by the fanatic Khomeini: capture of sixty hostages at the American embassy in Teheran. I feel it as the infamy of the white man who is digging his grave and the grave of our whole Western civilization. Europe is silent—afraid of losing Iranian oil, although a common action by civilized countries could quickly end this nightmarish barbarity. But these "civilized" countries not only can not, but do not want to do it. They are afraid; they fall on their knees and tremble. One is sick from it all. What have we come to? America has literally no power to defend its sixty American citizens. How many mistakes have been made: first, an impetuous support of the Shah, then Leftist delight about the Islamic revolution, and now—a broken trough (cf. fairy tale…).

### Friday, November 9, 1979

Growing agony of the hostages in Teheran. All the television news programs report it continuously. Carter looks like death itself. Demonstrations all over the States. What can be done? If only Khomeini were simply a barbarian, but here we see the horror of a diabolical religious fanaticism. A lesson to all the sweet preachers of rapprochement with Islam. As if its whole history were not a history of slaughter—in the literal sense of the word. And life continues: the faces of the hostages with bound eyes are followed by advertisements about the best lingerie or fresh orange juice, and at night all the stadiums will be full!

### Monday, November 12, 1979

Ninth day of the Teheran tragedy and the same dead end. Again, a fanatical speech by Khomeini condemning the Pope along with Carter. As I listen and read, I think more and more that this tragedy will not end well; that Americans and the West in general do not understand that they are dealing with a totally different logic. This is when one feels and realizes that Christianity, though just a glimmer, is still alive: a certain common language which must be used even by those who do not, in fact, acknowledge, not only Christianity, but the values coming from it. Whereas here—a wall, an absolute conviction in one's right. Even the Communists must maintain some kind of facade. In Iran, under Khomeini, no facade; a full, icy sincerity. A frightening thirst for revenge, a special kind of suffering from unrequited vengeance.

They *need* to hang the dying Shah. Fast, prayer, murder belong to the same reality. And in the West, so many people sincerely believe that all religions are the same.

Although Christianity has become distorted, it will never cease to denounce the lies, the anti-humanity of crowds, of masses; that is of religious fanaticism, totalitarianism, fascism; of a nation as a "conciliar personality," as a carrier of virtues higher than those of an individual person, of religion as "opium for the people," as creating idols, etc...

### *Thursday, November 15, 1979*

Liturgy yesterday at the Staten Island old-age home (Feast of SS. Cosmas and Damian). There is something frightening in this assembly of old men and women in one place, in a house where, because of the requirements of hygiene, everything is absolutely impersonal, clean, shines with some kind of dead brightness. Against the background of this cleanliness—the sight of disintegrating life. Present at the Liturgy and taking Communion were Metropolitan Ireney and three very old priests, literally human ruins. But if I were meeting each of these individuals—who might be close to me in some way, were a part of my life—in some different situation, warmed by life, I am quite sure I would not have this awful impression. The impression is not only of a death cell, but precisely of the devilish absurdity of such a gathering, of every "settler" condemned not only to his decay and his dying, but also to the sight—life in a mirror—of the same decay and dying all around. Man must die at home! There must not be this awful isolation, this multiplication of dying, of disintegration. But there is the question: How does one resolve this situation in practice in this frightening and unfeeling world, totally dependent on economic possibilities and impossibilities?

Teheran tragedy. The American government is upset by the silence of the allies. And really, one cannot help being horrified by the ostrich blindness of the world, the cowardice that has become its flesh and blood. This world is literally "choking" on the cursed oil on which its well-being, its whole strength is built. Frightening how nothing—neither the experience of the past, nor a rational approach, nor Munich, nor the October Revolution, nothing teaches anyone anything! The same blindness, the same destructive logic of self-preservation.

### *Sunday, November 18, 1979*

In a café in the Tulsa airport after two days of unbelievable exploitation: yesterday, 12 hours in church: Liturgy, talks, lectures, Vespers, common

Confession. But also great joy: yesterday I served with three former students, now parish priests. Great joy to be in communion with them in unity in the essential. A few students from Oral Roberts University converted to Orthodoxy. In spite of extreme fatigue, I am conscious of the usefulness of these immersions into the "real" Church. And, as usual, in awe when looking at the vast spaces at this huge sky!

The Teheran tragedy continues and there does not seem to be any way out. The same feeling of feebleness, baseness, meanness of the developed world, especially Europe. All of it like Ionesco's Rhinoceros...

### Sunday, November 25, 1979

*Paris*

I came here on Friday and from the airport went to visit Mother in her "home." On Saturday, I spent the day at a meeting of the Russian Student Christian Movement, trying to pull it out of all the arguments and injuries connected with Ivan M[orozov]'s death. Thank God, the meeting was successful, but extremely trying. This morning I attended Liturgy served by Père Placide, a French spiritual father—nice man, but serves according to Mt Athos rubrics with closed royal doors and even a closed curtain, silent Eucharistic prayers—and he defends this practice.

In Teheran, the situation is getting worse and worse. Khomeini has declared a holy war.

How will it end? It is simply awful!

Paris is gray, wet, November-like. Today I saw—far far away—patches of a gray-blue sky.

### Monday, November 26, 1979

*Paris*

Last evening we finished rather well all the business that was the goal of my flight here. Spent a few hours with Mother, very cozy, even fun! She is searching for words, can't remember any names, and conversation with her is like a guessing game. We even laughed about it.

As usual in Paris, I feel like a winded horse!

### Thursday, November 29, 1979

Every morning I took an early train—it's gray and hazy before sunrise—to visit Mother. Then the day is filled with appointments with friends and colleagues. A television interview at the cathedral on rue Daru, then a trip to the monastery in Bussy. Wonderful sunny day, Indian Summer, typical French countryside, little villages, fields, woods, little bell towers. The convent itself is charming, and its appearance *and* the joy of its nuns radiate a wonderful spiritual feeling. Back to Paris in dense fog. Finished the evening with Andrei at the restaurant *Dominique*—friendly and cozy.

Morning walk on a somewhat foggy day all over Paris. I have the feeling that every year Paris is becoming more and more beautiful.

Evening flight to New York. Rejoicing to come back home to L., although continuously conscious of the frightening dead end in Teheran.

### Tuesday, December 4, 1979

Days overfilled with work, but on Sunday I finished (after a year!) "The Sacrament of Thanksgiving"—a part of my *Eucharist*—and sent it off to Paris. As usual, while rereading it for the last time, I thought that maybe it's very, very bad. But, in spite of these doubts, I am happy to have sent it.

Afternoon at the Chancery for the Pre-Council Commission meeting. L. is in Baltimore for some checkups. Soon it will be the anniversary of her operation. The first Christmas lights have appeared.

### Monday, December 10, 1979

On Friday there was a Christmas party at the seminary. Two students played a long excerpt from Mozart's Clarinet Concerto. I am always impressed; reduced to tears by the transfigured faces of the players. How false are our usual superficial comments: "he or she is beautiful," whereas on a certain level of life, in those rare moments when life is "alive," a handsome man can be offensively ugly, and an ugly person—beautiful. It is when they look inside and upward, and give themselves to what they see and hear.

A vacation is near—I long for it as a deliverance from all that fills my life.

Maybe one should never reread what one wrote and published. One day I dug up some of my old stuff and was quite discouraged. Was it worth it?

The most vital of all prayers: "Help us, save us, have mercy upon us, and keep us, O God, by Thy grace." It is the prayer that defends us from the old Adam in us, as an infection permeating our whole being and poisoning it.

### Tuesday, December 11, 1979

On television yesterday, we watched the awarding of the Nobel Peace Prize to Mother Theresa. Her short, marvelous—I would say light-bearing condemnation of abortion. Saints do not solve problems; they take them away, making obvious that the problem itself is from the devil.

### Monday, December 17, 1979

Made a trip to the New Skete Monastery—three and a half hour drive along sunny roads in New York State. I am always impressed by the singing at the monastery; full of praise and beauty. I told L.: "I think that it's precisely the singing that defines and expresses the tone of this extraordinary monastery": no turn on one's self that is so typical in contemporary Orthodox monasticism, no occupation with one's self, no continuous introspection. Really—immersion in something quite genuine here.

### Thursday, December 20, 1979

"A quiet and silent existence" is the summit of intelligence, of wisdom, of joy, and—I don't know how to say it better—of "interestedness." Humility is not to be crestfallen, dejected, nor to be a bigot. It is a royal and kingly virtue because humility stems from wisdom, from knowledge, from contact with life overabundant. The contemporary man is a man who constantly jumps to action. Our whole civilization is an energetic "jump to action"—and man finds himself exactly where he was before he jumped. More and more often I think that what is most needful now is not scientific and sweet books about ascetic theology, but a humble, divine sense of humor. If the world were able to burst out laughing at the sight of the bearded face of Khomeini and the foolish crowd of students shaking their fists for a whole year, screaming slogans; if the world would understand how foolish and funny are the words "people," "revolution," "history," then... I don't know what would happen. But this laughter, I do know, would be more intelligent and probably more effective than the insane, serious analyses of every word by Mitterand and the like. The specific areas of foolishness are: politics, religion, problems of education, sociology, psychology. It is a weight of foolishness on humanity. I don't know any man professionally connected with one of these areas who does not start foolishly to jump into action!

### Monday, December 31, 1979

Last day of the year—a year which seemed to fly by faster than past years. Spent three days in the city reading students' papers. Went twice with L. to the Metropolitan Museum. Joy from contact with art—a different air to breathe. Festive crowds everywhere, while in the world—the same. Iranian insanity, Soviet troops in Afghanistan, in America—total dismay.

Today, Serge and his family are arriving in Russia. How will it be?

Sunny, rather warm days. One more year. Life is not just running; it's running away.

"My soul, my soul, arise. Why are you sleeping? The end is drawing near…"

# CHAPTER VIII

# 1980

∾

### *Wednesday, January 2, 1980*

Glanced over my notes for the year: the same "variations on a theme"—complaints and consolations. I am never fully at home in what I do. Strange state to be in. Always waiting for something to end: talks, meetings. I know quite well that before anything else it's weakness, laziness, lack of love, etc. But I think, I hope—*if only...*

### *Thursday, January 10, 1980*

I woke up today in a cold fury, thinking: Why has this nightmarish power been reigning in Russia for sixty years, and why is not the world amazed, why does it not scream about it?

Today again in the *New York Times*, an article saying that if the USSR did not feel encircled and threatened, then, maybe, the tension inside would weaken. Russia is half of Europe, half of Asia—and it is all a complex of self defense!

The main topic in American newspapers is the hardship that the embargo on grain will cause the farmers.

### *Friday, January 11, 1980*

Amazing—this general hatred for America. It's truly irrational. By analyzing it and understanding this irrationality, one can perhaps begin to explain the contemporary world. I am convinced that America's wealth and well-being are not the source of this hatred. Deep down and precisely in its irrational source, this hatred is caused by the fact that America is *different* from everything else in the world and because it is different, it is threatening. Just by touching it, America changes and—in some way—disintegrates any perception, any structure of life. The essence of that threat is not only that America carries in itself a different way of seeing and doing things and offers change that always produces resistance, but essentially America proposes *change* as a method of life. Every-thing, all the time, is in question, everything ceases being stable, obvious, thus reassuring. The paradox is that Americans don't talk at all about "revolution," whereas Europeans, and now the Third World, made this word the basis of all their discourse. The reason is that Europeans understand "revolution" as a re-placement of one system by another system; in other words—start with the system, the idea. But an American does not believe in any system and is there-fore repelled by an idealistic revolution, although he is, in his very nature, a revolutionary. Even the American Constitution, in the final analysis, is nothing other than a permanent "revolution." It is not by chance that the main occupa-tion of the courts in America is to test the legality of its laws, i.e., of any "sys-tem." A continuous revolution, guaranteed by the Constitution!

This is something that cannot be understood or accepted by all oth-ers—whether rich or poor, civilized or not. And these "others" cannot be un-derstood by Americans because an American perceives life itself as a continuous change (and strives for it, even when change is unnecessary). A Eu-ropean perceives change as something radical, grandiose, comprehensive, scary, even if wished for—it's his "revolution." How ridiculous, therefore, that the most non-conservative, the most revolutionary society in the world—Amer-ica—is hated as a conservative society and as anti-revolutionary.

### Wednesday, January 16, 1980

Wonderful letter from Serge, his first from Moscow. About the Christmas celebration at the cathedral, where they all received Communion; about his reactions to people—how, despite everything, he feels Russian.

Continuous paroxysm of insanity in the world. A feeling of total impo-tence of the West, amazing blindness and fear. Terrible surprise at the behav-ior of the Soviets...Meanwhile life continues.

### Friday, January 18, 1980

Same tension in the world. In the newspapers, cascades of analyses, progno-ses, evaluations, explanations. The general impression, however, is that the West is swinging its arms rather than preparing for a decisive rebuff. Europe obviously does not want a quarrel with Moscow; neither does Japan. The foolish Third World continues to see in America the "Enemy No. 1." All around: cowardice, betrayal, stupidity. But, reading American and European newspapers, I can understand the irritation with America: now it is forcing everybody to détente; now it demands an immediate support against the So-viets; now it takes away all arms; now it almost thrusts them on everybody.

The impression is one of a complete absence of planning, only reactions and reflexes. While there, they know what they are doing.

## Monday, January 21, 1980

Weekend in Washington, D.C. Very cozy dinner at the Grigorieffs'* where I spent the night. With passing years, I value more and more a disinterested friendship—a friendship that is not based on shared business or ideas but on "it's good to be together." Served the late Slavonic Liturgy at the cathedral, then lectured about "Solzhenitsyn accused." There were lots of people who seemed satisfied, but I was not; I don't even know why!

## Thursday, January 24, 1980

Yesterday, a warlike speech by Carter. Really, how could they so lightheartedly breed détente, believe everything? The whole foreign policy of the U.S. is based on wishful thinking. How little they really know or really think, how—usually—shallow are their analyses. Maybe now, they are waking up from their sweet dream!

Sakharov is under arrest. What the West needs to understand is that the Soviets always lie, and, more simply, *cannot but lie.* But this simple truth is debunked by Western intelligentsia as a primitive anti-communism: *l'anti-communisme primaire.*

I traveled all these days: Sunday in Washington; Monday and Tuesday in Richmond, VA at a Presbyterian seminary (night at the very nice DeTranas); Wednesday in Fort Wayne, Indiana, with the Bulgarians. A familiar, and, in a way, even beloved world of airports, solitude in the midst of crowds, a sort of recess. And these spaces, these American cities, America—in its mysterious essence, less determined than the essence of any other nation; where everyone is at home, and nobody is not at home. Where along with a very sincere togetherness—easy laughter, communication, closeness—there always shines through, always resounds (as a ringing ear), loneliness. Where everything is so noisy (voices, advertisements, music) because always one has to "out-voice," stifle the silence of that loneliness and fear.

## Friday, January 25, 1980

Old age? I have noticed how gradually grows a certain estrangement from me of our young ones. Not hostility, God forbid, no; and in difficult times they need me, but I have less time than ever. I simply possess a subconscious

* Grigorieff, Father Dmitry—Professor of Russian at Georgetown University; subsequently Dean of St Nicholas Cathedral, Washington, DC, until his retirement in 1998.

feeling that their hour has come, and it is right, it must be so. There is nothing worse than clinging to participation, to influence, to power. The positive result of this normal process should be a certain deliverance for me in order to work on what is most important for me (as modest as it is), i.e., on what is given to me; what I must do. Quite disruptive when one remains neither here nor there. And the disorder of my life, its difficulty, is precisely because I am neither here nor there. I hamper them *and* am needed at the very same time. I quite often think about it; i.e., how to get out of it, but can not find a way. Hence this irritation and lack of peace in my life.

### Tuesday, February 5, 1980

I have been following Sakharov's saga with ever-growing admiration. No rhetoric. No "I am going to Golgotha." Calm, courageous, firm, clear.

### Thursday, February 7, 1980

Yesterday, at Spence School, L. was awarded the *Palmes Académiques* by the French government. Touching and sober, with "style." And what an ovation for Liana!

### Friday, February 8, 1980

Long conversation with L. this morning about spiritual talks: What I find very difficult and, frankly, boring and useless, is a sort of overly personal, spiritual intimacy. I freely admit; moreover, I am quite sure, that my dislike for spiritual conversations comes mainly from sinful selfishness, from indifference, laziness, etc. But, besides, there still remains a question ...!

### Monday, February 11, 1980

Second letter from Serge in Moscow—wonderful in its deep perception of life there, the combination of despair and hope.

### Thursday, February 14, 1980

Long talk with N. yesterday: "I came so that you would help me..." Help from what? From the same thing: a personal misfortune, drama, and immediately: "Where is God? Where is His mercy? For six months I couldn't, wouldn't take Communion..." And blasphemy of the happiness that was broken down... "so that everything was a deceit." How little help one gets from all that one has read, that seemed to be assimilated, that was part of one's vision of the world. How different is Faith, which is not the faith that is a search for help, for meaning, etc...

Tito is dying! I remember the days Stalin was dying and the enormous headline in the *Daily News:* "Stalin Sinking"—Literally drowning, sinking. So too with Tito. And it will become obvious that he created nothing these past forty years—"not even smoke, but only a shadow running from the smoke…"

On Public Broadcasting, talks with students, not about military service, but only registration. Aplomb, assurance, prophetic tone. I spent my whole life with students and, mainly, was a student myself. And when I think about my student years, I am usually, first of all, quite ashamed of the stupid things that I said, of self-adulation, of condemning my professors for their self-assurance. Happily for the world, no government, no radio station had then invited me to "judge and ordain." Whereas now, there is no more important source of wisdom than the students! Still the same capitulation of the civilized man, of the adult world, of parents, of writers. Of Christianity! We live in fear of being shouted at and we tremble.

I was closing this notebook when N. called. "Thank you"! But what did I really say?

### *Tuesday, February 19, 1980*

Great Lent! I spent the whole day in church. On Saturday, I went to Boston for prayers for the persecuted (Sakharov's stepdaughter and others attended). Met with the parish council: discussed the resistance of older Russian parishioners to any change; Communion; language; singing, etc. Same situation as in Montreal and Sea Cliff. Russians organically don't accept that "key"! Their Orthodoxy is illogical—in the sense of an absence of *Logos*, of meaning, in the literal understanding of the word. For them, the sacred is broken down by logic. The Church helps to overcome a difficult period of life, helps to come back to normal life—but to try to make meaningful even, say, that help, is considered totally unnecessary. At that instant, words about eternal life, or meeting with a dead wife are needed, and the Church did what it was supposed to do—that's all. No connection with a vision of life, however. One gets comfort and goes back to one's normal life!

Christianity is absolutely *exceptional,* unique. Its view of the world is a challenge to all other views and perceptions. Its demand to convert, is to literally turn upside down all that is habitual, and first, of course, "religion." However, its history is a history of compromises with this world, with its logic and demands. I thought about it all these days while reading technical papers about the history of the Liturgy. Where is the compromise? Essentially, it's when Christianity is perceived as needed, but ceases to hamper life; whereas the object, the essence of Christianity is only in one thing: to hamper, i.e., to keep the "flame" of Christianity in the world. But the Church has become the compromise that makes Christianity at the same time needed and *not* a hindrance.

The same frosty sunshine. Yesterday I walked to church in the sunset. Brightly lit walls of houses, tops of trees. And a fleeting feeling, extremely strong, that here, right next to me, along with our life, exists another life, whose essence is entirely in its connection with the "other," in its witness and expectancy. I had the same feeling in Boston where thick snow was falling, like a tale that nobody listens to. Amazing—in nature, in the world, everything moves. But in this movement (falling snow, branches lit by the sun, fields) each moment reveals a divine immobility, a fullness, in an icon of eternity as life.

Another strange thought: the whole world lives *at the same time*, the whole world lives *this* very minute, owns this minute; the rest is abstract numbers on a calendar.

### Thursday, February 21, 1980

Yesterday, the first Presanctified Liturgy; before and after, many confessions. I am trying to clarify for myself what is the meaning of confessions as they exist and are practiced. I can understand the Catholic Confession—violation of a law. But I have to clarify the Orthodox Confession dogmatically (sacrament of repentance) and spiritually. In confession, the metamorphosis of the Church and of Christianity is most evident. The Church was born as a reality in opposition, externally visibly—and even more, internally invisibly—to this world. This metamorphosis consists of the fact that the Church gradually became a religious servicing of the world. In the beginning the sacrament of repentance was totally focused on one thing: on the betrayal of the Church, betrayal of her incarnated and revealed reality. Sin was considered a betrayal of the new life, a falling out of it. Sin was a rupture, a defection, a betrayal; sanctity was understood not as a moral perfection, but as an ontological faithfulness to Christ and His Kingdom. The moral teaching of the Church is eschatological, not ethical. For Christians, the essence of sin is the betrayal of Christ, the falling away from Him and the Church. So the sacrament of repentance is a return, through repentance, confession and regret, to the new life, already given, already revealed. Nowadays, Confession is not directed at that; its essence is different. It is directed toward a certain moral regularization—putting in order—of life in this world, of its laws. In other words, the sacrament of repentance began by being referred not to a moral law, but to faith and to sin as a falling away from faith ("no one who abides in Him sins..." (1 John 3:6)). Now Confession is often a conversation about violations of moral laws, about weaknesses and sinfulness, but without referral to faith. And the answer is not about Christ, but something like, "Try to pray more, fight temptations…" As everything in Christianity, the sacrament of repentance is eschatological; it is the return of man to the longed-for Kingdom and to "the life of the world to come." What it has become, I simply don't know, nor do I understand in what "category" this absolution of sins falls after a few minutes' talk about one's weaknesses. I don't know!

## *Sunday, February 24, 1980*

This morning, before her departure, I talked with L. about our respective schools. As different as they are, they are both constantly full of tension, of meetings, of projects, so that everybody is bumping into everybody else; everybody is in a hurry; there is not enough time—neither for professors nor for students. This is America! I remember my Lyceé Carnot in Paris. There reigned a sort of invincible immobility, routine, a total absence of activism. Was it bad compared to an American school always in motion, with constant events and projects, continuous discussions, meetings, forced contacts? I'm not sure. If the goal and the responsibility of a school is learning and education, then my lycée was doing it very well, without unnecessary fuss. The problem of how to approach a child, a young adult, was never discussed. The school did not pretend to be everything and seldom worried whether "I am happy and content" etc., never intruded on my personal life, did not pretend to be "life." Yes, undoubtedly a rather wholesome boredom reigned there. But the school did what it had to do and demanded of me to do the same. At the seminary and at L.'s school, there are frequent dramas, problems, a sustained piano pedal. As a result, people take themselves so seriously, discussing their potential, their frustrations, and attaching to them the greatest importance. I remember the boredom and the cool atmosphere in the classroom, and the yellow walls without any "promising school work" exhibits—with gratitude. Everything was serious without unnecessary chatter and without hysterics. "It looks like a prison!" No, it looked like a school where one learned reading, writing, history, geography… Here, when I give a B, the student comes to find out: Why?

All this might well be just *my* feeling. Maybe others were not as happy in that cold boredom, which was never an obstacle to one's dream, which did not touch one's inner life, never creating unnecessary worries. But then, how many daily joys, daily little feasts!—to leave at 4 o'clock in the fall, the winter, the spring, under rain or sun, to go home, to look at the Parisian roofs, to feel free in my whole being, to feel young. School gave me a sense of routine, rhythm, backbone—which then allowed me to be free.

*Friday, February 29, 1980*

I sometimes feel (today, for instance) incredibly tired in my heart. I would like to understand it because this tiredness is so obviously tied with the Church, with religion. What is it? Is it despondency, spiritual emptiness, tied with a deficiency (rather, almost absence) of prayer, with laziness, with lack of discipline? Or, besides all this, also something else? Today, for example, the reason for a recurrent attack of despondency was an incidental little Orthodox paper with unavoidable articles about spirituality, an attack on someone, etc. The tone of such papers, as well as our seminary's tone at times, as well as the tone of religious dissidents, has become loathsome, as well as almost everything that is written about or from within the Church. I am tortured when I have to sit in my office at the seminary, to be the witness and participant in a churchly-religious confusion where I have to live. All these days I worked on my report to the Liturgical Commission of the Synod—about Vespers (amendments, proposals, etc.); but Lord, with what boredom, what effort over myself. I feel well only when I am outside of it all, alone. All this is not my life, and this life has grown wearisome. It seems to me that everyone is occupied with the wrong thing, talks about the wrong thing, is interested in something unnecessary, unimportant. But what is needed? I can't say even to myself. I don't know. I would like to know what the first Christians did every day, from morning to night—those Christians who did not deal with church affairs, theology, morning and evening services, rubrics, discussions about ancient icons, singing, and many volumes of literature about spirituality. What did it mean in their life to live "by faith"? I became a priest when I was 25 because it was obvious to me (without any reflection or deepening or checking) that there is nothing more interesting in the world. I dreamed about it, literally dreamed sitting at my desk in school. It was always a dream of another existence, a secret treasure of my heart. But now, I feel—and how often—like the hero of a Chekhov story, who, for the sake of fighting for freedom, became a servant in order to spy on someone, to investigate something, in one word, to *serve*, and gradually, did not become disenchanted, but somehow "fell out" of that service, felt that it was not needed. He longed for simple life—simply, for life. I have the feeling that I live in a false situation, in continuous rhetoric, in an artificial world; that I am covering up, essentially, pettiness, fuss, self-assertion, etc. I sometimes have the feeling that my childish and dream-like experience of "another existence" which led me *to* service, is now shadowed mainly *by* this service.

On Tuesday night, I spent five hours in the city with Metropolitan Theodosius. I enjoyed his simplicity and directness. He is never pretentious and enjoys his life like a child—precisely a child. Maybe the Gospel's "become like children" (Matthew 18:3) is what's missing in contemporary Christianity and Orthodoxy. Everything became heavy laden with problems; one constantly has to quote "authorities."

## Saturday, March 1, 1980

"March—spring beauty, sad and early..." (Who said it? I don't remember.) And *we* have frost and snow, and it's extraordinarily cold.

America is immersed in its pre-electoral passion. What a strange force comes from politics and from democracy! So much time is consumed by campaigning and fighting for election. Truly, the lust for power is a huge force—and to me quite difficult to understand.

Letter from Moscow from Mania about our son Serge who, after a period of excitement, of enjoying the novelty of it all, is now in total fury about everything Soviet. L. and Anya got their visas and are going to Moscow on the 15th of March.

In the paper today, an impressive enumeration of Turkish diplomats killed by Armenian terrorists. Also a list of 14 embassies, occupied by all sorts of guerrillas. Everybody is focused on one's own pursuit, and for the sake of "one's own," they kill, and kill, and kill. And everywhere—"liberation," "justice" and "revenge." So much that used to unify people seems to be crumbling, except one thing: nationalism—vital, blind, wild. My question is: Can one still talk about the universality of Christianity? A lost cause. Without supra-nationalism, i.e., without the feeling that the Church cannot be reduced to nationalism, Christianity is not Christianity any more!

## Sunday, March 2, 1980

Yesterday, late at night (after the vigil and confessions), a long phone conversation with Natasha Solzhenitsyn. Summary:

"We are alone; everybody is against us, i.e., against Russia."

Drama with Sakharov, whom they reject because he is "with them, the enemies..."

Breakup with most of the dissidents in the States, who "do not understand" and will not submit to the cause...

Rather funny: Solz. to me: "break up with N.!" N. to me: "Why can't you explain to Solz.!" Ch. & Co. to me: "How can you talk with N. and S.?"

What can I do, if that kind of "integrity"—partisan, factional, and rather repulsive—is not given to me. What is needed, what is essential, is absolute faithfulness only to Christ. It is freedom not from the world, but in the world.

### Monday, March 3, 1980

From Serge's letter about his trip to the Saint Sergius-Trinity Lavra: "…I must say that the old babushki are a bit vexing. These old women are an incredibly primitive and barbaric species, somewhat reminiscent of Zulu women, but unfortunately closely involved with our much suffering Church here. They are all over, muttering, haggling with each other, pushing, shoving and squealing in inhuman voices. But all this is un-Christian. To quote Turgenev: 'Babas are foolish people…'" But it is in these babushki that many people, if not everybody, see the depository of the religious revival in Russia and of Russia, the support and the criterion of Orthodoxy! And the tragedy, in all probability, is that they really are the support and, alas, the criterion. Even our intelligentsia (beginning with Solzhenitsyn), when converting, convert usually to this kind of Orthodoxy, and to the mysterious attraction of an elemental piety.

### Wednesday, March 5, 1980

One hears incessantly about prayer sessions for the spiritual revival of Russia and for the confessors of the faith; about the preparation for a hunger strike in front of the United Nations, etc., and I try to understand why, deep down, I am repelled by it all. Although I cannot explain it to myself, I feel that all this behavior is not fitting for Christians; that it follows the elemental ways of the world, and not Christ! Maybe it's my skeptical character. What does "pray for the spiritual revival of Russia" mean? What is the goal of that prayer? What is understood in the word "Russia"? Briefly—what are we praying for? And why—"hunger strike"? I don't know; it's all unclear, confused, spiritually ambiguous. Even martyrs can become an object of idle talk and, mainly, self-satisfaction.

Okay, since I seem to be wallowing in irritation: How torturous is the "churchly" language that one must speak in church—the tone, style, habit. It is all artificial; there is a total absence of a simple human language. With what a sigh of relief one leaves this world of cassocks, hand-kissing and church gossip. As soon as one leaves, one sees: wet bare branches, fog which floats over fields, trees, homes. Sky. Early dusk. And it all tells an incredibly simple *Truth*.

Recently somebody quoted to me the following: "mysticism and asceticism are incompatible" (or something to that effect), and I thought about it time and again. It's worth thinking about it. The "ascetic" does not see the truth, which I just wrote about (of the sky, wet branches, foggy dusk, etc.) or, rather, does not want to see it; pushes it away as something "sensual." The ascetic mostly closes his eyes, ears, all his senses, and fights them. The "mystic" is the one who sees it, for whom all the senses are—ideally—in communion with God. Is Christianity ascetic or mystical? In the Gospel: "…Consider the lilies of the field… But if God so clothes the grass of the field…" (Matthew 6:28-30).

Church. Sacraments. Glory. Magnificence. All of it is mystical save the Cross—"But far be it from me to glory except in the cross of our Lord Jesus Christ, by which the world has been crucified to me, and I to the world…" (Galatians 6:14). But crucified does not mean rejected. It is quite complex because on the one hand, mysticism demands cleansing and verification (asceticism), whereas the ascetic lives for God, to break through to Him through the flesh. Two different emphases are possible. Somewhere asceticism ceases to be Christian (since people who have that tendency do not "feel" the sacraments or the Church and are drawn to rigorism). Somewhere, of course, mysticism also can be ambiguous, can become hedonistic. One can't throw "senses" (i.e., the "five senses") out of Christianity, nor can one eliminate asceticism, i.e., simplify, the fight with one's self.

## Monday, March 10, 1980

I spent a whole peaceful, idle Sunday at home, reading the Sunday *Times* and contemplating the world. It seems that people, nations, groups want independence—to "find" themselves, to "be" themselves. What does that mean? Not much! As soon as they become themselves, they surrender to something else: socialism, nationalism, etc. Fight for survival, and Marxism is ready for them. Others fight for their right to freedom (speech, pornography, and self-expression…). For them, liberalism offers its services, as well as the fight for human rights—although for a long time already these rights haven't been defined. Everything goes under the banner of a fight for something to be realized that is seldom realized. Having lost God, having rejected Him, humanity as a whole and separately lives totally focused on self: selfishness in the literal sense of the word. But since it is impossible to live strictly by one's self, since it is a *reductio ad absurdum* of life—which is life because it lives with and by the other—one constantly invents dangers for one's self; the other is the enemy and life is a fight.

*Tuesday, March 11, 1980*

My main and constant feeling is that of *life*. It is quite difficult to express it in words. Maybe the closest to that feeling is the word *wonder*, the perception of each moment, each situation as a gift (rather than obvious, evident). Everything is always new, everything is not simply life, but encounter with life, and thus a revelation. I write this and realize that these are not the right words, but I can't find any others. I only know that this life as a gift demands attention, an answer from me; that life, in other words, is a continuous acceptance of a gift. Maybe everybody feels that way, but sometimes I don't think so. It seems that many people, maybe even the vast majority, live without noticing life. It is somehow for them a neutral, faceless frame, their substance, but not an encounter, not a gift. They don't see it, as we don't see a mirror when we look at ourselves in it. As in a mirror, we see ourselves, but not the mirror; so in life, one can quite easily not see life. Or, life is a transparent bag full of me, my work, my concerns, my interests, etc. And this fullness gives a feeling of life—"life bubbles over, is in full swing." But suddenly, in a moment of clear vision, comes despair. I thought about it when reading yesterday, late at night, Cummings' biography and this poem:

wherelings whenlings,
(daughters of if but offsprings of hopefear
sons of unless and children of almost)
never shall guess the dimension of
him whose
each
foot likes the
here of this earth
whose both
eyes
love
this now of the sky.

This is about life. And it seems to me immeasurably closer to what faith and religion are about than the theology books that clutter my desk. (I am preparing a lecture about the rites of ordination...).

*Wednesday, March 12, 1980*

To continue yesterday's thinking, does it not lead to a perception of death as also being a gift; an encounter, the last and decisive encounter with what alone made life alive, made life a gift? "For to me to live is Christ, and to die is gain," said St Paul. (Philippians 1:21) Yes, *if* life becomes Christ, *as much as it* becomes Christ, if He is that gift, then death is a gain, the blessed face-to-face with Him for whom one hungers. Fear, the horror of death, is focused on one thing: "everything will go on, but I won't be here; the sun will shine, people will be hurrying to their occupations, and I won't be here." This is the feeling that breeds fear and horror. "Faith in the eternal life" does not help. Then, so thinks the dying man, better nothing. And he is not helped, not comforted by sweet words about the "blessed state of pure spirits." Man wants only the felicity that he knows, and it is only here, in the experience of this life. Our eternity is found only here. And Christianity affirms that we find it in Christ. He came to us, to this life, so that it would be an encounter with Him, the ultimate encounter with Him—in death. Death becomes a gain. Then, "if you love Me…" becomes the obvious condition. One can't love either teaching or commandments or promises. One can love only if there is an encounter, if Christ becomes the gift of everything in life.

## Sunday, March 16, 1980

Friday night I took L. and our daughter Anya to the airport for their flight to Moscow. I am not used to being alone. I literally don't know what to do with myself. Strong feeling of an absence, its burden. Really, "it is not good that man should be alone" (Genesis 2:18).

Yesterday I went to Philadelphia; today to Wilmington.

My main *sin*: I don't deny myself anything. Maybe, compared to others, there is not much that I would like (as different from a moral and mental—I *want*). But to this "I would like," I never oppose any resistance. When I become conscious of it, I am afraid: total absence of light, of an invisible armor that is so often mentioned in all spiritual literature… Afraid because I feel the strength of my delusion. I convince myself that I not only want, but also like only light, good, joyous things (following the principle of: "where your treasure is, there your heart will be also" (Matthew 6:21), so that I disregard the conflict between "I want" and "I like"—the conflict that pushed Apostle Paul to despair:

> I do not understand my own actions. For I do not do what I want, but I do the very thing I hate. …I can will what is right but I cannot do it. For I do not do the good I want, but the evil I do not want is what I do. Now if I do what I do not want, it is no longer I that do it, but sin which dwells within me. …Wretched man that I am! Who will deliver me from this body of death? (Romans 7:15-24).

## Wednesday, March 19, 1980

Strange, unusual combination these days of crazy work and solitude. Really true is the saying: "One human being is missing and all is like a desert."

## Friday, March 21, 1980

I'm on a plane on my way to Seattle, then Alaska.

On Wednesday, I read the second dialogue of J.-P. Sartre with an interviewer in which he renounces Marxism and continually talks about the uppermost importance of fraternity, solidarity. And last evening I heard that he was dying. Among the French intelligentsia, hardly anybody irritated me as much as Sartre. But there is a special greatness in this repentance: "No, I do not think like that any more. I was mistaken."

How irritating and false is the contemporary theme of "youth" as carrier of salvation. I write and wonder, is this senile babbling? No, because I can't remember anything with more shame than the time when I was part of "youth." Shame for "I know it all," for spiritual arrogance, for lack of respect. I could continue that list...! But compared to contemporary youth, we were rather innocuous. In youth there is so much slavery, idolatry, surrender to fashion, to trends. Even its idealism is tied to its narcissism. I thought about it while reading an essay in *Time* magazine on "ageism" (the contemporary contempt for old age).

## Sunday, March 23, 1980

### Anchorage, Alaska

In Seattle, dinner at the D.'s; cozy, friendly. Then the Akathist—Hymns to the Theotokos. I was happy not to miss the service—beloved since childhood—albeit in an empty church. Evening ray of sun on the *iconostasis* and a moment of fullness. Then a very long evening with new converts, their questions, their excitement, their maximalism, their demands for Orthodoxy to be perfect (showing an undigested Western approach). Short contact with the very nice and very intelligent Professor Treadgold.

Off to Anchorage. I was met by Bishop Gregory, Fathers [Nicholas] Harris and [Michael] Oleksa, many Aleuts with children. Right there, at the airport, the singing of the *Kontakion* to St Herman. All of it unexpected, unusual. In the evening, wonderful Vespers at the cathedral, filled to capacity. Again, lovely Aleut children. There are many of them; a feeling of something genuine, quite different from American, even Orthodox, religiosity.

This morning, a joyous, full Liturgy. I preached yesterday and today.

Then, a banquet, gifts, etc. All very touching.

Drove to an Indian village thirty miles from Anchorage. Sunshine. Snowy mountains. Melting snow in the middle of birch and pine trees. And an old, old chapel.

## Monday, March 24, 1980

*Kodiak, Alaska*

It is my third trip here. From the airport, we went straight to the shrine of St Herman. There were welcoming speeches by Bishop Gregory and Father Joseph Kreta. Happy hugs from Father Bob and Suzy Arida, Joost van Rossum, Father Fryntzko. I feel surrounded by worry and apprehension because the school is in a crisis, so that I appear to them like an inspector-general! We will see. Complaints, rumors about abuse of authority, quite unpleasant. I prayed to St Herman to help me.

This morning, a flight on a tiny four-seat plane to the mountains. On the horizon, the blinding white Mt. McKinley. We flew over an amazing blue glacier. Magnificence of that nature. We landed on a lake (the plane had skis) where the pilot has a small cabin. Waiting for us was a superb lunch. Quiet, pine trees covered with snow, high gray-blue sky. A totally different world!

## Tuesday, March 25, 1980

*Kodiak, Alaska*

Talked this morning with Bishop Gregory and Father Kreta about cooperation between the seminaries. They seem to agree with everything quickly. I lectured about Holy Week. Trip around the inland grandiose, magnificent, a glorious view of the sea, white mountains and Spruce Island. "Full of Thy glory!" Extraordinary.

Television news: Reagan's victory over Carter.

A second lecture—about the Eucharist. I am beginning to tire.

After Vespers, before the lecture, I was in church and listened to the same singing that I heard as a child in Paris, as an adult at the seminary, and now here on Kodiak Island far from everywhere. Young Aleutian priests have the same pronunciation, the same melody, the same words. Eternity and joy of the Church. A source that never runs dry. Presence. It seemed that Orthodox Alaska was finished, but it came to life. Twenty priests. Young people singing in the choir. "I will not leave you desolate, I will come to you" (John 14:18).

Yes, of course, the same little intrigues, same clericalism. But what is all that compared to the miracle of the "never aging, always young…"

In five days, L. comes back. Never did the days seem so long.

Essentially, we people are the ones who prevent each other from being "good," from "liking" the goodness that is in each of us because of our indifference, our lack of trust—quickly and gladly seeing the bad in others, judging and condemning. To wish someone well is not enough; it's indifference. What is needed is a real encounter, even if not expressed in any way. So—to the lecture.

## Wednesday, March 26, 1980

### Kodiak

A blinding morning. Blue domes of the church against a background of snowy mountains. Yesterday, I lectured about the Eucharist. Full hall. Catholics, Protestants.

Evening tea with the bishop and others. How quickly one gets accustomed to people and begins to feel their life, whereby the defensive attitude that they have with each other suddenly disappears. Radiant people: kind old Fryntzko, an old Aleut, Father Khariton—short as a ten-year old boy (he pressed into my hand 200 dollars to cover my expenses !).

Aleut children.

A two-hour talk with twelve priests, then confessions. Presanctified Liturgy, a parish meal. Almost freezing, but clear. Huge seagulls, and sometimes huge eagles. A forest of masts. And everywhere, a background of snowy mountains. Why do I enjoy so much this immersion into strange cities; why this passionate interest in shops, windows. For years and for many generations, people are living here. I feel such joy when seeing that life, the fact of life; and I become troubled when thinking about how short time is, how fleeting is this immersion; and woven into that short immersion, the sense of imminent separation, of parting. Life is, before anything else, the denial of death, and life is pierced by death.

During the service, I could not stop staring at the children—fat cheeks, narrow black eyes—especially one little girl, not more than three years old, all round, a miniature, cheerfully marching up high steps towards the chalice. Humility and goodness exuded by the Aleuts. I felt as if I had spent my whole life with them. There is a live stamp on them of what's most important and unique in Orthodoxy. How have they kept it? I somehow had a sense of life being one steady flow of gifts.

## *March 29, 1980*

### *Lazarus Saturday*

Finally home! Came back after an endless flight. From Alaska remains a feeling of happiness, light, fraternity.

Today, a wonderful Lazarus service in the overfilled seminary church. A gray day with a light drizzle. Happiness, to be home, in peace. Now starts the count down until Liana's return—on Monday!! I will call her in Paris.

## *March 30, 1980*

### *Palm Sunday*

Last evening a magnificent Vigil—no way to describe it! Overwhelming enthusiasm, joy, solemnity—a feast in the deepest sense of the word. Also the Liturgy this morning: my much loved epistle: "Rejoice…; again I will say, Rejoice." (Phil. 4:4) An extraordinary feast. From childhood, all of life has been illumined by that feast.

## *Holy Monday, March 31, 1980*

Last day of March: wet snow, slush. Will I be able to drive to the airport where Liana and our daughter Anya are arriving?

Yesterday, the last day of my solitude, turned out to be quite "worldly." Breakfast, lunch and tea with guests; dinner at the Meyendorffs. Then, Bridegroom Matins in a completely packed church. Wonderful choir.

In the *New York Magazine,* an article by A. Schlesinger, Jr. about liberalism and conservatism; very intelligent and, it seems to me, quite true. The change from one to the other is a kind of biological cycle. A period of activism is replaced by a period of fatigue. Both are indispensable.

Another article about abortion. From 1973, when the Supreme Court of the U.S. had legalized abortion, 9 million abortions have been legally performed. This is a judgment over our contemporary world and its humanism, a sure sign of a mystical decay.

I continue reading in the *Russian Messenger* about Father Sergius Bulgakov, the theologian.

After all, his is a "capricious" theology, very personal and, in a sense, emotional so that it probably won't "survive." It seems to me that it can also be said about "the Russian religious thought"—about Berdyaev, Florensky, Rosanov. Bulgakov uses a thoroughly Orthodox terminology, everything is a sort of "brocade"—at the same time, romantic, almost subjective. "My" theology!—"There! I will impose on Orthodoxy my 'Sophia'. I will show everybody what they really believe in." And it wasn't imposed on anybody, not because people are ignorant, but because it's unnecessary; like Berdyaev's "freedom" is unnecessary. I see in all of it a desire to shock and impress. It all originates, maybe even unconsciously, from an original *choice:* of the theme, the tonality, the vision. Any heresy depends on that kind of first choice; it is always an imposition on the Church of "my" choice. In Bulgakov's theology, there is no humility. Whatever he touches, he must immediately change it into his own, explain it in his own way. He never blends with the Church; he always feels *himself* in the Church. He explains the Church to the Church; he tells the Church what is needed. Thus, his theology has success only with a small group of intelligentsia because intelligentsia is before anything else a hypertrophic "I."

## Monday, April 14, 1980

Holy Week! Pascha! Wonderful, undeserved joyous thirst-quenching days! L. and I just returned from Vermont where we spent two days with the Solzhenitsyns. Our best time together. Any tension has disappeared, any caution, armor. Simple, friendly, family-like. I was immediately laden with work—checking, verifying some points. A joyous paschal Liturgy on Sunday morning. A lot of light remains from these days and also a sense of his greatness.

Back to the seminary. Five more weeks—but it feels like five hundred years away! After a year, I feel "played out"! And Solzhenitsyn to me: "Do write for Russia!"—and his wife, Natasha: "Do you realize how much they love you there?" But back at my desk, I feel engulfed in many little cares and concerns—as in a swamp.

## Wednesday, April 16, 1980

Jean Paul Sartre, a man synonymous of our era, has died. Passionate radicalism, confused thoughts, cult of the masses, of revolutions, the Left—all of it is mainly very small. His whole life, Sartre was the slave of some a priori ideas and also an unimaginable chatterer. He himself was not frightening, but the fact that our times have made him into a dominant influence is. At the very end of his life, it seemed that he had begun to understand something, but even then with some reservations. What self-assurance, what hatred of God, what awful blindness!

I mentioned Solzhenitsyn's greatness: he sets a vast scope, and having spent a day with him, one begins to be troubled by all that is petty and small in this world, by blindness, prejudice, etc.

## *Thursday, April 17, 1980*

Yesterday I spent a thoroughly "clerical" day with Bishop Peter for lunch, and Metropolitan Theodosius, Frs Hubiak and Kishkovsky for dinner. Church affairs, agenda with the Greeks and the Arabs, etc.

In *Time* magazine last week, an article about a new attack by sexologists against the last taboo—incest! Supposedly, there is nothing wrong if within families there is closeness, contacts, etc. On the contrary, one must welcome it as one more liberation, as a broadening of rights. *Time* writes with some—rather artificial—anger, but precisely—*artificial*. I am tired of repeating it: putrid decay of our civilization. Abortion, homosexuality, and now incest. Our civilization cannot survive that, but anything opposed to that decay is considered literally funny!

## *Tuesday, April 22, 1980*

Faculty Seminar with theological discussions. Biblical criticism, its rapport with Orthodox theology, etc. While listening, I thought and felt that it's all beside the point, not "it"—But what is the point, and how to express it?

Magnificent Spring days. Transparent greenery everywhere.

"…the Cross of our Lord Jesus Christ, by whom the world has been crucified unto me, and I unto the world…" (Gal. 6:14). I talked about it last evening while lecturing about the feasts of the Cross. The Cross is the acceptance of an impossible calling of God to man, of His design. By the Cross, religions of escapism, on one hand, of therapy, on the other, are excluded. I lectured, feeling it very strongly, mainly for myself.

## *Friday, April 25 1969*

I feel quite discouraged and disgusted by reading newspapers, listening to news, and by all that is poured on us from outside. It seems that everywhere one praises decay, destruction, rebellion, debunking, a sort of elemental hatred and passion full of "against." For instance, in what does Sartre's genius consist? He was, always and in everything, mistaken. Yes, they say, but he searched, he hated bourgeoisie, he was the carrier of hope. This is the man who consciously justified Stalin's terror in the name of History. It's impossible to argue; one can only be surprised and ask one's self: how did this glorification of rottenness become possible?

Sensation today! The Americans tried unsuccessfully to liberate their hostages in Iran—which failed because of two American planes colliding! What a horrible farce.

*Friday, May 16, 1980*

I don't have time, not just to write, but simply to clip my nails! I have the feeling that I am lying under a mountain avalanche and have hardly time to protect myself from the next falling stone. Reading students' papers. It's so comforting to feel that so many have seen something, felt, understood. Yesterday forty students, spouses and guests at our home for a traditional dean's reception before Commencement. A truly family, friendly atmosphere.

Letter from Serge from Moscow about his meetings with dissidents and others. Dissidents, says Serge, have no base because the Soviet government is still—for the people—*their own*. People with power, as well as people in general, love country cottages, jeans, cars, easy life...

*Sunday, June 8, 1980*

End-of-the-year chaos. Then, from May 22 to June 2, ten wonderful days with Serge in Paris. Stayed at Hotel Récamier, with a view of the square and the Church of St Sulpice.

*Monday, June 9, 1980*

Thoroughly enjoyed being with Serge, his intelligence, tact, humor and conscience, which makes him constantly vulnerable. Stories about Russia, about the torturing weight of everything there.

Paris, all these days, was at its best: sunny, cool and festal decorations for the visit of the Pope.

Mother, in her home, is almost totally absent. Ruin of a life. Thought a lot about it.

*Wednesday, September 10, 1980*

Back to New York after a long Labelle summer. This year it was exceptionally wonderful, peaceful, in spite of four trips to New York. I wrote a chapter of my *Eucharist*—"the Sacrament of Remembrance" and almost finished the "Liturgy of Death." So restful!—same walks, the same very special Labelle world and peace, the same Canadian sky, lake, pine and birch trees. Mania and her children spent a whole month with us.

These last weeks were marked by the events in Poland, which we followed quite tensely, always hoping that maybe, just maybe, something would explode in the nightmarish Soviet organism, that something might start. And always, disgust with the truly rotten West.

In general, I feel more and more estranged, alienated from what I have to do. I play all my roles—seminary, theology, Church, Russian émigré, but literally "roles." I don't know how to evaluate these roles, what they are. Maybe simply laziness, maybe something deeper. To be honest, I don't know. I only know that this alienation does not make me unhappy. I am essentially quite content with my fate and would not want any other. In a way, I like each of these roles, each of these worlds, and would probably be bored if I was deprived of them. But I can not identify with them. I think roughly this way: I have an inner life, but my spiritual one is kept down. Yes, I have faith, but with a total absence of a personal maximalism, so obviously required by the Gospel.

On the other hand, all that I read about this spiritual life, all that I see in people who live it, somehow irritates me. What is it? Is it self-defense, is it envy of those who live it, and therefore a desire to denigrate it? Then, by chance, I read a quote from Simeon the New Theologian about the need to hate one's body, and right away I feel that not only the worst in me, but something else does not agree with this, does not accept it.

Simple questions about simple earthly human happiness: about joy overcoming the fear of death; about life to which God has called us; about why and for what the sun shines; about what Labelle's horizons are, its gentle hills covered with trees, its vast sky and bright rays of sun. Simple questions!

Why, in another context, has the spiritual trend resulted in the fact that believers somehow do not feel, do not want either the Church or the Eucharist, or do not feel gratitude, or joy; but they want fear, sorrow, an almost malicious denial of it all.

## *Monday, September 22, 1980*

*Monastery, Serbia*

I am writing this sitting in the enormous cafeteria of a Serbian monastery attending a consultation of Orthodox theologians. Never in my life would I have gone to this meeting had it not been held in Serbia, where I lived for a year just before the war. On the way to Serbia, I stopped for three days in Paris.

From the airport in Paris, my brother Andrei took me to Bougival, where he had just organized a Cadets' convention (our childhood military school). Andrei was so happy with the success of his convention. I never realized how important it was for him. What is this "treasure" that attracts him so strongly? Childhood? Escape? I rejoice at his happiness. Then a visit to mother. She hardly understands us, forgets names, but was obviously happy to see me.

Call to L. Her brother just had a massive stroke and is in critical condition.

## Thursday, September 25, 1980

*Belgrade*

After leaving Paris on Saturday the 20th, I arrived in Belgrade, enjoying the drive through old Belgrade—yellow, old, one-story Balkan houses painted in ochre. Then to the Patriarchate and off to the monastery—a three-hour bus trip, incredibly hot. Everywhere one feels the imprint of socialism, a sort of transcendental grayness, ugliness, conventionalism. But the next day, Sunday, was from beginning to end unforgettable and radiant.

At 6:00 AM we drove to a little country village where the Patriarch was to consecrate a church. More than an hour spent on little country roads, among hills, fields with corn. On the way, we passed old Serbian peasants in their wide cotton trousers, women all in black. The whole time in Serbia I was strongly impressed by people's faces, endlessly human, sad, in their own way—beautiful!

A four-hour service, incredibly hot. But gradually one is immersed in the feast, in the wonderful, inspiring and light singing of a huge choir of priests, in watching a crowd of a thousand people, simple people. Many nuns—simple, humble. Then a three-hour meal in the scorching heat of a huge tent. Speeches, thunderous music of a local orchestra.

On the way back, we stopped at a nuns' convent surrounded by a transparent light garden, in the coolness of a medieval church. Singing of a choir of nuns.

The Church is not "this", not "that" (as determined by theology), but— Grace. Simplicity, evidence, joy of this grace.

H. L. Mencken: definition of Puritanism: "a haunting fear that someone somewhere may be happy..."

I won't write about the conference itself. A sort of nominal, unnecessary and fruitless game. "Preaching and Teaching Christian Faith Today." Thirty people—some professionals from Geneva who can talk about anything, who have learned to perfection the technique of this sort of "consultation." Others—bishops, priests from all kinds of ghettos, for whom the escape to such a conference is a safety valve from their joyless, aimless existence (clergy from Poland, Russia, Czechoslovakia, Bulgaria, Romania), some Ethiopians, Copts, Armenians, some Greeks from Greece, Jerusalem and Cyprus, hardly *au courant*, but quite proud to be part of the Olympus. I headed a group, wrote drafts, but found it rather difficult in such heterogeneous surroundings.

All of that in a monastery, wonderful, genuine, under an autumn sun, with a view of open fields. Monastic services—in the same inexpressible, un-explainable *Grace.*

On Tuesday, a solemn reception at the Bishop's residence for 200 people, and there, one felt the humiliation of the Church. Two speeches by the chairman of the government commission on religion, i.e., an official Communist who controls the Church—a gorilla, resembling Brezhnev, a fat boor. But Lord, how they were concerned about this gorilla, bowing and sweetly smiling, thanking him with extreme enthusiasm for…? He was given the Medal of St Mark for Freedom and Peace while he was smoking a fat cigar and blowing smoke into the face of the bishop sitting next to him. Nauseating. But—what a choir! Right after the gorilla's speech (after thunderous applause) they sing the wonderful, sorrowful *kontakion* of the Canon of St Andrew of Crete: "My soul, my soul arise, why are you sleeping?" Then the striking appeal to the Mother of God: "Rejoice, intercessor and savior of Serbia, blessed Cross-bearing people…" It was quite obvious that the whole demonic vileness was defeated, destroyed by Grace—a grace untouched by it all.

Boredom—the frightening, deadly, lifeless boredom of everything generated by Communism—is an absolutely authentic proof of its demonic character. Belgrade is permeated with this boredom, which I felt immediately on getting my visa at the Serbian Consulate in New York. Only the Church, only that which is tied with the Church, is free of this evil boredom; is illumined by Grace.

From my room, I called L. in New York and acutely felt how much I miss her.

Tomorrow morning, flight via London back home and, as usual, sadness at parting with a life that, for a short while, had become mine. I will leave, but out of these ten days something unique will grow and will become a new layer, an image, an imprint on my memory—like Galilee and Mt. Tabor, Finland, Venice, Rome, Alaska… Maybe this endless, bottomless silence of the gardens in the women's monasteries. Maybe the last words of today's Gospel: "While you have the light, believe in the light, that you may become sons of the light" (John 12:36).

## *Thursday, October 1, 1980*

*New York City*

War between Iraq and Iran; malicious satisfaction from this mutual destruction. Above anything else: how stupid.

I am reading the memoirs of Mircea Eliade (*Les Promesses de l'Équinoxe, 1907-1937*)—Childhood and student years in Bucharest between the wars. Intellectual hunger and thirst, search for meaning of life, history of religion, all of it with a piano pedal pushed to the floor, with pathos, excitement. What is quite impressive is the accumulation of his experiences: mysteries, three years in India to study yoga—everything except Orthodoxy. About that, not a word, as if it did not exist, as if it had no connection to his search. Once, when we met, Eliade told me that his faith is the faith of a Romanian peasant, that he does not know theology. But his whole life he has been writing about the theology of other religions; he has created a whole school; he knows everything about the smallest Indian sect; but the theology of *his* faith remains outside his field of interest. I have read half the book; maybe further on he will say something about his faith. So far, nothing. I don't know why.

### Thursday, October 2, 1980

Last evening I lectured about "Church and Church Piety." In connection with the lecture, I thought about the fate of Orthodoxy. At this time, there is a triumph of monasticism both in theology and in piety. In Serbia, every revival is connected with a monastic experience, trend or teaching. I'm worried about this trend becoming identified with Orthodoxy. In America, we often see the reduction of Orthodoxy to icons, to ancient singing, to Mt. Athos books about spiritual life. Byzantium is triumphing without a cosmic dimension. I can't avoid thinking that it is all a sort of romanticism—a love for that image of Orthodoxy, love because that image is radically different from the images of the contemporary world. Escape, departure, reduction of Orthodoxy.

What is very significant for me is that wherever this trend is triumphant, the Eucharist, Communion, the meaning and the experience of the Church are lost. This meaning and experience are needed now more than ever. The Eucharistic Church identifies itself as "in this world, but not of this world." The monastic trend of the Church is that the parish, community, etc., give this world only an opposition, while departure from this world is shown as the Orthodox answer and the true Orthodox way. The monastic trend, as strange as it may seem, considers the Church as part of the world, so that one must leave not only the world but the Church.

My professor at the Institute in Paris once wrote, "...where is Christ, where are the Apostles, where is the Church? Everything is darkened by the enormous shadow of the *Staretz* (the Elder, the Counsellor)..."

Quite logically, this trend is easily and naturally connected with a romantic, nationalistic Holy Russia, i.e., with the past, its image, its style.

Once, Father John M[eyendorff] told me in a moment of candor that he can not understand why people are obsessed with the Fathers. So many people propagate this fashion, which prevents them from understanding anything in the real world, and at the same time are convinced that they serve the Church and Orthodoxy. I'm afraid that people are attracted not by the thoughts of the Fathers, not by the content of their writings, but by their style. It is quite close to the Orthodox understanding of liturgical services: love them without understanding; and inasmuch as they are not understood, come to no conclusion. We sit in our shell, charmed by a melody, and do not notice that the Church is suffering, and for a long time already has left the battlefield.

### Sunday, October 5, 1980

On Friday, I went to the hospital to see L.'s brother Michael [Ossorguine]. Will he ever come back to total consciousness, rationality? He is quite clearly tortured by his silent (inner) fight. L. says, and it's so true: "in Misha, there is something truly precious." Something happens (a stroke) and everything remains in place, in an eternal order: wife, children—this whole deep, unique and genuine layer of life.

Sunday peace. L. is sleeping. Outside my window, yellowing trees. I am looking over my "Sacrament of Remembrance." All the while, although unconsciously, I know that I have started my 60th year.

### Monday, October 6, 1980

I continue reading the memoirs of Mircea Eliade. He spent three years in India studying all sorts of Indian wisdom: yoga, Tan Tru, etc. He remained in a cell in an *ashram* for half a year. But nowhere, not once in this long book, is there any mention of God. Religion, yes, but not God. It is the search for "*my*" way. It's a tortured choice between holiness and creativity, an endless analysis of various types of spirituality, but without God. How far it is from the Gospel's "…if you love Me…"

In these religious structures, most important is that there is nothing, nobody to love except an abstract perfection (the quest for the absolute). It's hard to imagine in them the conversion of the thief on the Cross, or Zacchaeus, or the Publican. They must study prayer, seek perfection, be all the time turned into the self. For me personally, a kind of metaphysical boredom comes out of it all.

Meanwhile, in Iran and Iraq, people are dying for the sake of Islam. Blind submission to two insane men: the Ayatollah and Hussein. The whole world trembles. Begin, based on biblical foundations and promises, is building a secular Israel. In Paris, bombs explode in synagogues. Two chance people—Carter and Reagan—fight for the presidency

What, who should one be in this world? What is the meaning of life here on this earth? Understandable, true are the words of the poet Khodasevich: "…but then the words—a child, an animal, a flower…" We must feed, cultivate, "educate" a child, an animal, flowers. We are part of history, "in the sweat of our brow," in creativity and not in an immobile *ashram*. What remains, what is sure is a *simple sense of duty* (cf. the last words of a simple sailor in one of Bunin's short stories: "I think that I was a rather good sailor…") Simplicity, clarity, ontological modesty of Christianity, beauty of Christian humility. Without it, everything, including the quest for the absolute, is deception, self-delusion, falseness and evil.

Today, L. is 57.

### Wednesday, October 8, 1980

In connection with my little book, *The Liturgy of Death*, I constantly think and read about death—rather the Christian approach to death.

### Thursday, October 9, 1980

On some days I am attacked—not violently, but quietly and depressingly—by a lack of faith in myself, in what I am doing, writing, serving. On these days, everything I have written seems unnecessary, and all my work seems like a soap bubble.

I am in bed with a nasty cold, reading a few strange books without any feeling of satisfaction. Maybe my discouragement comes from that! To these authors, everything seemed alive, important, decisive. And then it becomes the property of academic worms, who write their commentaries, footnotes, analyses. Peace and pure joy from H. L. Mencken's *Anthology*. He is my American favorite! My friend.

### Friday, October 10, 1980

Fourth day—sick in bed, out of my usual routine. How quickly one becomes a vegetable and gets used to idleness as a normal way of life. The thought that I must go back to work makes me panicky!

Enjoyed watching "Faulty Towers" yesterday on Channel 13. Like fresh air! Intelligent, funny, fast. Then an interview with John Cleese, the author and actor. Enjoyed his very British manner. It seems to me that an Englishman does not necessarily have to be intelligent. The civilization that surrounds him is intelligent. In America, everything is characterized by an interest in self, by taboos (blacks, Jews, women, religion, politics). If one does not say the right thing, immediately there is a noisy reaction; lawyers, demands for equal time, etc. In England, the smoothing of sharp angles is achieved by a sense of humor. In this world, it's a huge achievement; one, I would almost say, of a spiritual order. Christianity demands before anything else denial of self—the most difficult of all achievements.

## *Saturday, October 11, 1980*

In Crestwood—first gray, wet, really autumn day—a day to stay inside. I continue fighting my disgusting flu.

This morning, L. and I had one of our usual, cozy debates. In reality, a lively conversation rather than debate (we just call it that), celebrating the freedom of a Saturday morning. We talked about women in the church (L. went to a meeting organized at the seminary by Father Tom to prepare for a women's conference in Cleveland, before the All-American Council). Our "thesis" (*ad hoc*):

—One must liberate this whole debate from clericalism, churchliness (in the bad sense of the word, i.e., a turning of the Church on itself), problems of women's rights in the Church, what a woman can "do," what is her service in the existing clerical structures. All these "problems" are dead ends, since they are all based on categories of "rights," struggle, etc.

—The reduction of life exclusively to structures, impersonal and "objective," is the sin of the male world, the male perception of life (Marx, Freud). Hence, the main mistake of contemporary feminism is the acceptance of these structures: fight for one's place in the world, in the Church, in the government, etc.

—The genuine mission of women is to show the insufficiency, one-sidedness, and hence the awful harm and evil of the reduction of life to "structures."

—The woman is *life* and not *about life* so that her mission is to return man from the form to the content of life. Her categories, which *a priori* do not belong to the "male" reductions of life, are beauty, purity, depth, faith, intuition. These do not exist; more importantly cannot exist in Marxism, Freudianism, or in sociology, etc.

—Man looks for rules; a woman knows exceptions. But life is a continuous exception to rules. Wherever there is genuine life, there reigns not a rule but an exception. Man fights for rules. Woman has a living experience of the exception.

—"Exception" is the depth of Christianity as life. In the life created and given by God, everything is an exception because everything is unique, unrepeatable, a spring sprouting from the depths.

—Sex is a "rule," love is an exception. The law of life and the truth of life is love and not sex.

—Man is called not to the implementation of rules but to the miracle of life. Family is a miracle. Creative work is a miracle. The Kingdom of God is a miracle.

—The Mother of God does not "fit" into any rules. But in Her, and not in canons, is the truth about the Church.

Inasmuch as a man is only a man, he is, above all, boring, full of principles, virile, decent, logical, cold-blooded, useful; he becomes interesting only when he outgrows his rather humorous virility. A man is interesting as a boy or an old man, and is almost scary as an adult; at the top of his manhood, of his male power.

A man's holiness and a man's creativity are, above all, the refusal, the denial of the specifically "male" in him.

In holiness, a man is least of all a male.

Christ is the boy, the only-begotten Son, the Child of Mary. In Him is absent the main emphasis, the main idol of the man—his autonomy. The icon of the infant Christ on His Mother's lap is not simply the icon of the Incarnation. It is the icon of the essence of Christ.

One must know and feel all this when discussing the issue of women in the Church. The Church rejects man in his self-sufficiency, strength, self-assertion. Christ proclaims: "My grace is sufficient for you, for my power is made perfect in weakness" (2 Corinthians 12:9).

## Thursday, October 16, 1980

Meetings with Bishop George Khodre from Lebanon, first at the seminary, then yesterday during celebrations in his honor at the Antiochian Chancery. He is awfully nice, refined, friendly.

## Monday, October 20, 1980

On Friday morning, a phone call from our son Serge from Frankfurt—and at 6:00 PM he is with us in Crestwood. Long talks, discussions about Russia. In his opinion, dissidents are finished, crushed, liquidated! Liquidated because from the very beginning they did not have any foundation, any roots in the people. There is actually a strong solidarity of the people with the authorities. Everybody fears war and sees its danger coming not from the authorities, but from the West. There is a peculiar well-being, based mainly on the experience of extraordinary changes that have occurred since Stalin's time. Life is easier. The machine, the apparatus itself, is schizophrenic (the head of the TASS news agency confesses to Serge that he listens to my weekly religious broadcasts!). The lack of success of the defenders of human rights is easily explained by a total absence of any *experience* of rights. The Russia of Solzhenitsyn, the Russia of Russian émigrés, etc., all of these are formulas, reductions. Serge is continually tortured by it and tries to break through to an objective truth—through myths, tremolos, exaggerations, etc. I am very much impressed and happy to see in Serge a constant effort to be fair and conscientious with a refusal to condemn even the Soviet regime.

For nearly two weeks I continue being sick. Penicillin, wobbly knees, cracked skin—mainly I'm unable to start any serious work. No conviction. I become filled with disgust for the role I have been playing for decades. I have fear and apprehension at having to immerse myself in the affairs of the seminary and the Church. I feel that everybody around me knows what to do and how and what for, but I only *pretend* to know. In fact, I don't know anything; I am not sure of anything; I am deceiving myself and others. Only when I serve the Liturgy am I not deceitful. And I will say it again: all of life flows out of—and is connected with—the Liturgy! I feel a collapse of any energy—especially spiritual. I would like to leave...!

## *Thursday, October 23, 1980*

Last evening, Serge showed us his slides of Russia: Suzdal, Moscow, Vladimir. Ambiguous feeling: yes, all these churches, with their shining domes, through birch trees and sunsets, have a very strong effect. But one feels almost frightened when wondering what for, out of what, consciously or subconsciously, comes this huge accumulation of churches? The abundance, inside, of heavily adorned iconostases, icons, ornaments, gold! A sort of bacchanalia of sacred "things"! And, next to it, dirt, poverty, mediocrity. The fascination with "the temple" coincides with some spiritual, religious experience, some obvious need. What need? Above all, everything is submitted to an external impression. The temple from outside, as a vision, a presence, a calling. But then—lack of correspondence of the internal with the external. Crowded, crammed inside. Although the temple, the edifice of the Church, somehow organizes, stabilizes space, becomes the center and the meaning of disorganized, shapeless expanse, inside, there is no space left, everything is so small and cramped and, even if not small, unavoidably crammed. One feels like looking at those temples, but with no desire to go inside. They are touching, comforting, inspiring, but not by what is going on inside. I will never stop asking myself why church piety has made consciousness of the Eucharist so much weaker; has moved the Eucharist away.

### Friday, October 24, 1980

A phone call from Serge: he has been hired by the *New York Times*. It made me think about America. Serge was accepted exclusively on merit because I don't know of a more modest man, incapable of intrigue, unable to "suck up" to anyone, to being partisan. And there, at the age of 35, he is reaching the top, so not everything is based on politicking, connections, money!

### Monday, October 27, 1980

While preparing my chapter on "The Sacrament of the Holy Spirit," I read and reread what has been written about the *epiklesis*, the consecration of the Gifts (Father Cyprian, Gregory Dix, Karabinov and others). What diversity and confusion! The best I think is Dix, but even he does not seem to see something. I think that there are very few examples in the history of the Church of such a gap between the Liturgy itself and its theological interpretation.

The first question is: When and how are the gifts consecrated. Many contradictory, insufficient and ambiguous interpretations exist—it started in the fourth century when the "moment" of the consecration began to be discussed.

All of it appears to me as a theological failure—the reason for that failure is quite clear. The Eucharist can be interpreted correctly only in eschatological categories. Performed *in time* (*not outside* of time), the Liturgy reveals *in time*; anticipates and gives the Kingdom of the age to come; so the Sacrament of the Eucharist, although consisting of a series of actions, is one, undivided sacrament.

While the Liturgy as a whole is related to time, is part of time, inside the Liturgy the categories of time are not applicable, because the essence of the Liturgy is in leaving the fallen, fragmented time and moving into a time restored in all its fullness. In that sense, the whole Liturgy is in the Spirit. Christ is present; He assembles, offers and distributes *through* the Holy Spirit, as at the Last Supper. On the day of the Last Supper, there was no *epiklesis*, and the Last Supper shows the glorification of the Son by the Father in the Spirit, so that the distinction in the Eucharist of the actions of the three Persons of the Holy Trinity is *wrong* and leads to dead ends. Each Person of the Holy Trinity is acting "Trinitarianly."

Absent in all these dead-ends is the main question: What is *consecration*? If it consists of creating sacred "realities" (of the Body and the Blood of Christ, for example), of making "the sacred," then it is natural and evident to attribute the "consecrating" function to the Holy Spirit. But if the consecration is the revelation, the evidence, the gift of the Kingdom of God, of Trinitarian life, then consecration is always the communion with the Kingdom as the grace of the Son, the love of the Father and the Communion of the Holy Spirit. The Father reveals the Son, who reveals the Father, who sends the Spirit—as knowledge, relation, communion.

In the Eucharist, everything (the Kingdom of the Father, the Son and the Holy Spirit) is *accomplished* by the Son, and *revealed* by the Holy Spirit.

Thanksgiving has taken us, the Church, up to heaven, to the heavenly altar. In heaven, there is no other Food, no other Drink, than God, who gives us, as our life, His Son. So bread and wine are transformed *by our rising up* in the Son to the Father. And the Holy Spirit reveals Him to us as perfect, full, complete—given to us as Communion.

The goal of creation is fulfilled and revealed. What happens with the Bread? It is "fulfilled." "This is My Body…" What does that mean? It means that it is what the Bread was meant to be: everlasting, existing before time, Divine, fulfilled. It joins us in Christ to God; it makes us into what we are created for. It means that in this world, in its categories, nothing happens to the bread because what is happening is *spiritual,* in the Spirit. All the talk about the substance, the talks about the "moment," does not clarify anything. But then, "blessed are you who see…" It is impossible to objectively fit the Kingdom of God into frames, laws, connections of this world. That is why the disciples did not recognize Christ "objectively" but *knew* that it was He—*spiritually.* The early Church, therefore, never mentions the Eucharist detached from the Church, from the Assembly.

To explain the Eucharist separate from what is happening in it, first of all with the Church, is impossible. Therefore as soon as such an explanation is begun, it unavoidably leads to a dead end.

But how to say it in my chapter on the Holy Spirit? I feel, realistically, the impotence of words. Here, one also needs to be "in the Spirit." But I am convinced that it is all very important now. Everything in the Church depends on it.

Yesterday I went with L. to Nyack to visit her brother in the hospital. Autumn sun, golden hills over the Hudson, the huge expanse of the river. How much I love this autumn beauty permeated with sadness and humility, but also with some mysterious triumph.

### Saturday, November 1, 1980

*Denver, Colorado*

In Denver for a retreat. All these days, while working on church affairs, I thought about something that I call in my mind "Romantic Orthodoxy." It seems to me that this title is appropriate because it includes many disconnected manifestations and tendencies of contemporary Orthodoxy:

—nominalism (e.g. non-existing Patriarchates)

—blind liturgical conservatism

—cult of the past

—theological preoccupation almost exclusively with the Fathers

—"apocalypticism"

—hatred for the contemporary world (not for *this* world in general)

—emotionalism

—cult of externals (beard, cassocks, prayer ropes, style)

In other words, it includes all that makes Orthodoxy weak, that makes it into an internal ghetto (and not an appeal, a fight, life).

Romanticism, in life and in culture, is, above all, a dream, the primacy of the heart over *discernment* and *truth*. It pushes reality away for the sake of an *imagined* reality; it is belief in illusions.

### Wednesday, November 19, 1980

Spent last week in Detroit at the All American Council—the first three days with Liana. We had a room on the 28th floor overlooking the river and the Canadian plains beyond; skyscrapers, busy streets. All these days, all the time, everything flooded with sun. The usual hustle, assemblies, talks and meetings behind the scene, interviews. But every morning a Liturgy with an enormous choir, and every evening Vespers. In spite of the hotel atmosphere and the hustle and bustle, there was always a feeling of *the Church*. Everything went smoothly and well. A slightly troubled feeling remains from a small but aggressive group of fanatics, from their screams into the microphone, from their foolish maximalism. The eternal awful pole of religion: fanaticism, fear, blindness, self-admiration. Added to that a profound foolishness and narrow-mindedness. But it was a small group, while the majority of the Sobor is healthy.

A huge victory for Reagan, which America can't digest yet. Defeat not only of Carter, but of the pillars of liberalism—Senators Church, McGovern, *et al.* A deep protest against the rottenness of their kind of liberalism. And right away cries about the danger of religion, about its intervention into politics. I am happy about the signal, but worry whether it will be heard correctly and what will result from it all.

## *Monday, November 24 1980*

Two quiet peaceful days at home. Walked with L. all over Crestwood—a dark November day. In the evening, the Meyendorffs and Father Tom and Anya came to celebrate my namesday. The usual talks about some Moscow bishops who just left; about our bishops, about the whole empirical state of the Church, with all its passions large and small. It used to worry, irritate and torture me, but I'm beginning to feel a growing detachment. A human analysis is not only not applicable to the Church, it is by definition partial and not definite. According to *human* reasoning, the whole of our Orthodoxy hasn't got a chance. If the Pope cannot cope, what about us? So, to worry about the Church that so obviously does not want to be saved by my recipes, by *our* recipes, is sinful in the final analysis; it comes from pride. For God has chosen what was totally meaningless and worthless.*

Ambiguity of intelligence (pride) and its main function—analysis. In an intelligent analysis, everything is usually right, but on the whole, almost unavoidably, it is dark, destructive and flat. Intelligence knows only one dimension, so that finally it is like an analysis by the devil—all is right and all is a lie. Judged by that intelligence, not only poetry but also theology must be slightly foolish. Intelligence is the carrier and the breeding ground of *pride*; that is what caused the Fall. Intelligence destroys the world of God, unless it becomes "foolish in the Lord."

Tomorrow I am going to Paris for five days for a meeting of the Russian Student Christian Movement to try to clarify this second empirical area of my life—Paris, troubles and difficulties.

Have I been trying to write an apology for foolishness? No, because foolishness in our fallen world is also from the devil and is also pride. What about Marx, Freud, Hitler, Stalin: were they intelligent or not? Also—Nabokov, Valery, Gide, Hemingway, etc.

---

* 1 Corinthians 1:26-29: "But God chose what is foolish in the world to shame the wise, God chose what is weak in the world to shame the strong, God chose what is low and despised in the world, even things that are not, to bring to nothing things that are, so that no human being might boast in the presence of God."

In relation to what is essential, they were foolish; in relation to what is unimportant, they were intelligent. In the fallen world, intelligence is a grandiose and demonic operation, masking a basic and essential foolishness, that of pride.

It means that in the world, intelligence and foolishness are not opposed to each other (they presuppose each other, are rooted in each other); but intelligence/foolishness (i.e., pride) is opposed to *humility*. Humility is divine because it overcomes and defeats intelligence/pride and foolishness/pride.

### Wednesday, December 3, 1980

On Monday, December 1, I returned from Paris where I spent five days—half of them attending the general assembly of the Student Movement. It seems that everything finally turned out well—new statutes were accepted, harsh resignations were avoided—but the general impression is sad. Several groups of people still remain full of enmity, without any perspective or desire to find a solution.

I visited Mother twice. Very sad. She has lost a lot of weight, recognizes people with difficulty and has attacks of hallucinations. Left with a feeling of powerless pity.

Paris was cold, and dark. The only joy was a dinner with brother Andrei in the Russian restaurant Dominique. We always enjoy being together.

At the seminary, meetings of the building committee and the Board of Trustees. After Paris, it feels like fresh air.

New York City: bright sunshine, blue sky and strong, ice-cold winds knocking people off their feet.

Anna Akhmatova (Russian poet who suffered under the Soviet regime; her son perished in a concentration camp):

> Gold's luster fades and steel corrodes,
> marble crumbles. All for death prepared.
> Most durable on earth is grief
> And eternal—the majestic word.

Lord, how beautiful!

The difficulty, truly the uniqueness of Christianity, lies in the fact that it is addressed to the individual, but gives him or her, as its fulfillment, the Church.

The individual, the person who does not accept the Church distorts Christianity, transforming it into spiritual narcissism and selfishness. The Church, not accepting the individual, distorts Christianity, reducing it to a mass religion. In such a Church, the individual is replaced by a pious stamp (a pious person), while in such an individual, the Church is perceived, at best, as a giver of spiritual nourishment. This confusion, temptation and deception are constant—but in our days, especially clear. On one hand, search for a personal spirituality; on the other, some Church activism, Church as activity, as "collectivism." The Church becomes the reflection of these two contemporary illnesses: individualism and collectivism. The mystery of Christianity is to hold an internal unity with everybody. But precisely inside one's self, and not in a religious collectivism.

One must always remember that in the categories of this world, Christianity *cannot be not* paradoxical. Where there is no paradox, Christianity is somehow damaged and substituted by something false. The combination of the individual and the Church is one of those basic paradoxes.

## *Saturday, December 6, 1980*

Yesterday, at dinner, conversation with Father Tom about Western theologians (the majority) who proclaim as something self-evident that, in view of the cultural mutation of our times, one must radically rebuild the whole theology and the whole life of the Church. Theology must face this; must draw proper conclusions from what has happened, what *is*. My question: what exactly did happen, what is the content of that mutation? It seems to me that before coming to conclusions and starting to "rebuild," theologians must analyze this question. But I see only two reactions in the West (Orthodoxy does not count because it is not even aware of any mutation, does not know it): One is the acceptance, unconditional and without any preliminary analysis of that mutation. The other, just as unconditional, is a complete denial of any such mutation.

Another preliminary question arises, about the essence of theology itself. It seems to me that in the West, theology, when it first became a science (i.e., since the appearance of scholasticism), became dependent on "this world"—on its categories, words, concepts, philosophies in the broad sense of this word. Hence a constant need of an adaptation, a verification—not of this world by the Good News of Christianity and the Christian experience, but *of* the Good News itself and its content—by this world and its "mutations." This time, "mutation" deals with faith itself, therefore the panic arising from a lack of correspondence between faith and this world with its wisdom is especially sharp. This panic leads to two orientations, two choices: *Either* the dissolution of faith in this mutation (as in the theology of liberation), the affirmation that this mutation corresponds deep down with Christianity; *or* a spiritual escapism, the liberation of Christians once and for all from any interest in *any* mutations; or, simply, for the world and man's fate in it. The first choice is realized by reinterpreting faith (which, if understood correctly, must justify sex, abortion, euthanasia and revolution). The second choice is realized, for example, by reducing the whole Christian tradition, to, say, rubrics. Is Christianity addressed to the world by the Good News, or by theology? *To be continued...*

### Monday, December 8, 1980

Last evening we went to a meeting of all the Russian organizations dealing with the defense of human rights. All the leaders were there. The general impression is one of pure and dedicated action moved by compassion and pity addressed to the unjustly treated person.

*Good News or Theology (continued).* I call Good News *not* the "Bibleism" of all kinds of sectarians, but the testimony about the experience of the Church, about the faith—not just setting forth what the Church believes, but also its joy, its life, the knowledge that all is saved in God. For example, victory over death, resurrection in the flesh, etc. It is remarkable that scientific theology somehow keeps these major topics in the background.

### Thursday, December 11, 1980

Change life, a project of society! Impossible, unbearable to live a life built on "sleep subway work" (in French, "*dodo metro boulot*") Week after week, year after year, the same lamentations, accusations, demands addressed to politics to radically change life, to change relations among people, to liberate the woman, liberate children, liberate love; this in the belief that such liberation is possible through political and economical help.

"We can't live like this any more..." While half of all magazines which cry out for such a liberation are at the same time full of programs for concerts, exhibitions, spectacles, television shows, movies, sports, etc. There is an endless supply of things to do. But everybody—old or young—hates this society, dislikes schools, jobs, professions, and expects some miraculous liberation. Nobody describes or defines the positive content of this "new life." On the contrary, all those who supposedly were liberated are drowning in despair and boredom. Or, with some incredible blindness, they worship either the Soviet Union (e.g. the Western intelligentsia of the 'twenties and 'thirties) or Mao Tse-Tung and China, or some other revolution which turns out to be a stinking, bloody mess. One part of Christianity has agreed to it; another—the radical one—examines and rejects the world itself as irreparable, and any dream of its improvement as sinful and diabolical.

How does one find words to tell the truth in this confusion, in this awful lie on both sides—right and left? This truth—as any truth—is at the same time simple and complex, so that while stating it, one has to fight an unnecessary complication as well as an unnecessary simplification (both are possible temptations). Truth about life is simple in its essence and complex in its application to concrete life.

## *Friday, December 12, 1980*

First thesis:

Christianity is happiness, and creates, gives birth to a happy man. The definition of this happiness: "Joy which no one can take away from you"; knowledge of God in Christ; of Christ; of the Holy Spirit; knowledge of the "meaning of life"; knowledge of Christ's victory; knowledge of eternal life; "death consumed by victory..."

> What seems to contradict this happiness:
> weakness and sin;
> knowledge of people's suffering;
> evil of this world;
> The clarification of this contradiction:...

## *Thursday, December 18, 1980*

...There is a clarification—by life, by God, not by reasoning. Last Monday, at Johns Hopkins Hospital, doctors examined L. and came to the conclusion that a tumor has grown on her pituitary gland and are deciding now whether or not to operate. And again, a pity—which corrodes the whole of life; L.'s attacks of despair; a presence of grief, invisible but so obvious. Everything is changed; the elemental joy of life disappears, and an internal fight for light, for acceptance, for purification of the soul from despair and doubts begins. And all of it washes out the heart, and, while washing, *Love* is revealed in all its wonderful, miraculous, joyful power. *That is clarification!* We are amazed at how many people in the West blindly do not understand it.

Excruciating writing and rewriting of my chapter ...

Since Reagan was elected, there is for the first time in decades a serious discussion about the "right" and the "left," or, in American terminology, between conservatism and liberalism. The discussion is not ideological but about vision. For fifty years—since Lenin and later Hitler—the right was only defensive, while initiative, monopoly of ideas, of plans, belonged totally to the left. Suddenly the world became amazed at seeing the fruits of liberalism: political, economic, moral, spiritual—fruits that can be characterized by one word: rotten! A general decay. Added to it: hypocrisy, self-satisfaction, Pharisaism. The left managed to identify the right with "indecency," stupidity and evil. Suddenly there begins an awakening. Alas, there is no guarantee whatsoever that the resurrection of the right will bring good fruits. For the time being, neither the right's ideas nor its principles are victorious, but there is a growing disgust with the left. It is not clear at all whether the "rightists" have ideas and principles, except "get rich."

I am writing all this sitting in a small student room at St Tikhon Monastery. We are burying Bishop Kyprian. Last evening a three-hour funeral service. Beautiful choir. Ten bishops. The joy, the clear "evidence" of that service. This morning, sunny frost. Before the service, I preached. Only no, I strongly feel that in spite of frequent irritation with Bishop Kyprian, of making fun of him, he was a part of our life, and there was in him goodness, divine light, kindness, and, in the best sense of the word—"churchliness."

On Saturday, December 13, Serge, Mania and their children arrived in New York and moved into our apartment. Serge has a break between AP and the *New York Times*. I can listen forever to Serge's tales about Moscow and Russia in general, never ceasing to wonder, how can it all be possible?

# CHAPTER IX

# 1981

∾

*Monday, January 5, 1981*

These weeks without notes were filled with three matters:

*L.'s illness.* Three days before the New Year, Doctor Nager of Johns Hopkins Hospital called to say that the operation is unavoidable. The tumor has grown. Since then, the presence of this heaviness, fate. L. is wonderfully courageous and in control. But—suddenly—attacks of fear, of grief! And then I feel such pity, such an acute wish that anything would happen to me, but not to her. And because of that, over our whole life there is a haze of sadness, but also of something high, purifying.

*The Feast.* Pre-festal services, vigils, liturgies. So familiar, so loved since childhood, but because of our grief, everything sounds, purifies, lifts in a new way. "Christ draws near!"

Writing "Sacrament of the Holy Spirit" with inner enthusiasm and torture. How can I express everything that is so evident to the mind, the heart, the soul?

Presence of Serge and his family. Father John Tkachuk, Masha and Vera. Christmas tree. New Year. Snow. Frost. Incredible feeling of a fight between mortal life and life everlasting. Knowledge of that life and, at the same time, of the weakness, the tragic weakness, almost the impossibility of living by it.

Today—Liturgy of St Basil the Great, eve of Epiphany, blessing of water in a church flooded with a cold sun. Joy which does not exclude, but absorbs in itself worry, pity, and compassion.

*Friday, January 9, 1981*

Difficult days. All the time a presence in the air of this coming operation.

Since Tuesday, in New York at my desk writing my chapter. Lord, how slowly it moves; how almost impossible it is to find the necessary words and phrases for a clear understanding of what I want to say. Sometimes I feel like giving it all up, liberating myself from this heavy burden hanging around my neck. So much effort is needed to return to my desk, to sit down and again immerse myself in a torturous search.

## Thursday, January 15, 1981

Farewell speech by President Carter. Sober, lofty, about America's ideals. "America did not create human rights... human rights created America..." Although rhetorical, this is not a lie. There is, indeed, one key: the individual, the person. If not built on that cornerstone, nothing happens.

Letter from Paris:

"...the milieu of francophone Orthodoxy does not give much hope. Everyone is suspected by his neighbor... because each wants to expand the sphere of his influence...."

## Tuesday, January 20, 1981

Yesterday, a whole day of suspense about the epilogue of the hostages in Iran. Will they or will they not release them before Reagan's inauguration?

Two nuns left convent A (which had 8 nuns), went to convent B, then went further to create convent C. And so, all the time, everywhere, "*sketes* of Transfiguration," and pretty soon each of them will have one monastic. There will be as many *sketes* as there are monastics!

More and more often it seems to me that reviving the monasticism that everybody so ecstatically talks about—or at least trying to revive it—can be done only by liquidating first of all the monastic institution itself, i.e., the whole vaudeville of *klobuks,* cowls, stylization, etc. If I were a *starets*—an elder—I would tell a candidate for monasticism roughly the following:

—get a job, if possible the simplest one, without creativity (for example as a cashier in a bank);

—while working, pray and seek inner peace; do not get angry; do not think of yourself (rights, fairness, etc.). Accept everyone (coworkers, clients) as someone sent to you; pray for them;

—after paying for a modest apartment and groceries, give your money to the poor; to individuals rather than foundations;

—always go to the same church and there try to be a real helper, not by lecturing about spiritual life or icons, not by teaching but with a "dust rag" (cf. St Seraphim of Sarov). Keep at that kind of service and be—in church matters—totally obedient to the parish priest;

—do not thrust yourself and your service on anyone; do not be sad that your talents are not being used; be helpful; serve where needed and not where *you* think you are needed;

—read and learn as much as you can; do not read only monastic literature, but broadly (this point needs more precise definition);

—if friends and acquaintances invite you because they are close to you—go; but not too often, and within reason. Never stay more than one and a half or two hours. After that the friendliest atmosphere becomes harmful;

—dress like everybody else, but modestly, and without visible signs of a special spiritual life;

—be always simple, light, joyous. *Do not teach.* Avoid like the plague any "spiritual" conversations and any religious or churchly idle talk. If you act that way, everything will be to your benefit;

—do not seek a spiritual elder or guide. If he is needed, God will send him, and will send him when needed;

—having worked and served this way for ten years—no less—ask God whether you should continue to live this way, or whether change is needed. And wait for an answer: it will come; the signs will be "joy and peace in the Holy Spirit."

On the first page of the Baltimore Sun, four pictures of President Carter falling while jogging. Was this necessary? Why this cruelty?

Edward Kennedy's divorce. Sad, unworthy epilogue to the Kennedy saga. But the press seriously discusses whether it will harm his candidacy in 1984! What else is needed?

*January 26, 1981*

*Baltimore*

Sixth day after Liana's operation. Medically, thank God, everything seems to be all right. But poor L.! Awful room, deafening noise of the television, a blocked "packed" nose, breathing only through her mouth, dry, painful. I am torn inside, feeling such pity at L.'s despair. But, all the time, thank God for the main result.

I just called Spence (L.'s school) and the seminary. It feels strange to what an extent I am enjoying this forced detachment from my normal world. I already fear that soon I will have to plunge into that "normal" world again, into all its cares and concerns.

With passing years I hear them not better but worse. Here in the hospital in its Sunday sunny emptiness, on strange streets, in the solitude of my ho-tel—I feel the "Tout est ailleurs" of Julien Green: "all is elsewhere." By na-ture, I am a wanderer. Not a dreamer, but a wanderer. A dreamer does not notice the surrounding world; he lives in his dream. I don't have a dream. I don't need it. On the contrary, I like to notice everything—houses, win-dows, a reflected light, a ray of sun on a rooftop. I like to feel unmoving time ("temps immobile").

A wonderful fact remains from all the hassle with the hostages, the big sentimental shows for the crowds: not one of them cracked, or was defeated, or behaved unworthily. It is a testimony to the hidden strength of the *Homo Americanus.*

### Tuesday, February 17, 1981

Three days in Boston for a retreat. Time flies; no time for anything. Received from Paris the *Vestnik* with my chapter about "The Sacrament of Remem-brance" (for my *Eucharist*). I am rather happy with it.

### Thursday, February 25, 1981

Crisis at Spence School. I feel it to be the Lord's sign for L. to stop her hard labors there. A totally senseless crisis: a complaint by three paying clients, i.e., parents, and panic ensues, along with a petty settling of accounts. Disgust from it all, and real admiration for L's patience and courage. L. beaten up by her operation, weakness, the pettiness of her friends—and remains like a cork —upright and in control. Today a decisive meeting.

Sudden death in Paris of my childhood friend, Repnin. He had a very special place in my life, one hard to understand. If it were not ambiguous, I would call him "my first love." When I was 9-13, in our boarding military school, we lived in the closed atmosphere of an educational institution, full of high ideas, dreams, hopes for the future. The sacred mythology of Russia reigned in our school, its service, its salvation. The school was not for us; not to prepare us for life, not to teach, not to educate. The school was for Russia, to serve Russia. Day and night, we were inspired by our teachers, spending our days in the symbolism of that salvation, its sacred character. The goal and the content of our lives was totally clear and totally elevated: serve Russia, and, of course, die for Russia ("and death is as clear as the cross on our chest..."). We lived—not realizing it—in a threatening, radiant, hopeless world, and this atmosphere defined in our subconscious our personal rela-tionships, made them romantic. It's not that we considered our friendship as "of service to Russia," but that friendship subconsciously made "the other" a comrade, the friend more than just a pal. In other words, added to all other childish dimensions, our friendship had a higher, a different dimension. It reflected the high friendship on which Russia was founded—so we were taught—a friendship "illumined, strengthened on the fields of battles by dying for each other, dying together, a friendship of army comrades…"

Friendship, by its very nature, cannot be impersonal. It is incarnated in the other, in the friend; it is hard to understand, it is absolute. Repnin was that friend during those few years that now seem endlessly long, an almost eternal period of my life. Then, soon after, he disappeared from my *real* life, despite regular encounters and his studies for a while at St Sergius Institute. He did not have any place in my real life, nor I in his. But we both remembered our friendship as an important mark in our lives. Whenever I went to Paris, we met with two other school friends, sat in cafés, talked, but only little, since we had very few common interests. I knew that Repnin had a mentally ill wife for whom he cared with total dedication and heroic devotion. He met her under the big clock at the St Lazare Station after seeing an advertisement for "lonely hearts" in a third-rate paper, and married her. They lived in a maid's room in an attic on Île St Louis in the center of Paris (hard to believe this soap-opera situation…). We met and parted, fulfilling a sort of self-evident duty impossible to define in words. It was like communing with a friendship free from anything worldly; free, almost, from life itself. If one can say about friendship, as about love, that a real, genuine friendship is unique, then a unique friend in my life was Repnin.

## Sunday, March 1, 1981

Through my love for biographies and autobiographies, I read a book about the last years of Edmund Wilson, whose books in the fifties were my introduction to American literature (Richard Hauer Costa: *Edmund Wilson, Our Neighbor from Talcotville*; U. of Syracuse, 1980). Like Walter Lippmann's biography, I was struck by Wilson's—he was a dominant influence, a creator of reputations and trends; by the shakiness, if not the absence, of any integral vision of the world, and therefore a criterion, a perspective, of all that is needed for the ability to judge and to understand. Enthusiasm for Communism, disenchantment with Communism, cheap hatred for the American system (mainly because of clashes with income tax authorities). Capricious likes and dislikes in old age, alcohol, pornographic movies, and in spite of all of this, general admiration for greatness! Emptiness, knowing one's own emptiness and building on it (without hesitation) some evaluating principles, etc. Endless circling around religious themes (Pasternak, *Doctor Zhivago*, Dead Sea

Scrolls) with a lack of desire—not impossibility—to think anything through. Endless filling of emptiness. Sad. "The religious drama of the West"—its difference from the religious drama of the East: nowadays, it is a central basic topic.

The West: not rejection of God (as one usually thinks), but a rift inside religion between the transcendent from the immanent, from the eschatological essence of Christianity. Identification of Christianity either with "other-worldliness" or with the world and history. As a result, a loss of the other-worldly *and* of the worldly. Emptiness as a result of this division, culture as an attempt not to overcome that emptiness, but to get around it through a lot of explanations. Essentially, schizophrenia. The new Western culture is schizophrenic, and therefore clinical; always on the edge of insanity, self-destruction, self-explosion. The most pitiful, the most lacking in it is its rationalism ("a rational discourse"). If only I had time to really think about all this!

Difficult days for L. at her school, but a foretaste of a future liberation from all that mud!

### Wednesday, March 11, 1981

I haven't been writing because of the main concern of these days: L.'s difficulties at her school. Yesterday she decided to leave on the first of July. What a liberation! It was an experience of pure evil, irrational, impossible to understand. Finally, relief from the dreadful triumphant evil created by an inexplicable situation. I feel so sorry for her, offended in her best intentions.

From the 5th to the 7th, in Montreal for a retreat organized by Father John. All these days a great, pure joy; this time, contact with goodness and light. A lot of young people, wonderful services. All of it in a Canadian wilderness, right next to Montreal. Quiet, white snowy convent garden. Walks in the cemetery with narrow rows of nuns' graves.

Today, third day of Great Lent. Student retreat at the seminary. Today, while making 12 prostrations during "O Lord and Master of my life…" I clearly felt that I am sinful with *all* the main sins.

### Friday, April 10, 1981

Writing between trips. Yesterday, in Terryville, clergy confessions. I served the Presanctified Liturgy alone, and that, after our usual crowd in the seminary chapel, was quite unusual. I spoke about the joys and sorrows of priesthood, then had a friendly dinner with other priests at Father Koblosh's. Contact with the essence of the Church.

I drove there on a rainy day, but full of spring, and I thought how much I love this America of old "used" towns, and how many memories I have accumulated over the past thirty years.

Today—the Akathist to the Theotokos, which I have to miss to fly to Pittsburgh.

## *Monday, April 13, 1981*

Yesterday, Sunday, worked on our taxes, then celebrated Serge's birthday: 36 years old.

Their departure for Moscow—parting again—is near, and quite sad.

Friday night retreat in Pittsburgh. Bright impression from Father Matsko, from people clearly "hungry and thirsty." As usual, great joy from contact with the Pittsburgh people, with this special America of immigrants, their churches—not beautiful as much as touching. Everything is rather shapeless: houses, streets, buildings; but then I feel that some mysterious, happy wind is blowing over it all. A lot of suffering, a lot of prayer. And, in spite of the limitations of that Orthodoxy, how much more genuine everything is than in the new aseptic suburban parishes!

I firmly know that before dying I must finish my *Eucharist*, since in that book I must talk about the experience of the Church, theology, words (theology as the comprehension of the incomprehensible, not its explanation), uncovered in the experience of the Church, experience which makes words come alive. But my misfortune is that I am drowning in little concerns which I do not have the right to refuse. So it's up to God. If needed, I will write it. If not needed, if I am unworthy, I won't. It's as simple as that!

## *April 17, 1981*

This morning we drove Serge and his whole family to the airport for their flight to Moscow. I can't get used to the fact that my son will be living and working in Moscow.

Last day of Great Lent. "On the morrow, Christ comes to raise his departed brother."

## *Holy Monday, April 20, 1981*

Lazarus Saturday and Palm Sunday services were especially joyful. On Palm Sunday, baptism of little Andrew Drillock. And the Epistle of all Epistles: "Rejoice… and again I say, Rejoice!" Truly the Kingdom of God is among us, within us. But why, except for a momentary joy, does all of it not have *more* effect? How much anger, mutual torture, offense. How much—without exaggeration—hidden violence. What is it that man wants? For what does he thirst? If he does not get it, he is transformed into an evil person, and if he *does* get it, it makes him hungry for more. He wants recognition, that is, "glory from each other." To be "somebody" for the other, for others, "something": an authority, power, object of envy, etc. Here is, I think, the main source and essence of pride. And this pride transforms brothers into enemies; it kills the joy to which yesterday's Epistle calls us.

*In* the Church, because it is a microcosm and because it is called to reveal in this world the *New Life,* in the Church whose life, source, essence is not pride, but love (of your enemies)—all of this particularly visible. Outside the Church, in "this world," pride—as well as death, power, lust—is lawful. Forms are found for them that are sublimating them, transforming them into a well-founded phenomenon. Hence, nowadays, the fuss with "rights," democracy, etc. The main moving force, nowadays is not "freedom" as one usually thinks, but *equalization.* It's a passionate denial of hierarchy in life, the defense not at all of the right of each one to be himself, but a subconscious affirmation that essentially all are the same, that is, there are no "first," no irreplaceable, no unique, no called.

Nonetheless, in our fallen world, rights and democracy are relatively good, they are a relative regularization of everyone's fight against everybody else. They are evil only if their relative characteristics disappear and are "deified" so that they are *good* in a totalitarian racist government, but become evil where they are victorious and become a goal in themselves, that is, an idol. They become an idol every time they stop being a defense of the weak and become an instrument of equalization and, thus, of spiritual dehumanization; finally of pride.

In the Church, rights, equalization, and fights are inapplicable since the Church knows no other law but the law of love; or rather love itself. If love is denied or weakens, if one falls away from love, it is pride (lust of the flesh, lust of the eyes, worldly pride—1 John 2:16). Love, as the life of God—in that life there is no pride. The Father is always the Father, but He gives everything to the Son. The Son does not claim the right to be the Father and is eternally the Son, and the Holy Spirit is Life itself, Freedom itself, ("The wind blows where it wills" (John 3:8) is Love itself of the Father to the Son, of the Son to the Father, the divine gift of self and obedience. God gives that love, God makes man part of that love and that communion is the Church. Thus, in the Church, there are no rights, nor connected with those rights, no equalization. No equalization, hence no comparison—which is the main source of pride. The call to perfection addressed to each person is the call to find one's self , but not by comparing, not by self-analysis (where is my potential?) but in God. Hence, a paradox: one can find one's self only by losing one's self and it means in identifying one's self totally with God's calling, design for one's self revealed not in one's self but in God!

To love—one's self and others—with God's love: How needful this is in our time when love is almost completely misunderstood. How profitable it would be to think more carefully and more deeply about the radical peculiarity of God's love. It seems to me sometimes that the first peculiarity is its *cruelty*. It means—*mutatis mutandis*—the absence of the sentimentality with which the world and Christianity have usually identified that love. In God's love, there is no promise of earthly happiness, no concern about it. Rather, that love is totally submitted to the promise and the concern about the Kingdom of God, that is, the absolute happiness for which God has created man, to which He is calling man. Thus, the first essential conflict between God's love and the fallen human love. "Cut off your hand," "pluck out your eye," "leave your wife and children," "follow the narrow way…"—all of it is so obviously irreconcilable with happiness in life. This is what turned off this world from total love and what filled it with hatred. But—and this is so important—the world became turned off when in the Church itself something changed, something was "turned off." But about that I might write some other time. I must go to church and join in the Holy Week…

## Holy Tuesday, April 21, 1981

What has Christianity lost so that the world, nurtured by Christianity, has recoiled from it and started to pass judgment over the Christian faith? Christianity has lost *joy*—not natural joy, not joy-optimism, not joy from earthly happiness, but the Divine joy about which Christ told us that "no one will take your joy from you" (John 16:22). Only this joy *knows* that God's love to man and to the world is not cruel; knows it because that love is part of the absolute happiness for which we are all created. Christianity (*not the Church in its mystical depth*) has lost its eschatological dimension, has turned toward the world as law, judgment, redemption, recompense, as a religion of the future life; finally forbade joy and condemned happiness. There is no distinction here between Rome and Calvin; the world rebelled against Christianity in the name of earthly "happiness." The world's inspiration, all its dreams, utopias and ideologies (does it really have to be proven?) are essentially an earthly eschatology. The paradox of the history of Christianity: Having ceased being eschatological, it made the world eschatological.

The world is created by happiness and for happiness and everything in the world prophesies that happiness; everything calls to it, witnesses it by its very fragility. To the fallen world that has lost that happiness, but yearns for it and—in spite of everything—lives by it, Christianity has *opened up* and *given back* happiness; has fulfilled it *in Christ* as *joy*. And then dismissed it. So that the world began to hate Christianity (the Christian world) and went back to its earthly happiness. But having been poisoned by the incredible promise of an absolute happiness, the world started to build it, to progress toward it, to submit the present to this future happiness.

Now Christianity, in order to win back its place in the world and in history, accepts this earthly eschatology, begins to convince itself and others that it was always striving for this earthly happiness, that neither Christ nor the Church have ever taught anything else.

Christianity is divided between the conservatives (longing for a religion of law and recompense) and the progressives (serving a future happiness on this earth). What is interesting is that both groups hate nothing so much as a call to joy, as the reminding of a great joy announced and given at the beginning of the Gospel, which is the life of Christianity ("Rejoice in the Lord, and again I say Rejoice"), for which Christianity longs. Some say, "How can one rejoice when millions are suffering? One must serve the world." Others say, "How can one rejoice in a world lying in evil?" They do not understand that if for just one minute (that lasts secretly and hidden in the saints) the Church has overcome the world, the victory was won through Joy and Happiness.

Dead end of the world with its "progress." Dead end of religion with its laws and therapeutics. Christ has taken us out of both these dead ends. The Church eternally celebrates it, and people as eternally reject it and are deaf to it.

"I am going up to My Father and to your Father
to My God and to your God, and I will raise you to the mountain in
Jerusalem on high, to the Kingdom of Heaven..."
(Holy Week *stikhera*).

### Holy Thursday, April 23, 1981

Christianity is beautiful. But precisely because it is wonderful, perfect, full, true, its acceptance is before anything else the acceptance of its beauty, i.e., its fullness, divine perfection; whereas in history, Christians themselves have fragmented Christianity, have started to perceive it and offer it to others "in parts"—quite often in parts not connected with the whole. Teaching about some things, some doctrines. But in this fragmented state, Christianity loses the essential since the meaning of every part is to make us participants of the whole.

## *Holy Saturday, April 25, 1981*

I am writing before leaving for my most beloved of all loved services: *the Baptismal, Paschal Liturgy of St Basil the Great*, when "Life sleeps and Hades shudders…" I write just to say it again. It is the day of my conversion—not of unbelief to belief, not of "out of Church" to "Church." No; an internal conversion of faith, within the Church, to what constitutes the treasure of the heart—in spite of my sins, laziness, indifference, in spite of a continuous almost conscious falling away from that treasure, in spite of negligence, in the literal sense of the word. I don't know how, I don't know why—truly only by God's mercy—but Holy Saturday remains the center, the light, sign, symbol, and gift of everything. "Christ—the New Pascha…" And to that New Pascha, something in me says with joy and faith: "Amen."

## *Bright Monday, Monday, April 27, 1981*

Wonderful Pascha: joyful, solemn, bright spring days. A crowd of young people celebrating Pascha with such force; with their whole being. After a long Saturday and a long night, the same crowd comes to Sunday Pascha Vespers and today to the Liturgy.

Spent Pascha evening in the happy noisy crowd of our grandchildren at the Hopkos. Serge and Mania called from Moscow. (Today in the *New York Times* his article about Pascha in Moscow). Masha and Father John called; enthusiastic about Pascha in their Montreal parish.

Approaching my 60th birthday, I think constantly about the various components of my life, about its layers, periods, conditions which make up a synthesis, if there is such a one! I think about what remains, what played a role in one way or another, what lives on a hidden level, always a part of the present and active in it.

*Early childhood*—1921-1929—Estonia, where I was born; Belgrade and one year in Paris before the Corps of Cadets school. I remember very little, a few instances. Then…

*Corp of Cadets School*—1929-1936—Childhood and young adulthood. Very important—Russia, birth of a two-layered experience of life. Also—the Church (Father Zosima, Father Savva); literature and poetry (General Rimsky-Korsakov, head of the school, and his reading from his notebook of poems, which we had to memorize).

*Paris and France*—1936-1940—Lycée Carnot (high school). Life at home and, at the same time, rue Daru (the Cathedral St Alexandre Nevsky), serving, church life.

293

*St Sergius Theological Institute*—1940-1951—Studies—Marriage—first parish in Clamart—theology.

*America*—(a) New York. Florovsky and the seminary. Russian New York literary circle at our house, monthly lectures in Russian, Bridgehampton summers, Labelle summers, new friends. (b) Crestwood, Orthodox America, Solzhenitsyn...

*The present*—Books, dreams. The past, the future—synthesis.

Thinking about it, my life turned out, literally up to little details, as I wanted it, as I visualized it (as I dreamed, quite bored, behind my desk in the French *lycée*). Life turned out essentially harmonious (the Church) but also many-faced, many-layered (Carpatho-Russian Ohio; Solzhenitsyn Russia; France; America). What should I be especially grateful for (in addition to the gift of life itself)? For *freedom from idols*. For a constant feeling in life of the Other, of the most important present in everything, but not identified with anything, for *joy*. What should I primarily repent about? Self-preservation, escape from heroism and suffering, indifference, hence, compromise.

### Sunday, May 17, 1981

Back to what I wrote on Thursday, the falsity and fear that make my work at the seminary so difficult...Where does falseness come from? From the psychological style of Orthodoxy—a style quite foreign to me, not only to my nature but to my perception of Orthodoxy. I am not a so-called "pious" man. Not only do I feel alien, feel repelled by the unctuous, grief-stricken mixture which constitutes the style of Orthodoxy and which our students take to so easily. But one must live in that style, thus—falsity, mannerisms, a necessity to pretend. Hence, fear, a faint-hearted fear that I will be caught, that people will see through me, what I really am. I feel "at home," I am myself, only while lecturing. It seems to be my only talent.

The rest—confessions, guidance, spiritual help—it all follows someone else's example, and therefore it's quite burdensome. I am always surprised that I lecture as much to myself as to the students. While lecturing, I don't ever compromise with my conscience because somebody else is in me lecturing. Quite often I am simply surprised: Well, so that's how it is! That's the faith or the teaching of the Church! Sometimes I feel like getting up and saying, "Brothers and sisters, whatever I have to say, whatever I can witness to—it's all in my lectures. I don't have anything else, so please don't look for anything else from me." In everything else, it's not that I lie, no, but I don't have the "anointing" which is needed to be genuine. Maybe that's what the Apostle Paul meant when he said that God sent him not to baptize, but to "spread the good news."

All of this is to explain why everything is so troublesome for me the whole year long. My soul hides from people and all that I do, except "spread the good news," is so difficult. I play a role, and I cannot not play it. "Father, teach me to live a spiritual life." This is where my difficulties start with this spirituality that everybody talks about. Here I am blind and deaf. I don't have any "spiritual talent." Spirituality has become an academic discipline and nobody seems to chuckle at the title, "Spirituality 101."

The church bulletin at the French parish in Paris is filled with quotes from the *Philokalia.* I know people who regularly fly to London for confession with Metropolitan Anthony Bloom because he is their "guide." One of our students wrote a 300-page dissertation about "Solitude in the Ascetic Tradition," and so on. Here I stumble against some kind of wall—not only because my intuition tells me that this student is possessed by fear of solitude and a passionate longing for friendship and love; not because I never saw tangible results from this spiritual guidance; on the contrary, I saw quite a few spiritual catastrophes—but because I consider erroneous the singling out of this spirituality as a thing in itself (*Ding am Sich*), into a sort of (or does it only *seem* to me?) refined narcissism in all of this.

"Become as a child..." But are children spiritual? On the other side, hasn't Christianity conquered the world with its childishness? Having created "moral theology" and "spirituality," has it started to lose it? One can acquire spirituality from Buddhism and, if pushed to it, from various William Jameses, but the childlike joy only from Christianity.

The more they come to confession, the more intensely they study (!) spirituality, the stronger the religious madness which I loathe.

## Tuesday, June 2, 1981

Reading newspapers here and there, talks about Russian, American, Polish and other affairs, about *the* world crisis, about all kinds of "what's needed..." ("needed, have to, wake up...") And indeed, it's all rather interesting and perhaps needed. But, behind it all, I always feel detachment, estrangement, even surprise that people would actually believe that so many various things are "needed." As I grow old, I feel more and more that the Church and the Eucharist in the Church remain and exist in the world so that there would be, *could* be, this estrangement, detachment, so that deep down, when we aren't even conscious of it, our life could be "hid with Christ in God." "I hope for the Lord, Who saves me from faintheartedness and tempest." Remember these words and be amazed: do we need any other prayer?

295

## Wednesday, June 3, 1981

### Leave-Taking of Pascha

Just returned from church after a wonderful Paschal service and I simply want to reaffirm what I wrote yesterday: yes, that is why and in some way only why the Church remains in the world; so that again and again we could say: "Lord, it is good for us to be here."

More and more often I think that priesthood should not be a profession; that is, priests should work, have another occupation. Otherwise they transform church life into some occupation or rather activity which is simply not needed. They create it because they have nothing to "do," and it is awkward to get a salary for doing nothing. What did the first Christians do between their meetings in church? Nothing is said about that in all the documents that have reached us. Probably they created families and tried to live in a Christian way; that is, mainly relate everything to the one thing needful, to the presence of Christ among them, to the experience of the Kingdom of God. It's all beautifully shown in Chekhov's *Bishop*. The joy of the Church and the heaviness and despondency and nonsense of church fuss. Everything that the Church has to say and reveal is in the church services, in the assembly, the self-fulfillment of the Church. In our days, while searching for church occupations, we are down to parish Bingo and dinner dances—all of it caring for the Church.

I know full well that what I write will seem impossible.

## Friday, June 5, 1981

Tomorrow I fly to Santa Barbara for five days for meetings with the heads of the Evangelical Church.

## Sunday, June 7, 1981

### Santa Barbara, California

Last evening I arrived here from Los Angeles and immediately plunged into the world of these Orthodox Evangelicals who seriously want to come into our Church. It started with dinner with six of their nineteen bishops; friendly, happy, simple. It dispelled my fear that I would find some double fanatics; of American Evangelism *and* Orthodoxy. No, thank God, nothing of the kind. There was genuine seriousness, a desire to speak honestly and openly, without diplomacy.

This morning I attended their service. First, they meet in their Family Center; *synaxis,* prayers, Psalms, readings from the Bible and sermon. Then they all go to homes where the Eucharist takes place. Of course, externally, all this is quite far from Orthodox liturgical piety, especially the Eucharist, and in particular the absence of a temple, hence of any sacred character (except the vestments of the "priest," which seems almost strange in that context). But if one overcomes that first impression, one finds the same seriousness and even more, a healthy piety. In my head (since I had to discuss all of it for two days with a Synod of nineteen bishops) I had a question: Is the Orthodox Church able to see their Orthodoxy, an Orthodoxy without "Byzantinism," without "mysteriousness"? Another question: What do they clearly lack? Today is their Pentecost. Their bishop preached about the Holy Spirit, and preached well. What was absent was the experience of Pentecost, which is so beautifully given by the service of that day.

## *Tuesday, June 9, 1981*

### *Santa Barbara, California*

I just finished my business here. What remains is a last dinner and a farewell reception. A lot of thoughts, intuitions, impressions, but still chaos. The main question remains the same: Will our Church be able to seriously relate to these Orthodox Evangelicals, to discern the genuineness of their thirst for Orthodoxy; not exotic, Eastern, but also genuine?

Yesterday I visited Bishop John [Shakhovskoy] of San Francisco. Such a bright impression. Truly the spiritual beauty of old age. I could never read his writings without mild irritation because of their "artsy" complexity, but he is a man full of light, a man of God and of Christ. Will I ever see him again?

## *Thursday, September 10, 1981*

I did not take this journal to Labelle, so I will start this first fall day by writing a summary of the summer:

Mother's death. She died on August 17 after a few weeks in a coma. We knew she was dying and expected the news. This news strangely grows in my mind as if I was hearing it again every day.

L. and I went to Paris on the 18th. On the 19th, the Feast of Transfiguration (Old Calendar), she was put in her coffin. We still saw her in her bed. Then, the Transfiguration Liturgy, the blessing of fruits, the joy of the Feast. Funeral at the Cathedral of St Alexander Nevsky on rue Daru— i.e., at the heart of our childhood. Burial in the Russian cemetery of Sainte Geneviève. Rain. Evening at Andrei's house with close relatives. L. and I spent a week in Paris. Beautiful, cool, sunny days.

Perhaps it is strange, but after her death, I felt closer to Mother; she some-how became part of my life, a presence. These last years, especially since she moved into a nursing home, there was pity, bitterness, sadness from witness-ing her unhappiness, the decay of her life. Now she is with me again, whole, in me, in the unmoving time ("temps immobile") that is already gathered for eternity. Death of a mother—it is truly a return to childhood, a repossession; by the end, it is a revival of the beginning!

### Saturday, September 12, 1981

Tomorrow I will be 60! Old age. Do I feel old? No, not really. Do I feel that I am 60? Yes, I do. It is not the same thing. I am beginning to feel time—fragile, precious. Life becomes more tangible—as a gift. And of course death becomes tangible—my death, death as a question, an examination, as a kind of call.

Beautiful long summer—but also a short summer in Labelle. Walks every day. Three weeks with Andrei. Some growing need, necessity of that daily communion with "the Sweet Kingdom of this earth." Hours at my desk, blissfully suffering over the "Sacrament of the Holy Spirit" (still unfinished).

L. is happily building our new life, carefree and peaceful in our Crestwood home—just the two of us!

### Saturday, September 19, 1981

What amazes me in the constant difficulty experienced by various convents and monasteries is the lack of gratitude. All these monks and nuns are so of-ten unhappy—they feel misunderstood, unable to practice their vows, offended, etc. One crisis after another, quite often egocentric.

I talked about the Church with Father N. So many intrigues, offended ambitions, fights and mainly the extraordinary pettiness of all these prob-lems. All of it because the Church is perceived as a continuous, feverish activ-ity. Multiplication of departments, commissions, meetings, assemblies. A flow of documents, memoranda, information. Money is needed for these ac-tivities; to get money, one needs constant action. A sort of vicious circle.

In its present situation, the Church is a caricature of the world, with the difference that in the world, fights, institutions and so forth are real. In the Church, they are illusory because they are not related to anything. For salva-tion, this fussy activism is not needed; for joy and peace in the Holy Spirit—not needed either. The question is, What is the Church needed for? This question must be asked by the Church all the time, before any action. The Church is the connection with Christ and the relation of everything to Christ. It is often absent precisely because it is considered obvious. Why talk about it? Let's start with money, or organizational problems—or a jubilee—then everything becomes pierced with a horrible clerical boredom.

I set up some family pictures on my desk. My father—the last year of his life, sitting on a little bench at the cemetery and contemplating the cross and the grave where he is lying now. Mother in Labelle with both my daughters, Anya and Masha "…more and more blissful to breathe the air of the past on this earth…"

On the 1st of November—officially—the Synod of the Russian Orthodox Church Outside of Russia will canonize the "new martyrs" and with them, the Tsar and his family. I am constantly asked what I think about it. I think, before anything else, that what's important is not *who is canonized* but *who is canonizing them.* I do not recognize in those who will glorify them the right to do so. Not juridical right, but moral, spiritual. They do it not for the Church, not for Russia, but for themselves. It is an act of self-affirmation, or—in a spiritual language—of pride.

## *Monday, September 28, 1981*

Four days in Alaska—from the 22nd to the 26th. Diocesan Assembly, beginning of the school year, pastoral seminar. As usual, an impression of light, grace, joy. Especially the services in a packed church. An unforgettable trip to Spruce Island. All the time, everywhere "…it is good to be here."

## *Wednesday, September 30, 1981*

These past few days I was tempted by the thought that my life is going by and I am spending it not in doing "my own thing"—writing, leaving something after I am gone, and so on—but on other things; trips, lectures, seminary. This morning an answer came in the Epistle to the Galatians: not to consider one's self "something" or "somebody." Just what I needed!—and the temptation is gone. How many times have I noticed that if I listen to the Holy Scriptures as to a personal answer, a personal call, it always is just that!*

---

* "Bear one another's burdens, and so fulfil the law of Christ. For if any one thinks he is something, when he is nothing, he deceives himself. But let each one test his own work, and then his reason to boast will be in himself alone and not in his neighbor. For each man will have to bear his own load. Let him who is taught the word share all good things with him who teaches. Do not be deceived; God is not mocked, for whatever a man sows, that he will also reap. For he who sows to his own flesh will from the flesh reap corruption; but he who sows to the Spirit will from the Spirit reap eternal life. And let us not grow weary in well-doing, for in due season we shall reap, if we do not lose heart. So then, as we have opportunity, let us do good to all men, and especially to those who are of the household of faith." (Galatians 6:2-10)

## Friday, October 2, 1981

Yesterday, a faculty meeting in my office to review our curriculum. Everyone made useful, interesting suggestions. But I kept thinking a preliminary question: What is theology, academic theology, and can it be taught, say, like chemistry.

I strongly feel that theology is the transmission in words—not of other words and beliefs, but of the experience of the living Church, revealed now, communicated now. The theology that is being taught has estranged itself from the Church and from that experience; it has become self-sufficient and wants above all to be a science. Science about God, about Christ, about eternal life; therefore it has become unnecessary chatter.

## Sunday, October 11, 1981

Yesterday I spent a blissful day at my desk. After a two-month interruption, I came back to my book (*Eucharist*). I started by rereading a pile of drafts and could not understand what I am writing about; what is it that I cannot express? Little by little the thought started working. If only I could have one such day each week! The tragedy of my life is that I don't have it; that I live in constant fear of a phone call, meetings, talks, etc.

Today, a deluge of confessions. Father P[aul] L[azor] was serving. I heard confessions until the Great Entrance. I sometimes think that the highly overdeveloped feeling of sinfulness has weakened the feeling, the understanding, the consciousness of sin. The Gospel saying, "I have sinned against heaven and before You" (Luke 15:21), has lost its clarity. Predominant are "my defects," "my weaknesses," all kinds of introspection.

Sin is first of all unfaithfulness to the "Other," a betrayal. For a long time now, sin has become reduced to morals. And nothing leads away from God, from thirst for God, as precisely these morals. All morals consist first of all of bans and taboos. "I quarreled with my wife"—but in a quarrel with your wife whom you love the reason and content of the quarrel is almost always unimportant. What is important, painful, unbearable, is the rupture, the breach, as short as it might be. And you make peace with your wife not because you find who is right and who is wrong, but because you love each other, because each one's life is in the other. A Christianity reduced to morality, to norms, is impossible to practice because; not one of Christ's commandments is fulfilled without love for Christ. "If you love Me, you will keep My commandments" (John 14:15).

There is a kind of moral person with a passion for cleanliness, who runs to confession because for him any little spot is unbearable, just as it is unbearable for any well-dressed man of the world. But this is not repentance; it is closer to a feeling of human decency. But one can't say about a saint, "He was a thoroughly decent person." A saint is thirsty not for "decency," not for cleanliness, and not for absence of sin, but for unity with God. He does not live interested in himself (the introspection of a clean fellow), but in God.

Morality is directed toward one's self. Concern for rubrics is the equivalent in the Church. But in morality, there is no treasure about which it is said that "where your treasure is, there will your heart be also" (Matthew 6:21). The Church: Its call is not to morality, but to the revelation and the gift of the *Treasure*.

## Thursday, October 15, 1981

I received the magazine *Kontinent* with an article about Radio Liberty (where I speak weekly to the USSR):

> Maybe the greatest achievement of this radio station has become the radio broadcast on religious themes. The main credit belongs to Father Alexander Schmemann.... The phenomenal distinction of Father A's broadcasts is the fact that they are directed equally to believers and non-believers; even to convinced atheists. As soon as this intelligent man pronounces the first sentence, as if thinking aloud, your attention is riveted; it is simply impossible not to listen to the end. His God is true Love, but there is also the thought, the courage to penetrate the very depth of human doubts. (Vol. 29, pp. 351-352)

Why hide it? It is always pleasant to get praise, although I well know (at age 60) the value of these passing praises. This quote for me is not only a praise. Reading this article, I am happy that M. S. has felt what I meant in my scripts. It means that, at least partly, I succeeded.

## Friday, October 16, 1981

Yesterday, L. forced me to go to see *Moscow Does Not Believe in Tears*, and I'm very happy that she did! Many defects—a sort of soap opera with lengthy passages and unnecessary details. But despite that, a warm, very Russian, Chekhovian, humble and kind atmosphere—something one would not find in our sophisticated West. I felt it quite strongly while reading Auden's biography. I felt the emptiness of that world, the decay in the midst of snobbish brilliance.

This morning, during Matins, another one of those miracles. My thoughts were somewhere far off in some fuss, some suspicions, in something rather low. And suddenly, through this sticky fog, as if piercing it, comes "loud and clear" one Gospel sentence, a few words of Christ, and in them, literally a direct answer, a call, a solution to all questions. Amazing!

God never leaves the Church but, so to say, does not "encourage" the Church either. The strength of God in the Church is accomplished only in weakness. Thus, all external successes are harmful, since each success is food for pride and, finally, for the death of the soul.

I love biographies. But seldom have I read a biography of a man more unpleasant than Auden. I am reading it because it had a great review in the *New York Times,* and also because I met him several times in the 'fifties. Everyone considered him then a great Christian poet. So far I have not reached the Christian aspect.

I always want to ask the majority of Christians: Do they rejoice in their faith?

## Sunday, October 18, 1981

Drove today, after the Liturgy, to Wappingers Falls, to the Vinogradovs. Bright red, golden yellow leaves on a rainy grayish background. Sunday emptiness. Good!

Today I preached on the text from Corinthians, "...for God loves a cheerful giver...," and the Gospel text about St Peter, "Get behind me, Satan! ...for you are not on the side of God, but of men" (Matthew 16:23). God's generosity: out of water—wine; twelve baskets of bread remained after everybody was fed; so many fish that the fishermen's boats began to sink. Everything, and life itself, in plenty!

How many thoughts, how many revelations occur while lecturing. Yesterday ("Liturgy of Death") I talked about the subjects of salvation, resurrection, the non-baptized. Suddenly it became completely clear to me that the question is not whether or not they know Christ, whether or not they believe in Him, or were baptized, but rather that Christ knows them and gave Himself to them and for them, so that their death also is absorbed by victory because for them also it is the encounter with Christ. So is the judgment. It is not about dogmatics but about the treasure of the heart. The judgment is their encounter with Christ.

## Tuesday, October 27, 1981

Just came back from a trip to New Paltz with David Drillock and George Dworetzky, who wants to give his property there to the seminary. Beautiful place: a lake, four hundred acres, cozy stone building. It was foggy without any wind, complete silence. It all came as an obvious consolation. But the main consolation is David Drillock, his friendship, his trust, his generosity.

### *Wednesday, November 4, 1981*

Today is the 35th anniversary of my ordination to the deaconate. The Gospel is about Christ sleeping in the middle of a storm, the disciples in panic. "Where is your faith?"(Luke 8:25). So am I—despondent, offended, angry. Fear for the Church, for the seminary. Today, from the morning, I repeat to myself, "Where is your faith?"

Yesterday I spent almost the whole day sorting out my books, putting them on new shelves. I was arranging them and thinking, how much has been written! How much effort, how much passion and time was put into each of these books. And how swiftly they disappear, or stay on the shelves like in a book cemetery. A few hundred or maybe a few thousand remain alive, but for each of these, hundreds of thousands are hopelessly forgotten. All together, they were creating culture; each one, about something, in somebody, somehow, added either light or darkness to the world. How seldom I read the poet Blok, or even Pushkin. But would I be the same had I not read them at some time? Pushkin and Blok—yes! But even Maigret (the detective of Simenon's mysteries) with his rainy Paris has become part of me, of my vision of life.

I fear for our young people who seldom read, who live without memory, outside of memory, but are "interested in the Church." What can be "interesting" in the Church that causes their interest to be diluted in clericalism, in gossip about the bishops, and so on? Christ never dealt with culture? Not true! Each of His words about the Kingdom of God, about David, about the elders, presupposes the knowledge, the understanding, the memory of what He spoke about, of where He called us, of what He denounced.

Reports in the papers about the glorification of the New Martyrs, the Tsar's family and many other victims of the Revolution: "Russian sect canonizes Nicholas II…" How can one not understand, not feel, that to canonize the Tsar in New York with a banquet at the Hilton is not possible?

### *Saturday, November 7, 1981*

In Boston for two lectures to newly arrived Russians. Enjoyed the thoroughly, hopelessly (!) Russian atmosphere, a mixture of "Russian soul" clinging to the past and a lazy discontent with the present.

## Thursday, November 10, 1981

I read in snatches Nabokov's *American Lectures* about Russian literature. Talented, intelligent and hopelessly superficial. So much of it for effect.

Report in *Time* magazine about the canonization of the New Martyrs. Sarcastic, described as an eccentricity—"we are seeing all kinds of things in New York!" I feel like running away from this kind of Orthodoxy with all its cassocks, headwear, pointless ceremonies, unctuousness and slyness; to be myself, not to play some artificial, archaic, dull role. One consolation: the Epistle to the Colossians, which is read in church in these days. ("Set your minds on things that are above... let the peace of Christ rule in your hearts... and sing psalms and hymns and spiritual songs with thankfulness in your hearts to God" (Colossians 3).

## Monday, November 23, 1981

I spent Friday and Saturday in Springfield, Vermont, at an old desolate parish with a young and active priest. Several times I had promised him that I would come and always failed. I am so glad that this time I went. There is something acutely touching in these ethnic parishes, half dead, but never dying. And how utterly happy are these people that finally someone paid them some attention! It is an old church where there used to be a convent and an orphanage—with a somewhat sad and ugly end—and now a young convert tries to pour life into these ruins. Vespers—for more than two hours. A tiny choir. And gradually one enters their life. Above all, one feels that there is a life. We spent all Saturday in church, a liturgy and lectures, and at night we parted in joy and the feeling that, with the Grace of God, something good had been accomplished.

Attending the Saturday Liturgy and the first lecture were Natasha Solzhenitsyn with two sons. "I don't understand everything in English, but enough to know that it's all wonderful!"

For me, the main thing was the trip itself on a dark November day through an empty spacious Vermont. Sunset through clouds. Silence! Contact with "le temps immobile"—unmoving time.

On Sunday, after the Liturgy at the seminary, I had an interview about my understanding of Ecumenism. An hour and a half, and finally I begin to have a clearer idea of what my understanding really is.

After lunch, L. and I drove to Princeton for a solemn memorial service for Father Georges Florovsky. We arrived early, walked around Princeton and had dinner in a cozy little Italian restaurant. Freezing cold—all store windows are already lit up with Christmas lights, gifts, the feast. How I love these times of falling out of life; even fleeting, but an immersion in something "other."

The Memorial Service itself was very solemn—three bishops, thirty priests, seminary choir, and many people in a huge Gothic chapel. After the service there was a reception, but we happily left and went home.

I know that I am grumpy, but when facing the Church's empirical state, I am at my lowest. The last thirty years of my life I spent fighting... I know that in me there is a darkness to which I yield, which at times does not allow me to see much good or positive. Fight on...!

### Wednesday, November 25, 1981

Beginning of the first school vacation—Thanksgiving. I think that teachers and professors love vacations, expect them, rejoice in them as much, if not more than, children and students. Having left the seminary at 1:00 PM, I was so happy—as happy as I used to be in Paris, leaving my Lyceé Carnot on the eve of All Saints' Day or Armistice Day.

In *Nouvel Observateur* (French weekly magazine) I read the dialogue of Jean-Paul Sartre and Simone de Beauvoir, shortly before Sartre's death. Strange man. A combination of very genuine freedom and an equally genuine enslavement to ideas and abstractions. In his last talks, like in the *Dialogue*, a very true *humility*. To think: What if a man with such talents was, in our sad time, a witness to *Christ*? Where does this wall come from, this stony insensitivity, this giving of one's life to pettiness, to nonsense? The result is that whatever it was that made him universally famous—existentialism, excessive Leftism, etc.—will be the reason he is forgotten. Only something that witnesses to the eternal, that is involved in the eternal, does not age. I do not necessarily mean something religious in the narrow sense of the word. Chekhov, for instance, will not grow old or antiquated, nor will those little people under a little autumn rain he described, because they are eternal, not as "little" but as *people*.

### Monday, November 30, 1981

Thirty-fifth anniversary of my ordination to the priesthood at Saint Sergius Institute in Paris.

### Wednesday, December 2, 1981

Confessions. Quite often one talks about a certain state of mind that I can't remember from my own youth. Quite often a state of fear. Fear of life itself. Fear to miss something, to fail. It seems to me that this fear is the direct result of our contemporary cult of success, which causes constant rivalry and comparison. People literally fall to pieces; they are broken up by this fear. Another reaction is arrogance, self-affirmation by condemning others. A student, whom we asked to leave, arrogantly replied to our humble, well-meaning Prof. K[esich]: "I know it all. It's all lower than my level. I expected more from the seminary…" He is 30 and still boasting, showing off.

Our contemporary youth is unhappy above all because it lives in a world whose main criterion is success. Hence an incredible flow of all sorts of self-appointed guides, teachers, leaders. In the Church, it leads to an ever-growing "elder-guruism" among the young!

I don't mean to say that my own generation was free from self-glorification or boasting. We all loved to show off. But alone with ourselves, we knew quite well that deep down it was fake.

"Power over souls" is apparently an awesome and insatiable passion which devours the soul of whoever is possessed by it.

Recently I read a letter by one of these young "elders." The student who received it gave it to me because he had doubts about the teachings of this thirty-year-old teacher of spirituality. What incredible self-assurance, what an absolute self-identification with Truth. Having read the letter, I was literally frightened. If only it had been an isolated occurrence. No, I could, without effort, name ten such spiritual advisers who hopelessly maim hearts and souls with their pseudo-maximalism. As if they had never read that "God opposes the proud, but gives grace to the humble" (James 4:6).

### Thursday, December 3, 1981

I started working again on my "Sacrament of the Holy Spirit" (for the *Eucharist*). Suddenly, it became clear to me that I had put it aside out of laziness and faintheartedness. Also, lack of faith. Why, every year, does it become harder and harder for me to write? I ponder for the longest time over every sentence. One of the reasons, I think, is that with the passing years I feel that theology—that is, theological expression—is an art, and for that art I do not have enough strength or talent.

Yesterday, leaving my desk to go lecture about the Sacrament of Holy Unction—which I did not have to prepare since I read it numerous times—it suddenly struck me that the whole liturgy of the Sacrament (the Epistle, the Gospel, the prayers) reveals this healing—the Church itself—as the new life, where sickness and suffering are transformed. Outside of the Church they are a defeat; *in* the Church they are a victory and the testimony of the Kingdom.

*Friday, December 4, 1981*

Yesterday, almost suddenly, it became clear to me what my mistake was in the "Sacrament of the Holy Spirit." I found myself reducing everything in the debate about the *epiklesis* to a conflict between East and West. It is not right, and hence a dead end. One must discuss it this way: if the eschatological understanding of the Sacrament (and it means, of the Church itself) becomes weaker or disappears, then the questions of the moment and the mode of the transubstantiation of the Holy Gifts become necessary and logical, as well as the concept of the transubstantiation. This weakening of the eschatological essence of the Christian faith began very early, and not only in the West. Cyril of Jerusalem in the fourth century is already an example of that weakening. Then immediately the Holy Spirit and His action in the Eucharist begin to be understood as instrumental. Therefore I have apparently written an incredible number of pages in vain! Now, with fear and trembling, I start writing from the very beginning, following approximately this plan:

—The debate abut the *epiklesis* as a meaningless debate;
—The Church and the Holy Spirit
—The Holy Spirit in the Sacrament of the Church—of the Eucharist
—The Eucharist and Time
—The Eucharist and the Transubstantiation

*Monday, December 7, 1981*

I spent the weekend with a friend, tortured by family and love and hopeless entanglements. A disrupted life.

In connection with that, I thought about personal happiness. A paradox: on one hand, the absolute uniqueness of each life; on the other hand, the application to each life of the one and same spiritual law, its inner truth. In N.'s case, a difficult and unsuccessful marriage, an empirical dead-end. There is only one solution to such a dead end: to accept it, be patient, suffer through it, be victorious. But for that one needs to have spiritual strength. All of it sounds like a cliché. But it's true. Christianity is the overcoming of dead ends. The sin of our civilization is to deny the possibility of such an overcoming. There is the conviction that having rejected the dead end, one can somehow find happiness with another in a different way. The eternal truth of Anna Karenina: it is impossible to find it.

Two days of continuous storms and also of incredible sunsets.

## Tuesday, December 8, 1981

Last evening I had my last lecture on the "Liturgy of Death." Now I have to start putting it in order. When?

Thinking again about N.'s crisis. Besides everything else, there is a colossal self-centeredness. "We fell in love with each other…" I felt like asking rather rudely: "…and so what?" Marriage is love given and love to be fulfilled. "We fell in love" is love that fell on one's head. Marriage demands effort and strength. "We fell in love" demands capitulation. I know it's easy to say…!

## Saturday, December 12, 1981

For the first time in many weeks a quiet sunny morning at home at my desk. I continue working on my "Sacrament of the Holy Spirit"—mainly working on overcoming in myself some spiritual paralysis, laziness, idleness.

## Wednesday, December 16, 1981

Happy days in Baltimore where I came with L. for her hospital checkup. Thank God, all is well. I feel endless gratitude. Johns Hopkins Hospital—with its beautiful huge statue of Christ in the entrance hall—will always remain blessed for me.

## Thursday, December 31, 1981

Last day of the year. Gray, cold day with a hanging snow storm. In our living room—our Christmas tree. And as usual on this day, the feeling of time: its essence, its experience as an end and a beginning!

# CHAPTER X

# 1982

$\infty$

*Tuesday, January 5, 1982*

*Eve of Epiphany*

New Year. Christmas celebrations went well with relatives and grandchildren—happily, joyfully. L. and I, it seems to me, never appreciated our cozy home as much as this year.

One sad thing: my work. There are periods when it does not move. Although in my head I have not only many thoughts but I know more or less what I want to say, I just don't know how, and it's torture.

Old age: I am forgetting names and I can't always find words.

I have to write an article (12,000 words) about contemporary Orthodox spirituality. I woke up today and thought with total horror about *what* to say and write.

Preliminary thoughts:

1. Maybe the uniqueness of contemporary spirituality lies in the fact that it is singled out, has become a "thing" in itself. The reason is the alienation of the Church from the contemporary world. Spirituality is one such alienation. The Church is not only the way to God, but an escape from the *contemporary* world (not from the world, but into a past world).

2. Fragmentation, pluralism of spirituality
3. One type is academic spirituality (a nun: "I can't be a nun without having thoroughly studied Origen...")
4. The *starets*.
5. Non-Eucharistic spirituality
6. Form and content
7. Western influence—charismatics
8. Revival: Mt. Athos
9. Snobbish attitude

10. Positive and Negative

11 Ambiguity

12. The way: Where? What is needed? etc.

## Monday, February 1, 1982

If anything became clear during this last month of fuss and work, it is the realization that the time of constant compromises which I have lived with in the church has come to an end. Not on my initiative, a very long period of my involvement and influence in the church as an "*éminence grise*" has ended. The powers that be have decided to get rid of all counselors, and mainly me. At first I felt—I can't conceal it—that it was offensive, unfair, a rejection of my "merits," etc. But now, after a month of fighting with myself; that is, fighting with putting myself at the center of everything, with sadness and mixed feelings in my heart, I feel somehow liberated. Since 1966 I always felt responsible for everything in our Church. And now it is as if someone had taken away that responsibility. At first it was difficult not to give advice, not to interfere... But now it's easy.

Another compromise that has ended is a theological compromise; more precisely Eucharistic. It suddenly became clear to me that ultimately, deeply, there is a demonic fight in our Church with the Eucharist—and it is not by chance! Without putting the Eucharist at the very center, the church is a "religious phenomenon," but not the Church of Christ, the pillar and bulwark of the Truth (1 Timothy 3:15). The whole history of the Church has been marked by pious attempts to reduce the Eucharist, to make it "safe," to dilute it in piety, to reduce it to fasting and preparation, to tear it away from the church (ecclesiology), from the world (cosmology, history) from the Kingdom (eschatology). And it became clear to me that if I have a vocation, it is here, in the fight for the Eucharist, against this reduction, against the de-churching of the Church—which happened through clericalization on one hand, and through worldliness on the other.

## Tuesday, February 2, 1982

Clericalism suffocates; it makes part of itself into the whole sacred character of the Church; it makes its power a sacred power to control, to lead, to administer; a power to perform sacraments, and, in general, it makes any power a "power given to me"! Clericalism separates all "sacredness" from the lay people: the iconostasis, communion (only by permission), theology. In short, clericalism is *de facto* denial of the Church as the Body of Christ, for in the body, all organs are related and different only in their functions, but not in their essence. And the more clericalism "clericalizes" (the traditional image of the bishop or the priest—emphasized by his clothes, hair, e.g., the bishop in full regalia!), the more the Church itself becomes more worldly; spiritually submits itself to this world. In the New Testament, the priest is presented as an ideal layman. But almost immediately there begins his increasingly radical separation from lay people; and not only separation, but opposition to lay people, contrast to them.

Again, the most obvious form of this separation is the exclusion of lay people from communion as the fulfillment of their membership in the body of Christ. Instead of "a faithful image" (1 Timothy 4:12) there appears the image of a "master of all sacrality" separated from the faithful, dispensing grace as he sees fit.

This is the root of opposition to frequent communion by some clergy—the protection of communion by confession, by remission, by the "authority given to me..." etc. This fight is so clearly becoming stronger now under the influence of some clergy possessed by their power, their "sacredness." Nothing is as threatening to their authority as the return of the Eucharist to the Church, its revival as the "Sacrament of the Church," and not as "one of the means of sanctification..."

The tragedy of theological education lies in the fact that young people who seek priesthood are—consciously or unconsciously—seeking this separation, power, this rising above the laity. Their thirst is strengthened and generated by the whole system of theological education, of clericalism. How can they be made to understand, not only with their minds, but their whole being, that one must run away from power, any power, that it is always a temptation, always from the "devil" ("Christ flees us from that power— All authority in heaven and on earth has been given to me..." (Matthew 28:18)—by revealing the Light of power as power of love, of sacrificial self-offering. Christ gave the Church not "power," but the Holy Spirit: "receive the Holy Spirit..." In Christ, power returned to God, and man was cured from ruling and commanding.

In the sixty-first year of my life, I suddenly ask myself: How has it all has become so perverted? And I become afraid!

*Wednesday, February 3, 1982*

Poor Father N. has a hard time with his nuns. One of them can't listen to lectures at the seminary because she says that she has the gift of tears. Father N. suggests that she should talk with an older nun. "Never"! Total denial, hatred. From where does that passion come, this strange perversion which so often attacks spiritual people? What is the source of their continuous crises, their searches for new dwellings, conflicts? It seems that someone who has the "gift of tears" should rejoice! No, that gift is a "problem." This so-called spirituality is dark, angry, denies all others, constantly discusses monasticism. I remember my own experience with Matushka N. in the fifties: constant phone calls, temptations, falls, denials, suspicions—and all for the sake of the magic words: "spiritual life."

Somebody told me yesterday about N., an American who first became a Melchite, then an Orthodox, studied a few months with us, then amidst curses and turmoil, joined the Synodal Church and is now an archimandrite and the head of an Old Calendar Greek sect! The question is, why this irrepressible striving in a young, normal man for these extremes, for these continuous attacks and accusations, for a sectarian spirit? Yes, America is full of sects, but the same is happening in Europe. Why? I don't know. I only know that it's not without the devil. I know that religion is as much from God as it is from the devil. And that there is nothing more frightening than the thirst for power over souls. It's the thirst of the anti-christ.

### Thursday, February 18, 1982

Spent yesterday at my desk and, right away, a totally changed mood. At night L. was convincing me not to give in to irritation (in connection with church affairs), to grumbling, negativism, not to be acrimonious. She is right. The worst thing would be to lower myself to the level at which these "affairs" are dealt with. The best remedy is work; to try to incarnate a few images that make up my sense of the world.

The temptation of activism in the Church. Father Tom told me yesterday about one of our former students, a priest with only twenty parishioners, who tirelessly sends them circulars, forms, and questionnaires and demands their reactions in writing. Nowadays, especially in the U.S., the Church is perceived as an enterprise, an activity. The priest constantly harasses people to do something for the Church. And their activism is measured in quantitative criteria: how many meetings, how much money, how much "doing." I'm not sure it is all necessary. What is dangerous is not the activity itself, but the reduction of the Church, the identification of this activity with life in the Church. The idea of the Church, the sacramental principle of its life, lies in taking us away from activity ("let us put aside all earthly cares"), in making us commune with a new life, eternity, the Kingdom. And the idea of the Church, the principle of its life, *also* demands that we would bring *into* the world this experience of a new life so that we would purify this world, illumine it with the non-worldliness of the experience of the Church. Quite often the opposite happens: we bring activism into the Church, the fuss of this world, and submit the Church, poison its life with this incessant fuss. What happens is not that life becomes Church, but the Church becomes worldly.

Today, after Matins, a talk after confession with one of our seminarians. Pathological fear of not being popular, of falling out of the social micro-organism to which one belongs. How much in America depends on pseudo-friendship, pseudo-interest in each other, on a sort of ritual, symbolical unity. All of it comes from a pathological fear of being alone, even for a short time. There is so little inner life in people in these times. It is stifled by this necessity to be "with it." And when an inner life manages to break through, man is seized by total panic and rushes to some analyst. It also concerns marriages. A marriage either breaks up or is held by a tortured, panicky dependence on each other. The reason is the pursuit from childhood of an adjusted life. People are taught about it in their family, in kindergarten, in school and in college, so that any falling out of the established "*socium*" is perceived as a threatening symptom of maladjustment, demanding an immediate cure. I often ask myself—even wrote about it: Why is there so much tension at the seminary? The answer is simple, I think. Because everyone lives depending on the other. They think it's Christian love. But it's neither Christian, nor love. It is a selfish concern and fear about one's self; a fear of not having a witness in the other, a confirmation of one's own existence.

## *Wednesday, February 24, 1982*

Went to Baltimore yesterday for a lecture at Loyola College. A radiant day—the first genuine spring day! I arrived early and walked from the train station for four or five miles. Enjoyed the sunshine, the morning city life, my solitude. I felt gratitude for everything I was seeing. A good lecture, then a cozy lunch with professors, a lively conversation, serious and genuine, with people who have questions about the Church, the world, without any unctuous triumphalism, without any "spiritual" pretense.

"Woe to you, scribes and Pharisees, hypocrites! For you traverse sea and land to make a single proselyte, and when he becomes a proselyte, you make him twice as much a child of Hell as yourselves" (Matthew 23:15).

Stormy love affair between N. and NN. Listening to their effusions, I think that history has never taught anyone anything. Personal experience and any accumulated wisdom is irrelevant. In the midst of a life storm, one is alone, impervious to any outside wisdom, any outside experience. Each person must go through all the stages of human history.

## Monday, March 1, 1982

### Great Lent

Yesterday was Forgiveness Sunday with its services and preaching. How very difficult it is to break through the usual words to the genuine essence of forgiveness—forgiveness as a divine creative "event." What does it mean: "God will forgive"? In the Church one is in contact all the time with something essential, ultimate; or rather this essential has a hold on you. But very soon, alas, one falls out of it…!

## Tuesday, March 2, 1982

### First Day of Great Lent

A long Matins and, as usual, amazement at the force, the beauty, the extraordinary uplift of the Psalms and then of the Old Testament hymns. Yesterday we sang the first one—the Song of Moses. There is the living God, and the "I" who cries out to the generous Lord—the living man, the whole man, everything in him. The whole world is included in this praise, this fight, the despair, the joy!.

In the evening, the Canon of St Andrew of Crete. Again, I am convinced that it is impossible to translate it for the contemporary man. Eastern Orthodoxy remains and cannot not remain foreign to the Western ways that are dominant in the world. Encounter with the West, conversion of the West, can occur through contact with the Bible and the Eucharist; and in no way through contact with Byzantine mysteriology.

During the day I spent a few hours of torturous thought about the *epiklesis* and its problems. More and more I am convinced that the root of the evil about which I wrote (i.e., the isolation of the Eucharist from its eschatological, hence cosmic and historical meaning) is not in the West, but in Byzantium, in undigested Platonism, in the platonic heresy about time.

In the *New York Times*, almost every day, there are articles by my son, Serge. Where does he get his invincible spiritual health, his knowledge of how to be truly objective, truthful, honest?

## Wednesday, March 3, 1982

Cold, even freezing, but already a spring sunshine. I started again to work on the "Sacrament of the Holy Spirit" since it has become so absolutely clear that until now I was on the wrong path. Maybe the antithesis of East-West (Western heresy, Western approach, Western categories) does not have, cannot, must not have such a universal efficiency. In my case, I feel every year more and more strongly my own Westernism—not metaphysically, not dogmatically, but in the West I feel at home, while I have the impression that the East is hopelessly entangled in itself. Yesterday I had this feeling while listening to the Canon of St Andrew of Crete. This flow of words, this deluge of allegories, metaphors, various ornaments is rather tiresome. But once in a while a simple, deep, bright thought comes as a breath of air on a hot exhausting day.

An Orthodox person will not say, will not acknowledge that Orthodoxy can be decadent, that a great part of the heavy volumes of the liturgical *Menaion* consists of imitative and often meaningless rhetoric. An Orthodox person will condemn that very thought as heretical and sinful. Thus a man who comes close to the Church, who has become churchly, constantly struggles to fit into a very narrow garment not of his size, while assuring himself that he is right and despising anyone who does not yet question anything, but might do so. Such a man easily burns what he adored; leaves and throws everything away.

Confessions. Good boys, good girls. But one feels a continually pushed pedal, an inability to have a simple, clear vision, an exaggerated importance given to self. They speak not of sins but of failures; a word pierced with pride, speaking of one's own success and not God's success in one's self.

## Saturday, March 6, 1982

I just came back from the first Lenten Saturday Liturgy and felt the particular joy of these Saturdays which my mother always shared with me.

Consolation! Two letters: one from the president of Syndesmos: "...I want to assure you, Father, of the immense pleasure of knowing you after having reread many times your writings. The prophetic aspect..." etc.—too lazy to copy any further. And another from a woman from Israel: "Only a few lines to thank you for what you share..." And so on... And a phone call thanking me for a chapter from *Great Lent*. What can I say? It's very nice!

## Sunday, March 7, 1982

### Triumph of Orthodoxy

Yesterday I received from the Chancery a thick package containing reports to the Synod of Bishops from the various departments, committees, treasurer and others. So we have apparently reached what we were dreaming of. We have achieved the reduction of the Church to successful bureaucracy, administration, to a paper waterfall, all of it rather dull. Bureaucracy is costly (meetings, traveling expenses, secretarial expenses). So the pathos of this bureaucracy is mainly directed to its financial aspect. But the financial techniques demand people, specialists in appeals and fundraising. Hence, one needs more money. A vicious circle—"bureaucratization of charisma." After a breath of fresh air that seemed to blow over our Church, normalization has begun.

Each nation has its own totem, a system of symbols, of archetypes, symbolic language, and its own specific center. In France, this totem is political; political essence and music, not necessarily ideas. In America, the same music flows from the word "business." For Americans it is not prosaic but on the contrary romantic, esthetic, the treasure of the heart. In the reception room of the great investment company Brown Brothers, there is on display a luxury edition of the history of the bank. It is written in a key of *mysterium tremens*, as could be written the history of the Crusades or the Order of Trappists. The word "business" is of a sacramental category and tonality. Therefore the transformation of the Church into a "business" is not felt as profanation. It is the only known sacramental language. I am writing this without any irony because money, indeed, has a sacramental character and indeed the Church needs it. The whole question is only how money is made and for what; or rather, what happens to money inside the Church. And now we can see what is happening to the Church when it submits its language and its essence to money.

### Wednesday, March 10, 1982

*The Truants* by William Barrett:

> "Genius, Nietzsche once remarked, is a will to stupidity... N. had in view a certain type of mind so intent on its own purposes that it closes the doors to any influence that might deflect from those purposes..." (p. 207) It fits Solzhenitsyn and his fixation on "Russia."

Monday night I spent one hour with N. and his "instant" romance with NN. Then another hour with Y. and her stormy romance with YY. Why does it fall in my lap? I never felt any vocation nor ability to counsel in concrete life's problems. Maybe because I, myself, never felt any desire for such counseling. On the contrary, any intimate conversation has always been for me quite embarrassing. I try my best...!

Yesterday I read the *Church Hierarchy* of Pseudo-Dionysius the Areopagite. What can it mean in our contemporary world? What could it have meant in a world where it was written? What does the success of this *corpus* mean in Byzantium? If one would apply the Gospel's basic principle, "for the tree is known by its fruit"(Matthew 12:33), to the history of the Church, one would see that what happened was the reduction of the Church to a mysterious piety, the dying of its eschatological essence and mission, and, finally, the de-Christianization of this world and its secularization. But, it seems that there is an impulse precisely to return to this very legacy.

It's time to acknowledge to myself: I feel part of this secularized world and I feel strange and hostile in the world that calls itself Christian. The secular world is the only one that is real. Christ came into this world and spoke to this world; in it and for it He left us the Church. If one would speak in paradoxes, one could say that any religious world, as well as the Christian world, easily manages without God, but can not spend a minute without gods, i.e., idols. Little by little, the Church and piety and the way of life and faith itself become such idols. The secularized world, by its denial, clamors for God. But, captivated by our holiness, we do not hear that clamor. Captivated by our piety, we despise this world, escape it with priestly jokes and hypocritically pity those who don't know "our" churchliness. And we fail to notice that we, ourselves, failed and are failing all our exams—of spirituality, of piety and of churchliness.

## Saturday, March 13, 1982

Liturgy with an ordination. Each time that I participate in an ordination, while the man is kneeling at the altar and has his head covered with an OMO-PHORION and on his head lie the bishop's hands, I think and ask myself, what is happening, what is being accomplished? On one hand the tremendous depth of the uninterrupted succession for two thousand years! On the other, the weakness of that succession, the human limitation of its interpretation, experience, realization.

Just called Moscow. L. and M. arrived and are about to eat borscht—in Moscow! Strange that they are in the same Russia that I never saw, although it determined my whole life. Beginning with the emotion I felt as a child when listening to the romance, "You are buried under snow, my Russia," or reading poetry:

Russia: the ringing of little bells
the sweeping rush of a troika
the dark music of the poet
in the sparkling falling snow...

And now, tourism, borscht! Maybe that's why I don't want to go to Russia as a tourist because I am afraid of losing the Russia whose sweetness was in its distance, snow, birches, etc.

During the litany, I vividly remembered today—somehow all at once—so many people who "accompanied" my life: Father Cyprian, friend and confessor (under a light Parisian drizzle on our way to the metro); V. A. the warden at the rue Daru cathedral, and others. And I remembered them not abstractly, but each one in a real instance of a real day. To remember that occasion, to incarnate it again, to live it, can be done because it *is* real, it *exists*, and all of these instances together, if I really remember and relive them, make up my "resurrected body." The Church is the memory and the remembrance, but in the light of the Resurrection.

### Sunday, March 14, 1982

Today, during the Liturgy: "…May I never abide, Giver of Life, alone, apart from You, my breath, my life, my joy, for You are the True desire and the ineffable joy of those who love You, O Christ our God, and all creation sings Your praise forever…" The Eucharist is the fulfillment of everything in the Holy Spirit. Here is the real meaning of the *epiklesis*, the uniting with Christ through the Spirit.

Is it possible, is it necessary to overcome lack of discipline, laziness, lust for power and sin by *joy in the Lord*? Yes!

### Monday, March 15, 1982

It occurred to me that I should write not just memoirs—it sounds pompous—but a sort of report, testimony about how generously, throughout my whole life, God gave me gifts; about the ray of light which I almost always felt and saw.

On the train last evening, returning from Wilmington, I had a long conversation with a black woman; nice, modest mother of five. She was going to Trenton where her daughter was having surgery. How often I marvel at the genuine "aristocratism" of black people. Compared with this woman, successful, white suburbanites are vulgar and common.

What an effort to start a new week and get involved in fuss, conversations and life's tension. As the poet Valery said, "The wind is beginning to blow; one must attempt to live…"

I know that I am lazy, often discouraged…and I have many sins! But I love the Church and earnestly long—if only in my heart—for the Church's fulfillment.

### Saturday, March 20, 1982

This morning I came back from Washington. On Friday I celebrated a

Presanctified Liturgy and lectured. Many young people. In the afternoon I went for a short while to the National Gallery to look at the Rembrandts. Spring and feast in the air.

After the lecture I was asked to sign my books. Such a joy! Somebody read it, liked it, it was useful. I think that this joy is—almost—without vainglory. I say "almost" because I am sure that there is some vainglory somewhere. But the first surge of joy is quite pure.

### Wednesday, March 24, 1982

Phone call from L. from Moscow after three days in St Petersburg. Happy and deeply impressed.

### Thursday, March 25, 1982

I am more and more impatient to have L. back. What burdens me is not my solitude but her absence. It's a big difference!

I like solitude very much, that is, being outside of human contacts and fuss. But L.'s absence is abnormal, is a "flaw," a loss.

Sin is only in being torn away from God, in betraying Christ. A clear eye—in general—the theme of vision in Christianity.

### Friday, April 2, 1982

"Faintheartedness and storm"—alas, there is no other description for what is going on in my heart when I think about our Church, all the Church affairs, and also the seminary. I am deadly tired—spiritually—of it all. I am tired of the religious fuss in which I lived my whole life. As I am growing old, I feel how unnecessary and harmful it is. Christ was killed and is being killed by religion. Religion is the organ in us which, strange as it may seem, is at the same time intensifying and hiding from us our deepest passions and sins: pride, hypocrisy, self-admiration, self-satisfaction, etc. Religion is our constant self-justification before God, the effacing for ourselves of our sins and temptations.

Father Tom told me about a certain N., a Protestant who converted to Orthodoxy and was a deacon in T. where I met him two or three years ago. It seems that he left his wife and children and lives in some Synodal *skete* and writes little brochures (among other things) about Kallistos Ware,* accusing

* Ware, Father Kallistos—Spaulding lecturer in Eastern Orthodox Studies at the University of Oxford, UK, and fellow of Pembroke College. In 1982 consecrated Bishop of Diokleia (Ecumenical Patriarchate).

him of not being sufficiently Orthodox. I ask myself: why and how could it happen? Why is it that the closer he came into contact with Orthodoxy, the stronger was his longing for this dark, strange fanaticism, for accusations and cursing? If only he was the only one, but it happens with so many converts and also with so many cradle Orthodox people who fall into "acute churchliness." Is it a reaction against the minimalism of the Church, of parishes? At some point they begin to hate the light and the joy of that faith, and it is so frightening.

Some priests only accuse, only frighten, only threaten, and nothing else. Why? All right—we live in a frightening world. But isn't it just as bad as it was when it crucified Christ? What can be added to that horror, that fear? Didn't Christ give Himself to be crucified so that we could walk in a New Life? —life, and not religion. The Savior freed us from the fear, legalism, power of religion. What did people do between the fulfillment of the Church attending Christ's banquet and in His Kingdom? They lived—each lived the life and the duty that God gave to him. Yes, N. will say, but Christ said that if we want to be perfect, we must leave everything and follow Him, so "I left my family and followed Him." Does that mean nowadays to become a priest, a monk, a theologian? Does it require institutional change? I think that in the context of the Gospel, it means just the opposite because the One we follow is *not* leaving but coming. He is coming so that we would have life and life in abundance. What needs to be abandoned in order to follow Christ is identified by Christ with property and family. And truly, in the fallen world, these are the two burdens which bind man, which are obstacles to his following Christ because they become "idols." That is why Christ talks about them, because these two essential coordinates of life have been distorted, and in this distortion is revealed the whole depth of the fall of man and of the world, of their falling away from God. In reality, property and family are from God. When God created the world He gave it to man to possess, so that it would become man's possession "...to till it and to keep it..." And when He created man, He created a wife because "it is not good that the man should be alone..." But then, here is the fall (the original sin): Man wanted the world as a possession for himself and not for God, not for life in Him; and man made his wife an object of love torn away from God's love, again for himself. And then Christ Himself gives away, leaves His life in order to resurrect it, to free it from death, so that life would cease being the source of death, so that life would reign and death would be trampled down. Does it mean that God calls us to kill ourselves? "Leave" the world, give away one's possessions, leave the family—all of these do not mean that they (possessions, family) are identified with evil, in which case they should be thrown away, but that they mean their liberation and their transfiguration into what God had created them to be. The one who gives away his property in reality becomes richer because he makes the world again (given away, dispensed) divine. "Leaving" one's family is its resurrection, its cleansing, its transfiguration, but not its annihilation. How could the Church perform the sacrament of marriage if marriage was evil? Marriage is a sacrament because through it is accomplished its gift to God, to Christ, to the Holy Spirit—where everything is *light*, as it is in Christ's call: distribute, leave, all is positive, all is light and not darkness and destruction.

## Saturday, April 3, 1982

### Akathist to the Theotokos

"The return to God"—more and more is being written about it, a religious revival. It would seem that one should rejoice. But I do not feel any joy. I wrote yesterday about N. (who left his family to follow Christ). He is not at all a unique occurrence. "Return," the one I see, is a sort of emotional wave, pseudo-mysticism, fanaticism, and finally hatred: hatred directed against the world, hatred against those who think differently, sectarianism and pseudo-spirituality. Those outside of Christianity escape into Buddhism or into some dull mysticism.

The reason for this "return to God" is, of course, the collapse of rationalism, the collapse of foolish optimism and the utopias that are the result of rationalism, so that "they run to the mountains." People run toward any "*credo quia absurdum*," toward any *typikon* or Talmud, any "spirituality." What is typical is that the more educated a man, the more he has tasted of rationalism and positivism, the more he chooses foolish religiosity. In America, suspicious sketes and rather meaningless charismatics are sprouting like mushrooms, in which everybody is condemning everybody else and trying to outdo the other.

All of this is not only not joyful, but frightening—an atmosphere of joyless, panicky apocalypse. Here is what all these neo-religious people do not understand: Yes, rationalism, positivism, optimism have collapsed, and have collapsed in serving the devil. However, without wisdom, without the light of wisdom, Christianity is not Christianity but anti-Christianity. The Church Fathers were never against wisdom and reason, and neither the Church nor Christianity fought anything as persistently as false mysticism, as pseudo-maximalism (Docetism, Manichaeism, Montanism, Donatism, etc.). Christianity—to say it simply and exactly—fought with religion, with religiosity *per se* and lost the battle when it transformed itself—in the Middle Ages—into a "religion." (cf. LeGoff's book about Purgatory) And this extreme brought the opposite extreme—rationalism—and its offspring, humanism. Christianity has not yet discovered this truth about itself, has not accepted it. And now, Christianity joyfully welcomes the "religious revival."

How amazing, how joyful the Akathist to the Theotokos sounded yesterday! "Rejoice, you full of shining joy…" How little of that joy shines over the world and how often we betray it.

### Thursday, April 8, 1982

On Tuesday—a blinding snowstorm—unheard of in April. A blanket of snow and freezing cold.

Yesterday morning I had a phone call from Bruce Rigdon in Chicago, who incited me in 1963 to write *For the Life of the World*. He has become an important man in ecumenism and in the Presbyterian Church. The Presbyterians are now—says he—revising their teaching about the sacraments, especially about baptism. Their main help is my *Of Water and the Spirit*. He invited me to come to a conference in October where the revision will be debated "on a high level." He says he is constantly rereading my books, that they changed and defined his theological conscience.

Such consolations—it's really strange—come to me when I myself, as in recent days, am rather discouraged. I am discouraged because of rumors that I, supposedly, am leaving the seminary; that I am almost about to go to Paris! I know that it's all nonsense, but I feel quite disturbed. I have a strange premonition of an approaching crash. I know and I understand that it is all good, it is God pointing to me to know my pride, my habit of being "important," if not "unique." I even feel a sort of liberation. But the old Adam in me is saddened and distressed. And then God sends comfort. Look, you didn't live for nothing…even Presbyterians…!

A real torture, my *Eucharist* book. I know exactly what I want to say, but as soon as it comes to "how," I constantly reach a dead end.

A growing collision between England and Argentina. As in a fairy tale, a British fleet is going to the Falkland Islands, occupied by Argentina. Argentina has offended England's honor; England is fighting for its honor. Silly to say, but I am quite happy! When did we last hear about *honor*—and not about commerce and oil? It's as if instead of Freud and other psychopaths, one would read an old adventurous novel. I am all for England and I only fear whether they will have enough stamina.

L. tells about Russia, Moscow, Leningrad—closeness, blood closeness with Russia and at the same time, horror…!

## Friday, April 9, 1982

### End of Great Lent—Lazarus

While looking for a passage in the Gospel of St John, I read in Christ's last discourse to his disciples His consolation. They will not see Christ any more, and "so your hearts will be filled with sadness." But "I will not leave you orphans. I will come to you…"(John 16)—like a bolt of lightning. Everything in Christianity depends on love for Christ. Death is the encounter with Him and so it is all joy! But, O God, how far we are from such love—His love that defeated death, the love that defeats death in us.

## Holy Monday, April 12, 1982

Palm Sunday: the Feast of the Kingdom, the feast of the reign. Everything is so clear during that feast. All of Holy Week is the revelation of the Kingdom. The Lord's Entrance into Jerusalem is the revelation of the King. The Last Supper—the revelation of the Kingdom. The Cross—the reign, the victory of the King. Pascha—the beginning of the eternal Passover, the entrance into heaven. "And He opened for us the gates of paradise…"

I find more and more difficult contact with people in an unavoidably fussy dimension of life: decisions, talks, plans. More and more I thirst for "time unmoving." From the place where I stand in the sanctuary when I am not serving, I can see a high, very high bare tree. If I look at it for a long time, I begin to feel its mysterious presence as if it is performing for me, for us, something very important that we hardly notice in the midst of our bustle. Right now, while I am writing, I "see" behind my window the sunny silence of empty Crestwood. Somewhere a bell is slowly ringing. One can say that all of nature, all that is "natural"—the ocean at Montauk Point, the rays of sunset and shadows, walks in Labelle—everything is condemning our enslavement to fuss—life's decay, a flame running along life as a thread…

## Holy Tuesday, April 13, 1982

Yesterday I read J.-F. Revel's little book, *La grâce de l'Etat* (*The Grace of the State*) published after the Socialist victory in France. Why don't people see the obvious, frightening evil of socialism? Because socialism is the goodness of the anti-christ and the devil himself preaches it and attracts to it.

Socialism is the liberation from selfishness (profit, gain), but by the killing of the person. A person, if he is alive, must become richer, but richer in God. However, if one has fallen away from God, one will not be saved.

## Holy Friday, April 16, 1982

Yesterday, the Twelve Gospels. Before that, the Liturgy of the Mystical Supper—"I will not speak of Thy mystery to Thine enemies." Today, the Burial service and the immersion into "This is the Blessed Sabbath..." How many times in my life? Always in these days memory resurrects that time, that moment? that year? I do not know when it was all revealed in my life, when it became so beloved, so "absolutely desirable," and even though hidden in my heart, so decisive an event: rue Daru, the Cathedral of Alexander Nevsky in Paris, spring, home, youth, happiness. Then the key to everything was given me. As priest, as theologian, as author, as lecturer. I essentially witness only to "that." I almost never pray in the conventional sense; my spiritual life—as heroic feat, rule, spiritual guidelines—is zero, and if it exists, it does so as a constant consciousness, a subconscious feeling that all is elsewhere. On the other hand, deep down, I live only by it, or rather it lives in me.

Simple questions:

What does God want from us?

That we would love Him, accept Him as the source, the meaning, the goal of life: "the heart of my heart and my King..."

How can one come to love God? Where is the locus of this love?

In His self-revelation to us in the world and in life.

The summit and the fulfillment of this self-revelation is Christ.

Everything relates to Him. The Incarnation, the entrance into the world of nature, of time, of history is for Him.

It follows that love for God is Christ.

Joy in Him.

Love for Him.

The reference of everything to Him.

The gathering of everything in Him.

Life in Him, by the knowledge of Him in everything through the Holy Spirit.

The Church: the possibility and the gift of this love and life.

Amen.

## Bright Monday, April 19, 1982

Wonderful Pascha. Radiant Spring. Wonderful evening with Anya's family.

## Bright Tuesday, April 20, 1982

Letter from Oxford from one Dr. Nicholas Dewey, newly converted to Orthodoxy: "…thus, I came to read *Of Water and the Spirit, Great Lent* and *The World as Sacrament*. Your historical sense and deep understanding of the liturgical origins and the marvelous way that your knowledge is related to the present needs of the Church—and indeed, of the world…" This last sentence makes me very happy, but also saddens me, because all around me I see a general regression into a narrow, fanatic, self-satisfied Orthodoxy or into a cozy corner with chatter about Byzantium and vestments.

John M[eyendorff] is dismayed at letters from Russia which defend and extol the canonization of the Tsar and his family. To me it seems quite normal, at least from a "guilty intelligentsia." For Russians this is always the case: either apostasy, or a hysterical maximalism. Russians are certainly not given the "light of wisdom."

Strange, how detached I feel this past year from this fuss—spiritual, canonical, liturgical—which is so evident in contemporary empirical Orthodoxy.

The British fleet is nearing the wretched Falkland Islands. Argentina is rattling its weapons and threatening to form an alliance with the USSR. Israel is bombing southern Lebanon. The Arabs are trembling because of Iran's growing strength and its propaganda of the Islam revolution. Today or tomorrow, the execution of Godzabe, the Minister of Foreign Affairs, whose face has become quite familiar to us as we watch the crisis of the hostages, will take place in Tehran. In Poland, no respite. In America, whooping for Reagan. In the whole world, a growing clamor and uproar of long-haired fools who defend peace. But nobody—in any case in the free world—has any real idea, any plan. Petty people, petty world, armed with nuclear bombs…

## Monday, April 26, 1982

Yesterday, Alexis B[outeneff]'s wedding in Baltimore. We drove there on Saturday after the last Paschal Liturgy. Wonderful trip: everything is suddenly green; beautiful spring days. After the wedding in the Greek Cathedral, while the mostly non-Orthodox guests, sincerely charmed by our service (weddings have an unfailing effect), lined up to congratulate the newlyweds, I thought once again about our own decline, negligence, dying. In the morning I had a long conversation about it with Alexis Vino[gradov]. I said, the first thing that should be clarified is why Orthodoxy has ceased to have an effect on the Orthodox themselves. Whether it's Russians, Carpatho-Russians, Greeks, Arabs, Albanians, Serbians or Romanians, there stands between them and Orthodoxy (their own faith) a sort of *wall*, impossible to breach with preaching, books, or any religious educational activity. And it is so because this wall essentially represents their perception of the Church (already in existence for centuries), of liturgical services, of spirituality, of faith itself. It is not only emptiness, an absence of knowledge or interest. No. It is a kind of fullness beyond measure, forbidding any intrusion into their conscience of anything new.

One could and probably should put together a sort of typology of these walls since the Russian wall is different from the Greek one, as are all the others. Their correspondence, however, lies in a deeply hidden, organic denial of meaning, an inexplicable fear of any meaning: "Keep away from me!" Orthodoxy, in this perception, is reduced to feeling, whereas feeling is defined, created by all kinds of reasons, but not by knowledge or faith. For example, the rite of Marriage is perceived as being quite unrelated to the meaning, to the faith, to the teaching that created it; one can say—to Christ! Everything else, including Pascha, Liturgy, funerals, etc., is perceived in the same way. Having become a religion, Christianity has irresistibly become a "natural" religion.

On Friday night I lectured at a rather frightening gathering. I found myself there at the recommendation of Sister Cora Brady, whom I have known for a long time. It was neither more nor less than a school of *startsy*, i.e., of spiritual guidance. About 30 people, mostly mature women. Lord, what nonsense they talked! Apparently they expected the same kind of nonsense from me. I have understood for a long time that it is very easy to recognize pseudo-spirituality: It is accompanied by a strange, ineffable boredom.

How clear and obvious in this nonsense is a passion for spiritual power, for guidance of souls. I could hardly sit there for two hours, and escaped, having first, instinctively, talked about "demonic" spirituality. I don't know, but I don't think they understood anything, as they were truly bewitched.

### Thursday, April 29, 1982

A certain N., 37 years old, asked me to prepare him for Orthodoxy. He is well educated, has traveled all over the world, visited Mt. Athos, India, the New Skete, and is working as a taxi driver. Such calm, such joy and peace emanate from him. I anticipated him with boredom but ended seeing him off as a human being close to me.

The British started landing on the Falkland Islands. Why does it worry me so much that I grab a newspaper and rush to the television set? I'm afraid, or rather I know that it's not out of Christian feelings, which should be pacific, but out of disgust for the attempt to fatally harm Great Britain. I remember so well how worried I was in the 'forties, when the Germans seemed to be about to invade England. The British have many sins, but there is something in them that is only in them, and it seemed to me that its disappearance, its defeat by the coarse mechanized German army, would mean the irreparable ruin of a world in which one can live and breathe. And now I passionately hope that this old ragged lion will survive.

In the magazine *L'Express*, an article by Solzhenitsyn. Same topic: the West does not understand Russia, the essence of Communism, etc. Everything sort of true, but it will not have any effect. Furthermore, it will be counterproductive. Why? Because everything in the article is permeated with dislike of the West, of America; with an undisguised contempt for anything Western. The reader can't miss it. Whereas in Russia, he suggests that everything is serious, deep, real. And in the seventy-year domination by the Bolsheviks, everybody is guilty, except Russia and the Russians ...

## Friday, April 30, 1982

Yesterday I went to N.—an old parish where the parishioners (who do not speak Russian) want to increase readings and singing in Slavonic; where one finds the same gossip, the same meaningless contest with the priest, the same ghetto that I wrote about yesterday. A Kafkaesque world! A wall that nothing can crush. On the other hand, in the parishes where that wall has come down, all seems to be well, but one finds the same dead-end. Is it not because, outside of an organic Orthodox world, the Church incarnated itself—and could not do otherwise—in a parish, i.e., an organization with clearly defined membership with the necessity to care for property, with authority, administrative concerns, etc. The Church became an organization among organizations, an activity among activities that the Church never used to be. In the early Christian period, in the time of its denial by the world, the Church was an eschatological reality; it did not have any specific worldly activity and could not have it. The center of its life was the Eucharist, the Sacrament of transformation not only of bread and wine into "heavenly food" but of the world, life itself, into the anticipation of the Kingdom. Therefore the Eucharist was the Sacrament of the Church—the Church as community (synaxis), the Church as love (mercy, agape), the Church as knowledge (the Divine Word), the Church as fulfillment of everything in Christ.

Then a "Christian epoch" ensued. In a given nation, everybody became

Christian, and the laity appeared as a new form of Christian life. A lay person is not one who is outside the Church (as in early Christianity), but one who, distinguished from the clerics (full time officers of the Church), lives the life of the world, illumines it with faith, knowledge, prayer, etc. Sanctifies the world by an other-worldly faith, time by eschatology, and the earth by heaven. The Church sanctifies the lay person by making him a communicant of the Kingdom of God and sanctifies his life in the world by showing him—be it ideally—the meaning of life. Yes, the Church has become a Temple, a cult, but this temple, this cult, this "contact," this eschatology, are related to the world as revelation, as gift, as the possibility of a new life, as knowledge of life itself, as "new creation."

This Christian world, the world connected with the thirst for the Kingdom of God, has fallen before our eyes. But the paradox and the tragedy of this fall, of this decay, lies in the fact that it fell in the same degree that the Church renounced its eschatological function in the world, that it joined in its activism, identified itself with that activism; that it literally became part of the world, its organization and activity.

The secularization of the world started as a liberation from the Church, not from the faith; from clericalism, not from lay people. But the Church is guilty because in a way it did away with laity; it did so on one hand by transforming them into "customers" of the clerics, and clerics into priests servicing their spiritual needs. On the other hand, the Church, demanding religious activism from the laity, made them into members of a Church organization, servicing the needs of the Church.

So here are the two poles of a layman's psychology, especially obvious in the *diaspora*, that is where even the ruins of an organic Christian world are absent:

(a) It is, first, the psychology of a consumer who decides himself what he needs from the Church, and in what form. He can demand that the Church be his tie with his native land, his childhood, etc., or that the Church be, say, totally American. Either he wants a Russian Pascha at midnight, or a Carpatho-Russian one with the Liturgy in the morning, etc. *ad infinitum.* And since he is the customer, paying for everything and supporting with his money the clerics who service him, any opposition by the clergy, any reference to some inexplicable and totally unnecessary rules or to discipline seem to him, the customer, absolutely unnecessary; an ill-will of the priest, a manifestation of his lust for power.

(b) Secondly, it is the psychology of a Church activist who helps the Church, who is an active member of that organization. The Church has told him that the essence of his being a layman is in servicing the needs of the Church, that he must help the Church. So, he helps. But since his work is administrative, financial, etc., he does not understand why a cleric must manage it.

The goal of the Church has become the Church itself, its organization, its welfare, its success!

## Saturday, May 1, 1982

*Continued from April 30...*

The Western Church has understood its participation in the life of the world as a clerical power over the world. But when the world rejected that power, the Church resorted to direct participation in politics—first right, then left. But this participation condemns the Christian West to a sort of schizophrenia. The politics in which the Church participates have as their horizon, necessarily, only this world. Eschatology is reduced to utopia, but utopia, from a Christian point of view, is not only a mistake, but a heresy, the real heresy of our time. A heresy because the emphasis is transferred from a person, from the human being, to "structures"—social, ideological, etc. It is not by chance that those Christians who totally give themselves over to utopia and fight for it and accept Marxism, beginning with class struggle, totally accept the emotional essence of utopianism. The genuine Christian eschatology is not only silenced but denied and condemned as a shameful blot on the historical Church. The eschatological essence and function of the Church (in this world, but not of this world) is hushed up and the Church is gradually identified as one of the means in the fight for freedom, equality and fraternity, for the defense of the third world, for any utopia inscribed on this and that banner.

For the Orthodox, this departure into struggle and utopia remains alien—not because they have remained faithful to the eschatological antinomy of Christianity, but because of a gradual transformation of Orthodoxy either into a clerical ritual and magic religion, or into a spirituality which denies the world. By "clericalism" I mean here not the power of clerics over lay people (that kind of power has long disappeared) but the focus on Church, administration, etc., that I wrote about yesterday. The goal of the Church community is itself. It is not by chance that it is fashionable these days to discuss "lay ministries"; laymen as a sort of diluted clergy. What occupies the centers of the Church, the Synods of Bishops, the departments, etc.? Church "affairs"—diplomacy, finances, the appointments and transfers of priests, etc. Hence, the bottomless dullness and poverty of the Church press, the reduction of the content of Church life to ceremonies, jubilees, meetings, etc.; a kind of game with wooden soldiers, beginning with the language of the Church—"of all America and Canada..." It would seem that these words should raise questions; unless explained, it sounds comical. But nobody laughs!

My perpetual conclusion: if theology, spirituality, etc. do not return to a genuine Christian eschatology (and I don't see any signs of one) then we are fated not only to remain a ghetto, but to transform ourselves, the Church and all that is within it, into a spiritual ghetto. The return—and this is my other perpetual conclusion—starts from a genuine understanding of the Eucharist, the mystery of the Church, the mystery of the New Creature, the mystery of the Kingdom of God. These are the Alpha and Omega of Christianity.

War between England and Argentina: a real war with hundreds dead. Majestic fairy tale—battleships sinking! Everything in this war seems unreal; it's like a nightmare!

People are tearing me to pieces. Dramas between N. and NN. Complications in Alaska. Constant phone calls. Tomorrow a trip to West Virginia. I awake with the sense of a frightening, heavy weight. If one looks at our blossoming planet, one sees blood and darkness in Iran, blood and darkness in Afghanistan, blood in Lebanon and Palestine, terrorism in Poland, Bolshevism in Russia, crazy Khadafy in Libya, war in the Sahara, in the South Atlantic, terror in Central America. And quiet, rational advice about it all in the editorials of the *New York Times*: "Let's sit down and talk a while about compromises and all will be well..." Yes, and I forgot the Armenian resistance which has decided to kill all Turkish ambassadors around the world!

What is real? All that I enumerated earlier, or this moment:

An empty house flooded with sunshine; trees in full bloom behind the window; far away little white clouds floating in the sky; the peace of my office; the silent presence—friendly, joyful—of the books on my shelves.

### Thursday, May 6, 1982

The first anniversary of Mitterrand and Socialism in France. Again and again I am surprised how can one believe in socialism, even with its dream of a radiant future. It all ends up being dull gray chewing gum!

For several days on television we are shown demonstrations in Poland by hundreds of thousands of people who refuse to be slaves. Clear and simple. But Western socialists will affirm that even there, salvation is in socialism. Is it not obvious that after a first real contact with socialism, man's nature rejects it, because it can only be thrust on people by force? The most "fallen" possession is closer to God's design for man than malicious egalitarianism. Possession is what God gave me (which I usually use selfishly and sinfully), whereas equality is what the government and society give me, and they give something that does not belong to them. Equality is from the devil because it comes entirely from envy, which is the essence of the devil. What is the right to equality? Nobody fights with such frenzy for titles, private offices, etc. as the champions of equality. Is it not all clear and obvious?

## Monday, May 10, 1982

Last evening, while having dinner at the Hopkos (Mother's Day), Father Tom told me about his theological discussions with N. Tragic, hopelessly meaningless and also evil. Denunciation, a tone of irreconcilable indignation—and about what? About whether or not the Holy Spirit is "life hypostasized" or is "life the Son." An example of such theology: "All attributes that are not clearly witnessed by the Scriptures—to which Person of the Trinity do they relate—must automatically be related to the Father..." Theological chatter.

Unpleasant, painful happenings with N.'s engagement. And, at the same time more and more often, I have a strange feeling: a feeling of estrangement deep within, of freedom from all the tension of my life. It is as if it doesn't touch me any more; as if I am already on the other side of a crest, not totally a participant in these storms. Quite recently they were my life and I painfully felt that they were my duty, my responsibility. And now this burden is somehow melting, is becoming transformed into an object of contemplation, but from without, not within. It would be prideful to say, as did the poet Khodasevich, "and freely breathes the air of heaven, my soul, almost free..." No, alas, not heaven yet, but already not life's travails, not the struggles of an ant, not life with ebbs and flows. What is it—old age? If it is, then I sometimes feel a close contact with its blessedness.

Pride, flesh, laziness: triune source of sin; three basic dimensions of the fall of the world and the fall of life. They are destroyed only by Divine Love flowing into the heart: love-humility; love-purity; love-doing—

"If you love Me..."

"...ourselves and each other and our *whole* life..."

## Wednesday, May 12, 1982

Spent the whole day with N. talking about her troublesome engagement. Thought a lot about the "pastoral counseling" that so many people talk about, though I, personally, don't really know what it entails. Maybe it consists of only one thing: struggle for light; not for solving difficulties, but for altering the level of the heart. On the level where those difficulties or even tragedies occur, they are impossible to resolve. To solve them, one must rise, and any counseling should help this "rise," not rummage in all sorts of miasmas of our fallen world.

I read yesterday the 1943-1944 correspondence between Zaitsev and Bunin, two émigré writers. How well I remember the atmosphere of those years in Paris. Constant air raid warnings, fear, shopping lines, rumors, etc. I also remember how easy it all was for us, the youth, quite different from the older generation. January 1943—our wedding; January 1944, Anya's birth. I don't remember being hungry, although I do remember what trash we ate! I remember how much we danced, had fun, and how little we thought about what was going on; how we lived in a staunch optimism, firmly believing that all would end well.

### Tuesday, May 18, 1982

Long letter from Father K[ostoff]: "I would like to at least—though superficially—let you know how absolutely important my three years of study under your guidance and in your presence were to me both intellectually and spiritually. I eagerly absorbed or attempted to do so to the fullness of my capacity, that vision of the Church and simply of life itself which you presented to us at all times in the chapel and classroom. For me, personally, and Deborah has expressed the same feelings, this was an encounter with an authentic vision, thereby making it not only inwardly convincing but also lasting and influential."

From the Preface to Father G's thesis:

"…particular credit must go to my advisor, Father A. S. Not only did he provide the topic and incentive, but the whole study is permeated with his vision of the Church…"

I am writing this here because such testimonies help me fight the most terrible of all my doubts: Is it all for nothing? How can anything break through these walls, this deafness and blindness (clergy, parishes, the whole imperium of our Church). And in the midst of this doubt come these testimonies, like a drink of cold water.

Last evening we celebrated Father Tom's doctorate. Only the closest and most faithful—the Drillocks, the Lazors, the Bazils. Joyful feeling of closeness, unity, of a real family!

Little miracles: This morning in New York, I had just given my old Parker fountain pen to be repaired and sat waiting to have my shoes cleaned. A man, my neighbor at the shoe place, gave me a gift: a magnificent new silver Parker pen. So surprising!

## Tuesday, May 25, 1982

Long walks all over Oxford. Visited the Bodleian Library. Oxford is cool and sunny. I visited Father Kallistos Ware. He will be consecrated bishop on Pentecost. He seems quite happy. But I am always worried because of the inexplicable transformation that often occurs when a man becomes a bishop. Ambiguity and temptation of sacerdotal power!

Lunch with J. F[ennell*] at New College. Exceptional coziness of these living rooms, dining rooms, old fireplaces, old professors reading their papers. Wonderful gardens, old trees surrounding buildings with bell towers and stone walls.

In the evening I lectured about Orthodoxy in America. Two hundred people made me rather nervous. It seemed to me that the lecture went worse than I intended, but apparently the people were pleased.

Then off to London. I am quite exhausted, though I have two more working days ahead of me.

## Tuesday, June 1, 1982

Returned from London on Saturday, May 29. The whole trip gave me great joy, in particular since it took me away for a week from all the concerns of the seminary, the difficulties and little problems. What remains in my memory is Oxford in the month of May with its towers, gardens and flowers, and London, which I had not seen since 1948, and which was for me an immersion into the past, youth, the "beginning."

## Wednesday, June 2, 1982

From the very beginning of the Church, dark, fanatic maximalisms spring up time and again: Montanism, Donatism, Bogomils, Chiliasts, Old Believers, *et al.* From the very beginning and right up to our times: apocalypses, all kinds of Feraponts. It is probably natural for Christianity; perhaps for religion in general.

The reason is the ambiguity of Christianity. Christianity is by definition ambiguous: on one hand, "...for God so loved the world..."; on the other:

* Fennell, John—Professor of Russian History, University of Oxford, UK.

"Don't love the world, nor what is in the world." This basic antinomy not only was never transformed into an existential experience; into an understanding of life, an ideal of life, by the historic and Orthodox Christianity (the Fathers, the Church, etc.), but it was refused. The Church became happily organized in the world—covered with gold and silver crosses, miters, icons; it swelled and became rich; it became a way of life; *but*—and here is the whole paradox—continued to tirelessly call on all "not to love the world, nor what is in it," ignoring, so to say, the love of God Himself for the world ("...for God so loved the world..."). If "God so loved the world" is unrelated to "do not love the world," it becomes a dark negative maximalism and a true heresy. But the Church is unable any longer to discern this heresy since the key to that discernment (and I will repeat it to my dying hour) is in the eschatological essence of Christianity. It means, precisely, to discern—here and now, in our midst—the coming Kingdom in the joy of Christ who ascended into heaven, "not being parted from those who love you" but remaining with them, in the mystical transfiguration of the world and the creature. The heresy of all maximalisms is the refusal of "love which conquers fear." It is all given and opened to those who love Him—"crying to those who loved Him: I am with you and nobody will be against you." Hence the two dead-ends of contemporary Christianity: Love of "this world" (i.e., without "don't love the world") and hatred of this world (i.e., without "and God so loved the world"). Two dead-ends, two apostasies, two heresies.

### Saturday, June 5, 1982

Last night Johnny Hopko's graduation from Fordham Prep. The speech by the university president—an old Jesuit—was all "sucking up" to youth: you have rejected our antiquated theologies, you are for life, not for death, you are independent. And all in that tone. Even the text of Deuteronomy about the choice between the way of life and the way of death turned out to be a justification for contemporary pacifism. So flat; not a single call to "lift up our hearts," to an inner struggle, to witness for Christ. Everywhere the same saccharin "love" flooding everything like a sickly gravy.

Today is Memorial Saturday. For me, the remembrance of the dead at the *proskomedia* before the Liturgy is becoming more and more meaningful, more and more joyful. It gives a feeling of real unity with them. As I remember them—childhood, military school, Lycée, Theological Institute, Paris, America—it seems that my whole life gathers up and becomes reality, again alive.

## *Monday, June 7, 1982*

### *Day of the Holy Spirit*

I am dragging myself along; I am at the end of my rope—completely exhausted. Yesterday, Pentecost. Many confessions. A beautiful service!

Last night I started thinking about four keynotes for our Summer Institute. As usual, my first feeling is that I do not understand anything in the topic: "Proclaiming the Word of God." I do not understand the question itself and do not know what should and can be said. I started leafing through books—not finding in them anything clear, ultimate. Each time I have a painful encounter with something huge, decisive, essential and each time I have the feeling that I have to rediscover everything anew. What is the "Word of God" and what does "…and the Word was God" mean? Literally thousands of books have been written on the subject and it is still incomprehensible. The point is not some technical theological question, not something secondary but the essence of the faith. But an essence must be simple, since God revealed it not to scientists, nor to theologians.

> In the beginning was the Word,
> and the Word was with God,
> and the Word was God…

> In him was life, and
> the life was the light of men…

> And the Word became flesh
> and dwelt among us,
> full of grace and truth; …
> (John 1)

## *Wednesday, June 9, 1982*

Tomorrow we leave for Labelle, Canada—only for ten days, but we *leave*. I am completely exhausted. For three days I have had terrible headaches and nightmares. I remember the poet Valéry who wanted to have written on his grave: "Killed by others." I know that I have been dragging the same dull tune for years, but sometimes it is unbearable, and then I feel darkness moving in.

War in the Middle East. The Israelis are closing in on Beirut. Syrian planes are shot down. The whole world is in a helpless state of panic. War of England with Argentina, of Iran with Iraq, other little wars where probably the killing is more efficient. Bombs explode in many capitals, diplomats are killed. The Armenians—against the Turks; others—without signature. Between the news, television shows, basketball finals, new cars, advertisements for travel and all sorts of mundane entertainment. "Bread and spectacle!" Life continues. And this contrast more than anything else creates an atmosphere of insanity.

Meeting of the Orthodox Theological Society at the seminary. I attended—although without any strength in me—and read two lectures. Then, while listening, I thought that theology (words about God, growth into the essence of faith) presupposes an indispensable condition; either a genuine level of culture, or holiness in simplicity, humility, etc. Culture is not just knowledge; it is communion with the inner life of the world, with the "tragedy" (in the Greek meaning of the word) of human history, the human race. Theology is always an answer, or rather its answer is the Good News, the Good News as the answer. It is not by chance that in our Orthodox Theological Society, theology has been transformed into an interpretation of administrative texts—first canonical (mixed marriages, their number, etc.) Young priests sit there and energetically write down "recipes" (and then will use them to beat unhappy, confused people, and thus will prove their Orthodoxy). One melody is never heard in this sort of administrative theology: "I came to release the tormented ones to freedom…" A meeting of theologians is a meeting of angry people defending their points of view. There is no air, no wish to introduce people to life, to joy, to the reality of the Church. Everything is built like a police station (protocol of a crime), a hospital (psychological digging in the subconscious), a trial and condemnation. God is "interested" in the world and the man. We are interested in the problems of the Church and its administration—all of it hopelessly dead and boring.

I thought about it yesterday during the funeral of General S. A group of old Russians, rather churchly. But Lord, what complete estrangement from the service itself, from the words, the rites. They all firmly believe that this is the way it has to be; one has to observe all that is prescribed. But what is needed and why: no thought is given to that. In these cases, I always feel that I am a tribal, heathen priest who knows some complex manipulations—be it baptism, wedding, or funeral—but keeps them hidden from the profane.

### Monday, June 14, 1982

*Labelle*

Thirty-second summer! We arrived on Friday afternoon and since then managed to go to three villages for shopping or just walks. As every year, it's a real encounter after separation, and a recognition. Nowhere in the whole world am I so delighted with a simple pure happiness as here; the special and acute happiness in these first days of slowly "getting in gear."

I immediately started working on my keynote lectures for our Summer Institute on "Proclaiming the Word of God." As usual, I found myself in total confusion. I don't know where and how to start; how to find what to say without acting against my conscience and without hiding my ignorance through academic tricks. How does one answer the question, What does "the Word was God" mean? Rather, how to answer so that something would open the heart to faith, to conscience, and not only to reason?

## *Wednesday, June 16, 1982*

All these days I am immersed in the preparation of my lectures. I am rather pleased with my work, with the joy, with the meaning, with the life that is uncovered for me while I work, while I think about things that I seldom thought about until now. Amazing—and I always feel it—that, in theology, I do not reveal, express or transmit something that is already in me, that I know, that belongs to me, but, on the contrary, something is revealed, is given *to me*. And my whole task consists only of transmitting it to others as faithfully, as fully, as convincingly as possible. Theology, in that sense, is only the search for words fitting to God, and the rejection of false words.

Between hours of work, we take long walks in familiar places that every year become like a communion, a certainty, a revelation of what is the most important, and the encounter—a sort of Liturgy: "The gentle kingdom of the earth."

When I work intensely on something, as I am these days, I cannot, am not able to read anything serious and related to my work. So I took from my shelf a two-volume biography of Sainte-Beuve, written by A. Bailly. I bought it long ago but never even cut the pages. Here is another man who stood all his life close to faith, in contact—as a critic, as a historian of ideas and of experience—with people of faith, and who found peace in a certain "wise skepticism." What an amazing, mysterious occurrence is the rejection of faith, the liberation from it in the 19th century—the rejection of faith as of some leprosy; the worry of Roger Martin du Gard in his novel *Jean Barrois* for his hero not to succumb to faith at his dying hour, the anger provoked by André Gide's religious funeral, the indignation of Simone de Beauvoir about a tiny, frail link of God, of faith in dying Jean-Paul Sartre. This anger, this worry, this fear does not belong to indifferent people, but to believers and defenders of their own faith. It is a belief in non-belief as the main, the decisive condition of the importance of their action, their convictions, their dominion over people's minds. This is why it is essential for Christians above all never to cease simply confessing their faith. For the horror of what is happening to

Christians in the West is the acceptance of this non-belief only as a "misunderstanding."

Why do I enjoy so much reading those who have renounced faith, who believe in their non-belief—Loisy, Roger Martin du Gard, Gide, Léautaud, etc.? I think that in them the genuine meaning of my faith is revealed to me. All that they deny, I deny also, and then not only what my faith affirms but what its presence clearly implies is revealed to me.

### Monday, June 21, 1982

Four days in Crestwood. Thank God—cool and sunny, not humid or stifling.

### Tuesday, June 22, 1982

Last evening a dialogue with priests participating in the Institute. As usual, I feel quite vividly a deep kinship, a mutual responsibility. They complain and criticize as usual, but behind it all is the most important: these people stand at the Lord's altar, and, 2,000 years after the Last Supper, they fulfill it in the Eucharist. And this joy will never be taken away from them!

### Wednesday, June 23, 1982

After my second lecture, I met with many of our former students. Each one has his own difficulties, even tragedies. But the general impression is very good; I would say joyous and grateful. They all live by something high, even at a time when nobody, even in our culture, calls to it; something that not only is rejected, but is simply non-existent.

The whole week is cool and sunny. Last evening I felt so tired that my head was simply not working anymore!

### Sunday, September 5, 1982

One more summer in Labelle has ended. I will be 61 in a week. Somehow, surprisingly for myself, I was amazed. I always thought that I had many, many years ahead of me, and I suddenly remembered what it meant for me when people said: "Oh, he is over sixty!" Old age, old man. And it has become part of me, often unconsciously; it is present in me, it colors everything.

Andrei came to Labelle for three weeks. As usual we walked, talked, had discussions at lunch and dinner.

From Labelle I came back to New York for a Preconciliar Commission meeting. From the Church, or rather, from the church establishment, I get the same impression of some metamorphosis into a game, a flow of ambitions, bureaucracy and chatter. Something has snapped; maybe also in me. But everything has become strange, uninteresting.

*But*, in Canada—I wrote! And although the result is not too great—25 pages of the same chapter, "The Sacrament of the Holy Spirit"—I have all the time a joyous feeling from the presence of the topic in me, its hidden life in my soul, my heart, my reason.

Liana went to Italy at the end of August to travel with our granddaughter Liana Hopko as she did with our own children. I was in Labelle quite alone, and felt quite acutely what solitude is, how much I miss common life, contact, a constantly incarnated unity. Thank God she is coming back on Wednesday.

Our son Serge came for only ten days. But what a joy! What a wonderful person he is; what a wonderful family: Serge, Mania and the children. Serge worked with enthusiasm organizing his new house on the lake, right next to ours.

Labor Day—then immersion into the seminary business.

I spent the evening with Father Paul L[azor]. We had a long conversation about religious and spiritual education and what a heavy responsibility it is. We talked about the need to review the goal and the methods. We discussed the reasons for so many failures. Besides the confusion of our time, I see also an acute ambition which our culture is trying to plant. In religion itself, there is no peace, no silence—a lot of problems and all of them personal.

## Tuesday, September 7, 1982

I read yesterday the translation into Russian of my For the *Life of the World*. Good, but not is impossible to explain. This book is all in a certain "key," and the translation does not convey it. Some work to do!

Yesterday I spent the day at my desk, and at night a barbecue at the Drillocks. Long talks with David D[rillock] and Paul L[azor]. I feel so good with them.

Since the beginning of the summer, something has gone to pieces in my health—a constant headache, and now some dizziness, lack of balance when I walk, and, finally, a catastrophic weakening of my memory: names, words, facts. Today, for the first time, I was worried. What is it: old age, or sickness, or both?

## Thursday, September 9, 1982

Because of my headaches and strange dizziness I am going from doctor to doctor. Saw my general practitioner, then an eye doctor. All seems to be in order. But then where do these headaches and that dizziness come from? On Monday I have an appointment with a neurologist.

## Monday, September 20, 1982

Spent two days in East Hampton. Beautiful weather, but I felt so badly, I couldn't move.

## Saturday, September 25, 1982

Fourth day at the New York Hospital. Several tumors in my head, lots of tests. It is boring to write about it, and it would be too long. Letters, flowers, a feeling of something undeserved… How simply, how incredibly simply, in one moment, the whole perspective changes. There was a simple world, clear and simple, and since then. St Sergius Day. I am expecting Father Michael A[ksenov] with Communion.

## Sunday, October 3, 1982

Thirteenth day at the hospital. Tests and more tests. In general, thanks to God, calm, silence, peace. Presence of L. and the girls, Anya and Masha. Letters, cards. Behind my window, an extraordinary view of New York, Queensboro, Midtown, the river, skyscrapers. And sunshine, every day sunshine. All around me, love and worry!

Father Michael just left after Communion: "…where the voice of those who feast is unceasing, and the gladness of those who behold the goodness of Thy countenance is unending…" Faith, hope and love.

## Monday, October 4, 1982

Fourteenth day in the hospital. I am in a room flooded with sunshine and am waiting for a decision about treatment. Yesterday, as well as every day, visitors came. So many kind words, so much love, prayers. I feel it almost physically. Yesterday, a phone call from Serge in Moscow, from my brother Andrei in Paris, from my cousin Father Michael Ossorgin in France. Presence of L. and Masha. Almost happiness.

Yesterday I made a first attempt to work; started working on the "Sacrament of the Holy Spirit." What prevents me from working? An inner agitation created by the hospital. I am waiting for something all the time and that waiting prevents me from concentrating.

# CHAPTER XI

# 1983

∾

*Wednesday, June 1, 1983*

For eight months I have not written in this journal. Not because I had nothing to say; on the contrary, never, I believe, did I have so many thoughts and questions and impressions; but because I was constantly afraid of the height where my sickness had lifted me, afraid of falling from it. In the first months, before Pascha, I wrote and worked. I suddenly wanted so much that my English books would appear in Russian, although, alas, they are not written in a Russian tonality, and a translation hardly conveys what I think needs to be said.

Active presence of L. Had she not been with me, I believe that I would not have had these essentially peaceful and deep eight months.

Andrei came three times.

Serge came three times.

Masha and Father John came again and again...

What happiness it has all been!

# AFTERWORD*

⟩

Father Alexander celebrated his last Divine Liturgy here with us on Thanksgiving Day on November 24. Those of us who prayed with him in this Chapel on that day remember how, at the end of the Liturgy, he called on all of us to give thanks to God—for the Liturgy which we had just celebrated, for the joy and communion which was given to us in the holy Church, for our common ministry at St Vladimir's Seminary, for our family joys, for the children around us, and even for the noise they occasionally make in church.

This last Thanksgiving was so characteristic of Father Alexander's personality! More than anybody I ever met, he was always able to acknowledge and to celebrate the gifts of life, and to understand his own personal functions, as priest and as theologian, in thanking God for these gifts. Is not "thanksgiving" (*eucharistia*) at the very center of Church life? Father Alexander was ready and happy, until practically his last breath, to thank God for all, and by so doing, he won an obvious victory, a clear triumph over suffering and death itself.

But was that Liturgy on Thanksgiving day really his "last" Liturgy? Our Christian faith tells us clearly: no, indeed. For we know that, every time the Eucharist is celebrated, it unites in Christ the living and the dead, the saints of all times, and all our brothers and sisters who were—or still are—dear to us. So, always, in this chapel, Father Alexander will continue to give thanks to God with us, and we will be one with him in this Thanksgiving.

As we pray today for the repose of his soul and for the remission of his sins, voluntary or involuntary, and as we ask God to forgive our offenses against him, it is our first duty to join him in this continuing thanksgiving.

* Originally published as "A Life Worth Living," by Father John Meyendorff, *St Vladimir's Theological Quarterly*, vol 28, no 1, 1988.

This is the best way to follow the example which Father Alexander gave us.

Let us, therefore, first of all, thank God for having given Father Alexander to the Church, to the Seminary, and to each one of us personally.

It is truly extraordinary to realize how many people very personally were reached by him in his ministry—throughout this country, both Orthodox and non-Orthodox—and also, certainly an even greater number in the country of his ancestors, through his preaching in the Russian language on Radio Liberty. All of them, known and unknown, he succeeded in uniting around himself in Christ. For this, let us give thanks.

Here, at this Seminary, his colleagues, his students, and all the alumni were kept together, against so many odds, around Father Alexander, but always in Christ. For this, let us also give thanks.

His is a wonderful family, united as ever—Juliana, children and grand-children—and he always stood in the middle, gathering them around himself, in Christ. This unity is not ended today, so that we can give thanks for it.

In this fallen world, our every step is being watched by the Divider (*diabolos*), Satan, who thrives only in enmity, separation and death. All of us will be judged by our ability to resist that evil spirit. It is through his ministry of uniting people in Christ, that Father Alexander, in his last days with us, has been able to demonstrate, not only in words but in deeds, so obviously and so triumphantly, that Death was indeed overcome by Life, that the risen Christ has trampled down the powers of Satan.

For the model and the example he thus leaves for us, let us give thanks, not only in words but in deeds, so that—in the Spirit of God—we may continue to share in that communion, in that joy, and in that courage, of which Father Alexander remains for us our ever-living image. Amen.

The thoughts and feelings expressed by those who had the opportunity to speak at Father Alexander Schmemann's funeral services—hierarchs, colleagues and friends—reflect all that needs to be said in these first weeks after his untimely death on December 13, 1983. Others perhaps will eventually undertake a more thorough evaluation of his thought and writings, including that which remains unpublished. My task here is only to point to the main periods of his life, without pretending to be exhaustive. As one writes about a very close friend—almost a brother—it is, however, impossible to be totally objective, to avoid being somewhat subjective and impressionistic in interpreting what was truly significant in Father Alexander's life—a life truly worth living! For this subjectivity I apologize in advance.

Born in 1921 into a Russian family, with Baltic German ancestors on his father's side, Father Alexander moved to France from Estonia in his early childhood. The life of the Russian emigration in Paris became his life until his departure for America in 1951.

The "Russian Paris" of the 1930s was a world unto itself. Numbering tens of thousands and including intellectuals, artists, theologians, grand dukes and former tsarist ministers, publishing daily papers and settling political divisions in hot arguments, Russian émigrés still dreamt of a return home. Children were reared in Russian schools, somewhat in isolation from the surrounding French society (which actually was not always very hospitable to them). The young Alexander (or Sasha, as he was called by family and friends) tasted something of that secluded Russian education: he spent several years as a "cadet," in a Russian military school in Versailles, and then transferred to a *gimnaziya* (high school). Whatever the merits of that initial schooling, it hardly satisfied his mind and aspirations. Even then he felt that the best in the great legacy of Russian culture (particularly Russian literature) was not closed to the West, but was, on the contrary, necessarily "European" in scope. Dostoevsky's famous "Pushkin speech" represented for him the only valid understanding of Russia and of Russian civilization. He refused to accept its artificial limitation, and pursued studies at a French lycée and the University of Paris.

Already as a teenager, Alexander discovered his true spiritual home in the Church. His initiation to Orthodoxy and its authentic spirit took place not so much at the dull, compulsory religion classes given at the military school or the *gimnaziya*, but rather through active participation in the liturgy at the monumental St Alexander Nevsky Cathedral on rue Daru, as an altar boy and later as a subdeacon. Inspired by the eminently wise and always gracious personality of Metropolitan Evlogui, by a clergy a little "old régime" but also enlightened and open, by the dedicated leadership of Dr Peter Kovalevsky (who headed the large staff of "minor" clergy at the cathedral), Alexander understood the value and dimensions of the liturgy and even developed a certain love for pomp and ceremony, which remained with him all his life.

The years of World War II and the German occupation of France were years of decisive options. Providentially sheltered from the tragedies of war, Alexander studied at the Theological Institute of Paris (1940-1945) and married Juliana Ossorguine (1943), then a student in classics at the Sorbonne and a member of a traditional, church-oriented Russian family. It became quite clear in those years, to all his friends and acquaintances, that Alexander had found his true vocation, and also that God had blessed him with successful marriage and family life. The inspiration and joy that he found then contributed much to the power with which, in all later years, he was able to communicate their content to others.

The Orthodox Theological Institute in Paris—"St Sergius," as it is frequently called—had gathered a somewhat heterogenous but remarkable faculty, which included representatives of the old theological establishment of prerevolutionary Russia (A. V. Kartashev), intellectuals who came to Orthodoxy during the revolution (V. V. Zenkovsky) and former students at Belgrade (Father Cyprian Kern, Father Nicholas Afanassieff). The school was still dominated by the personality of Father Sergius Bulgakov, a former Russian seminarian, then a Marxist philosopher and finally—through the influence of Vladimir Soloviev and Paul Florensky—a priest and a theologian. During the war years at St Sergius the students were few, but the enthusiasm and the hopes for an Orthodox revival remained strong.

Never attracted by the "sophiological" speculations of Bulgakov—for whom, however, he had the greatest personal respect—Alexander Schmemann was primarily seeking specialization in church history. He became a pupil of A.V. Kartashev, whose brilliant lectures and skeptical mind matched Schmemann's own tendency to critical analysis of reality around him. The result was a "candidate's thesis" (equivalent to an MDiv) on Byzantine theocracy. Having completed the five-year program of studies at St Sergius, Schmemann became an instructor in church history, first as a layman, then as a priest, following his ordination by the then Archbishop Vladimir (Tikhonitsky) in 1946, who was heading the Russian Exarchate of Western Europe under the jurisdiction of the Patriarchate of Constantinople.

Besides A.V. Kartashev, two other members of the St Sergius faculty exercised a decisive influence upon Father Schmemann. Archimandrite Cyprian (Kern), his spiritual father and friend, also took him as his assistant in the SS Constantine and Helen parish in Clamart, near Paris. Father Cyprian taught patristics at St Sergius, but his love was for the liturgy and his liturgical taste had a lasting influence on Father Schmemann. Both also shared knowledge and appreciation of Russian classical literature. Intellectually more decisive, however, was Father Schmemann's acquaintance with and devotion to the ecclesiological ideas of Father Nicholas Afanassieff, a professor of canon law whose name will be forever attached to what he called "eucharistic ecclesiology" and whose ideas are reflected in many of Father Schmemann's writings.

As a young instructor in Church History, Father Schmemann planned to write a doctoral dissertation on the Council of Florence. He eventually abandoned that topic, but the publication of a short treatise by St Mark of

Ephesus on "The Resurrection" remains from that initial interest in Byzantine studies. Actually, the Church itself always stood at the center of Father Alexander's spiritual and intellectual interests and commitments. His discussion of Byzantine theocracy, and his readings in Church History in general—as well as his initial dissertation topic—come from his concern with the survival of the Church, as Church, during the centuries of an ambiguous alliance with the State, and the survival of Orthodoxy in its medieval confrontation with Rome. But, perhaps, he lacked the necessary patience for remaining concentrated on the Church's past: the existential today was that which really mattered. And today, the Orthodox Church could not be alive either as a defense of the State, or cultural appendix of "Russianism": it was alive in and through the Liturgy. Here, the ecclesiology of Afanasieff provided the direction (although not really the model) for Father Alexander's further orientation as a theologian.

It is quite clear that Father Alexander's theological worldview was shaped during his Paris years. But, although the influence of some of his teachers at St Sergius was decisive, he always lived in a wider spiritual world. The forties and fifties were a period of extraordinary theological revival in French Roman Catholicism—the years of a "return to the sources" and a "liturgical movement." It is from that existing milieu that Father Schmemann really learned "liturgical theology," a "philosophy of time" and the true meaning of the "paschal mystery." The names and ideas of Jean Daniélou, Louis Bouyer, and several others are inseparable from the shaping of Father Schmemann's mind. And if their legacy was somewhat lost within the turmoil of postconciliar Roman Catholicism, their ideas produced much fruit in the organically-liturgical and ecclesiologically-consistent world of Orthodoxy through the brilliant and always effective witness of Father Schmemann.

Orthodoxy in France was not made up only of intellectual or theological pursuits. The breakdown of all reasonable hopes for a swift return to Russia raised the immediate issue of a permanent survival of Orthodoxy in the West and involved the question: Why did an Orthodox "diaspora" occur at all? Together with most representatives of the "younger" generation of Orthodox theologians, Father Schmemann saw no other answer and no other meaning for the existence of the "diaspora" than the establishment of a territorial, eventually French-speaking local Church in France. His opposition to a return to the jurisdiction of the Moscow Patriarchate was primarily based on the hope that the Ecumenical Patriarchate, under whose protection the Russian "Exarchate" of Western Europe had placed itself in 1931, would initiate and sponsor such a gradual Orthodox unification according to canonical norms. Most Russians, however—including the older generation of St Sergius professors—rather saw the Constantinopolitan allegiance negatively, as a shield against Moscow's control—not as an opportunity for a mission to the West. Here lies one of the important elements which eventually encouraged Father Alexander and his family to look to America for better conditions of realizing a more consistent Orthodox ecclesiology in the concrete life of the Church.

The decisive factor which determined the departure of Father Alexander for the United States, was the return to Paris from Eastern Europe of Father Georges Florovsky, and his eventual appointment as Dean of St Vladimir's in New York.

Father Florovsky had taught at St Sergius before the war, but his relationships with his colleagues were not easy. This uneasiness was partly due to his criticism of the sophiology of Father Bulgakov (a criticism which, however, appears only indirectly in his writings). Rescued from Soviet-occupied Czechoslovakia in 1947, through the mediation of ecumenical friends, Father Florovsky could not reassume his chair of Patristics at St Sergius (it was now occupied by Father Cyprian Kern). He taught Moral Theology for a short while and then accepted the post at St Vladimir's in New York (1949). Father Schmemann became fascinated by the brightness of Florovsky's theological mind, by his vision of the Orthodox mission to the West, by his criticism of accepted nationalistic stereotypes, by the fact that he succeeded in being both rooted in the Church's past and fully open to the best theological movements of Western Christendom.

The fact that Father Schmemann left for America (1951) and joined the faculty of St Vladimir's then being built up by Father Florovsky, was felt at St Sergius as something of a betrayal, especially since it was eventually followed by similar moves by S. S. Verhovskoy (1953) and, later, by John Meyendorff (1959). The subsequent history and development of Orthodoxy in America does appear to show that the moves were justified, especially since St Sergius itself, although deprived of some of its faculty, not only survived, but eventually turned its programs and orientation in the Pan-Orthodox direction, which made survival possible.

The early fifties were not easy years for St Vladimir's Seminary, then located in the extremely modest quarters of Reed House, on Broadway and 121st Street. Conflicts of temperament and style are at the bottom of the regrettable resignation of Father Florovsky (1955), who by the mere prestige of his personality had placed St Vladimir's on the academic and theological map of the country. Only in 1962, when the Seminary acquired its present campus in Crestwood, NY did Father Alexander assume the post of Dean, which he held until his death in 1983.

It is probably too early to speak in detail of the last and longest period of his life in America, associated with the Seminary and with the Church at large. Perhaps the single most obvious contribution of Father Alexander to the life of St Vladimir's was that he succeeded in integrating the school within the very texture of ecclesiastical life. During his tenure, it ceased to be simply an academic institution, respected in ecumenical circles, but rather heterogeneous to the life of dioceses and parishes. St Vladimir's produced priests, and these priests, serving not only within the "Russian Metropolia," but also in other jurisdictions (particularly the Antiochian and the Serbian) were taught the spirit of a universal and missionary Orthodox Church, transcending purely ethnic concerns. Also, St Vladimir's became the center of a liturgical and eucharistic revival, which is recognized and praised by both Metropolitan Theodosius and Metropolitan Philip. Fully committed to his work in America, Father Schmemann did not break links with Europe. It is there at his alma mater of St Sergius that he obtained his doctorate in 1959, with Father Nicholas Afanassieff and the present writer acting as examiners.

A real watershed in Father Alexander's career in America was the establishment of the autocephalous Orthodox Church in America in 1970. If there was any commitment which was constant in his life, already in France, it was the hope that the uncanonical overlapping of "jurisdictions," which was the single most obvious obstacle to Orthodox witness in the West, would be replaced by local Church unity in conformity not only with canons, but with the most essential requirements of Orthodox ecclesiology. Father Alexander—and those of us who were committed in the same fundamental aspirations—hoped that the Ecumenical Patriarchate of Constantinople would contribute to (and possibly lead) Orthodox unity in America, for example through the "Standing Conference of Orthodox Bishops." But a role for Constantinople in such a process of unification would have required the consent of all the other Orthodox Churches including the patriarchate of Moscow, whose jurisdiction in America was never denied by the Metropolia and was always sustained by American civil courts. On the other hand, Constantinople, very demanding in theory, was in practice quite inconsistent (it terminated its jurisdiction over the Russian diocese of France and called it to return to the Patriarchate of Moscow in 1965). The other churches would clearly not even envisage transferring their "diasporas" to the Greek patriarch. Realistically, the basis for Orthodox unity was rather to be found in the policies which the Russian Church always followed in principle, since it first established Orthodoxy in North America. Its canonical and missionary aim had always been a Church for Americans, established with the blessing of the Mother Churches and inviting all those who were interested freely to join in. This last offer implied, of course, that unity could not be established unilaterally, that the free consent of all was required. Of course, the Patriarchate of Constantinople was still welcome to assume leadership in an eventual unification process.

During the negotiations leading to autocephaly, a remarkable personal link was established between Father Alexander and Metropolitan Nikodim (Rotov) of Leningrad, whose full understanding of the historical opportunity for Orthodoxy in America and singlehanded effectiveness in realizing the common goal made possible the signing of the Tomos of Autocephaly on April 10, 1970 by Patriarch Alexis of Moscow. This act, however, was understood both by the Mother Church of Russia and its daughter-church in America, as the first—and not the last—step towards Orthodox unity to be realized through conciliar assent of all Orthodox Churches.

In the midst of his work as teacher and his involvement in the life of the Church—with lectures, articles, addresses and meetings all over the country—Father Schmemann never lost another concern which he held since his youth: the fate of Orthodoxy in Russia. The opportunity he had for years to address a weekly sermon in Russian on "Radio Liberty" made his name known to many among the ghettoized and repressed Christians in Russia. One of them was Alexander I. Solzhenitsyn, whose writings, smuggled abroad, were for Father Alexander—as for many others—a breath of fresh air from the depressing flatness of Soviet reality, a witness to the spirit of "true" Russia and an authentic miracle of spiritual survival. About Solzhenitszyn's attitude to Russia, Father Alexander coined a great word: the author of the "Gulag Archipelago" and of "August 14" had a "seeing" or "lucid" love of Russia, as opposed to the "blind" nationalism of so many. Father Schmemann was particularly indignant at those—Russian and Western—critics of Solzhenitszyn, who saw in him precisely that "blind" nationalism, which the criticism of pre-revolutionary Russia in "August 14" refutes so obviously. However, Father Schmemann also responded negatively to some of Solzhenitsyn's enthusiasms, for instance his (passing) admiration for the Old Believers.

Be it as it may, it seems to me that if there is a talent which Father Alexander did not have the time to develop fully in his published writings, it is his extraordinary grasp of Russian literature (and Western, particularly French), his ability to discern what was "true" and what was "false." His few writings (and lectures) on literary topics were among the best in his entire legacy.

A full biography could mention other aspects of Father Schmemann's career: his involvement, still in France, as Vice-Chairman of the Youth Department of the World Council of Churches; and his brief passage in the "Faith and Order Commission;" his lecturing as Adjunct-Professor at Union, at General and at Columbia; his later involvement with more conservative Christian circles (the "Hartford Appeal").

A great master of the spoken word, a man able, better than anyone, to relate and to sympathize authentically, but first and foremost a priest committed to the Church always seen, in spite of all human deficiencies, as an anticipation of the Kingdom and as the only authentic token of immortality, Father Alexander Schmemann occupied so great a place in the life of so many! His legacy will not disappear, not only because his friends will not forget him, but because he obviously remains in the Eternal Memory of God, as a faithful servant in this vineyard.

# OTHER TITLES BY FATHER
# ALEXANDER SCHMEMANN

Ω

*Great Lent: Journey to Pascha.* (Crestwood: St Vladimir's Seminary Press, 1969).

*For the Life of the World: Sacraments and Orthodoxy.* (Crestwood: St Vladimir's Seminary Press, 1970).

*Liturgy and Life: Christian Development Through Liturgical Experience.* (New York: DRE, 1974).

*Of Water and the Spirit: A Liturgical Study of Baptism* (Crestwood: St Vladimir's Seminary Press, 1974).

*Introduction to Liturgical Theology* (Crestwood: St Vladimir's Seminary Press, 1975).

*The Historical Road of Eastern Orthodoxy* (Crestwood: St Vladimir's Seminary Press, 1977).

*Ultimate Questions: An Anthology of Modern Russian Religious Thought* (Crestwood: St Vladimir's Seminary Press, 1977).

*Church, World, Mission: Reflections on Orthodoxy in the West* (Crestwood: St Vladimir's Seminary Press, 1979).

*The Eucharist: Sacrament of the Kingdom* (Crestwood: St Vladimir's Seminary Press. 1988).

*Liturgy and Tradition: Theological Reflections of Alexander Schmemann.* (Thomas Fisch ed.) (Crestwood: St Vladimir's Seminary Press, 1990).

*Celebration of Faith: I Believe...,* Vol 1 (Crestwood: St Vladimir's Seminary Press, 1991).

*Celebration of Faith: The Church Year,* Vol 2 (Crestwood: St Vladimir's Seminary Press, 1994).

*Celebration of Faith: The Virgin Mary,* Vol 3 (Crestwood: St Vladimir's Seminary Press, 1995).